Aksum

An African Civilisation of Late Antiquity

Dedicated to the late H. Neville Chittick

Aksum

An African Civilisation of Late Antiquity

Stuart Munro-Hay

Edinburgh University Press

Edinburgh University Press
22 George Square, Edinburgh

Set in Lasercomp Times Roman
and printed in Great Britain by
The Alden Press Limited
London and Oxford

British Library Cataloguing
in Publication Data
Munro-Hay, S. C. (Stuart C), *1947–*
Aksum : an African civilization of late antiquity.
1. Axumite Kingdom, history
I. Title
963.4

ISBN 0 7486 0106 6 (cased)

Contents

Chronological Chart.

	Period 1. Early Aksum until the reign of GDRT. 1st- 2nd centuries AD.	
100 AD	Zoskales	Periplus
		Ptolemy
c.150 AD		
	Period 2. GDRT-Endubis. Beginning of 3rd century AD to c. 270 AD.	
200 AD		
	GDRT, BYGT	South Arabian inscriptions
230 AD	‘D̲BH, GRMT	
	Sembrouthes	
260 AD	DTWNS and ZQRNS	
	Period 3. Endubis to Ezana before his conversion. c.270 AD to c.330 AD	
270 AD		
	Endubis*	Coinage begins
300 AD		
	Aphilas*	
	Wazeba*	
	Ousanas*	
	Ezana*	Inscriptions.
	Period 4. Ezana as a Christian to Kaleb. c. 330 AD to c. 520 AD.	
330 AD		
		Christian inscriptions and coins.
		Anonymous Christian coins
350 AD		
	MHDYS*	
	Ouazebas*	
400 AD		
	Eon*	
	Ebana*	
	Nezool*/Nezana*	
500 AD	Ousas*/Ousana(s)*. Tazena	
	Period 5. Kaleb until the end of the coinage. c.515 AD to early C.7th AD	
	Kaleb*	Inscription
		Yusuf As’ar
530 AD		Sumyafa’ Ashwa
	Alla Amidas*	Abreha
	Wazena*	
	W‘ZB/Ella Gabaz	
	Ioel*	
575 AD		Persians in Yemen
	Hataz* = ‘Iathlia’*?	
	Israel*	
600 AD		
	Gersem*	
614 AD	Armah*	Jerusalem falls to Persia
619 AD		Egypt falls to Persia
		End of Aksum as capital

	Period 6. After the end of the coinage	
630 AD	Death of Ashama ibn Abjar	
640 AD		Arab expedition in Red Sea, Egypt falls to Arabs
705–715 AD	Reign of al-Walid, Qusayr Amra painting	

The symbol * denotes issues of coins

Preface.

Perhaps the most frequently quoted remark about Ethiopia occurs in a brief excursus on the Ethiopian church which Edward Gibbon included in his monmental work *The Decline and Fall of the Roman Empire*, written at the end of the eighteenth century; 'Encompassed on all sides by the enemies of their religion the Æthiopians thiopians slept near a thousand years, forgetful of the world, by whom they were forgotten'. Gibbon further accorded brief mention to those few events in Aksumite Ethiopia's history which touched the larger theme of the history of the Roman empire. In this he still remains relatively unusual, for however one might nowadays view the Ethiopians' 'sleep', Gibbon's last phrases still ring true. Of all the important ancient civilisations of the past, that of the ancient Ethiopian kingdom of Aksum still remains perhaps the least known.

When this book was in preparation, I wrote to the archaeology editor of one of Britain's most prominent history and archaeology publishers about its prospects. He replied that, although he had a degree in archaeology, he had never heard of Aksum, and didn't think it would arouse much interest. If anything, this points the more strongly to the need for an introductory history to one of Africa's most fascinating civilisations. In most of the recent general histories of Africa or of the Roman world, Aksum is either not mentioned at all, or is noted in brief summaries culled from earlier works. Only in Connah's 1987 book *African Civilisations* does Aksum, though still dealt with in one brief chapter, begin to take its proper place as an important part of Africa's history. Certainly there have been books on Aksum, or on Ethiopian civilisation in general, mainly in German, French, Italian and Russian; but since the last of these was published much new work has been done, and a well-illustrated and up-to-date general coverage of Aksumite Ethiopia is now the more urgently required.

It is hoped that this book, the result of nearly fifteen years study of Aksumite history and civilisation, will at least partly fill the gap, and encourage interest in Aksumite studies. Ancient Ethiopia is a fertile field for future researchers, and if this book attracts the attention of even a few towards this neglected but richly rewarding subject, it will have served its purpose adequately. It is worth adding that Ethiopia, and especially

Aksumite Ethiopia, is an elusive entity, and I cannot hope to have always plumped for the correct interpretation in some of the more debated themes of its history. Theories and arguments which I may seem to have left aside could prove to be of great importance to future study. In most cases where a choice between opposing theories has been made, it is nevertheless with a profound consciousness of the stimulation afforded by the points-of-view of colleagues who share the opposite opinion, and with the certainty that the last word has not yet been said, that I have leaned towards certain conclusions. I have not infrequently drawn on my own earlier publications for certain sections of this book, sometimes with radically different results; alterations indicative of the progress made by more recent research.

I am extremely grateful, as the dedication indicates, to the late Dr. H. Neville Chittick for introducing me to Aksumite studies during the important excavations which he directed at Aksum between 1972 and 1974, and for his continued subsequent encouragement. His excavations at Aksum completely altered many concepts about Aksumite Ethiopia, clarifying certain points and, inevitably, raising new questions. In 1985 I was invited by the British Institute in Eastern Africa, under whose auspices Neville Chittick had worked, to publish in their Memoir series the excavation report his death prevented him from undertaking; and it was during this work that the idea of the present book, less specialist and wider-ranging, was suggested to me by Glen Kania. The British Institute in Eastern Africa also kindly gave permission for the reproduction of some of the photographs taken during the excavations. A number of friends and colleagues helped in the preparation of the book; I would particularly like to thank Dr. Bent Juel-Jensen and Dr. David Phillipson for reading and commenting on the typescript at different stages, and for supplying illustrations; Roger Brereton and the late Ruth Plant for other illustrations; Chris Tsielepi for information from the Horniman Museum; Michael Grogan for the maps and Glen Kania for his usual patience and assistance in editing and word-processing, for the fourth time, a book on an Aksumite theme.

Aksum's obscurity, and the impossibility of visiting the site at present, seem to have had a discouraging effect on funding institutions. However, awards which have greatly helped me in the writing of this book, and in my Aksumite studies in general, came from the Twenty-Seven Foundation and the Spalding Trust; to these organisations I am extremely grateful, particularly since they have both assisted my work in other fields as well.

Stuart Munro-Hay

St. Orens-Pouy-Petit, France. December 1988.

I

Introduction

This book is designed to introduce the ancient African civilisation of Aksum to a wider readership than has been catered for by specialist publications currently available. The Ethiopian kingdom centred on Aksum in the northern province of Tigray during the first six or seven hundred years of our era, is still very little known in general terms. Its history and civilisation has been largely ignored, or at most accorded only brief mention, in the majority of recent books purporting to deal at large with ancient African civilisations, or with the world of late antiquity. Perhaps, considering the paucity of published material, authors of such syntheses can hardly be blamed for omitting it; those who do include it generally merely repeat the same vague outlines of Aksumite history as are found in much older works. The excavations of the 1950s-70s in Ethiopia, and the studies of a few scholars in recent years, have increased the scope of our information about the country's history and civilisation, and the time has now come when a general introduction to Aksum should be of value to interested readers and students of ancient history alike.

The Aksumite state bordered one of the ancient world's great arteries of commerce, the Red Sea, and through its port of Adulis Aksum participated actively in contemporary events. Its links with other countries, whether through military campaigns, trading enterprise, or cultural and ideological exchange, made Aksum part and parcel of the international community of the time, peripheral perhaps from the Romano-centric point-of-view, but directly involved with the nations of the southern and eastern spheres, both within the Roman empire and beyond. Aksum's position in the international trade and diplomatic activity which connected the Roman provinces around the Mediterranean via the Red Sea with South Arabia, Persia, India, Sri Lanka, and even China, tied it too firmly into the network of commerce to be simply ignored (Ch. 3: 6).

Whether or not Aksum, as is sometimes claimed (Ch. 4: 5), gave the final coup-de-grâce to the ancient Sudanese kingdom of Meroë in the modern republic of Sudan, it nevertheless had an important influence on the peoples of the Nile valley, and also on the South Arabian kingdoms across the Red Sea (Ch. 3: 6). As far as the history of civilisation in Africa is concerned, the

Map A. Map showing Aksum with Ethiopia, Sudan. the Red Sea, Arabia, Persia, India and Ceylon.

position of Aksum in international terms followed directly on to that of Pharaonic and Ptolemaic Egypt and Meroë; each was, before its eclipse, the only internationally recognised independent African monarchy of important power status in its age. Aksumite Ethiopia, however, differs from the previous two in many ways. Its economy was not based on the agricultural wealth of the Nile Valley, but on the exploitation of the Ethiopian highland environment (Ch. 8) and the Red Sea trade; unlike Egypt and Meroë, Aksumite Ethiopia depended for its communications not on the relatively easy flow along a great river, but on the maintenance of considerably more arduous routes across the highlands and steep river valleys. For its international trade, it depended on sea lanes which required vigilant policing. Most important, Aksum was sufficiently remote never to have come into open conflict with either Rome or Persia, and was neither conquered by these contemporary super-powers, nor suffered from punitive expeditions like Egypt, South Arabia or Meroë. Even the tremendous changes in the balance of power in the Red Sea and neighbouring regions caused by the rise of Islam (Ch. 4: 8) owed something to Aksum. It was an Ethiopian ruler of late Aksumite times who gave protection and shelter to the early followers of the prophet Muhammad, allowing the new religious movement the respite it needed (Ch. 15: 4). Ethiopia, the kingdom of the '*najashi* of Habashat' as the Arabs called the ruler, survived the eclipse of the pre-Islamic political and commercial system, but one of the casualties of the upheaval was the ancient capital, Aksum, itself; various factors removed the government of the country from Aksum to other centres. The Ethiopian kingdom remained independent even though the consolidation of the Muslim empire now made it the direct neighbour of this latest militant imperial power. But eventually Ethiopia lost its hold on the coastal regions as Islam spread across the Red Sea. Nevertheless, the Aksumite kingdom's direct successors in Ethiopia, though at times in desperate straits, retained that independence, and with it even managed to preserve some of the characteristics of the ancient way of life until the present day.

The Aksumites developed a civilisation of considerable sophistication, knowledge of which has been much increased by recent excavations (Ch. 16). Aksum's contribution in such fields as architecture (Ch. 5: 4-6) and ceramics (Ch. 12: 1) is both original and impressive. Their development of the vocalisation of the Ge'ez or Ethiopic script allowed them to leave, alone of ancient African states except Egypt and Meroë, a legacy of written material (Ch. 13: 1, Ch. 11: 5) from which we can gain some impression of Aksumite ideas and policies from their own records. In addition, uniquely for Africa, they produced a coinage, remarkable for several features, especially the inlay of gold on silver and bronze coins (Ch. 9). This coinage, whose very existence speaks for a progressive economic and ambitious political outlook, bore legends in both Greek and Ge'ez, which name the successive kings of Aksum for some three hundred years. The coinage can accordingly be used as a foundation for a chronology of the kingdom's history (Ch.4: 2).

It may be as well to outline briefly here Aksumite historical development, and Aksum's position in the contemporary world, discussed in detail in later chapters (Chs. 4 & 3: 6). Aksumite origins are still uncertain, but a strong South Arabian (Sabaean) influence in architecture, religion, and cultural features can be detected in the pre-Aksumite period from about the fifth century BC, and it is clear that contacts across the Red Sea were at one time very close (Ch. 4: 1). A kingdom called D'MT (perhaps to be read Da'mot or Di'amat) is attested in Ethiopian inscriptions at this early date, and, though the period between this and the development of Aksum around the beginning of the Christian era is an Ethiopian 'Dark Age' for us at present, it may be surmised that the D'MT monarchy and its successors, and other Ethiopian chiefdoms, continued something of the same 'Ethio-Sabaean' civilisation until eventually subordinated by Aksum. A certain linguistic and religious continuity may be observed between the two periods, though many features of Aksumite civilisation differ considerably from the earlier material.

The Aksumite period in Northern Ethiopia covers some six or seven centuries from around the beginning of our era, and was ancestral to the rather better known mediaeval Ethiopian kingdoms, successively based further south in Lasta and Shewa. The Semitic-speaking people called Aksumites or Habash (Abyssinians), centred at their capital city Aksum (Ch. 5) in the western part of the province of Tigray, from there came to control both the highland and coastal regions of northern Ethiopia. They were able to exploit a series of favourable situations, some of which we can only guess at at this stage, to become the dominant power group in the region and to develop their very characteristic civilisation in an area now represented by the province of Tigray, with Eritrea to the north where they gained access to the Red Sea coast at the port of Adulis (Ch.3: 2).

Aksumite inscriptions (Ch. 11: 5), an important, and for Africa this far south, very unusual source of information, mention a number of subordinate kings or chiefs, and it seems that the developing state gradually absorbed its weaker neighbours, but frequently retained traditional rulers as administrators (Ch. 6) under a tribute system. The title *negusa nagast*, or king of kings, used by Aksumite and successive Ethiopian rulers until the death of the late emperor Haile Sellassie, is a reflection of the sort of loose federation under their own monarchy (Ch. 7) which the Aksumites achieved throughout a large part of Ethiopia and neighbouring lands.

In the early centuries AD the Aksumites had already managed, presumably by a combination of such factors as military superiority, access to resources, and wealth resulting from their convenient situation astride trade routes leading from the Nile Valley to the Red Sea, to extend their hegemony over many peoples of northern Ethiopia. The process arouses a certain amount of admiration; anyone familiar with the terrain of that region can readily envisage the difficulties of mastering the various tribal groups scattered from the Red Sea coastal lowlands to the mountains and valleys of the Semien range south-west of Aksum. One Aksumite inscription, the so-called *Monumentum Adulitanum* (Ch. 11: 5) details campaigns undertaken in environments which, in a range of only some 250 km across Ethiopia, varied from the snow and frost of the Semien mountains to the waterless salt plains of the eastern lowlands. The highest point in the mountains reaches about 4620 m and the lowest, in the Danakil desert, is about 110 m below sea level, and although the campaigns would not have touched quite these extremes, the diversity of the country the Aksumites attempted to subdue is well illustrated. The same series of campaigns continued to police the roads leading to the Egyptian frontier region and over the sea to what are now the Yemeni and Saudi Arabian coastlands.

The Aksumite rulers became sufficiently Hellenized to employ the Greek language, as noted quite early on by the Greek shipping guide called the *Periplus of the Erythraean Sea* (Ch. 2: 2), a document variously dated between the mid-first and third centuries AD with a concensus of modern opinion favouring the first or early second centuries. Somewhat later, Greek became one of the customary languages for Aksumite inscriptions and coins, since it was the *lingua franca* of the countries with which they traded.

The Aksumites grew strong enough to expand their military activity into South Arabia by the end of the second or early third century AD, where their control over a considerable area is attested by their Arabian enemies' own inscriptions (Ch. 4: 3 & 4); a direct reversal of the earlier process of South Arabian influence in Ethiopia already mentioned.

As the consolidated Aksumite kingdom grew more prosperous, the monuments and archaeological finds at Aksum and other sites attest to the development of a number of urban centres (Chs. 4 & 5) with many indigenous arts and crafts (Chs. 12 & 13: 3) demonstrating high technological skills, and a vigorous internal and overseas trade (Ch. 8). The inscriptions and other sources imply a rising position for Aksum in the African and overseas political concerns of the period. In the towns, the lack of walls even at Aksum seems to hint at relatively peaceful internal conditions, though the inscriptions (Ch. 11: 5) do mention occasional revolts among the subordinate tribes. Exploitation of the agricultural potential of the region (Ch. 8: 2), in places probably much higher than today and perhaps enhanced by use of irrigation, water-storage, or terracing techniques, allowed these urban communities to develop to considerable size. Perhaps the best-known symbols of the Aksumites' particular ideas and style are the great carved monoliths (Ch. 5: 6), some of which still stand, erected to commemorate their dead rulers; they also record the considerable skill of the Aksumite quarrymen, engineers, and stone-carvers, being in some cases among the largest single stones ever employed in ancient times.

The prosperity which such works bespeak came from Aksum's key position in the exploitation of certain costly luxuries, either brought from areas under Aksum's direct control, traded locally, or transhipped from afar

(Ch. 8: 4). We have accounts of trade in such precious items as turtle-shell from the Dahlak Islands near Adulis, obsidian, also from Red Sea islands, ivory from across the Nile, rhino-horn, incense, and emeralds from the Beja lands in the Red Sea hills. Gold from the Sudan was paid for by salt from the Danakil desert, cattle, and iron. Other commodities such as civet, certain spices, animal skins, and hides seem also to have been among Aksum's exports. Royal titles on inscriptions attest (Ch. 7: 5) to Aksum's claim to control the catchment area of some of these exports, including parts of such neighbouring regions as the old Kushite or Meroitic kingdom, the lands of the Noba and Beja peoples, other now-unidentifiable African districts, and even parts of South Arabia. To some extent such claims may be wishful thinking, but the general prosperity and reputation of the country led the Persian religious leader Mani to label Aksum as the third of the kingdoms of the world in the later third century; and something of this reputation is substantiated by the production of an independent coinage (Ch. 9) at about this time. It paralleled the country with the few other contemporary states with the wealth and political status to issue gold coinage; Rome, Persia (to a lesser degree), and, into the third century, the Kushana kingdom in northern India.

Aksum's considerable imports (Ch. 8), ranging from wines and olive oil to cloth, iron, glass and objects of precious metals, are reported by various ancient writers, but containers for the foodstuffs and examples of some of the others have also been found in tombs and domestic buildings excavated at the capital and other towns. From such discoveries some ideas can be suggested concerning the social structure and way of life of the Aksumites (Ch. 14), while the tombs reveal something of their attitude to death and expectations of an afterlife. There was a radical change in this sphere in the second quarter of the fourth century, when the Aksumite king Ezana, previously a worshipper of gods identified with such Greek deities as Zeus, Poseidon, and Ares, was converted to Christianity (Ch. 10). From then on the coins and inscriptions show royal support for the new religion by replacing the old disc and crescent motifs of the former gods with the cross, though it may have taken a considerable time for Christianity to spread into the remoter regions under Aksumite control. Aksumite inscriptions from this period are in three scripts and two languages; Ge'ez, the local language, written both in its own cursive script and in the South Arabian monumental script (Epigraphic South Arabian, or ESA), and Greek, the international language of the Red Sea trade and the Hellenized Orient.

The adoption of Christianity must have aligned the kingdom to some extent towards the Roman empire, but this seems not to have been a slavish obedience for political ends. The Alexandrian patriarch Athanasius appointed, about 330AD, a Tyrian called Frumentius, who had lived in Aksum for some years, as Aksum's first bishop (Ch. 10: 2), and this apparently founded a tradition of Alexandrian appointments to the see of Aksum. In about

356AD the emperor Constantius II wrote to Ezana trying to persuade him to submit Frumentius to doctrinal examination by his own appointee to Alexandria, the bishop George of Cappadocia, who, with the emperor, subscribed to the Arian heresy. In such matters of church politics, Aksum seems to have followed Alexandria's lead, and refused to adopt Constantius' proposed changes. After the Council of Chalcedon in 451 the international church was divided, and Aksum, with Egypt and much of the east, split from the so-called melkite or imperial church and followed the monophysite interpretation of Christ's nature which Ethiopia still retains.

Little is known about fifth century Aksum, but in the sixth century king Kaleb (Ch. 4: 6 & 7) reiterated Aksumite claims to some sort of control in the Yemen by mounting an invasion. This was ostensibly undertaken to prevent continued persecution there of the Christians by the recently emerged Jewish ruler, Yusuf Asar, though interference with foreign traders, and perhaps fears of a new pro-Persian policy in Arabia, may have been strong incentives for Aksum, with Constantinople in the background, to interfere. The invasion succeeded, and Kaleb appointed a new ruler. However, Aksum does not seem to have been able to maintain its overseas conquests, and a military coup soon deposed Kaleb's client king, who was replaced by a certain Abreha. The latter maintained himself against subsequent Aksumite invasion forces, and is said by the contemporary historian Procopius to have come to terms with Kaleb's successor.

In any event, as the sixth and seventh centuries progressed Aksum's position grew more difficult. The independence of the Yemen was followed by its conquest by Persia during the reign of the Sassanian king Khusro I (531-579), and further Persian disruption of the Roman east followed with the conquest of Syria and Egypt under Khusro II. This seems to have dried up some of Aksum's flow of trade, and the kingdom's expansionist days were over. Arab conquests followed in the mid-seventh century, and the whole economic system which had maintained Aksum's prosperity came to an end. Christian Ethiopia retained its control of the highlands, but seems to have turned away from the sea in the centuries after the advent of Islam and begun to look more southwards than eastwards during the following centuries.

The centre of the kingdom being moved from Aksum, the city became a politically unimportant backwater (Ch. 15). In the archaeological excavations conducted there (Ch. 16), nothing significant was found in the tombs or buildings which could certainly be attributed to a later date, and it seems that by about 630 the town had been abandoned as a capital, although it continued on a much reduced scale as a religious centre and occasional coronation place for later dynasties. The large residences in the town were first occupied or built around by squatters, in some cases, apparently, even during the reigns of the last coin-issuing kings, then gradually covered by material brought down by run-off from the deforested hills. The exhausted state of the land, and climatic changes (Ch. 15) combined with a number of other factors must have compelled the rulers finally to shift their capital elsewhere. Ge'ez accounts suggest that the *najashi* (*negus* or king) whose death is noted by Arab records in 630, and who was a contemporary with Muhammad, had already done this. He is said to have been buried at Weqro (Wiqro, Wuqro) south-east of Aksum rather than in the ancient royal cemetery. The names of other Ethiopian capitals begin to be mentioned by Arab authors from about this time (Ch. 4: 8).

It seems, therefore, that the city of Aksum probably lasted as an important centre from about the first to the seventh centuries AD. The wealth it gained from its control of much of highland Ethiopia, and its rich trade with the Roman world maintained it until the late sixth century, but after that first Persian and then later Arab conquests first disrupted this commerce and then prevented any re-establishment of the Red Sea route from Adulis to the Roman world. Though a powerful Ethiopian state continued in the highlands, the old centre of Aksum, its trading advantages gone, and its hinterland no longer able to support a large population, shrank to small town or village status, with only the particularly sacred precincts of the cathedral of Mary of Zion, the stelae, mostly fallen, and a vast store of local legends about its history (Ch. 2: 1) to preserve its memory.

II

Legend, Literature and Archaeological Discovery

1. The Legends of Aksum

The town of Aksum is today only a small district centre, not even the capital of the northern Ethiopian province of Tigray in which it is situated. However, despite this relative unimportance in modern times, Aksum's past position is reflected by the prime place it occupies in the fabric of legends which make up traditional Ethiopian history. For the people of Ethiopia, it is even now regarded as the ancient residence and capital city of the queen of Sheba, the second Jerusalem, and the resting place of the Ark of the Covenant. One text calls the city the 'royal throne of the kings of Zion, mother of all lands, pride of the entire universe, jewel of kings' (Levine 1974: 111). The cathedral of Maryam Tseyon, or Mary of Zion, called Gabaza Aksum, was the holiest place in the Ethiopian Christian kingdom, and is still said to house the Ark, supposedly brought from Jerusalem by the first emperor, Menelik. Tradition says that he was the son of king Solomon of Israel and the queen of Sheba conceived during the queen's famous visit to Jerusalem. Although no information survives in the legends about the ancient Aksumite rulers who really built the palaces and erected the giant stone obelisks or stelae which still stand in several places around the town, these monuments are locally attributed in many instances to Menelik or to Makeda, the queen of Sheba or queen of Azab (the South). Such legends are still a living force at Aksum today; for example, the mansion recently excavated in the district of Dungur, west of Aksum, has immediately been absorbed into local legends as the 'palace of the queen of Sheba' (Chittick 1974: 192, n. 28).

In the tales describing life in Ethiopia before the reign of the queen of Sheba, Aksum holds an important place. A tale about a local saint, Marqorewos, states that Aksum was formerly called Atsabo (Conti Rossini 1904: 32). The *Matshafa Aksum*, or 'Book of Aksum' (Conti Rossini 1910: 3; Beckingham and Huntingford 1961: 521ff), a short Ge'ez (Ethiopic) work of the seventeenth century or a little earlier, says that the town was formerly built at Mazeber ('ruin') where was the tomb of Ityopis (Ethiopis), son of Kush, son of Ham, son of Noah. A structure called the 'tomb of Ethiopis' (Littmann 1913: II, taf. XXVII) is still shown near Aksum, a little to the west of the modern town in an area where the ruins of many large structures of

1. Painted miniature from a XVth century Ethiopic *Psalter* depicting king Solomon, reputed ancestor of the Ethiopian monarchy. Photo B. Juel-Jensen.

the ancient capital still lie buried. Makeda next moved the city to the territory called 'Aseba, from whence she is said to have gained her name queen of Saba (Sheba). The third building of the city is stated to have been accomplished by the kings Abreha and Atsbeha (Ch. 10:3). An Arab writer of the sixteenth century, describing how the *tabot* or Ark was removed from the cathedral of Aksum to a safe place when the Muslim armies approached, says of Aksum *'it is not known who built it: some say it was Dhu al-Qarnayn* (Alexander the Great). *God alone knows best'*! (from the *Futuh al-Habasha*, or 'History of the Conquest of Abyssinia' by Arab-Faqih; de Villard 1938: 61-2).

Several modern authors (eg. Doresse 1956, 1971; Kitchen 1971) have speculated as to whether Tigray or the Ethiopian-Sudanese borderlands, instead of Arabia or the Horn of Africa, may have been the legendary 'God's Land' of the ancient Egyptians. This land of Punt, producer of incense and other exotic treasures, where the pharaohs sent their ships, may at least have been one of the regions included at some time in the Aksumites' extended kingdom. Egyptian expeditions to Punt are known from as far back as Old Kingdom times in Egypt, in the third millenium BC, but the best- known report comes from the New Kingdom period, during the reign of queen Hatshepsut, in the fifteenth century BC. She was so proud of her great foreign trading expedition that she had detailed reliefs of it carved on the walls of her funerary temple at Dayr al-Bahri across the Nile from the old Egyptian capital of Thebes. The surviving reliefs show that the region was organised even then under chiefly rule, with a population eager to trade the recognisably African products of their lands with the visitors. Aksum is still today a sorting and distibution centre for the frankincense produced in the region, and it is not unlikely that the coastal stations visited by the ancient Egyptians acquired their incense from the same sources. Punt is suggested to have been inland from the Sawakin-north Eritrean coast (Kitchen 1971; Fattovich 1988, 1989i), and, apart from the great similarity of its products with those of the Sudan-Ethiopia border region, an Egyptian hieroglyphic text seems to confirm its identity with the Ethiopian highland region by reference to a downpour in the land of Punt which caused the Nile to flood (Petrie 1888: p. 107). The inscription dates to the twenty-sixth Egyptian dynasty, and knowledge of Punt seems to have continued even into the Persian period in Egypt, when king Darius in an inscription of 486-5BC mentions, or at least claims, that the Puntites sent tribute (Fattovich 1989ii: 92). One extremely interesting Egyptian record from an 18th Dynasty tomb at Thebes actually shows Puntite trading boats or rafts with triangular sails (Säve-Söderbergh 1946: 24), for transporting the products of Punt, indicating that the commerce was not exclusively Egyptian-carried, and that local Red Sea peoples were already seafaring – or at least conveying goods some distance by water (Sleeswyk 1983) – for themselves.

Returning to more specifically Aksumite matters, the *Book of Aksum* states that Aksumawi, son of Ityopis (Ethiopis), and great-grandson of Noah, was the founder of the city, and the names of his descendants (the 'fathers of Aksum') gave rise to the various district names. His son was Malakya-Aksum, and his grandsons Sum, Nafas, Bagi'o, Kuduki, Akhoro and Fasheba (Littmann 1913: I, 38). In other legends (Littmann 1947), it is said that once a serpent-king, Arwe or Waynaba, ruled over the land, exacting a tribute of a young girl each year. It may be that the tale reflects memory of a serpent-cult in the region. Eventually a stranger, Angabo, arrived, and rescued the chosen girl, killing the monster at the same time. Angabo was duly elected king by the people, and one of his successors was Makeda. Sometimes the legends say that it was Makeda herself who was the intended sacrifice and inheritor of the kingdom. The essential element of all this was to appropriate for Aksum, one way or another, the legends which referred to the remote origins of Ethiopian history. The Englishman Nathaniel Pearce, who lived in Ethiopia in the early nineteenth century, related (Pearce 1831) how these stories were still current amongst the Ethiopians; *'In the evening, while sitting with Ozoro, she told me a number of silly tales about Axum, among others a long story about a large snake which ruled the country...which sometimes resided at Temben, though Axum was the favourite residence of the two''*. Pearce was later shown what seems to have been a fruit press, but which he interpreted as being *'made by the ancients to prepare some kind of cement in for building'*; his Ethiopian friend told him that this had actually been designed as a container for the snake's food.

The origins of these legends hark back to some unknown time after the conversion of the kingdom to Christianity in the reign of king Ezana of Aksum in the fourth century AD, or in some cases perhaps to an even earlier period when some Jewish traditions had entered the country. Such legends had their political use in providing pedigrees for national institutions. It was believed in later times that the state offices from the king downwards were descended from the company which had brought the Ark to Aksum from Jerusalem (Budge 1922: 61). Doubtless the Christian priests, searching for a longer pedigree for their religion to impress pagans and unbelievers, would have been interested in developing these tales which connected Ethiopia with Solomon and Sheba. The Ethiopian kings themselves, anxious to acquire the prestige of ancient and venerable dynastic ancestors, could scarcely have hoped for a more august couple as their reputed progenitors. Even in the official Ethiopian Constitution, up to the time of the end of the reign of emperor Haile Selassie, the dynasty was held to have descended directly from Solomon and the queen of Sheba through their mythical son, the emperor Menelik I.

The real events in Ethiopia's history before the present two millenia are lost in the mists of antiquity, but valiant attempts were made by Ethiopian chroniclers to fill in the immense gap between the reign of Menelik I and the time of the kings of Aksum. The king lists they developed (all those now surviving are of comparatively recent date), name a long line of rulers,

2. Built into one of the walls of the cathedral of Maryan Tseyon at Aksum, the so-called Stone of Bazen, surmounted by the Stele of the Lances.

covering the whole span from Menelik through the Aksumite period and on to the later Zagwé and 'Solomonic' dynasties (Conti Rossini 1909). There is little point in reciting the majority of these names, but some of the most important of the reputed successors of Menelik I are worth noting for their importance in Ethiopian tradition.

The legendary king Bazen was supposed to have been reigning at the time of the birth of Christ in his eighth year (one modern interpretation even depicts him as one of the Three Kings who came to Bethlehem). A tomb is attributed to him in the south-eastern necropolis of Aksum, at the entrance to the modern town on the Adwa road. Near the cathedral is a stone on which is written in Ge'ez *'This is the sepulchral stone of Bazen'*, but when this inscription was actually carved is unknown (Littmann 1913: IV, 49); evidently after the arrival of Christianity in Ethiopia, since it begins and ends with a cross. Two rulers preeminent in Ethiopian tradition were Abreha and Atsbeha (Ch. 10: 3), brothers who are said to have ruled jointly. They were converted to Christianity by the missionary Frumentius, and their example was eventually followed by the entire nation. Another hero in Aksumite legend was king Kaleb, also called Ella Atsbeha (Ch. 4: 7). He was regarded as a great conqueror and Christian hero whose expedition to suppress the persecution of his co-religionists in the Yemen by the Jewish king there caused his name to be famous throughout the Christian world. He is recognised as a saint in several church calendars. Two sons of Kaleb, called Gabra Masqal and Israel, are said to have succeeded him, and their rule is supposed to have encompassed both the physical and the spiritual worlds. Local legend in Aksum attributes an unusual double tomb structure to Gabra Masqal and his father Kaleb (Littmann 1913: II, 127ff); but Gabra Masqal is also supposed to be buried at his monastic foundation, Dabra Damo, to the north-east of Aksum. Finally among the legendary accounts come Degnajan, Anbessa Wedem and Dil Na'od, the kings in whose reigns, according to tradition, the collapse of Aksum eventually occurred (Sergew 1972, 203ff). It seems that in reality the stories about these three rulers refer to a time after Aksum had ceased to be the capital, and the traditions, interestingly, associate all of these theoretical 'kings of Aksum' with activities in Shewa, Amhara, and other southern regions, even mentioning details implying a shift of the capital.

Much of this legendary literature is, of course, based very broadly on actual events and personalities. The story of Kaleb's conquest of the Yemen is at least a genuine historical occurrence (Ch. 4: 7), and, although there seem to be various distortions, the main theme of the conversion of the kingdom to Christianity by Frumentius also has independent historical confirmation (Ch. 10: 2). When more information is available about Ethiopian history in the period of Aksum's zenith and decline, it is very probable that the reality behind many other legends will be decoded into more prosaic form.

Legendary accounts for the fifth century are particularly rich, since it was then that the so-called Nine Saints (Sergew 1972, 115ff) and other foreign missionaries arrived in Ethiopia. Some of these would appear to have been Roman subjects from the Syrian provinces, probably seeking safe exile from the persecutions suffered by followers of the monophysite interpretation of the nature of Christ. They settled in various districts of the Aksumite kingdom, and began, it seems, the real Christianisation of the Ethiopian countryside population as apart from the official, royal, conversion of the fourth century, whose influence was no doubt somewhat limited. Around the missionaries' work a large and fascinating cycle of legends, full of miraculous happenings, developed, and is reported by the various *gadlan* ('lives', literally 'struggles') of the saints. Their arrival and activities are set in the reigns of the fifth and sixth century kings Sa'aldoba, Ella Amida, Tazena, Kaleb and Gabra Masqal. The legendary accounts certainly contain elements of truth, and it seems that the missionaries who worked to convert the Aksumite population left traces of themselves in the Ge'ez language itself, since they used certain Aramaic/Syriac words in their translation of the Bible which remained in use ever afterwards (Ullendorff 1967).

One of the stories related about the end of Aksum, the tale of the foreign queen, called Gudit, Judith or Esato, seems also to have actual relevance to Ethiopian history in the last half of the tenth century. Gudit is said to have attacked the Aksumite kingdom, and driven the king out. Her armies harried the royal forces, destroying cities and churches as they went, and collecting plunder on a large scale. In Aksum they are said to have caused immense destruction, damaging the cathedral, smashing the altars, and even toppling some of the great stelae. Certain Arab historians corroborate parts of the tale; one, Ibn Hawqal, (Kramers and Weit 1964) states that, in the later tenth century, a foreign queen was able to take over the country, eventually killing the king. Another simply notes that a Yemeni king, sending a gift to the king of Iraq, included a female zebra previously sent to him by a queen who ruled over Habasha (Abyssinia), dating this event to AD969-70 (el-Chennafi 1976). The *History of the Patriarchs of Alexandria* preserves a letter from an unnamed Ethiopian king to George (Girgis) II of Nubia, in which the king, attacked by the 'Queen of the Bani al-Hamwiyya', bemoans his fate, attributing his distress to a rift between the monarchy and the patriarchate, and begs the Nubian king to intercede for him with the Alexandrian patriarch (Atiya et al. 1948, 171-2; Budge, 1928ii: I, 233-4). Though the origin of this queen is obscure, it is possible that she was ruler of one of the pagan kingdoms to the south, such as Damot.

The Portuguese father Francisco Alvares, whose book on Ethiopia was written by 1540 (Beckingham and Huntingford 1961), reported that Aksum (which he calls *"a very good [big] town named Aquaxumo")..."was the city, court and residence (as they say) of the Queen Saba [whose own name was Maqueda]"*... He also wrote that *"Aquaxumo was the principal residence of Queen Candace* (the title of the queens of the ancient Sudanese kingdom of Kush or Kasu, whose capital was Meroë), *[whose personal name was Giudich]* (Judith or Gudit), *who was the beginning of the country's being Christian...they say that here was fulfilled the prophecy which David spoke "Ethiopia shall arise, and stretch forth her hands to God"* (Psalm lxviii.31). *So they say they were the first Christians in the world"*. Alvares has conflated the pagan/Jewish queen Judith with Candace (Kandake) the 'queen of the Ethiopians', whose eunuch treasurer was converted to Christianity by the apostle Philip (Acts, ch.8), and whom the Ethiopians claim was actually a ruler of Ethiopia rather than of Meroë; in such ways do the legends grow more and more confused. Alvares also mentions the *"large and handsome tower....a royal affair, all of well hewn stone"* (the pre-Aksumite Sabaean temple at Yeha, Ch. 4: 1), as another edifice which *"belonged to Candace"*.

Ethiopian Christian chroniclers have sought to connect their country with several other events and prophecies mentioned in the Bible. The kingdom was referred to in ancient documents as 'Aksum' or the country 'of the Aksumites', after the capital city and the ruling tribal group or clan. The people, or perhaps a group of peoples including the 'Aksumites', were also called 'Habasha', and the name for their country, Habashat, is that from which we derive the now out-of-fashion name 'Abyssinia'. However, already by the fourth century AD the Aksumite king Ezana, in his long list of titles in a bilingual inscription (see Ch. 11: 4), uses the word 'Ethiopia' in the Greek version as the translation for 'Habashat'. The original use of the Greek designation 'Ethiopia' was either as a general designation for the black peoples south of the Egyptian border (as the Arabs later used 'al-Habasha' or its plural 'Ahabish' for groups like the Zanj, Beja, and Nubians as well as the Abyssinians; Tolmacheva 1986), or more specifically as a reference to the kingdom of Kush or Kasu, with its capital at Meroë on the Sudanese Nile. But after the eclipse of this state, the kings of both Aksum and Nubia (Munro-Hay 1982-3) used the name 'Ethiopia' to refer to their own countries and peoples. Thus the mentions of Kush in the Bible have been attributed to Aksumite 'Ethiopia', instead of Meroitic/Kushite Ethiopia, by those Christian interpreters determined to bestow a long and prominent tradition, beginning with Kush, grandson of Noah, on their country.

By the fourth century AD Aksumite pilgrims began to appear in Jerusalem, and St. Jerome noted their presence (Cerulli 1943: I, 1). A few fourth-century Aksumite coins have been found there and in Caesarea (Barkay 1981; Meshorer 1965-6). Later the Ethiopians had a religious house at Jerusalem (Meinardus 1965) which helped to spread the growing interest in Ethiopia in subsequent centuries, and also played its part in disseminating the legendary history of Ethiopia in the west.

The Ethiopian traditional king-lists and chronicles are important in that, late as they are in their present form, they show how vital the legends concerning Aksum have been to the Ethiopians throughout their history. They are unquestionably erroneous, since there are widely differing versions both of the king-lists and the lists of metropolitan bishops of Aksum starting with Frumentius. They also fail to name those kings and bishops who are known from inscriptions, coins, and other sources except in a very few cases. Although it has been suggested that, in the case of the kings, this could be in part due to the Ethiopian rulers' custom of employing several names (as, for example, a personal name, a throne name, a 'tribal' name and so on; see Ch 7: 5), the differences in the lists are not to be so simply explained. Nevertheless, the compilation of the lists, the collection of anecdotes and chronicles, and the attempts to root Ethiopian tradition in the remote past connected with eminent persons, places and events, clearly indicates the importance of the country's past history to mediaeval and even to more modern Ethiopians. Such texts remain a testimony, whether their contents be partly legendary or not, to the efforts of Ethiopian scholars over the centuries to understand and interpret their own history.

2. Aksum in Ancient Sources.

Some details about the political and military history of Aksum have been preserved in ancient documentary sources, some Aksumite and some foreign. A number of Greek and Roman geographers and scholars noted small snippets of information about contemporary Aksum, and certain travellers, merchants, ecclesiastics and ambassadors added various facts about the country in their writings. None of them seems to have acquired any really substantial knowledge about the kingdom- certainly no-one appears to have left us more than the briefest accounts- but at least we are afforded some slight glimpses from time to time.

The Roman writer Gaius Plinius Secundus – Pliny the Younger – , whose notes on Ethiopia in his *Naturalis Historia* were probably completed in their present form in AD77 (Rackham 1948: 467-9), mentions only Aksum's 'window on the world', the Red Sea port of Adulis, through which the kingdom's international trade passed. Another document, called the *Periplus of the Erythraean Sea*, notes the *'city of the people called Auxumites*' (Schoff 1912: 23) or *'the metropolis called the Axomite*' (Huntingford 1980: 20), or *'the metropolis itself, which is called Axômitês'* (Casson 1989: 53), and gives details of the trade goods imported and exported. This anonymous report, which modern scholars view as either an official report, or a merchants' and sailors' guide to the known Red Sea and Indian Ocean ports, dating perhaps somewhere between the mid-first and the early second century AD, also describes the ruler of this region. This monarch, almost certainly the Aksumite king himself (but see Cerulli 1960: 7, 11; Huntingford 1980: 60, 149-50; Chittick 1981: 186; Casson 1989: 109-10), was called Zoskales; he is represented as a miserly man, but of good character, who had some acquaintance with Greek literature. The famous Greek astronomer and geographer, Claudius Ptolomaeus – Ptolemy – of Alexandria, describes Aksum in the middle of the second century AD as the seat of the king's palace (Stevenson 1932: 108); and the existence of a prospering trading centre at Aksum at about this time is confirmed by the latest archaeological investigations (Munro-Hay 1989).

The Persian religious leader Mani, founder of the Manichaean religion, who died in 276 or 277 AD, is reported by his followers to have described the four most important kingdoms of the world as comprising Persia, Rome, Aksum and Sileos, the latter possibly China (Polotsky 1940: 188-9). This remark shows that Aksum's repute was spreading in the contemporary world. It was about this time that the Aksumites produced their own coinage, an excellent way of bringing their country into prominence abroad, since only the greatest of contemporary states issued a gold coinage.

Around 356AD, the Roman emperor Constantius II wrote a letter to Ezana, king of Aksum, and his brother Sazana, on an ecclesiastical matter. The letter has been preserved in the *Apologia ad Constantium Imperatorem* of the famous Alexandrian patriarch Athanasius (Szymusiak 1958). Aksum is also mentioned in the account (Philostorgius; ed. Migne 1864: 482ff.) of the travels of an Arian bishop, Theophilus 'the Indian', who was sent by Constantius to try to convert the Arabian kingdoms; he later seems to have visited Aksum. It has been suggested that possibly it was he who carried the letter from Constantius to the Aksumite rulers, but Schneider (1984: 156) points out that according to Philostorgius Theophilus returned from his mission not long after 344AD. The ecclesiastical historian Rufinus (ed. Migne 1849: 478-9), writing at the end of the fourth century, gives an account of the conversion of the country, apparently taken directly from bishop Frumentius of Aksum's erstwhile companion, Aedesius of Tyre.

Very little is known of the fifth century history of Aksum, but in the sixth century the dramatic events following upon king Kaleb of Aksum's expedition to the Yemen greatly interested the Christian world. Several ambassadors from Constantinople, sent by the emperor Justinian to propose various trading and military arrangements, have left accounts of their embassies. One ambassador described the king's appearance at an audience (Malalas, ed. Migne 1860: 670). Another Greek-speaking visitor, Kosmas, called 'Indikopleustes', who was in Ethiopia just before Kaleb's expedition, was asked by the king's governor at Adulis to copy an inscription so that it could be sent to the king at Aksum. He complied, and preserved the contents of the inscription, together with various other interesting details about Aksumite life, in his *Christian Topography* (Wolska-Conus 1968, 1973).

After the time of Kaleb, foreign reports about Ethiopia grow much sparser. The Byzantine historian Procopius mentions (ed. Dewing 1961: 191) that Kaleb's successor had to acknowledge the virtual independence of the Yemeni ruler Abreha, but all the rest of our information on the later Aksumite kings comes from inferences drawn from their coinage. For the followers of the recently-arisen prophet Muhammad, the Muslims, the country was important because the reigning *najashi* gave asylum to the prophet's early followers (Guillaume 1955: 146ff). Muhammad is said to have mourned when he heard of this king's death. However, the *najashi*, Ashama ibn Abjar, though he was the ruler of the territories of the Aksumite kingdom, may no longer have used that city as his capital. There is reason for thinking that by the time of Ashama's death in 630 AD, the centre of the kingdom may have shifted elsewhere. If this is so, the portrait of a *najashi* or *nigos* (the picture is labelled in both Greek and Arabic), preserved on the walls of a hunting lodge at Qusayr 'Amra in Jordan, built and decorated at the command of the Caliph al-Walid (705-715 AD), would be of one of the successors of Ashama ibn Abjar who was no longer resident at Aksum (Almagro et al 1975: 165 & pl. XVII).

In the ninth and tenth centuries, Arab historians still noted the vast extent of the territories of the reigning *najashi* (see Ch. 4: 8), but situated the capital at a place called Ku'bar or Ka'bar, a large and prosperous trading town. Where this was, we do not know at present, but presumably it was situated in a place more favourable for the exploitation of trade and for participating in current political events than was Aksum. The legends about the fall of Aksum to Gudit, which seem, from the accounts of the Arab authors, to have derived from events in the later tenth century, do not really militate against this. Aksum, as Ethiopia's pre-eminent ecclesiastical centre, and perhaps coronation city, (a function restored to it in later times), may have suffered from Gudit's armies, but was not necessarily the country's administrative capital at the time. The great wealth of its cathedral, the ruins of its palaces, and the giant funerary monuments of its former kings, might well have attracted the attention of invaders in search of loot. Several of the kings mentioned in Ethiopian historical texts are said to have moved their capitals, doubtless reflecting the memory of a real event, unless they were already by that time nomadic tented capitals as was customary later in Ethiopian history.

3. THE REDISCOVERY OF AKSUM IN MODERN TIMES. Whatever was the cause of the end of the former Aksumite kingdom, a new centre eventually appeared in the province of Lasta to the south under a dynasty, apparently of Cushitic (Agaw) origin, later regarded as usurpers, called the Zagwé (Taddesse Tamrat 1972: 53ff; *Dictionary of Ethiopian Biography* 1975: 200ff). The existence of a long and a short chronology for this dynasty indicates that the Ge'ez chroniclers were in some confusion as to the precise events occurring at the end of the 'Aksumite' period until the advent of the Zagwé. The Zagwé capital, surely one of the world's most remarkable sights with its marvellous rock-cut churches, was at Roha, later renamed after the most famous of the Zagwé kings, Lalibela, who seems to have died around 1225. It still bears his name.

The Zagwé dynasty was eventually superseded by the so-called 'Solomonic Restoration' in 1270, under king Yekuno Amlak. This new dynasty held to the legalistic fiction that Yekuno Amlak was a direct heir to the old Aksumite kings, whose line had been preserved in exile in the province of Amhara until strong enough to regain their inheritance by ousting the Zagwé monarchs. By the time of this restoration, and for a long period afterwards, the highland kingdom was involved in struggles with the constantly encroaching power of the Muslim states which had become established along the seaboard, and were pushing inland and up onto the Ethiopian plateau. In spite of some successes, the kingdom was in great distress when the first westerners began to renew the old contacts formerly maintained with the Ethiopian highlands by Greek, Roman, Indian and Arab traders.

Though there is a mention of Aksum (Chaxum) in a Venetian merchant itinerary (Crawford 1958: 28) of the late fourteenth century (which specifically notes Aksum's status as a coronation city and the magnificence of its basilica, richly ornamented with gold plates), it was, in fact, the Portuguese who first made real contact. A number of Ethiopian kings, such as Widim Ar'ad (1297-1312), Yeshaq (1414-1429), and Zara Ya'qob (1434-1468), had previously tried to communicate by sending missions to Europe, and as a result a certain interest was aroused.

In the early fourteenth century the now-lost treatise written by Giovanni da Carignano, who obtained his information from an Ethiopian embassy which stopped at Genoa in 1306 while returning from Avignon and Rome, had declared that the legendary Christian king Prester John was to be found in Ethiopia (Beckingham 1980). It is, of course, possible that Jacopo Filippo Foresti of Bergamo, who summarised Carignano's work in 1483, interpolated this idea, but a map of 1339 already shows Prester John in Ethiopia.

Aksum appears on a map by Pizzigani in 1367 as Civitas Syone, the City of Zion, appropriately enough in view of its cathedral dedicated to Mary of Zion. At the end of the fourteenth century Antonio Bartoli of Florence was in Ethiopia, and in 1407 Pietro Rombulo arrived there, remaining for a very long time. Envoys of Yeshaq reached Valencia with letters from the king to Alfonso of Aragon in 1428. In 1441 Ethiopian monks from Jerusalem attended the Council of Florence (Tedeschi 1988) and some of their remarks about their country, recorded through an Arab-speaking interpreter by Poggio Bracciolini, constitute the first more or less credible description of Ethiopia printed in Europe (1492). Embassies sent by Zara Ya'qob to Cairo in 1443 and 1447 were also reported in Europe. In 1450 Rombulo went to Italy as ambassador for Zara Ya'qob to Alfonso of Aragon, and met Pietro Ranzano, who recorded some of his account in his very muddled description of the land of Prester John (this work is still unpublished). Alfonso replied, mentioning that on a previous occasion the artisans and envoys he had sent had all died. Ethiopian maps were produced, such as the Egyptus Novelo of c. 1454 (which does not include Aksum) and that of Fra Mauro, 1460, which shows it under the name 'Hacsum'. From 1470-1524 the Venetian Alessandro Zorzi was collecting his *Ethiopian Itineraries* (Crawford 1958), some of which mention Aksum or Axon (*'great city of Davit, prete Jani of Ethiopia'*)

The Portuguese, beginning their expansion in the East, envisaged allying with Prester John against the Muslims, who were natural enemies of Portuguese trading development. Portuguese sailors, soldiers, and priests began to penetrate into Ethiopia in the later fifteenth century, and their accounts renewed interest in the history and legends of the country, and also brought to notice the ruins of the ancient capital of Aksum (Rey 1929; Caraman 1985; de Villard 1938). This was a fascinating period in the history of Ethiopia. The tales told by the Portuguese missionaries and envoys, and the absolutely extraordinary journeys, made willingly or not, which they undertook, are well worth the reading; but they are not, alas, within the compass of a work purely on Aksum. It was they, however, who reintroduced the ancient Ethiopian capital to the world, and some of them described the ruined town with a certain amount of detail. The best of these accounts are quoted *in extenso* below, Ch 5: 3.

In the last years of the emperor Eskender (1478-1494) Pero de Covilhã, the first of the Portuguese envoys, who had been sent to the east by his king João II, reached the country. He was never allowed to leave, and he remained in Ethiopia until he died. By 1502 king Manoel I of Portugal had adopted the resounding title 'Lord of the Conquest, Navigation and Commerce of Ethiopia, India, Arabia and Persia', a manifesto of intentions towards Ethiopia which were never to be realised. Perhaps the conquest of Goa and Ormuz had raised expectations elsewhere. In 1507 Covilhã was joined by João Gomes, a priest sent by Tristão da Cunha. Both of them were still there when the priest Francisco Alvares, to whom we owe a great debt for his description of the Ethiopia of his day (Alvares, ed. Beckingham and Huntingford 1961), arrived with the Portuguese fleet bringing the ambassador Rodrigo de Lima in 1520 (Thomas and Cortesão 1938). In 1512, the first reply to these embassies was sent by the Ethiopian queen-regent Eleni (Helena), through a certain Matthew, apparently an Armenian, who eventually managed to get to Portugal and return with the 1520 embassy, dying just afterwards. The military successes of the emperors Na'od (1494-1508) and Lebna Dengel (1508-1540) led the Ethiopians to make little of the opportunity for alliance offered by Rodrigo de Lima's embassy, a grave error since almost immediately after the embassy's departure in 1526 the attacks of the amir of Adal, Ahmad Gragn (or Grañ; 'the left-handed'), began to wreak havoc in the kingdom. This continued until 1542, but already in 1541, in response to renewed appeals, the Portuguese soldier Cristovão da Gama, son of Vasco da Gama, had arrived with his troops. The Portuguese (though da Gama himself was killed in 1542) helped the new emperor Galawdewos or Claudius (1540 -1559) to rescue his country from the depredations of the amir of Adal, who eventually died as a result of wounds inflicted in battle. Galawdewos himself later perished in battle, but the Ethiopian Christian state was from this time on in less danger from its Muslim enemies than before.

During his campaigns Gragn, like queen Gudit, had sacked Aksum and it was probably he who burnt the famous cathedral of 'our Lady Mary Zion, the Mother of God'. Sartsa Dengel (1563-1597) was the next king after Zara Ya'qob to celebrate his coronation at Aksum, and perhaps at this time he built a small church in the ruins, which probably perished in its turn during the Galla war of 1611. There may have been some restoration of this structure, before the present church was constructed by the emperor Fasiladas (1632-1667) with Portuguese or Indian influenced architects; it seems to have been dedicated in 1655. Though the ancient cathedral disappeared as a result of Gragn's destruction, there is preserved among the Portuguese records Francisco Alvares' description of its appearance a decade or two before (Ch. 5: 3).

In spite of the harmony of purpose beween Ethiopians and Portuguese in the mid-sixteenth century, the latter's influence in Ethiopia was brief. By the time of the emperor Susenyos (1608-1632), religious disputes had grown up between the Catholics and the Ethiopian Orthodox church, and Jesuit arrogance destroyed the atmosphere of trust. As a result the Portuguese were expelled from the country by Susenyos' son Fasiladas. It was, however, this Portuguese episode in Ethiopia which first revealed the remains of the Aksumite civilisation to the outside world, through the writings and travels of the Portuguese ecclesiastics.

Francisco Alvares, the chaplain accompanying the embassy which arrived in 1520, left an interesting account in his book *The Prester John of the Indies*, published in Portuguese in Lisbon in 1540 (Beckingham and Huntingford

segundo vio e escreveo ho padre capellã del Rey nosso
senhor. por mandado do dito senhor em casa de
liureiro de sua alteza.

2A. The title page of Francisco Alvares 1540 book on Ethiopia. Though the book itself is rich in information about Ethiopia, including a valuable section on Aksum and its ruins, the illustrator has shown 'Prester John' with all the trappings of a contemporary European monarch.

1961). Apart from the description of the great five-aisled basilica of Maryam Tseyon, he mentioned the stone thrones nearby, and a reservoir which does not seem to be the well-known one called Mai Shum (Ch. 5: 1). He described some of the stelae, and visited the 'Tomb of Kaleb and Gabra Masqal', which he mentioned was supposed by some to contain the treasure chests of the Queen of Sheba. He also noted some information about Abba Pantelewon and Abba Liqanos, both churches on small hills near Aksum.

In 1603, the Spaniard Pedro Paez (Pero Pais) arrived in Ethiopia after extraordinary adventures in the Yemen, where he was a prisoner for seven years. He wrote a *History of Ethiopia* (Pais 1945-6), and also mentioned Aksum in his letters to a friend, Thomas Iturén, with whom he corresponded every year (Caraman 1985). Through João Gabriel, captain of the Portuguese in Ethiopia, who was present at the time, he was able to describe the coronation of Susenyos at Aksum on 18 March 1608 (Ch. 7: 6). He also mentions the thrones, the stelae, and the church, though he comments that this latter could not be compared with the ancient one. Paez even prepared a measured drawing of the 'Tomb of Kaleb' (Monneret de Villard 1938: 68).

Two years after Paez' death in 1622, Manoel de Almeida arrived. His *History of Ethiopia* (Huntingford 1954), which contained revised material from Paez' work, noted that about twenty stelae were still standing, and seven or eight fallen and broken ones were visible (Ch. 5: 3). He commented that it was said that these were overthrown by the Turks during the war of Sartsa Dengel with the viceroy Yeshaq (1578). Such an incident is not mentioned in the Ge'ez chronicles.

Emmanuel Barradas, who accompanied de Almeida's mission, also left some notes (de Villard 1938: 68-71) on Aksum's monuments, some of which were *'very large and of notable majesty'*, including *'high and beautiful columns or pyramids'*, evidently the stelae, which bore comparison with the biggest and best at Rome. He also mentions an inscription with letters on one side in 'Amharic' of an ancient style, and on the other letters which appeared to be Greek or Latin. The thrones are described, and also the 'Tomb of Kaleb and Gabra Masqal'.

In 1625, the new catholic patriarch Alfonso Mendes reached Ethiopia, bringing with him from Diu the Jesuit father Jerónimo Lobo, who had gone there after a courageous but abortive attempt to enter the country via Malindi, on the Indian Ocean coast (now in Kenya). Lobo remained nine years in Ethiopia; his account of his travels, the *Itinerário*, was first published in 1728 in a French translation by Le Grand, and later appeared in English translated by Samuel Johnson (1735). All he says of Aksum is

> *"and the place where she* (the Queen of Sheba) *had her court still exists today, with monuments of remarkable magnificence, as well as the town where they say she was born and which still today preserves her name, the land being called Saba by the Abyssinians, all of which I saw and traversed on several occasions".*

When James Bruce, (who detested the Jesuits, and who referred to Lobo as *'a grovelling fanatic priest'*) launched into one of his denunciations of Lobo's inaccuracy, he made the mistake of assuming that Lobo's 'Caxume' was Aksum, and ridiculed his geographical understanding (Bruce 1790). Actually, Lobo was referring to Qishn in Arabia.

Finally, in 1660 the Jesuit Balthasar Telles or Tellez published his *Historia geral de Ethiopia a alta*, at Coimbra in Portugal. This was an abridgement and revision of de Almeida's (unpublished) book, just as the latter depended to some extent on Paez. Translated into English, Tellez' *The Travels of the Jesuits in Ethiopia* was published in London in 1710. It contained a brief account of Aksum and its monuments (Ch. 5: 3).

The information imparted by the various missionaries who worked in Ethiopia in the sixteenth and seventeenth centuries, though full of semi-legendary material, allowed Job Ludolf, or Ludolphus, in 1681, to publish at Frankfurt the first full *History of Abyssinia*, (excluding the fabulous 'history' written by Tellez' *'Chimerical author'*, Luis de Urreta, published at Valencia in 1610 -a book about which Geddes (1696: 467ff), quoting an extract about vast and mythical Dominican convents in Ethiopia, noted *'though it is an octavo of 1130 odd pages, and a small print, there is not one syllable of truth from the beginning to the end'*). Ludolf's work was translated and printed in English the next year. It included, in Book II, a chapter (XI) entitled *"Of the Royal City of Axuma: and the Inauguration of their Kings"*. Ludolf has very little to add, beyond a number of sighs at the transience of material things, to the Jesuit reports, merely saying that

> *"of old this city was adorn'd with most beautiful structures, a fair palace, and a cathedral proudly vaunting her obelisks, sculptures, and several sumptuous edifices. Some of the pillars are still to be seen, with inscriptions of unknown letters, remaining arguments of their antiquity, now demolish'd by the wars, or defac'd with age. The city itself, now totally ruin'd, looks more like a village, than a town of note...only the ruins still remain to testify that once it was great and populous"*.

The next additions to our knowledge about the country came from travellers who for one reason or another managed to penetrate through what is now the Sudan or from the inhospitable coastlands and climb through the passes to the high Ethiopian plateau. The French doctor, Charles Poncet, journeyed to Aksum (which he called Heleni) in 1699, but limited himself to describing three pyramidal and triangular granite needles, covered with hieroglyphs, in the square in front of the church. He noted that they had bolts represented on them, which surprised him, since the Ethiopians did not employ them. However inaccurate the description, it is evident that he refers to the three largest stelae.

The Scottish explorer, James Bruce, arrived in 1769 and stayed in the country until 1772. In his book, *Travels to Discover the Source of the Nile*, he devoted some pages to the description of the antiquities of Aksum. He mentioned forty obelisks *"none of which have any hieroglyphs upon them"*, discussed Poncet's bolts, and suggested that the three largest stelae were the work of Ptolemy Euergetes. He also illustrated this part with a *"geometrical elevation, servilely copied, without shading or perspective, that all kind of readers may understand it"*. This illustration is very inaccurate, but does give an impression of the stelae. Bruce also mentioned one hundred and thirty three pedestals with the marks of statues on top; some of these pedestals still remain visible today. Bruce claimed that two of them still bore the statues of *"Syrius the Latrator Anubis, or Dog Star"*. These were *'much mutilated, but of a taste easily distinguished to be Egyptian"*. What these actually were is, alas, now a mystery, but his evidence, with that of Alvares, leads one to think that there must have been many more pedestals or thrones visible than can be seen today. He also saw other pedestals *"whereon the figures of the Sphinx had been placed"*. He commented on the *"magnificent flights of steps"* of the platform of the former church *"probably the remains of a temple built by Ptolemy Euergetes, if not of a time more remote"*, and dismissed the cathedral as a *"mean, small building, very ill kept, and full of pigeons dung"*. He also added that the king himself told him that the Ark of the Covenant had been destroyed by Gragn with the church, *"though pretended falsely to subsist there still"*. He saw the various pillars and thrones (or at least so one supposes from his description of *"three small square inclosures, all of granite, with small octagon pillars in the angles, apparently Egyptian; on the top of which formerly were small images of the dog-star, probably of metal"*). Bruce found, below the coronation stone, another stone with a defaced inscription which, naturally, he announced *"may safely be restored"* with the Greek letters reading 'King Ptolemy Euergetes'. He further alludes to the Mai Shum reservoir, and estimates the town to have amounted in his time to some six hundred houses. Oddly enough, in view of his particular desire to see most of the monuments as Egyptian, Bruce was, while in Tigray, actually presented with a late Egyptian (possibly XXXth Dynasty or Ptolemaic) *cippus* (a small stele bearing magical texts) of Horus, which he illustrates in two engravings. This is one of the very rare Egyptian or Meroitic objects known from Ethiopia, but a standing figure of the same deity shown on the cippus, Horus-the-Child or Harpokrates, is also known from a cornaline amuletic figure found at Matara (Leclant 1965).

In spite of Bruce's curious interpretations of the Aksumite monuments visible in his time, his publication, though a certain amount of incredulity greeted his account of what he had seen and done, attracted interest in Ethiopian history and antiquities. He was soon followed by Henry Salt, who travelled to Ethiopia with George Annesley, viscount Valentia, in 1805, and again as British envoy in 1809. In the last volume of Valentia's three-volume account (1809), Salt contributed a chapter on Aksum, and first published Ezana's inscription as well as other antiquities; the folio acquatint companion volume to Valentia's work contained a picture of the stelae, the first nineteenth-century illustration of Aksumite antiquities. Salt also published *A Voyage to Abyssinia* in 1814, illustrating it with a copy of Ezana's famous trilingual inscription. With Salt, who cleared the base of this inscription, we may say that archaeology had arrived at Aksum, although it was not until 1868 that a deliberately planned excavation, amateurish though it seems to us today, was undertaken. This occurred when soldiers accompanying the British military expedition, sent to relieve the prisoners kept by the emperor Tewodros (Theodore) at Magdala, opened some trenches at the site of the port of Adulis. They were theoretically under the distant supervision of R. R. Holmes, the British Museum's agent, who actually remained up-country endeavouring, unsuccessfully as it transpired, to obtain permission to visit

3-4. Prints after one of Bruce's sketches, showing the Egyptian Cippus of Horus given to him in Ethiopia.

Aksum (Munro-Hay, 1989). Other visitors of various nationalities followed, including Theodore Bent who, in 1893, was able to add a certain amount to the description of Aksum and its surroundings in his *Sacred City of the Abyssinians* (1896). The Italian archaeologist Paribeni, in 1906, and the

4. See Figure 3 Caption

Swede Sundström, also excavated at Adulis and found impressive ruined structures, with a number of coins and other objects (Paribeni 1907: Sundström 1907).

With the beginning of archaeology in the country, the potential for discovering more about the Aksumites' way of life was immensely increased. Details about technological and agricultural affairs, or urbanisation, not available from any other source, now began to emerge. The major event in Ethiopian archaeology until the excavations of modern times, was the arrival of the Deutsche Aksum-Expedition, led by Enno Littmann, in 1906 (Littmann et al.

5. The Greek version of the trilingual inscription of king Ezana of Aksum first published by Salt. Photo BIEA.

1913). The German team explored Aksumite sites along their route across Ethiopia, and surveyed the whole Aksum region; they dug for the plans of major structures, and meticulously planned, drew or photographed whatever they cleared. Almost immediately after their return a preliminary report appeared (Littmann and Krencker 1906). The German team also presented, in their copiously-illustrated four-volume publication in 1913, sketches, photographs and descriptions of everything of interest both ancient and modern. This included a number of Aksumite inscriptions, which were translated and so offered some primary material for speculations about chronology and other aspects of Aksumite history.

The foundation which they laid has been built upon, though very modestly in comparison to work in other countries, by subsequent expeditions. Archaeological and survey work has been done by Italian, French, American and British teams, and by the Ethiopian Department of Antiquities (most of it only published in preliminary reports in the *Annales d'Ethiopie*, but see also Chittick 1974 and Munro-Hay 1989). The surveys and excavations have revealed numerous structures and domestic material of Aksumite date in many parts of northern Ethiopia. As a result, some idea can now be obtained as to the extraordinary civilisation developed between about the first and seventh centuries AD by the Aksumites at their capital city and other urban centres. Though the archaeological study of the kingdom is still in its infancy, the results are very impressive, and we can now put Aksum firmly into its place among the great civilisations of late antiquity.

III

The City and the State

1. The Landscape

A traveller arriving at Gabaza, the coast station and customs point for the port city of Adulis (Ch. 3: 4) a short distance inland, may well have looked westwards towards Aksum from the hot and humid coastal plain by the Red Sea shore with some trepidation. As James Bruce (1790) put it

> *"The mountains of Abyssinia have a singular aspect from this* (coastal plain)*, as they appear in three ridges. The first is of no considerable height, but full of gullies and broken ground, thinly covered with shrubs; the second, higher and steeper, still more rugged and bare; the third is a row of sharp, uneven-edged mountains, which would be counted high in any country in Europe"*

The traveller would know that Aksum lay in those highlands, several days journey from the top of the escarpment, in a different climatic zone, and to all intents and purposes in a different world.

Adulis, with its prosperous international trading community, and sizable buildings in the Aksumite style, was the first important town on the journey to the capital. It evidently became 'Aksumite' in terms of architecture and government, but may well have already had a long history before that. During the Aksumite period, it was probably still rather different from the inland towns, as one would expect from a community exposed to many foreign influences. Paribeni (1907) found there many objects apparently imported from the Graeco-Roman world or even India.

Immediately on leaving Adulis on the Aksum road, a traveller would have seen the famous monument left by an unknown Aksumite king, and a stele belonging to one of the Egyptian Ptolemies (Chs. 3: 4 and 11: 1). From here the journey to Aksum took eight days, according to the *Periplus* (Huntingford 1980: 20), or twelve days according to Procopius (Dewing 1914: 183). The difference doubtless refected either some change in the route, or in the season of travelling, if it was not simply caused by the greater haste of merchants in comparison to ambassadors travelling in a comparatively leisurely manner. The journey took travellers through two of the three climatic zones recognised by the Ethiopians nowadays; the first is called the *kwolla*, below 1800 m and with a hot tropical climate (26°C or more), and the second the *woina dega*, from 1800-2400 m, with a sub-tropical climate and average temperatures of 22° C. Aksum itself lay at about 2100 m. The final climatic zone was the high *dega*, above 2400 m with an average temperature of 16° C.

The climatic extremes or differences were mentioned by ancient travellers such as Kosmas (Wolska-Conus 1968: 362), who particularly noted that it was the rainfall in Ethiopia which formed the torrents which fell into the Nile. The ambassador of Justinian, Nonnosus (Photius; ed. Freese 1920) noted the two zones;

> *"The climate and its successive changes between Aue and Aksum should be mentioned. It offers extreme contrasts of winter and summer. In fact, when the sun traverses Cancer, Leo and Virgo it is, as far as Aue, just as with us, summer and the dry weather reigns without cease in the air; but from Aue to Aksum and the rest of Ethiopia a rough winter reigns. It does not rage all day, but begins at midday everywhere; it fills the air with clouds and inundates the land with violent storms. It is at this moment that the Nile in flood spreads over Egypt, making a sea of it and irrigating its soil. But, when the sun crosses Capricorn, Aquarius and Pisces, inversely, the sky, from the Adulitae to Aue, inundates the land with showers, and for those who live between Aue and Aksum and in all the rest of Ethiopia, it is summer and the land offers them its splendours"*

Frequently, because of the possibility of the name Aue being a Greek rendition of the name Yeha, the two are identified (see for example Bent 1896: 143ff). But Nonnosus specifically says that Aue is mid-way between Adulis and Aksum, and this note, with the climatic information, seems to place it among the first towns of the highlands when the plateau is reached, possibly Qohayto, Tekondo, or Matara (if the latter is not identified with the Koloë of the *Periplus*). Schneider (1982) has already suggested that Aue lay on the edge of the plateau.

After following the winding rocky passes up and up into the cooler zone of the highlands the traveller would reach one of these towns, set in the broken scenery of the high Ethiopian plateau, scored by rivers and valleys sloping westwards to the Nile valley and scattered with strange-shaped mountains. Flat land is relatively rare here, but the plateaux on the tops of the mountains, called *amba*s, are utilised for cultivation, and also act as natural fortresses. Balthasar Telles (Tellez 1710: 31) mentioned their advantages;

> *"Some of these mountains, which the natives call ambas, stand by themselves apart from all others, are prodigious high, as it were in an impregnable fortress..."*

Vegetation and streams abound, and there must have been a considerable variety of wildlife in ancient times. Alvares, who described part of his journey as passing *"through mountains and devilish jungle"*, populated his jungle with lions, elephants, tigers, leopards, wolves, boars, stags, tapirs and *"all other beasts which can be named in the world except...bears and rabbits"*. His tigers

6. The mountainous scenery of northern Ethiopia. Photo R. Brereton.

may have been hyenas, as Bruce suggested (Beckingham and Huntingford 1961: 67) or perhaps cheetahs. Telles and Alvares mention crocodiles and hippopotami in the Takaze river, as well as the electric fish, called the torpedo or cramp-fish (Tellez 1710: 20–21).

On entering the highlands of Eritrea and Tigray, the heartland of the Aksumite kingdom, it is the mountains which most impress. To quote Bruce again,

> *"It is not the extreme height of the mountains in Abyssinia that occasions surprise, but the number of them, and the extraordinary forms which they present to the eye. Some of them are flat, thin and square, in the shape of a hearth-stone, or slab, that scarce would seem to have base sufficient to resist the action of the winds. Some are like pyramids, others like obelisks or prisms, and some, the most extraordinary of all the rest, pyramids pitched upon their points, with the base uppermost, which, if it was possible, as it is not, they could have been so formed in the beginning, would be strong objections to our received ideas of gravity".*

Telles commented that there were

> *"almost continual mountains of a prodigious height, and it is rare to travel a day's journey without meeting such steep, lofty and craggy hills, that they are dreadful to behold, much more to pass over".*

The northern Ethiopian scenery, enhanced by the startling shapes of the imposing *euphorbia candelabra* trees on the slopes, is both beautiful and formidable. Nowadays, however, when the rains have not arrived, the area around Aksum can seem as desolate as a moonscape, inhospitable and without a blade of grass anywhere; the results of climatic changes and man's improvidence (Ch. 15).

All along the main route south, from the head of the valleys where one finally entered the highlands, were Aksumite towns. A traveller must have passed at least one major town, Matara, and many others with impressive stone buildings, before he turned west to Aksum. From the plateau of Shire, behind the ancient capital to the west, descend two river valleys, the Marab in the north and the Takaze in the south, both doubtless used, at least in the dry season, as routes into the Sudan. Beyond the Takaze rise the Semien mountains, described in one of the Aksumite inscriptions as covered with snow and freezing mists. This inscription, the *Monumentum Adulitanum* (Ch. 11: 5), also describes campaigns against the tent–dwelling Beja in the inhospitable hills of the Red Sea coast, against some mountain-dwelling peoples, and against the tribes living in the immense waterless plains of the Danakil region. The account given in the inscription gives a good idea of the extreme contrasts in the geography, climate, and population groups of the area which the Aksumites controlled, and instills a certain amount of respect for the rulers who, albeit tenuously, managed to link such disparate parts into a functioning political and commercial system for several centuries.

2. Origins and Expansion of the Kingdom.

Aksum was, oddly as it might seem at first, situated in the western part of the future Aksumite kingdom. This, however, must reflect the prevailing political, economic and commercial conditions long before Aksumite ambitions could have reached to an outlet on the Red Sea coast, and probably implies that the original significance of the site derived from its command over certain local resources and interior trade–routes, one important one most likely leading to the Nile Valley and using the Marab and Takaze river valleys which drained westwards towards the Nile. Eventually Aksum lay at the heart of a series of routes. One lay between the Nile and Adulis, another led to 'the Cataracts' (Aswan), a journey of 30 days according to Kosmas (Wolska-Conus 1968: 356). This route leading to Egypt was also mentioned by the anonymous king who raised the *Monumentum Adulitanum* (Ch. 11: 5), and by Procopius (ed. Dewing 1914: 185); *"From the city of Auxomis to the Aegyptian boundaries of the Roman domain, where the city called Elephantine is situated, is a journey of thirty days for an unencumbered traveller"*. A third route may be surmised as leading south from Aksum to the *"extremities of*

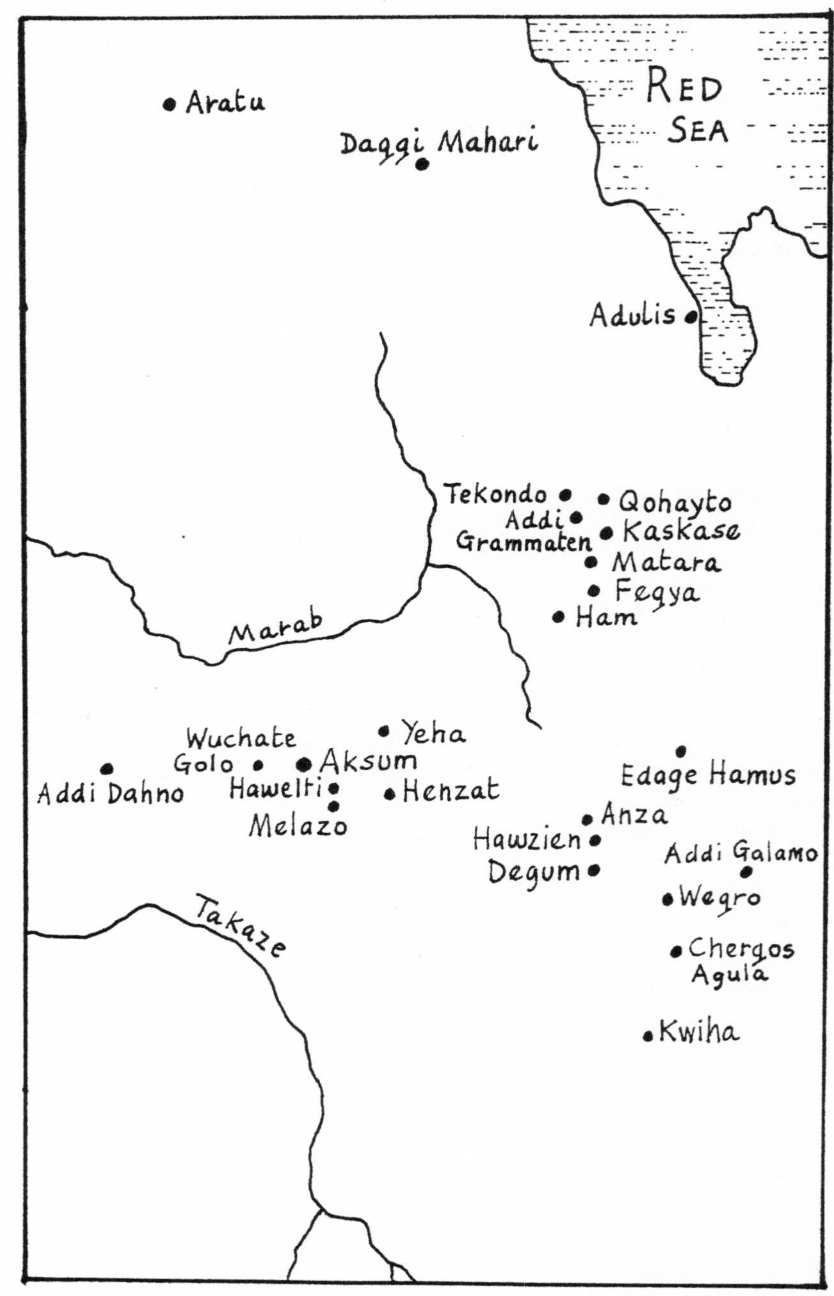

Map B. Map of Aksumite Ethiopia.

Ethiopia", defined by Kosmas as "*to the land of incense called Barbaria*" (apparently the Somali coast where incense can still be found), some 30 days distant. A final route was that known for the gold trade, running through the Agaw lands towards Sasu, which took six months to go and return, including five-day stops for trading (Wolska-Conus 1968: 362).

In addition to its advantageous position for trade, the site, facing the plains of Aksum and Hasabo and with the plateau of Shire behind it, enjoyed abundant rainfall, with a long rainy season from late June to early September. There were probably a number of streams and springs, and fertile soil very likely capable of producing more than one crop a year. In the environs of the future city were good agricultural areas, such as the plain of Hasabo (Hazebo, Atzabo) to the east. Michels (1988: 2–3, map 4), in a very useful survey, interviewed farmers in the Aksum-Yeha region in 1974 as to soil qualities, and studied local topography and irrigation potential. He was able to classify four ecological zones, and found that the immediate environs of Aksum and Yeha belonged in his Zone A; *"low gradient, highly fertile land that is optimal for plow cultivation, requires no fertility intervention other than crop rotation, and relies upon seasonal rains"*.

This evidently favourable region was, it seems, already populated when Aksum was founded. Though there are earlier sites with ruins dating to the Sabaean-influenced pre-Aksumite period nearby (such as Hawelti, Melazo – with Gobochela and Enda Cherqos – and Medoge) so far no firm evidence has been found to indicate that the site of Aksum itself was occupied before about the beginning of our era. However, the pre-Aksumite 'Sabaean' cultural area certainly extended along the route from Adulis and into the Aksum region.

Recent work by Italian archaeologists in the Kassala region, noted by Fattovich (1988), has hinted that certain aspects of Aksumite culture may have come from the western lowlands even before this. Fattovich observed features on pre-Aksumite pottery resembling those on pottery of the Sudanese peoples labelled by archaeologists Kerma and C– group, and suggested that even such cultural features as the stelae, so characteristic of later Ethiopian funerary customs, might perhaps have derived from early Sudanese prototypes. Some of these features date back to the late 3rd and early 2nd millenia BC, and the discovery of evidence of fairly complex societies in the region at this early date may suggest, to quote Fattovich, *"a more complex reconstruction of state formation in Northern Ethiopia"* (see also Ch. 4: 1).

At the moment, however, the early history of Aksum is almost unknown and there is little evidence available relating to the formation of the Aksumite state. However, we can suggest a possible course of development. It would seem that the favourable position of the future capital both from the trading point of view, and from that of local food-production and other resources, allowed increasing prosperity to come to the settlement. With this prosperity there was possibly a rise in the local population, and, concomitantly, an increase in potential military strength. Expansion to secure either new resources or various trade-routes was possible with the development of a military machine which, as we may surmise from later events, became very efficient. What other incentives may have arisen to encourage the Aksumites to exploit their new potential we do not know, but there could have been such impulses as the need to repel a possible threat from nearby peoples, or the rise of an exceptional leader. Aksum was not a great colonial power, arriving with superior weapons to fight ill-equipped locals; though they did exploit the possibilities of imported weapons, as the *Periplus* mentions, it was, if we can hazard a guess, increased manpower, organisational ability, speed and capable generalship which eventually gave Aksum the dominant military role in the region.

How the governmental system of the earlier polity functioned can only be suggested. Possibly it was based on some sort of tribal council, which eventually made way for a single leader, or possibly traditional organisations based on such examples as the ancient chiefs of Punt and the *mukarrib*s and kings of the earlier South Arabian period had already left the heritage of a system of chiefly control. Aksum must have begun to take its place as an ever more important part of the local political scene, partly by the exercise of military initiative, and partly, perhaps, by developing treaty-relationships with neighbouring tribal groups and gradually assuming the position of *primus inter pares*. We have no idea about the Aksumites' attitudes towards these surrounding peoples until later, when they were definitely considered to be subordinate; but presumably the dominance the Aksumites eventually achieved was not easily gained, and even in the heyday of Aksum one or other of the lesser tribes occasionally made a bid for freedom, described in the official Aksumite sources as 'rebellions'.

Absorbtion of neighbouring tribal groups seems to have followed the initial impetus for expansion, often with the traditional rulers left in power as sub-kings, until in the end the Aksumites controlled a very large area of modern Ethiopia. Under the umbrella of Aksumite control, we can envisage a number of older systems of government still functioning, and perhaps themselves in some ways influencing the Aksumites politically and culturally. The kings' titles on inscriptions list a number of regions, certainly those which constituted the most important provinces of the empire, but the many smaller polities mentioned in the body of the inscriptions, with their local kings, were evidently not considered significant enough to merit this special mention in the titularies. They may, by this time, have been subsumed under the general term 'Habashat', or even, in some cases, 'Aksumites', and, as it were, been transformed from foreign tribesman to Aksumite citizen. The designation 'Habashat' may originally have referred to the population of the prosperous eastern area of Tigray. Probably, after their submission, levies from the various tribes or their clans would have swollen the Aksumite potential for putting armies into the field, and might even have given the names to some of the military regiments known from the inscriptions (Ch. 11: 2).

Whether the Aksumites had formed a concept of the state as comprising these communities of the central region, but excluding those particularly mentioned in the titularies, is uncertain. The primary title, *negus* in Ge'ez or *najashi* in Arabic, (signifying king or military leader) of Aksum, or 'of the Aksumites', seems to refer to the nucleus of tribal groups taken in to form a single polity, quite aside from the more 'foreign' peoples and regions later subordinated to Aksumite control. But the inscriptions still continue to refer to revolts in the inner territories for as long as we have records from Aksumite times, and we have little idea what was regarded as constituting the 'Aksumite' ingredient of the state. The land belonging to the subordinate tribes was perhaps not considered part of 'Aksumite' territorial jurisdiction, land-rights remaining vested in those tribes and the payment of tribute reserving a measure of autonomy. These neighbours did not, then, immediately become united in a political sense to the Aksumites by the merger of their lands and institutions with those of Aksum, though their eventual disappearance from the record indicates that ultimately absorbtion was inevitable. It would evidently have been in the interest of the security of the Aksumite crown to diminish the power of provincial authorities, eliminate provincial royalty, and reduce the provinces to the direct control of the monarchy, but only if the monarchy itself were capable of controlling the areas thus acquired; but it may well be that the continued existence of the smaller units reflects the central government's inability to do this adequately. Aksum may have been obliged by necessity to tolerate an imperfect situation for some time, until through a policy of gradual replacement by Aksumite officials of hereditary rulers with a hold on local loyalties, the separate identity of the smaller entities was slowly eroded away.

This retention of a separate identity by certain tribes for some centuries after their submission to Aksumite authority might help to explain the revolts reported in Aksumite inscriptions, since if we presume that there were neither Aksumite garrisons nor royal retainers with land in the tribal areas, such risings would have been easier to foment. It is interesting to note that Procopius (Dewing 1914: 183) still refers to Adulis as the 'harbour of the Adulites' using the ethnic name Ptolemy (Stevenson 1932: 108), had used much earlier. Other writers, like Epiphanius (ed. Blake and de Vis 1934), who in the late fourth century listed nine kingdoms of the 'Indians' including 'Adoulites', also recognised a difference between Adulites and Aksumites, though they are subsumed together in the Latin version; *"Aksumites with Adulites"* (Cerulli 1960: 16–17). It may have taken a considerable time before formal incorporation into the Aksumite state altered established social patterns.

In due course there must have been changes in the Aksumite's own political outlook, too, perhaps partly resulting from the exposure of the country to Graeco-Roman and other influences, particularly after the development of the Red Sea trade and Aksum's entry into a wider network of commerce. By around AD200 the Aksumite kings were able to intervene militarily in internal struggles in South Arabia, and in the fourth century we have evidence for at least theoretical suzerainty over several groups in the Sudan, such as the Kasu, Noba, and the Northern Cushitic-speaking Beja tribes (see the titulature on the inscriptions, Ch. 11: 5). Here, Aksum had to some extent taken over the imperial role of Meroë. In the south, Agaw (Central Cushitic-speaking) peoples also became subject to the Semitic-speaking Aksumites. The expansion to the Adulite coastal region now permitted Aksum to convey goods originating in districts beyond the Nile or its tributaries to their own port on the Red Sea coast, and the rulers doubtless hoped that their projects across the Red Sea would eventually lead to control of some of the immensely rich trade of the Arabian kingdoms. With Rome as a powerful ally and trading partner, Aksum's prosperity was based on firm geographical and historical realities, and was maintained until these altered in the late sixth/early seventh century.

The Aksumite cultural province, as far as reported sites can indicate, was centred in Eritrea and Tigray, particularly the districts of the Akkele Guzay, Agame, and the region around Aksum, Adwa, and Shire. Traces have also been found in Enderta, Hamasien, Keren, and as far as the Rore Plateau (Conti Rossini, 1931), and even in Wollo (Anfray 1970). Some of the largest extensions suggested for the kingdom seem unlikely; Doresse, for example (1971: 84), includes among 'the largest Aksumite ports' not only Adulis but Deire, on the coast at the Bab al-Mandeb, and also notes (p. 90) Mathew's statement that a structure excavated at Amoud south of Berbera suggested Aksumite building work. Such ideas, probably based on the *Monumentum Adulitanum* account of the campaigns of an Aksumite king, cannot yet be confirmed.

The Akkele Guzay and Agame area seems to be distinguished from the western Tigray sites by differences in pottery and other elements. From the tentative observations of Francis Anfray (1974), it seems, from the cluster of sites on the north-south route from Qohayto to Agula, Degum, and even to Nazret, that this eastern 'province' may have become the most prosperous in later Aksumite times. Aksum and the sites of the west, from Addi Dahno to Henzat and the Yeha region, may have enjoyed prosperity in the pre-Christian period (many stelae are associated with the sites), but this compared unfavourably with the east later on. In such a case, Aksum may, even by the fifth and sixth centuries, have retained its position more by its prestige as the royal, eponymous city of the kingdom than by any continuing special merit in its situation. Possibly the Aksumites' expansion to Adulis, opening the western region to an already-established (pre-Aksumite?) trading system between the eastern highlands and the Red Sea, reflected in trading terms more favourably on the eastern towns, and in some ways made the city's own place in the system more tenuous. Even by the beginning of the second century Koloë was 'the first market for ivory', only three days from Adulis. Possibly the end result was that the eastern towns grew richer, whilst the remoter west, though the site of the capital, participated less in the new influx of wealth.

3. The development of Aksum: an interpretation

A different, and extremely interesting, interpretation of Aksumite history was proposed in a recent paper by Joseph Michels (1986; revised 1988), who conducted surveys in the Aksum-Yeha region in 1974. His conclusions can be compared with the historical outline proposed below (at the end of Ch. 2: 4). He identified seven historical phases in the area, from the end of the Late Neolithic through the pre-Aksumite South Arabian period to Late Aksumite, c. 700BC–1000AD. By studying the spatial configuration of settlements, which were classified according to size and the types of structures observed (without excavation), Michels identified periodic changes in the settlement pattern, and, assuming that these signified shifts in the political and economic spheres, endeavoured to extrapolate to the historical record. Pottery and obsidian collections were made, the latter providing Michel's dating.

As a result of his studies, Michels identified three pre-Aksumite phases (Early, Middle and Late) dating from 700/400/150 BC, and three Aksumite phases with the same divisions, dating from 150/450/800 AD, with the Post-Aksumite from 1000 AD. The earliest phases are of some interest, as Michels' paper represents almost the first progress towards defining the sort of social structure in existence in Ethiopia before and during the period of South Arabian contacts. Michels found that his analyses suggested for the earliest period indigenous occupation at only village or hamlet level, with no special preference for situation in one or other of the ecological zones he identified. In contrast, the 'South Arabian' settlement pattern was identifiable by stone structures on high ground in proximity to both the fertile ploughlands and the alluvial valleys susceptible of being cultivated by using South Arabian irrigation techniques. Michels sees this primary experiment in Ethiopia as developing in the second pre-Aksumite phase from 400 BC to a much more dominant South Arabian character; *"They were no longer simply intrusive within a predominantly indigenous political and economic environment, but had profoundly altered the economic, demographic, and political landscape"*. He identifies four large South Arabian centres emerging at the expense of the former hamlets - *"the traditional autonomy of hamlet and village gives way to the more complex governmental systems and sociopolitical stratification associated with large, nucleated settlements, institutionalized religion, irrigation management, and long-distance trade"*.

It is evident that there is no place here for the pre-Aksumite Ethiopian D'MT monarchy (Ch. 4: 1). Although Michels emphasises that his first South

Arabian period (in which linguistic and palaeographic studies locate the Ethiopian and South Arabian inscriptions) was not necessarily an attempt to politically dominate the region, but just to exploit it agriculturally, he does say that the colonists *"did not have to confront and compete with an indigenous political adversary comparable in organizational complexity to the kind of polities then common in South Arabia"*. But this is just what the D'MT monarchy is suggested to have been, even though it evidently shared some South Arabian cultural tendencies. We may instead postulate that Ethiopians, under the control of the D'MT monarchy and its successors, lived in some of the communities identified in Michels' second period, rather than apart from them in the *"small villages"* to which he assigns them. Further, it is difficult to imagine that the second period could have lasted so long as from 400–150 BC.

Whatever the case, it is easy to agree with Michels' idea that after the South Arabian colonial zenith (or that of the D'MT monarchy), the earlier pattern of scattered villages and hamlets recurs. This is scarcely surprising, since whichever dominant power was in control, it evidently disappeared, and with it all signs of its political supremacy. There are no large nucleated communities or religious sanctuaries (nor, one might add, are there any inscriptions). Michels hypothesises that in this period of decentralisation Yeha alone remained a centre for *"an elite refugee community within a South Arabian cultural enclave, now largely isolated from the economic and political landscape of the region as a whole"*. This period is supposed to have continued until 150 AD; its latter part is contemporary with some of the early material found by the latest excavations at Aksum (Munro-Hay 1989), and well post-dates the current favoured date for the evidence from the *Periplus* (Ch. 2: 2).

After 150 AD, in Michels' Early Aksumite phase, changes in the settlement pattern are again noted. Michels suggests three levels of organisation. Small-scale chiefdoms appear, marked in the landscape by village communities with masonry structures representing chiefly dwellings, and there are also district-scale 'kingdoms' of c. 150-200 sq. km. denoted by very large nucleated communities with one or more élite residences, and at Aksum by the rough stelae erected near the town. The third level is the kingdom of Aksum, and here Michels' conclusions are of sufficient interest to quote the whole passage;

> *"Quite probably, the kingdom was a confederacy, one which was led by a a district-level king who commanded the allegiance of other petty kings within the Axumite realm. The ruler of the Axumite kingdom was thus "King-of-Kings" – a title often found in inscriptions of this period. There is no evidence that a single royal lineage has yet emerged, and it is quite possible that at the death of a King-of-Kings, a new one would be selected from among all the kings in the confederacy, rather than through some principle of primogeniture."*

(It may be noted here that Kobishchanov (1979: 202–3) had already proposed the idea of an elective Aksumite monarchy, using his analysis of the rites of coronation).

> *"By implication, therefore, there is reason to question whether Axum was invariably the location of the royal household, especially during the early part of this phase. Certainly the discovery of four large-scale elite residences at or near Axum and believed to date to this phase would suggest that probably by the end of the period, Axum was beginning to take on that function. But, by and large, one must conclude that during the Early Axumite phase, Axum, as the ceremonial or symbolic center of the kingdom, lent its name to the kingdom but had not yet emerged as its permanent secular capital"*

This very different view of the origins of Aksum concerns the considerable period between 150 to 450AD, when relatively little historical material is available. At first sight the idea that kings were chosen from among the rulers of an Ethiopian confederacy might seem an attractive solution to explain the 'Bisi'-title or ethnicon of the kings, meaning 'man of....' in Ge'ez, and different for each succeeding monarch. The title, however, persists even after the certain establishment of an Aksum-based hereditary dynasty, and there are other explanations for it (Ch. 7: 5).

Despite the dearth of information, Aksum's position as the secular capital by the very beginning of this period seems well-enough established from external sources. Both the *Periplus* and Ptolemy mention the town as a royal capital (Ch. 2: 2), a metropolis with a royal palace. One question which remains unanswered is; why should Aksum take on such a tremendous significance among numerous Ethiopian kingdoms that it became the ceremonial and symbolic centre, and kings of different regions would aspire to call themselves 'king of kings of Aksum'? The answer seems rather that it was local Aksumite rulers themselves who gradually became the 'kings of kings'.

By about 200 AD (about fifty years after the date Michels' proposes for the beginning of this phase), king GDR/GDRT was involved in South Arabian affairs, and his name and that of three other kings, 'D̲BH, DTWNS and ZQRNS are associated with the titles '*nagashi* of Aksūm', or '*nagashi* of Habashat and Aksum' (Ch. 4: 4), and with wars in South Arabia during the century. By the later third century, with the inception of the local coinage, the title 'king of the Aksumites' is given prominence on the coin-legends (Ch.9), and by the 330s a bishop of Aksum, Frumentius, had been consecrated (Ch. 10: 2). During the whole period important notice is given only to Aksum or Habashat (Abyssinia). Aksum was indeed set apart as the ceremonial centre, site of the royal tombs and inscriptions, but was also the kingdom's capital city, whose rulers and people were referred to as Aksumites after their town (Procopius, ed. Dewing 1914: 183) with its special and increasing predominance in the region. There are stelae and tombs at Matara and elsewhere which doubtless indicate the burial places of the local rulers of other disricts, whilst those at Aksum are surely more likely to belong to a dynasty centred in Aksum itself than to a series of kings whose capitals were actually at different places all over the country. Family emphasis (relevant to the question of a royal lineage and the succession – Ch. 7: 4) is quite prominent throughout this period. Both GDRT and 'D̲BH had sons fighting in South Arabia, and in the early fourth century Ēzana not only almost certainly succeeded his father Ella Amida but was guided during his minority by his mother the queen-regent. Later in his reign his two brothers fought for him in his wars. The unknown author of the *Monumentum Adulitanum* inscription (Chs. 11: 5 and 3: 4), certainly dateable to this period, calls attention to the fact that he was the first and only one among the kings his predecessors to make such conquests; and while admittedly he could be referring to previous 'kings of kings' from different lineages, the example of Ezana makes it much more likely that he alludes to his ancestors on the Aksumite throne.

It is hard to credit that *"district-level"* kings selected as the 'kings of kings' from different regions in succession, could have presided for some 300 years over a kingdom whose course was otherwise so unified in so many disparate fields; a regular policy of interference in Arabian affairs, the issuing of a continuous coinage, and the steady architectural and cultural developments at Aksum can scarcely be viewed from such a perspective. In short, it seems quite clear that the achievements of the period, in terms of military and naval organisation, coinage, monumental construction and so on, bespeak something far more centralised than a loose confederation of more or less equal petty kingdoms.

Very likely some other urban centres still existed in the Aksum region as the capitals of more or less independent political entities while Aksum began to consolidate its power; but they fell in due course under Aksum's hegemony. Even in the reigns of Ezana or Kaleb, groups near to the centre of the kingdom, like the Agwezat, continued to rebel under their own kings (Ch. 11: 5), and perhaps among the 'district-scale kingdoms' which Michels identifies are represented one or more of the local centres of such groups, contemporaries of, and subjects of, the kings of Aksum. The Aksumites, as suggested in Ch. 2: 2, may have much earlier been allied with neighbouring tribal groups, but by the period in question it seems that such disparate elements had been gathered under the control of one dominating centre: Aksum. Without further excavation we cannot detect signs which might illustrate this, such as the relative size of the elite residences in Aksum as compared to those in subordinate centres, or the increasing amount of imported luxury items in one place as compared to another; but from what work has been done Aksum seems without doubt to have been the 'central place' in Ethiopia from at least the first century AD.

From 450–800 AD Michels envisages an *"explosive growth in the number of settlements and in the size of the overall regional population...Axum itself must now be viewed as a metropolitan entity consisting of fourteen towns and villages within a three-kilometer radius"*. The district-scale chiefdoms have vanished, and almost all the élite structures are now within metropolitan Aksum. On Amba Beta Giyorgis above the town, and in other places, were workshops marked by the presence of flaked stone tools. These are identified possibly, and plausibly, as tools for dealing with the ivory brought into the town before its re-export abroad (though the presence of these stone scrapers might also indicate that the commerce in leather attested in later times had already begun, since such tools could be used for preparing the skins). In this period Michels now accepts the concentration of the ruling and merchant classes at Aksum, while in the surrounding territory were many village communities, practising dry-farming, defining the capital's immediate sustaining area.

Except for the dates, which take us long past the end of the coinage and into a period when the archaeological evidence indicates that many of the élite residences were in ruins or at least subject to squatter occupation (Munro-Hay 1989), the depiction of a large town, with its *"concentration of economic, demographic and political assets"*, represents Aksum at its zenith. But Michels also attributes to this period an 'explicit neglect' of the royal tombs of the 'confederate phase' which apparently *"dramatizes the consolidation of power by a single royal lineage"*.

A very different analysis of events is possible. In this book, the tombs and stelae, developing along traceable architectural lines, are considered to represent rather the continuity of a *"true state-level monarchy"* at Aksum over a long period, culminating in the great stelae and tombs of the late third and fourth centuries. Michels quotes Butzer (1981) in observing that the main stelae field was *"covered over by an extensive residential community during this phase"*. In fact, there were no dwellings among the stelae and platforms in the Stele Park except those very much later ones (ninteenth century?) found there by the DAE (Littmann 1913) which were removed around 1965 for the construction of the Stele Park. The French archaeologist, Henri de Contenson (1959i) – whom in his turn Butzer quotes for his information–specifically notes *"les rares éléments architecturaux attestés dans ce niveau"*. He found traces of occupation dating to after the fall of the largest stele in or after the time of the probably late fourth century king Ouazebas, in the form of a single room built near the main terrace wall on deposits covering the nearby large tomb called Nefas Mawcha (Ch. 5: 5). But this one structure, which was, it must be emphasised, not even in the cemetery as defined by the main terrace wall, but outside it, does not mean that the whole cemetery was abandoned, and in no way resembles the debris of an 'extensive residential community'. All that it indicates is that outside the cemetery wall, in the area above and north of the Nefas Mawcha – a tomb which was anyway designed to be buried (Ch. 5: 5), – there was some late fourth century occupation on the wash layers which had partly covered the terrace wall. It seems more likely that with the advent of Christianity and the collapse of the largest stele, which obviously demonstrated the impracticability of erecting yet larger monuments, a new type of mortuary structure, of a type illustrated by the Tomb of the False Door (Ch. 5: 5), was then adopted (Munro-Hay 1989). This may have meant that no more stelae were erected, but does not imply 'explicit neglect' of the older monuments, since it was built in the same cemetery.

The last Aksumite phase proposed by Michels, like the previous one, follows the expected pattern, but is far removed in its suggested date. Reduction of population, the end of the factory-scale workshops, and an emphatic shrinkage of the city boundaries, combined with the re-emergence of small-scale chiefdoms in the region, occurs in this phase. All of this would reflect the decline of Aksum, and the eventual departure of the government to another more suitable centre for the reasons proposed in Ch. 15 below.

An interesting detail noted in Michels 1986 paper was that in the Late Aksumite period a new factor was introduced; for the first time, consideration was apparently given to selecting defensive sites for the palaces or élite residences. If this was not caused simply by the fact that all the prime sites were by now occupied, it might have been in response to such troubles as those mentioned in the *hatsani* Danael texts (Ch. 11: 5). If the structures were built after Aksum ceased to be the centre of government, these dwellings might represent the remnant who stayed on to administer the region dependent on the old capital.

4. Cities, Towns and Villages.

Within the expanded Aksumite kingdom, a number of flourishing urban communities appear to have grown up. Adulis, the chief Aksumite, and probably pre-Aksumite, port, and Aksum itself are special cases; but it seems, from archaeological and literary evidence, that a number of other towns became established on trade routes or crossroads, or wherever particularly favourable conditions were encountered. Water availablility was an evident precondition (Anfray 1973i: 15, n. 5). The development of some degree of urbanism in Aksumite Ethiopia is an interesting phenomenon, but one which is not yet even partially documented. All that survives of many of the 'towns' are the traces of a few monumental structures such as temples, churches or élite residential/administrative buildings, and scatterings of pottery on the surface. These have been reported from the time of the earliest explorations in Ethiopia, but have only rarely been properly surveyed, much less excavated and planned. Excavation may yet provide some surprises, as it has already done at Matara, but in general these towns may not have been very large, perhaps of little more than large village status, though Matara certainly seems to have been a sizeable community (Anfray 1963, 1974; Anfray and Annequin 1965). Such communities were probably much more intimately associated with the surrounding countryside than are, for example, modern manufacturing towns. But even so their existence bespeaks an agricultural output sufficient to provide the surplus necessary to support at least some town dwellers engaged in specialist pursuits, and the availablility of more or less efficient exchange and transport facilities on a regional scale. The urban setting throughout Ethiopia, including port, capital and market or trading towns, implies the development of a social stratification. At the top we can envisage the occupants of the élite dwellings and elaborately-constructed tombs. Further ranks would have included the merchants, traders or middlemen who arranged the supply-system, or the architects, builders, and artisans who raised the buildings. The base of the system rested upon the labourers in the fields and the workers in other sectors. We can assume from the apparently long existence of the towns that reasonably stable conditions prevailed in the country both politically and otherwise. This at least partly urbanised Aksumite society was in sharp contrast to the situation in later Ethiopia, when travellers remarked that the country contained no cities or substantial towns, only the mobile tented 'capital' which followed the emperor, and was moved to another region when it had exhausted the resources of a particular spot (Pankhurst 1961: 137ff).

Aksumite cultural traits are found at many of the town sites, some of which may originally have been the local centres for tribal groups later conquered by the Aksumites. The port-city of Adulis, which eventually covered at least 20,000 square metres, according to Paribeni (1907: 443), with its harbour and customs point a short distance away at Gabaza (see below), appears to have originated as the centre for the coastal people called Adulitae. It was the first point on the long trade route into the Sudan, and, favourably situated as it was in a bay on the Red Sea coast, had obvious opportunities to acquire wealth by trading. Evidence of its prosperity came from Sundström's and Paribeni's excavations in 1906, where numbers of gold coins were found in several different occupation levels (Sundström 1907, Paribeni 1907). It was not necessarily the only Aksumite port or coastal city, and another coastal town to the north called Samidi is known (see below). In the Dahlak Islands off the coast, Puglisi (1969: 37ff) noted four typical Aksumite capitals or column bases and a chamfered column re-used in a building at Gim'hilé and more complex carved material at Dahlak Kebir; almost certain evidence for Aksumite activity on the islands. It is perhaps just possible that they could have been taken there later, but it seems inconceivable that the long Aksumite control of the coast would not have encouraged them to secure these islands on the direct path to their main port.

Defence was not apparently an urgent consideration for the people of Adulis; although it was not safe for foreign vessels to anchor in places directly accessible from the Ethiopian coast at the time of the *Periplus* (Huntingford 1980: 20), the town does not seem to have been walled. Paribeni (1907: 444) searched on all sides of the town for any traces of fortifications, but without success.

Adulis contained large and elegant buildings, churches, and smaller town houses of a few rooms (Paribeni 1907; Anfray 1974). It lay a short distance inland from the port installations at Gabaza. The *Periplus* and Procopius do not name Gabaza, but mention the distance of 20 stades from the actual harbour to Adulis itself (Huntingford 1980: 20; Procopius, ed. Dewing 1914: 183). Adulis' Ethiopic name may have been Zala (Caquot 1965: 225). The merchant Kosmas, who situates the town '2 miles' from the coast (Wolska-Conus 1968: 364), mentions that Adulis had a governor, Asbas (Wolska-Conus 1968: 368), and that merchants from Alexandria and Ela (Aela or Eilat) traded there (Wolska-Conus 1968: 364). On Kosmas' map, preserved in much later copies, the position of Adulis is shown with Gabaza a little to the south on the sea-shore, and Samidi to the north (Wolska-Conus 1968: 367). Paribeni wondered if perhaps Adulis had originally been on the sea-coast, and excavated a trench at the east side of the ruin-field to test for any such evidence; but the trench instead revealed a church (Paribeni 1907: 529).

Paribeni (1907: 444) also searched for the famous *Monumentum Adulitanum*. The monument, a sort of symbolic throne, seems to have been fairly elaborate in design. Kosmas describes it as placed at the entrance to the town, on the west side towards the road to Aksum. Executions took place in front of it. It was of good white marble, but not, Kosmas says, Proconnesian, with a square base supported by four slender columns at the corners and another, heavier, column carved in a twisted fashion, in the centre. The throne had a back, sculpted with images of Hermes and Hercules, and two arm-rests. Behind it was a basalt stele, fallen and broken, with a peaked top. Both monuments, drawings of which are included on Kosmas' map of the Ethiopian coast, had inscriptions in Greek on them, one of Ptolemy III (246–221BC) on the stele, and one of an unnamed Aksumite king on the throne (see Ch. 11: 5).

The name of Adulis' customs-point, Gabaza, has been preserved also in the *Martyrium Sancti Arethae* (Carpentier 1861: 747), where it is cited as the naval station for Adulis. In this account of the persecutions in South Arabia in the sixth century, a hermit called Zonaenus, originally from Aela, is said to have been living at the town of Sabi; this has been thought to refer to a coastal town near Adulis (Irvine, in *Dictionary of Ethiopian Biography* 1975: 217), and the king is said to have descended from it to Adulis after receiving the hermit's blessing. But it seems rather to refer to the hermitage of Abba Pantelewon, very close to Aksum (Boissonade 1833; Carpentier 1861: 748, 751). Carpentier drew attention to Telles' note about a place called Saba, when he wrote that *"Near to Auxum or Aczum, in the kingdom of Tigre in Ethiopia, there is still a small village called Saba or Sabaim, where they say the queen of Sheba or Saba was born"* (Tellez 1710: 71).

Ptolemy mentions a town called Sabat, which he situates to the north of Adulis (Stevenson 1932: 108, and map, where it is labelled Sabath). Perhaps it is identical with Kosmas' Samidi. Huntingford (1980: 100) suggested that Sabat might rather be identified with the town of Saue mentioned in the *Periplus*; this was three days inland on the Arabian side between Muza and

Zafar. Taddesse Tamrat, after Conti Rossini, identified Sabat with Girar near Massawa (1972: 14). Carpentier referred to *"Sabae, a port of Ethiopia on the Red Sea, noted by Strabo, and Sabat, a town of Ethiopia in the Adulitic gulf, mentioned by Ptolemy"*, Occasionally Adulis itself has been identified with Strabo's Saba, and Assab with his Sabai (Strabo XVI; Huntingford 1980: 168–70), and even older origins have been proposed for Adulis (see Munro-Hay 1982i). Until a great deal more is known about the earlier archaeological levels at the site of Adulis, the antiquity of its origins remains obscure; but Paribeni found archaeological deposits of over 10m. depth in one of his exploratory trenches (Paribeni 1907: 446ff, 566) and suggested that a considerable amount had been deposited before sustained contacts with other civilisations had developed.

After climbing the steep valleys, such as that of the river Haddas which led from the coastal plain where Adulis was situated up to the highlands, the town of Koloë, mentioned in the *Periplus* (Huntingford 1980: 20; Casson 1989: 53) was reached. Koloë town and Maste town were also noted by Ptolemy (Stevenson 1932: 108) as among the towns remote from the river in the interior. Koloë derived its importance from its position as the first inland market where ivory could be obtained (see also Ch. 8: 4). It is possibly to be identified with the present-day Matara in southern Eritrea. At this site the French archaeologist Francis Anfray, in a spectacular series of excavations (Anfray 1963, 1967, 1974; Anfray and Annequin 1965), found numerous large and splendid mansions surrounded by their dependencies, together with churches, tombs, and even some domestic buildings in humbler residential areas. With the structures he found the material remains of a very sophisticated way of life. The town's history, as revealed by the excavations, extends back into the pre-Aksumite period, though so far this earlier archaeological stratum has only been accessible in extremely restricted areas of the site, and has not therefore been thoroughly investigated. Another town, Qohayto, further to the north, which also has the ruins of impressive structures (Littmann 1913: II, 148ff), but which has not yet been excavated, might be another candidate for identification with Koloë. It is most remarkable for the dam, made of seven courses of dressed stone stepped back in typical Aksumite fashion, which still retains water after the rains.

From Koloë the route continued to Aksum and beyond; but although its southern extension led past many Aksumite communities, relatively few sites have so far been identified between Aksum and this main north-south route, and even fewer west of the capital. The eastern highlands, in contrast, contain the ruins of numerous towns and villages, and it is evident that this part of the Aksumite kingdom was a prosperous and populous region from pre-Aksumite days (Anfray 1973i: 20). Aksum itself, as is to be expected, lay within easy access of several villages whose produce was doubtless necessary to feed the capital's increasing population (Michels, in Kobishchanov 1979).

The general homogeneity of the architecture and material goods of these ancient Ethiopian towns is apparent, and, despite regional differences in, for example, building stone and pottery types, the overall 'Aksumite' nature of the civilisation is undeniable. The large mansions in the towns may have been the residences of sub-kings who had adopted the metropolitan style of living, or those of Aksumite governors and officials. No mansion has yet been identified as belonging to some local ruler known from the inscriptions, as for example the Agwezat kings who are mentioned in the time of Ezana and Kaleb (Ch. 11: 5), and information of such a specific character is likely to be very nearly impossible to obtain. But it is not impossible that the headquarters of the archon of Adulis, or that of the local controller at Matara, could be identified eventually. The mansion buildings at this latter place contained such symbols of wealth and authority as the Matara treasure (gold jewellery found in a bronze pot), an elaborate tomb, and apparently in one case the skeletons of prisoners still lying in their chains in basement oubliettes.

Not very much is yet known about the settlement pattern of the Aksumite kingdom, but it has been possible to identify a number of particularly well-populated areas. The towns and villages along the main tracks south and east from Adulis towards Aksum, like Qohayto, Tekondo, Matara, Zala-Bet-Makeda, Ham, Etchmara, Gulo-Makeda, Haghero-Deragweh, Yeha, Dergouah and Henzat, and those further south along the route west of the escarpment from Enda Maryam Tseyon Tehot and Maryam Kedih, or the branch via Anza, Hawzien and Degum, at least as far as Cherqos Agula and Nazret (Anfray 1970) must have developed along with the main trade and supply routes and at cross-routes leading into the interior. Such centres probably lay in areas of farming settlements, and acted as their market-outlet and exchange points, and some perhaps supplemented this activity with specific local products or, if suitably situated, could provide services connected with the movement of goods along the main routes.

Aksumite settlements also appear to the west and north of Adulis, and the inscription of Sembrouthes from Daqqi Mahari, the buildings and coins from Arato (Piva 1907), and even traces as far north as Rora Laba and perhaps beyond, confirm that this region belonged to the Aksumite milieu. However, it is impossible to suggest what the limits of the Aksumite kingdom may have been at its zenith in view of the lack of archaeological evidence. Conti Rossini (1931) notes ruins in northern Eritrea with possible Aksumite affinities, particularly the thrones at Dicdic and the carved stelae at Rora Laba with lion and ox sculptures, and Anfray (1970) describes apparently Aksumite columns from Qeneda in Wollo, as well as paralleling, tentatively, the lion sculpture at Tchika-Beret in southern Wollo with the well-known Aksumite lion-headed water-spouts. Anfray's survey is the most informative we have so far, but more work is required to define the limits of Aksumite penetration.

One feature often found in Aksumite town sites is the mansion-and-dependencies element (Ch. 5: 4). Such mansions were not only a feature of the towns, but also seem, at least in the case of Aksum itself, to have been distributed in their hinterland, perhaps representing local village centres surrounding landlord's houses. These élite residences are found in quantity, according to the survey by Joseph Michels undertaken in 1974 (Michels in Kobishchanov 1979; Michels 1986) in and around the capital and in the region of a number of villages as far as Yeha.

The term 'villa' for these mansion-and-dependencies groups is tempting (Anfray 1974: 761), but they are evidently not all country and/or farm-houses like the Roman villas. The largest ones at Aksum and other towns could have had a different function from the smaller, more scattered country ones, although the general plan might have been common to both; even this is not yet properly confirmed, since a number of town mansions have been excavated but none of the remoter ones. Michel's published information tells us very little about the possible function of the larger and smaller élite residences in the Aksum area, and we can only guess how to interpret them economically and socially. If we knew more about the chronological development of these mansions, we might be able to trace whether the type was developed at Aksum and moved from the city and royal context first to other towns and then was adopted as the model for the country mansions of a landowner class, a sequence which might be plausible. On the other hand, they may have originated elsewhere; in, for example, Adulis, with its greater exposure to foreign influences, and spread thence to Aksum and the countryside.

In those towns which became administrative centres of the Aksumite state, Aksumite institutions would of course be prominent. The largest mansions probably housed the ruler of the region and acted as governmental and ceremonial centres; their layout, with the separation of the imposing central pavilion on its podium and staircases, seems emphatically designed to impress. In such town mansions the outer ranges must have been partly used for occupation and partly for service activities. We are still archaeologically ignorant of what went on in the dependencies. Certain features, like ovens, would indicate domestic activities serving the central occupant and all his people; others, like a possible heating system under the floor, would seem to indicate a luxury dwelling. Some rooms may even have been used as manufacturies of items needed in everyday life. Francis Anfray excavated one of these mansions just to the west of present-day Aksum, the so-called 'Château de Dungur', and when the results of this excavation are completely published we will certainly have a much clearer idea of the nature of these structures (Anfray 1972).

The country mansions, one might think, were more likely to have been on agriculturally-based estates of the surrounding region, perhaps owned by city-dwellers who possessed the capital to build elsewhere as well. Land around Aksum or any other largish town must have become a good investment as the city grew and the demand for foodstuffs increased. Did some of

7. View of the Dungur villa, showing one of the facades of the central pavilion with a double staircase leading to the entrance. Photo R. Brereton.

these mansions lie in estates which were selected since they could produce sufficient surplus crops to serve the capital? Some of the mansions we know of were situated close enough to Aksum to exploit the constant demand the town-market must have created, provided there was a reasonable road and transport system to guarantee the preservation of perishables in transit; there may have been wheeled carts and porters employed for inland transport, and one made-up stone road, apparently ancient, has been found northeast of Aksum. Conversely this demand must have acted as a spur to production. In such circumstances one can well imagine the Aksumite noble or businessman deciding to try out an agricultural investment, and building on his estate the imitation of his town mansion. Such mansions would then have been in some sense dependencies themselves. Alternatively, perhaps, we should think in terms of a 'rural aristocracy' living and farming on their estates? In fact, we know nothing of such putative estates; only the existence of the mansions themselves allows us to postulate the estates.

5. The Inhabitants.

The population of the Aksumite villages probably resembled closely the inhabitants of the present day; Semitic speakers in the central region ('Aksumites, Habash') owing something of their cultural tradition to influences from South Arabia in earlier times, with Cushitic speaking peoples on the peripheries of the kingdom. We know that tribal groups, if they submitted to Aksum, were left under the control of their local rulers, and probably those not in the immediate vicinity of the capital managed to preserve something of their own social systems. But we also learn from inscriptions that forcible transportation for rebellious tribes was practised, and by this method some alien elements must have been introduced. Ezana, for example, removed some 4400 Beja tribespeople to a province called Matlia (Ch. 11: 5), seemingly a march of several months. It has been suggested that this move could have been the origin of the present province-name Begamder (Begameder), or 'Land of the Beja'.

No painted representations or statues of Aksumites survive to give us an idea of their appearance; except for the badly damaged picture of an Ethiopian ruler at Qusayr Amra in Jordan, and the pottery heads from jars found during excavations (Munro-Hay 1989: 280). Pirenne has noted that the coiffure of the latter resembles that of figures carved on the decorated roof-beams of the temple of Ma'in in South Arabia (1977: I. 255–7). Another sort of coiffure seems to be represented on a small mask-pendant from Aksum (Tringali 1987: Tav. VIa). No personal descriptions are available either, though one of the Byzantine ambassadors described king Kaleb's costume and ornaments on a state occasion (Ch. 7: 2). The kings' features on the coins are fixed from the very first issues, and tell us little about their actual appearance; the large eyes, straight nose and prominent lips and chin may owe as much to the die-cutter's conventions as to an idea of portraiture. The situation is, curiously enough, different for the pre-Aksumite period. Statues, fragments of statues, and relief sculpture, from the pre-Aksumite Ethiopian sites at Addi Galamo and Hawelti (Caquot and Drewes 1955; de Contenson 1963ii) show elegantly-robed female figures represented with tightly-curled hair, large, wide eyes outlined in the Egyptian fashion, and enigmatically smiling mouths. Two statues from Hawelti show women wearing full-length robes, apparently pleated, and adorned with heavy triple-necklaces; they are rather reminiscent of some South Arabian sculptures of goddesses (Pirenne 1977: I.439, I. 451). Another, from Addi Galamo, wears a fringed robe decorated with a repeated pattern of a dot with eight others set in a circle around it. A male figure carved on an elaborate covered throne from Hawelti wears a shorter knee-length kilt, a cloak knotted over his shoulders, and sports a jutting beard with his close-curled hair. From Matara (Anfray and Annequin 1965: pl. LXIII: 1) came only the fragment of a statue showing one of the heavily outlined Egyptian-style eyes, and tightly-curled hair. Aksum itself yielded, from the Maryam Tseyon area (de Contenson 1963: pl. XIII, d), the remains of yet another head, in basalt, with only the close curls of the hair visible. A human-headed sphinx, a very early example of a type later found in South Arabian art, came from Kaskase, found with inscriptions dating to perhaps the fifth century BC (Pirenne 1977: I. 468–9, fig. 1).

Very likely these pre-Aksumite statues represent much the same people as those who later formed the Aksumite population. We know from Ezana's 'monotheist' inscription (Ch. 11: 5) that the Aksumites recognised the Black (tsalim) and the Red (qayh) peoples, mentioning also the 'Red Noba'; but it is not clear where in these categories they fitted themselves. Littmann (1913) thought that the implication was of the 'red' people of the kingdom of Aksum in contrast to the 'black' Noba (and others), a differentiation which still applies today in the eyes of the northern Ethiopians. Both Drewes (1962: 98) and Schneider (1961: 61-2), whose particular study has been the pre-Aksumite inscriptions, have come to the conclusion that even in the time of the kingdom of D'MT this contrast was used. The expression 'the entire kingdom' was rendered in the geographical sense by the phrase 'its east and its west', while the different characteristics of its population were illustrated by the words 'its red (people) and its black (people)'. If this is correct, and the two phrases are intentionally balanced, it might indicate a predominance of the 'red' or semiticised population in the eastern and central part of the kingdom, as would be expected given the South Arabian influences apparent from the material remains found there.

6. Foreign Relations.

Aksum had diplomatic and commercial relations with many foreign countries, increasing as the kingdom's own importance developed. There are several accounts of ambassadors and messengers sent to or from distant or neighbouring powers, and even, occasionally, some clues as to the purpose of their missions. In addition, a number of archaeological or chance finds have produced objects which attest to contacts of one sort or another between Aksum and certain foreign countries.

Egypt.

All the proposed connexions between Aksum and (pre-Roman) Egypt remain very uncertain, and indeed it seems as if Aksum itself was only in its very earliest stages of development when the Ptolemaic dynasty fell with Cleopatra VII's death in 30BC. There are a few objects which might have come from Egypt, such as the cippus of Horus given to Bruce, and illustrated by him (Ch. 2: 3), and a few amulet figurines of blue faience (de Contenson 1963ii: 48, p. XLIX b and c) or cornaline (Leclant 1965: 86–7) found at various sites in Ethiopia. The latter, with its double-uraeus, could perhaps have come instead from Meroë. From Adulis came a glazed Egyptian scarab carved with a design somewhat resembling a ship, probably dating to a very late period (Paribeni 1907: 5, fig. 3). Other signs of contact between the regions are the inscription of Ptolemy III copied by Kosmas at Adulis and an 'ankh'-sign engraved on one of the stelae (Anfray 1972). It is not beyond possibility that the accounts of Egyptian expeditions to Punt may be the earliest extant references to peoples of the Ethiopian/Sudanese coast and interior; provided that Punt (Pwene) always meant the same thing to the Egyptians over the long period that mentions of the country occur in their records. If so, these are important witnesses to trade-links stretching at least

8. One of the rough stele in the Northern Stele Field at Aksum, with a carved symbol representing the ancient Egyptian word for life, *ankh*. Photo BIEA.

as far back as the time of the pharaoh Djedkare Isesi, eighth king of the fifth Egyptian dynasty, c. 2400BC, and still continuing in the time of Rameses III around 1200BC. Later contacts, under the Romans, are much better documented and are described below.

Meroë and Africa.

Virtually nothing is known of what sort of contacts Aksum had with its western neighbour, the kingdom of Meroë or Kasu and its large but probably loosely controlled area of more or less effective influence. It has been suggested that perhaps the famous rock-relief of the Meroitic king Sherkarer, at Jabal Qayli, the easternmost Meroitic monument known, was connected with some conflict with a rising Aksum, but there is no proof either way. Only a few objects to which a Meroitic origin has been attributed have been found in Ethiopia, most notably some bronze bowls from Addi Galamo (Atsbi Dera) -which could also have come from Roman Egypt (Doresse 1960: 425ff)-, possibly the diorite thumb-ring (archer's loose) found by the BIEA expedition at Aksum (illustrated by Chittick, 1974, PL.XIV), and a cornaline amulet of Harpocrates with the typical double-uraeus of the Meroites on its forehead (see above, Leclant 1965: 86-7). The most powerful evidence for contacts are the fragments of two Aksumite inscriptions from Meroë which may indicate that Aksumite campaigns reached the city; and also some Ge'ez inscriptions roughly cut on the pyramids there (Ch. 11: 5). When king Ezana of Aksum led his expedition to the Nile (Ch. 11: 5, DAE 11), the Meroitic kingdom had probably ceased to exist. Its successors, the Noba, apparently behaved insultingly to the Aksumite ambassadors sent to them, and were punished by a military expedition. Certain tribes, the Mangurto, the Barya, and the Khasa had asked for Ezana's support against these aggressors, and either regarded Aksum as a usefully powerful neighbour who could be invoked to help check Noba ambitions, or possibly even as a suzerain. Ezana's expedition also attacked the Kasu, the remnants of the Meroitic state. Both the Noba and the Beja, as well as the Kasu, were officially noted in the titulature as comprising part of Ezana's kingdom.

These records, and certain other accounts of military expeditions within or on the borders of Aksum, are almost the only fragments of information which have come down to us about Aksumite dealings with their African neighbours. There is a brief mention of some missionary activity in the southern Nubian kingdom of Alodia/Alwa (see Ch. 10), and Kosmas Indikopleustes wrote about Aksum's 'silent trade' with the gold-gatherers of Sasu (Wolska-Conus 1968). However, it seems likely that, unless the main elephant-hunting areas were already within Aksum's direct control, there must have been close and protracted trading contacts with the suppliers of ivory from beyond the Nile; an excellent reason for the maintenance of generally peaceful conditions to encourage this important commerce.

South Arabia.

The South Arabian states, such as Saba, Himyar, and the Hadramawt, had a long and special relationship with Ethiopia. Aksum seems to have been quite strongly influenced by the same cultural tradition as prevailed in these countries, and in language, religion, and other cultural traits the Aksumites belonged to something of the same milieu as their overseas neighbours. When the Aksumites first became powerful enough to assert themselves by intervening in the political troubles of the Arabian states is uncertain, but from the beginning of the third century AD there are several records of such expeditions (Ch. 4: 3–4). There was much diplomatic and military activity during the reigns of Gadarat (GRDT) and Adhebah ('DBH) in the first half of the third century, including the negotiation of a treaty with Saba and then with Hadramawt. In Adhebah's time a certain Shamir, called *dhu-Raydan*, 'he of Raydan', a prince of Himyar, sent for military aid from Aksum. At least from the time of Ezana, in the fourth century, the Aksumite king adopted the title of 'king of Saba and Himyar', asserting a suzerainty probably difficult to enforce in practice. It is very likely that there was continuous contact during the fifth and early sixth centuries between the two sides of the Red Sea; Procopius mentions that it took five days and nights to cross the Red Sea and that *"the harbour of the Homeritae from which they are accustomed to put to sea is called Boulikas"* – presumably somewhere near Mukha;- *and at the end of the sail across the sea they always put in at the harbour of the Adulitae"* (Procopius, ed. Dewing 1914: 183). In the reign of the Aksumite king Kaleb (Ch. 4: 7), the use of the Arabian titles was expanded to copy the current style in use there, a procedure no doubt justified by the impact of the king's successful Arabian expedition which destroyed the régime of the Jewish king of Himyar, Yusuf Asar. Kaleb set up a vice-royalty in the Yemen, but soon his viceroy was deposed, and the Yemen became more or less independent. Direct Aksumite influence was never reinstated. However, one of the inscriptions of the new king in the Yemen, Abreha, dated to 543AD and dealing with the restoration of the great dam at Marib, mentions embassies from various foreign countries (Aksum, Rome, Persia, and various Arab groups), putting that of the Aksumite *najashi* first in the list (Sergew Hable Sellassie 1972: 148–9), and Procopius notes Abreha's formal submission to the successor of Kaleb- a diplomatic solution which may have soothed the damaged pride of the Aksumites and did Abreha little harm (Procopius, ed. Dewing 1914: 191).

Mecca and the Quraysh.

It has been suggested (Creswell, see Ullendorff 1960: 154) that the man who re-built the Ka'ba at Mecca in 608 AD was an Aksumite. His name was Bakum, and he used the wood retrieved from a shipwreck to build a structure of wood and stone layers which sounds very like the typical Aksumite architectural style as represented by, for example, Dabra Damo church. In

615 AD, at the time of the prophet Muhammad's mission, the Ethiopians were involved in a certain amount of diplomatic activity with the Quraysh tribe, the mercantile rulers of Mecca. The reigning *najashi*, whom the Arab chroniclers refer to as Ashama ibn Abjar (see Ch. 15: 4), offered asylum to Muslim political exiles, who entered the country in two waves. The first *hijra*, or flight, in the 7th month of the 5th year of Muhammad's mission (615), consisted of eleven men and four wives, who came via the old port of Mecca, Shu'ayba. These returned after three months, due to the false report that the Quraysh had been converted to Islam. The second *hijra* eventually amounted to one hundred and one Muslims, 83 of them men, and these did not all return until 628 (Muir 1923: 69). The *najashi*, in spite of gifts and representations from the Quraysh, refused to hand the Muslims over.

At different times many famous names in Islam were to seek the *najashi*'s hospitality, including Muhammad's daughter Ruqayya, and two of his future wives, Umm Habiba and Umm Salama or Hind, who described Maryam Tseyon church at Aksum to the prophet on his deathbed (Ch. 13: 3). Umm Habiba's former husband was 'Ubaydalla, a Quraysh convert to Islam who emigrated to Ethiopia where he adopted Christianity, and died confessing that faith (Muir 1923: 36). It was the *najashi* himself who contracted the marriage of Umm Habiba to Muhammad, which occurred when she returned in 628. Another famous exile was 'Uthman b. Affan, who eventually became *khalifa* in 644AD. The conqueror of Egypt, 'Amr ibn al-Asi, was actually received into Islam, if one credits the tradition (Guillaume 1955: 484) by the *najashi* acting on behalf of the prophet. Because of this kindness to his followers, Muhammad is said to have exempted Ethiopia from the *jihad* or holy war of Islam. According to Muslim tradition, in AH.6/627-8AD Muhammad himself is said to have sent an embassy to the *najashi* and other rulers; the contents of his letter (which many authorities doubt was ever actually written) are reproduced by Tabari and others, and an actual copy of the letter, undoubtedly a forgery, was published by Dunlop (1940). All this occurred very close to the time when it is suggested that Aksum was abandoned as the capital (Ch. 15: 4).

Rome and Constantinople/Byzantium.

With the Romano-Byzantine world Aksum seems to have almost always had good relations. Possibly Rome had designs on Aksum in Nero's time (see Ch. 4: 3), but this is uncertain. Aksum may have had some cause to fear the recovery of Roman power from about the time of Aurelian (270–275), when Aksumite ambassadors are reported in Rome (see below) but the arrangements for the frontiers made by Diocletian in 298 must have put such fears to rest, since Rome set Elephantine (Philae) as the limit of its direct authority (Williams 1985: 82).

The land route from Aksumite territory to Egypt was mentioned by the author of the *Monumentum Adulitanum* inscription (Wolska-Conus 1968:

374), and it is known from Procopius (ed. Dewing 1914: 185) that the route from Aksum to Elephantine took thirty days for an unencumbered traveller (Ch. 3: 2).

Though the land-route may have been used at times, the most frequented route from the Roman world appears to have been down the Red Sea from Egyptian ports to Adulis. It is possible that the story of Frumentius, the Tyrian Christian who converted the country, reveals one break in the early fourth century in the otherwise generally peaceful Romano-Aksumite trading relations. According to the historian Rufinus (Migne 1849: 478–9), the ship in which Frumentius, then a boy, was travelling, landed at a port, presumably under Ethiopian control, for provisions. But apparently due to a rift in political relations, the vessel was seized and the occupants slain. Frumentius and his companion Aedesius were lucky, as they alone were spared, and subsequently taken to the king as prisoners. It is not impossible that such a breach in relations was caused by the death of one king and the succession of another, since in traditional Hellenistic monarchies (some elements of whose organisation we can detect in Aksum) treaties would lapse until confirmed by the ruler who next came to power. In this case, we might conceivably suggest that king Wazeba of Aksum had died, and Ousanas (Ella Amida) had just come to the throne (Ch. 4: 5). The lapse of the treaty might also reflect the uncertain conditions in the Roman world after the retirement of Diocletian in 305 until 323 when complete order was restored by Constantine's defeat of Licinius.

Apart from this story, there are no signs of anything but peaceful trade and occasional diplomatic activity. With the new order in the Roman empire, and no challenges on the frontiers between Roman and Aksumite ambitions, Aksum had nothing to look for from Rome/Constantinople but peaceful and profitable trading relations. There was a certain amount of diplomatic activity in the reign of Constantius II, with the mission of Theophilus the Indian. This ecclesiastic may also have delivered the letter of Constantius preserved in the *Apologia* of the patriarch Athanasius of Alexandria (Ch. 4: 3). During and after the Himyarite war which Kaleb conducted in the sixth century, there was an increase in recorded diplomatic activity, and several missions were sent by Justinian. Two of the ambassadors, Julian, and Nonnosus son of Abrames, are mentioned by historians of the period, together with some details as to their instructions from the emperor (Procopius, ed. Dewing 1924: 192–5; Photius, ed. Henry 1959: 4–5).

Palmyra.

The suggestion (Sergew Hable Sellassie 1972: 86) that Aksumites were taken prisoner by Aurelian (270–275 AD), the Roman emperor who conquered Queen Zenobia of Palmyra's armies, is unfounded. Zenobia's forces had benefited from the weakness of Rome under its ephemeral military emperors in the late third century, and she was in control of Syria and the great city of Antioch. In 269AD, she successfully invaded Egypt; by 270 her interest was turning to Asia Minor. In 271 she proclaimed her son Wahballat as Augustus. In spite of this widespread success, the Roman empire was at last recovering from its unhappy condition under a new emperor, Aurelian, and Palmyrene hegemony lasted only a few years; and in August 272 Palmyra itself fell to the emperor's armies.

The Aksumites mentioned in the (rather suspect) Latin 'Life of Aurelian' attributed to Flavius Vopiscus in the so-called *Scriptores Historiae Augustae* (Magie 1932: 258–61), seem to have been among the foreign envoys present at the celebration of Aurelian's triumph rather than defeated allies of Zenobia being led with the queen in the procession. They are included in a separate section with other representatives from different countries bearing gifts, and not among the captives from peoples against whom Aurelian is known to have conducted campaigns. There is no evidence that Zenobia was able to open any diplomatic relations with Aksum during her brief period of dominance, and none to indicate that she enlisted the support of the Aksumites in her wars.

Persia.

Towards the end of Aksum's period of power, the Persians conquered both Egypt (in 619 AD, holding it until 628) and South Arabia (in 575 and again, after a rebellion in Himyar, in 598), and it may have been this that began to destroy Aksum's trade in the Red Sea rather than the later Arab expansion. There is only a little information about Persian relations with Aksum. John of Ephesus, in his 'Life of Simeon the Bishop', states that when Simeon and his companions had been for seven years in the prison at Nisibis, the king of Ethiopia heard of it and made a successful request, through his ambassadors to king Kawad (d. 531AD), that they should be freed (Brooks 1923: 153). Kosmas mentions that merchants from Adulis and Persia both met in Taprobane (Sri Lanka), and that ivory was exported from Ethiopia to Persia by sea (Wolska-Conus 1973: 348, 354). Also in the sixth century, the emperor Justinian is supposed to have tried to use Aksum against Persia in both an economic war over silk supplies and a military tentative through Aksum's South Arabian possessions (Procopius, ed. Dewing 1914: 192–5). The inference is that Aksum would be ready to act against the Persians because of their community of religion with the Roman/Byzantine empire. After the loss of Aksum's direct influence in South Arabia, and the death of the *negus* Kaleb, the historian Procopius (ed. Dewing 1914: 190–1) informs us that the leader of the rebel government in Arabia, Abreha, agreed to pay tribute to Aksum. The Persian conquest would have terminated this arrangement if it still applied to Abreha's successors. It may be supposed, then, that after 575 Aksum had not only lost its tribute, but was also faced with a more or less hostile Persian dependency just across the Red Sea. Already there may have been an increase in the movement of hostile shipping in the sea-lanes on which Aksum depended for its foreign commerce.

A few links with Persia have been suggested at different times. It may be that certain figures, robed and with curly hair, depicted on the monumental staircase of the Apadana at Persepolis, are Ethiopians. They are shown presenting a giraffe, a tusk, and a vase. Some details of their appearance resemble the more-or-less contemporary Ethiopians as known from their statues and throne reliefs from Hawelti (Leroy 1963: 293-5). At a much later date, certain glazed wares, blue-green in colour, found at Aksum and Matara, have been classified, rather vaguely, as Sassanian-Islamic or Gulf wares (Wilding in Munro-Hay 1989; Anfray 1974: 759).

India and Sri Lanka.

Aksum also had trading relations with India and Sri Lanka (Pankhurst 1974). A find of Indian gold coins, issued by the Kushana kings (who ruled in north India and Afghanistan) in the earlier third century, at the monastery of Dabra Damo on the route between Aksum and the coast, confirms the contact from the Ethiopian side (Mordini 1960, 1967). There are also occasional allusions to ships from Adulis sailing to or from the sub-continent. Such instances occur in the accounts of the arrival of the future bishop Frumentius in Ethiopia (Ch. 10: 2), the journey of bishop Moses of Adulis (Desanges 1969) and in the *Christian Topography* of Kosmas Indikopleustes. Kosmas (Wolska-Conus 1973: 348–51) describes how a Roman merchant, Sopatros, who had gone to Taprobane (Sri Lanka) with merchants from Adulis, got the better of a distinguished Persian in the presence of a Sri Lankan king by comparing the gold coins of the Romans with the silver milarision of the Persians. A number of yellow pottery figures, apparently mould-made, were found at Hawelti, near the stelae there; de Contenson suggested that they were of Indian type, but this has not been authoritatively confirmed (de Contenson 1963ii: 45–6, pl. XLVIII).

The Far East.

There is no real evidence for contacts between China and Aksum, but it has been suggested that the Han dynasty records include a reference to the Aksumite kingdom (Sergew Hable Sellassie 1972: 71, 84–5). If, as seems possible, the Han ships were in contact with states beyond India, the kingdom which the chroniclers call Huang-Chi might have been Aksum (Fiaccadori 1984: 283, n. 30). Aksum grew to be an important power in the region of the Red Sea, and the Chinese merchants must, at the very least, have eventually come into contact with someone who knew of Aksum. If Huang-Chi was Aksum the contact is a valuable one for our chronology, since the usurper Wang Mang (1–6 AD) received in return for his gifts a live rhinoceros from the king of Huang Chi, thus attesting the presence of a dominant power group at this early stage, just when the rise of Aksum is postulated. However, Wang Mang's agents could equally well have contacted some other coastally centred pre-Aksumite group, like the Adulitae. Other products of Huang-Chi were tortoise-shell and ivory, both readily available to the Aksumites. The distances cited by the Chinese records put Huang-Chi well beyond India and it took twelve months to accomplish the voyage there. We can only say that the identification is tempting, but very uncertain. A suggestion that the Hsi-wang Mu of ancient Chinese records, who lived in the K'un-lun mountains, was to be identified with the Queen of Sheba living in the *qolla* of Abyssinia, was another attempt to find a point of contact in the even more remote past.

IV

Aksumite History

A useful divison for the study of the history of Aksum, in our present state of knowledge, is to separate the historical sequence into a number of periods based as far as possible on the coinage. The latter (Ch. 9) is the best criterion we have for suggesting a chronology. Since the history of Aksum obviously overlaps the issue of the coinage at both ends, the following divisions have been employed.

Pre-Aksumite. Northern Ethiopia before the rise of Aksum.
1. Early Aksum until the reign of Gadarat. 1st and 2nd centuries AD.
2. Gadarat to the first issues of coinage under Endubis. 3rd century AD until c 270.
3. The Pagan Kings; Endubis to Ezana. c 270 – c 330 AD.
4. Ezana (after his conversion) to Kaleb. c. 330 – c 520 AD.
5. Kaleb to the end of the coinage. c 520 – early seventh century AD.
6. The Post-Aksumite period. From the early seventh century AD.

The period begins with the reign of Ashama ibn Abjar and continues until the accession of the Zagwé dynasty c. 1137.

1. The Pre-Aksumite Period.

This period is not of major concern to us here, and in any case we have very little information about it; but some consideration should be given to the situation in Ethiopia before the rise of Aksum, since the source of at least some of the characteristics of the later Aksumite civilisation can be traced to this earlier period. Perhaps the most interesting phenomenon in this respect is that by around the middle of the first millenium BC – a date cautiously suggested, using palaeographical information (Pirenne 1956; Drewes 1962: 91), but possibly rather too late in view of new discoveries in the Yemen (Fattovich 1989: 16–17) which may even push it back to the eighth century BC – some sort of contact, apparently quite close, seems to have been maintained between Ethiopia and South Arabia. This developed to such an extent that in not a few places in Ethiopia the remains of certain mainly religious or funerary installations, some of major importance, with an unmistakeable South Arabian appearance in many details, have been excavated. Among the sites are Hawelti-Melazo, near Aksum (de Contenson 1961ii), the famous temple and other buildings and tombs at Yeha (Anfray 1973ii), the early levels at Matara (Anfray 1967), and the sites at Seglamien (Ricci and Fattovich 1984–6), Addi Galamo, Feqya, Addi Grameten and Kaskase, to name only the better-known ones. Fattovich (1989: 4–5) comments on many of these and has been able to attribute some ninety sites altogether to the pre-Aksumite period.

Inscriptions found at some of these sites include the names of persons bearing the traditional South Arabian title of *mukarrib*, apparently indicating a ruler with something of a priest-king status, not otherwise known in Ethiopia (Caquot and Drewes 1955). Others have the title of king, *mlkn* (Schneider 1961; 1973). Evidently the pre-Aksumite Sabaean-influenced cultural province did not consist merely of a few briefly-occupied staging posts, but was a wide-spread and well-established phenomenon. Until relatively recently South Arabian artefacts found in Ethiopia were interpreted as the material signs left behind by a superior colonial occupation force, with political supremacy over the indigenes – an interpretation still maintained by Michels (1988). But further study has now suggested that very likely, by the time the inscriptions were produced, the majority of the material in fact represented the civilisation of the Ethiopians themselves. Nevertheless, a certain amount of contact with South Arabia is very apparent, and had resulted in the adoption of a number of cultural traits (Schneider 1973; 1976).

Evidently the arrival of Sabaean influences does not represent the beginning of Ethiopian civilisation. For a long time different peoples had been interacting through population movements, warfare, trade and intermarriage in the Ethiopian region, resulting in a predominance of peoples speaking languages of the Afro-Asiatic family. The main branches represented were the Cushitic and the Semitic. Semiticized Agaw peoples are thought to have migrated from south-eastern Eritrea possibly as early as 2000BC, bringing their 'proto-Ethiopic' language, ancestor of Ge'ez and the other Ethiopian Semitic languages, with them; and these and other groups had already developed specific cultural and linguistic identities by the time any Sabaean influences arrived. Features such as dressed stone building, writing and iron-working may have been introduced by Sabaeans, but words for 'plough' and other agricultural vocabulary are apparently of Agaw origin in Ethiopian Semitic languages, indicating that the techniques of food-production were not one of the Arabian imports. Clark (1988) even suggestes that wheat, barley, and the plough may have been introduced from Egypt via Punt. Some of the graffiti found in eastern Eritrea include names apparently neither South Arabian nor Ethiopian, perhaps reflecting the continued existence of some older ethnic groups in the same cultural matrix. Various stone-age sites and rock-paintings attest to these early Ethiopians in Eritrea and Tigray. At Matara and Yeha, for example, archaeologists have distinguished phases represented by pottery types which seem to owe nothing to South Arabia, but do have some Sudanese affinities. The Italian archaeologist Rodolfo Fattovich, who has particularly interested himself in this study, has suggested that the pre-Aksumite culture might owe something to Nubia, specifically to C- group/Kerma influences, and later on to Meroë/Alodia (Fattovich 1977, 1978, 1989). Worsening ecological conditions in the savanna/Sahel belt might have induced certain peoples to move from plains and lowlands up to the plateau in the second half of the second millenium BC (Clark 1976), bringing with them certain cultural traditions. Evidence for early trade activity to regions across the Red Sea from eastern Sudan and Ethiopia at about this time has been noted by Zarins (1988), with reference to the obsidian trade. Extremely interesting results have lately come from work in the Gash Delta on the Ethiopo-Sudanese borderland, indicating the existence of a complex society there in the late 3rd-early 2nd millenium BC (Fattovich 1989: 21); possibly the location of the land of Punt there reinforces this suggestion (Kitchen (1971; Fattovich 1988: 2, 7). It seems that the new discoveries are of major importance to an understanding of the dynamics of state formation in the Ethiopian highlands. The latest work suggests that in the late second and early first millenium BC the eastern part of the Tigray plateau was included in a widespread cultural complex on both the African and the Arabian Tihama coasts of the Red Sea, in contact with the lowlands of the Sudan and perhaps with the Nile Valley, while the western part was in contact with peoples of the Gash Delta. These two regions of the plateau later became united culturally and politically under the D'MT monarchy (Fattovich 1989: 34–5)

It appears that there were undoubtedly some South Arabian immigrants in Ethiopia in the mid-first millenium BC, but there is (unless the interpretation of Michels is accepted) no sure indication that they were politically dominant. The sites chosen by them may be related to their relative ease of access to the Red Sea coast. Arthur Irvine (1977) and others have regarded sympathetically the suggestion that the inscriptions which testify to Sabaean presence in Ethiopia may have been set up by colonists around the time of the Sabaean ruler Karibil Watar in the late fourth century BC; but the dating is very uncertain, as noted above. They may have been military or trading colonists, living in some sort of symbiosis with the local Ethiopian population, perhaps under a species of treaty-status.

It seems that the pre-Aksumite society on the Tigray plateau, centred in the Aksum/Yeha region but extending from Tekondo in the north to Enderta in the south (Schneider 1973: 389), had achieved state level, and that the major entity came to be called D'MT (Di'amat, Damot?), as appears in the regal title '*mukarrib* of Da'mot and Saba'. The name may survive in the Aksumite titulature as Tiamo/Tsiyamo(Ch. 7:5). Its rulers, kings and *mukarrib*s, by including the name Saba in their titles, appear to have expressly claimed control over the resident Sabaeans in their country; actual Sabaean presence is assumed at Matara, Yeha and Hawelti-Melazo according to present information (Schneider 1973: 388). The inscriptions of *mukarrib*s of D'MT and

9. An inscription from Abba Pantelewon near Aksum, written in the Epigraphic South Arabian script and mentioning the kingdom of D'MT; it is dedicated to the deity Dhat-Ba'adan. It has been photographed upside down. Photo BIEA.

Saba are known from Addi Galamo (Caquot and Drewes 1955: 26–32), Enda Cherqos (Schneider 1961: 61ff), possibly Matara, if the name LMN attested there is the same as the .MN from the other sites, (Schneider 1965: 90; Drewes and Schneider 1967: 91), Melazo (Schneider 1978: 130-2), and Abuna Garima (Schneider 1973; Schneider 1976iii: 86ff). Of four rulers known to date, the earliest appears to be a certain W'RN HYWT, who only had the title *mlkn*, king, and evidence of whom has been found at Yeha, Kaskase, Addi Seglamen; he was succeeded by three *mukarribs*, RD'M, RBH, and LMN (Schneider 1976iii: 89–93).

The Sabaeans in Ethiopia appear, from the use of certain place-names like Marib in their inscriptions, to have kept in contact with their own country, and indeed the purpose of their presence may well have been to maintain and develop links across the sea to the profit of South Arabia's trading network. Naturally, such an arrangement would have worked also to the benefit of the indigenous Ethiopian rulers, who employed the titles *mukarrib* and *mlkn* at first, and *nagashi (najashi)* or *negus* later; no pre-Aksumite *najashi* or *negus* is known. The inscriptions dating from this period in Ethiopia are apparently written in two languages, pure Sabaean and another language with certain aspects found later in Ge'ez (Schneider 1976). All the royal inscriptions are in this second, presumably Ethiopian, language. A number of different tribes and families seem to be mentioned by the inscriptions of this period, but there is no evidence to show whether any of these groups lasted into the Aksumite period. Only the word YG'DYN, man of Yeg'az, might hint that the Ge'ez or Agazyan tribe was established so early, though the particular inscription which mentions it is written in the South Arabian rather than the Ethiopian language (Schneider 1961). Some of the other apparently tribal names also occur in both groups of inscriptions. The usual way of referring to someone in the inscriptions is 'N. of the family N. of the tribe N.', possibly also reflected later by the Aksumite 'Bisi'-title; 'king N. man of the tribe/clan (?) N' (Ch. 7: 5).

It seems that these 'inscriptional' Sabaeans did not remain more than a century or so – or perhaps even only a few decades – as a separate and identifiable people. Possibly their presence was connected to a contemporary efflorescence of Saba on the other side of the Red Sea. Their influence was only in a limited geographical area, affecting the autochthonous population in that area to a greater or lesser degree. Such influences as did remain after their departure or assimilation fused with the local cultural background, and contributed to the ensemble of traits which constituted Ethiopian civilisation in the rest of the pre-Aksumite period. Indeed, it may be that the Sabaeans were able to establish themselves in Ethiopia in the first place because both their civilisation and that of mid-1st millenium Ethiopia already had something in common; it has been suggested that earlier migrations or contacts might have taken place, leaving a kind of cultural sympathy between the two areas which allowed the later contact to flourish easily. The precise nature of the contacts between the two areas, their range in commercial, linguistic or cultural terms, and their chronology, is still a major question, and discussion of this fascinating problem continues (Marrassini 1985; Avanzini 1987; Pirenne 1987; Isaac and Felder 1988).

Jacqueline Pirenne's most recent (1987) proposal results in a radically different view of the Ethiopian/South Arabian contacts. Weighing up the evidence from all sides, particularly aspects of material culture and lingustic/palaeographic information, she suggests that *"il est donc vraisemblable que l'expansion ne s'est pas faite du Yémen vers l'Ethiopie, mais bien en sens inverse: de l'Ethiopie vers le Yémen"*. According to this theory, one group of Sabaeans would have left north Arabia (where they were then established) for Ethiopia in about the eighth or seventh century BC under pressure from the Assyrians; they then continued on into south Arabia. A second wave of emigrants, in the sixth and fifth century, would reign over the kingdom of Da'amat (D'MT), and would have been accompanied by Hebrews fleeing after Nebuchadnezzar's capture of Jerusalem; an explanation for the later Ethiopian traditions with their Jewish and Biblical flavour, and for the Falashas or black Jews of Ethiopia. These Sabaeans too, in their turn would have departed for the Yemen, taking there the writing and architecture which they had first perfected in Tigray. In the fourth and third century BC the remaining Sabaean emigrés would have left Ethiopia for the Yemen, leaving elements of their civilisation and traditions firmly embedded in the Ethiopian's way of life. This ingenious *mise en scène*, so far only briefly noted in a conference paper, must await complete publication before it can be fully discussed; but it is expressive of the highly theoretical nature of our conclusions about pre-Aksumite Ethiopia that so complete a reversal of previous ideas can even be proposed. Isaac and Felder (1988) also speculate about the possibility of a common cultural sphere in Ethiopia and Arabia, without giving either side the precedence.

It has also been suggested that the progress of the youthful Ethiopian state brought it into conflict with Meroë in the reigns of such kings as Harsiotef and Nastasen from the fourth century BC. Whilst there must have been some contact later, there is no real evidence from this early date (Taddesse Tamrat 1972: 12).

The altars, inscriptions, stelae, temples, secular structures, tombs and other material left by the Sabaean-influenced Ethiopian population occur in considerable numbers even from the few excavated sites; those attributed to the Sabaeans themselves occur more rarely. The monuments are dated from the 5th century BC by study of the letter-forms used on them (palaeography), and seem to appear in Ethiopia at about the same time as they do in South Arabia (nb. the reservations about the dating expressed by Fattovich 1989). The disc and crescent symbol used on some of the monuments (and very much later by the pre-Christian Aksumites) was also familiar on some South Arabian coins, and South Arabian altars; many of the same deities were being worshipped in the two regions. It was also during this period that iron was introduced into the country. In the present state of our knowledge, it is unclear how much of Aksumite civilisation was a direct continuation of a cultural heritage from pre-Aksumite times, or how much any South Arabian aspects might be better attributed to a renewal of overseas contacts in the period after the consolidation of Aksum as an independent polity in the first and second centuries AD. No clear evidence of connexions between the pre- Aksumite, Sabaean-influenced, period, and the earliest Aksumite period is at the moment available, though it seems intrinsically more likely that Aksum in some way was able to draw directly on part of the experience of its predecessors. At Matara, the archaeological evidence implies that there was a clear break between the two periods (Anfray and Annequin 1965), but this need not have been the case everywhere in the country. The solution to these questions can only await further clarification from archaeology.

The subsequent periods are those which represent the duration of the Aksumite kingdom proper. In the following table approximate dates for these periods, numbered 1–5, are indicated, together with the names of the known rulers, with notes about any references in texts or inscriptions, contemporary constructions (Ch. 16) at Aksum (using the terminology in Munro-Hay 1989), and significant international events with a bearing on Aksum.

2. Comparative Chronological Chart; Rulers, Sources and Sites.

Period 1. Early Aksum until the reign of GDRT. 1st- 2nd centuries AD.

	Zoskales?	Earliest platforms Lower Stele Park levels *Periplus*?
100 AD		
c.150 AD		Platform A, 1st platform extension Ptolemy.

Period 2. GDRT-Endubis. Beginning of 3rd century AD to c. 270 AD.

200 AD		
	GDRT, BYGT	South Arabian inscriptions
230 AD	'DBH, GRMT Sembrouthes	
250 AD		Nefas Mawcha Walls M2,M5,and M9 Gudit Tomb; Gudit, Southeastern, and GA stelae fields
260 AD	DTWNS and ZQRNS	

Period 3. Endubis to Ezana before his conversion. c.270 AD to c.330 AD.

270 AD		
	Endubis* Coinage begins	Main Stele Field
		Dressed stelae Wall M1
300 AD		
		Decorated stelae
	Aphilas*	
		Tunnel Complex, East Tomb, Sh.T.B
	Wazeba* Ousanas*	
	Ezana* Inscriptions,	Tomb of Brick Arches Anza stele, Brick Vaulted Structure,Mausoleum, Matara stele.

Period 4. Ezana as a Christian to Kaleb. c. 330 AD to c. 520 AD.

330 AD		
	Christian Inscriptions and coins.	

		2nd platform extension Wall M’1,East wall, East steps
	Anonymous Christian coins	
350 AD		
	Athanasius *Apologia* MHDYS* Ouazebas*	Sh.T.C Walls M7 and M8
400 AD		Fall of Stele 1 Kaleb I-IA buildings
	Eon*	Tomb of the False Door IW building
	Ebana* Nezool*/Nezana*	
500 AD		
	Ousas*/Ousana(s)*. Tazena	

Period 5. Kaleb until the end of the coinage. c.520 AD to early C.7th AD

	Kaleb* Inscription	Kosmas Indikopleustes Conquest of Yemen
	Yusuf As‘ar	Tombs of Kaleb and Gabra Masqal
530 AD	Sumyafa‘ Ashwa‘ Abreha Alla Amidas* Wazena* W’ZB Inscription, Ella Gabaz*	
		Sh.T.A.
	Ioel*	
575 AD		Persians in Yemen
	Hataz* = ‘Iathlia’ Israel*	Fill of ES building
600 AD		
	Gersem*	
614 AD	Armah*	Jerusalem falls to Persia
619 AD		Egypt falls to Persia End of Aksum as capital, Matara tomb

Period 6, After the end of the coinage.

630 AD		Death of Ashama ibn Abjar
640 AD	Arab expedition in Red Sea,	Egypt falls to Arabs
705-715 AD	Reign of al-Walid, Qusayr Amra painting	

The symbol * denotes issues of coins.

3. PERIOD 1: EARLY AKSUM UNTIL THE REIGN OF GADARAT. The process of development of the Aksumite state is obscure. The earliest surviving literary references to Aksum, in the *Periplus of the Erythraean Sea* (Huntingford 1980) and Ptolemy's *Geography* (Stevenson 1932), together with some finds of early date from the site itself (Munro-Hay 1989), indicate that the city was probably established at the beginning of our era. The dates of both the above references have been disputed. It has been suggested that the *Periplus* could have been written in the mid-1st century (Bowersock 1983: 70; Casson 1989: 7) or even as late as the 3rd century AD (Pirenne 1961), whilst one scholar proposed that the earliest surviving versions of Ptolemy's work relay information which was continually updated until the 4th century AD (Mathew 1975: 152). However, if they are accepted as early documents, their references to Aksum do seem to be backed up by the excavation there of certain features which can be satisfactorily dated to the first and second centuries AD. These include stone-built platforms, perhaps originally laid out with some funerary purpose since they were found below the deposits later formed by the main cemetery (now the so-called Stele Park; see Ch. 16). They have been dated by radiocarbon tests on material found in associated contexts to the first two centuries AD (Chittick 1974; Chittick 1976i; Munro-Hay 1989). Among the finds from this region were fragments of glass vessels of particular types, dateable to the first century AD; and certain types of glass were actually included in the list of imports into Aksum provided by the *Periplus*.

If we are right in thinking of the *Periplus* as a probably mid-first century document, we can hope to find at Aksum evidence of the *"city of the people called Auxumites"* (Schoff 1912: 23) – translated by Huntingford as *"the metropolis called the Axomite"* (1980: 20) – which it mentions, together with a comprehensive selection of such goods as it describes as being imported into Aksum. Ptolemy, if we accept that his reference is not a later addition, leads us to expect a city with a king's palace at some time around the mid-second century AD. Archaeology has so far revealed little of this, but the early platforms and glass indicate that further evidence for the existence of the city by the first century AD may now be expected. With more archaeological excavation, other early remains apart from the platforms may be discovered. Much of the other material excavated is at the moment difficult to date reliably and so remains inconclusive.

Accepting, with the modern concensus of opinion, that the *Periplus* dates to the mid-first century AD, we find that at this stage Aksum, under the rule of king Zoskales, was already a substantial state with access to the sea at Adulis. Zoskales is the earliest king of the region known to us at the moment (though Cerulli 1960: 7; Huntingford 1980: 60, 149-50 and Chittick 1981: 186 suggested that he was not king of Aksum but a lesser tributary ruler). In his time there was a vigorous trading economy, and already a notable demand for the luxuries of foreign countries. The monarchy was established; and Ptolemy confirms that Aksum was the royal capital by the mid-second century AD. This period, then, saw the rise of the city into the governmental centre for a considerable area of the Ethiopian plateau and the coastal plain. Such a line of development is to be expected since by the time of king GDRT (Gadarat) Aksum had attained a position which allowed it to venture to send its armies on overseas expeditions and even establish garrisons in parts of Arabia. The fact that the *Periplus* does not mention Aksumites in connection with South Arabia is another feature which seems to date it before the period of Abyssinian intervention there, and indeed the *Periplus* notes that the power of king Kharibael of Himyar and Saba, and the *tyrannos* Kholaibos of the southern coastal Mopharitic region (al-Ma'afir), reaching from their capitals of Zafar and Saue, was sufficient to allow them to control Azania, the east African coast to Tanzania, and its rich trade in ivory and tortoise-shell (Casson 1989: 61, 69). Though, by the early third century, Aksum had come to dominate al-Ma'afir, and much weakened the Arabian trading system, at the time of the *Periplus* the Ethiopians were not in a position to reach so far, and the Arabian port of Muza seems to have been rather more important than Adulis. Gradually, during the second century, Aksum must have begun to interest itself in weakening Himyarite maritime control, culminating in its allying with Saba (see below) and seizing certain areas formerly under Himyarite rule (Bafaqih and Robin 1980; Bafaqih 1983: Ch. 3).

One uncertain but interesting hint that Aksumite power may have been increasing notably in the 1st century AD comes from accounts preserved by Seneca (ed. Corcoran 1972), the Roman writer who became the emperor Nero's tutor, and Pliny (ed. Rackham 1952: VI. 35, 184). These authors record details about an exploration (or two separate expeditions; Shinnie 1967: 21-22) in 61 AD into the southern part of the Sudan. Certain Roman officers were able to penetrate as far as the great papyrus swamp region of the Sudan, the Sudd, it seems with a certain amount of help from the Meroitic king. Even in Augustus' time, according to Strabo (ed. Page 1930: 353) Aelius Gallus had been sent not only to explore Arabia, '*but also in Aethiopia, since Caesar saw that the Troglodyte country which adjoins Aegypt neighbours upon Arabia, and also that the Arabian Gulf, which separates the Arabians from the Troglodytes, is extremely narrow*' but this earlier effort came to nothing, it seems, since Gallus' expedition was a failure. It has been suggested that at the time of the Sudan expedition Rome, as Meroë's ally, was trying to assist in preventing the nascent Aksumite kingdom from seizing control of the routes formerly used by the Kushite monarchy's merchant caravans. Whilst we have no certain confirmation of this, there may have come a time when Meroë and Aksum clashed over their interests in the control of the Nile routes. Schur (1923) says that the emperor Nero intended to move against Aksum, and therefore sent an army to Ptolemais under Vespasian and Titus; but this can only be conjecture. Nevertheless, with the decline of Meroitic power and the fragmentation of authority in the region, Aksum would certainly have had a better opportunity for advancing its interests to the west and north than when Meroë was still a powerful state. The Meroitic relief at Jabal Qayli, close to the route leading to Kassala, where the king of Meroë is shown with slain enemies under the image of an Apollo-like deity, is the furthest actual trace of Meroitic influence to the east (Shinnie 1967: 50-51). This relief, bearing the name of king Sherkarer, is attributed to the early first century AD, but the Meroitic dates are not certainly fixed, and there is considerable leeway. It has been suggested that the distorted figures of the enemy represent slain Aksumites, but they could just as easily be depictions of any local group who had incurred Sherkarer's enmity.

4. Period 2: Gadarat to Endubis

This period may be characterised as Aksum's first 'South Arabian' period, since most of the information available comes from inscriptions found in South Arabia (Beeston 1937; Jamme 1962; Robin 1981). The inscriptions name the Ethiopian kings as '*nagashi* of Habashat (Abyssinia) and of Aksum(an)' and are written in the old South Arabian script and language. Since there are no vowels marked, the royal names mentioned by these inscriptions actually read GDRT, 'AD̲BH, ZQRNS and DTWNS, but for convenience here simple vowelling has been added, as for example, in the name 'Gadarat'. The letters GDRT could represent a Ge'ez name such as Gedur, Gadura, Gedara or the like, but until a correctly vowelled spelling is found we remain unsure of the precise pronunciation.

The inscriptions which refer to Gadarat and 'Adhebah (perhaps 'Azba or 'Azeba in Ge'ez), kings of Aksum and Habashat, come from the famous temple at Marib called by the Arabs 'Mahram Bilqis', after the Arab name for the Queen of Sheba. Mahram Bilqis was in fact the great temple of the moon-god Ilmuqah at the ancient capital of the kingdom of Saba, now in north Yemen. Dated inscriptions, using an 'era of Himyar' are now interpreted as providing a date for Gadarat around the beginning of the 3rd century AD. It was previously suggested (Munro-Hay 1984: 20) that these were fourth century rulers, on the strength of the reading of 'AD̲BH as WD̲BH, identified with Wazeba (WZB), one of the earliest kings named on the coinage, but since new discoveries about the dating of the inscriptions this theory has been abandoned.

The inscriptions which mention the Aksumite rulers were written as official accounts of wars and victories by the kings of Saba and Himyar. Since these kings were usually the enemies of the Aksumites, they do not deal very often with Aksumite successes. Nevertheless, we find that the military forces of the Aksumites were in control of certain regions of the Arabian peninsular, a situation doubtless partly facilitated by the political situation in Arabia, where the rulers of both Saba and Himyar at different times called in the help of Aksumite armies against each other.

The situation is still not entirely clear, but it appears that Arabia at the end of the second century was dominated by four states, Himyar (a relatively new polity), Saba, Hadhramawt and Qataban. Somewhere between c 160-210AD Qataban was annexed by Hadhramawt, while the Sabaean rulers tried to subjugate Himyar, then ruled by king Tharan Ya'ub Yuhan'im. The Sabaean king 'Alhan Nahfan, son of Yarim Ayman I, and his sons Sha'ir Awtar and Yarim Ayman II allied themselves against Himyar with Gadarat, *nagashi* of Aksum. This latter power was probably a relatively recent arrival on the Arabian scene, interested in curtailing Himyarite trading control in the Red Sea and beyond, and its assistance helped the Sabaeans to achieve a favourable balance of power. But it also brought a new factor into South Arabian politics, not finally disposed of until the Persian conquest centuries later; the Abyssinian presence ultimately protracted the conflict between Saba and Himyar for eventual control of the entire region.

This realignment occurred in the early part of the third century. The three Sabaean kings had previously allied themselves with Yada'ub Gaylan, the king of Hadhramawt. An inscription celebrating their treaty with Aksum declares that

> *'they agreed together that their war and their peace should be in unison, against anyone that might rise up against them, and that in safety and in security there should be allied together Salhen and Zararan and 'Alhan and Gadarat'.*

In this inscription what seems to be Gadarat's castle or chief residence Zararan, is mentioned in parallel to the palace of 'Alhan at Marib, capital of Saba, which was called Salhen; Zararan might even be one of the palaces whose ruins are still visible at Aksum (Ch. 5: 4).

After 'Alhan Nahfan's death his son Sha'ir Awtar (whose reign seems to date from about 210 to 230AD, linked for a time in co-regency with his brother Hayu'athtar Yada') abandoned this alliance. Frictions had doubtless begun to develop as Aksum grew more powerful in the region, and learned to play off the Arabian kingdoms and tribal allegiances against each other. By about 225AD Sha'ir Awtar had defeated and captured Il'azz Yalut, king of the Hadhramawt, and taken his capital, Shabwa. Il'azz was married to the sister of Sha'ir Awtar, and in 217-8AD the latter had helped put down a rebellion against the Hadhrami king; the enmity between Hadhramawt and Saba was a major change in policy. The Abyssinian position in these events is not clear. Sha'ir Awtar apparently used both Himyarite and Sabaean troops in this campaign, and the Himyarite ruler, Li'azz Yahnuf Yuhasdiq, whose reign may have overlapped with the end of Sha'ir's, also allied with the Sabaeans against Gadarat. Aksum suffered a defeat, and was expelled from the Himyarite capital, Zafar, which had been occupied and garrisoned under the command of a son of the *nagashi*, Beyga or Baygat (BYGT). However, Aksum still retained territory in Arabia in the reign of Sha'ir Awtar's successor Lahay'atat Yarkham, who had at least one clash with Habash troops. In any event, these activities, dating from perhaps the beginning of the third century to the 230's AD, are confirmation that Aksum had reached a new zenith in its power. Overseas wars, the occupation of territories in Arabia, military alliances, a fleet, and the extension of Aksumite political and military influence from the Hadhramawt to Najran in modern Saudi Arabia bespeak an important increase in the scope of the Aksumite state.

A peace may have been patched up between the contestants for a while, but it was only temporary. A little later, in the 240s, we find two rival dynasties calling themselves kings of Saba and Dhu-Raydan, one of which, represented by a certain Shamir of Dhu-Raydan and Himyar, turned for help to king 'Azeba or 'Adhebah ('ADBH) of Aksum, and his son Girma, Garima or Garmat (GRMT), with their allies from Sahartan and the tribe of Akk, against the Sabaean kings Ilsharah Yahdub and Yazzil Bayyin, sons of Fari'um Yanhub (who only called himself king of Saba, perhaps recognising that he was not in the same position of power as his two predecessors, who had employed the dual title 'king of Saba and Dhu-Raydan'). These kings considered that Himyar, the Abyssinians, and Sahartan were in breach of a peace-treaty during the ensuing war. Shamir Dhu-Raydan was almost certainly the Himyarite king Shamir Yuhahmid, who became an ally of Aksum under 'ADBH and the 'son of the *nagashi*' GRMT. He sent for help to the *nagashi*, and, though one inscription claims that

> *"Shamir of Dhu-Raydan and Himyar had called in the help of the clans of Habashat for war against the kings of Saba; but Ilmuqah granted...the submission of Shamir of Dhu-Raydan and the clans of Habashat",*

Shamir seems to have to some extent recovered Himyarite power. It may have been such a request for aid that eventually led the Aksumite kings to claim the much-used titles of 'king of Saba and Himyar' in their own titulature, asserting some sort of theoretical suzerainty over the Arabian kings. Incidentally, it is unknown whether the two generals entitled 'son of the *nagashi*' Baygat and Garmat were 'crown princes' who succeeded to the throne in their turn, or whether they were merely military captains under the *nagashi*s. Their names are unknown except for these inscriptions.

Around the end of the 240s until c. 260, the Himyarite king was Karibil Ayfa', who fought with Yada'il Bayyin and his son Ilriyam Yadum of the new dynasty in Hadhramawt, with the Abyssinians, and with Ilsharah Yahdub and Yazzil Bayyin of Saba; all the main forces then in the Yemen. One of the al-Mis'al inscriptions (no. 3) mentions that a son of the *nagashi*, unfortunately unnamed, came to Zafar with the troops of al-Ma'afir and the Abyssinians, and that a sortie was made against them.

A new gap now occurs in the records. Possibly it may be filled by one of the most mysterious of the Aksumite kings, Sembrouthes (Littmann 1913: IV, 3). He is known only from his Greek inscription from Daqqi Mahari, well north of Aksum in present-day Eritrea. The inscription is on a roughly shaped building block, and, for so brief a text, is filled with expressions of the royal self-esteem;

> *"King of kings of Aksum, great Sembrouthes came (and) dedicated (this inscription) in the year 24 of Sembrouthes the Great King"*

10. The Greek inscription of the king of kings Sembrouthes of Aksum, from Daqqi Mahari, Eritrea (courtesy of G. Tringali).

His substantial reign of at least 24 years, if correctly placed here, fills the period between the last mention of 'Adhebah and the next known Aksumite rulers, DTWNS and ZQRNS. Himyarite power was growing stronger throughout this period, and perhaps to curb this Aksum decided to act; in c. 267-8 Yasir Yuhan'im of Himyar (c.260-270) suffered an invasion led by two Aksumite kings. More South Arabian inscriptions, recently brought to notice by Christian Robin, (whose dating of the South Arabian eras, and general historical scheme (1981) we have followed here) come from the Yemeni site of al-Mis'al. One inscription (no. 5) deals with this war in which the two kings of Aksum, Datawnas (DTWNS) and Zaqarnas (ZQRNS), with their allies of al-Ma'afir, were involved. Whether these were co-rulers, or successive occupants of the Aksumite throne, is not certain, but they appear to have renewed or continued the Aksumite presence in South Arabia sometime during the years between 260 and 270 AD. The results of their efforts remain unclear; when the al-Mis'al inscriptions are fully published more may be known about the events of this period, but the fact that the Aksumite kings were still interfering in Arabian politics indicates that their interests in South Arabia were not lightly abandoned. An inscription of the last Sabaean king, Nashakarib Yuha'min Yuharib, also mentions Abyssinian incursions at this time, but it is notable that accounts of his wars in Sahartan do not mention the Abyssinians.

The subsequent events, culminating in a Himyarite victory over Saba, are conjectured to be more or less contemporary with the Aksumite kings Endubis and Aphilas, and are detailed below (Ch. 4: 5).

Sadly, nothing is known of these Aksumite kings of the third century from the Ethiopian side except for the discovery at Atsbi Dera of a sceptre or wand in bronze, which mentions the name of 'GDR negus of Aksum' (Caquot and Drewes 1955: 32-38; Doresse 1960). This appears in a short inscription which has been translated as either *'GDR king of Aksum occupied the passages of 'RG and LMQ'*', or *"Gedara, King of Axum is humbled before the [gods] Arg and Almouqah*"(Jamme 1957). GDR is very likely the same king called by the Arabian kings GDRT (Gadarat). In addition, some finds of Himyarite coins at Aksum may be attributed to this overseas intercourse (Munro-Hay 1978).

The stelae of two prominent Ethiopians of the late third century offer a little information about local matters (Drewes 1962: 67-8). One, the Matara stele, reads *'This is the stele which Agaz has made for his ancestors....'*, but no information is given about Agaz himself. The other, the Anza (near Hawzien) stele, was erected by Bazat (BZT) *negus* of Agabo, perhaps a local king. His stele seems to celebrate a 15 day festival, and 520 containers of beer and 20,620 loaves are recorded as a donation.

The Aksumite state at this stage appears fully-fledged as a militaristic monarchy with wide-reaching foreign connexions. The interest in South Arabia may have been encouraged by the need to keep the Red Sea efficiently policed so that vessels of the Aksumites or their trading partners could come and go safely. Aksum may also have been concerned to be included in the enormously profitable trade in incense and other valuable goods along the routes which crossed Arabia to the markets of the Roman empire. Sembrouthes' inscription attests Aksumite power as far north as Daqqi Mahari, and confirms that he controlled subordinate kings, since he uses the title 'king of kings'. His inscription is in Greek, the language Zoskales also knew. It remains possible that Sembrouthes should be situated at an earlier date, though the elevated title of 'king of kings' does perhaps tend to support the dating proposed above.

5. Period 3: Endubis to Ezana

From the reign of king Endubis we are fortunate in having the newly issued coinage, in gold, silver, and bronze, to guide us in tracing out a framework for the history and chronology of Aksum (Munro-Hay, loc. var.; Hahn 1983). The issue of a coinage (Ch. 9) is of very great importance in itself, and for Aksum the issue of an independent gold-based currency was a move which announced that the state considered itself on a par with its great neighbours at least in so far as sovereignty was concerned. It further enabled the rulers to employ a powerful propaganda instrument, simplified trade, and, not to be forgotten, was profitable.

As far as publicising themselves and their state was concerned the

10a. Drawing of a silver coin (d. 12mm) of king Wazeba with its alternative reverses, the right-hand example belonging to king Ousanas and perhaps indicating joint tenure of the throne.

Aksumite rulers were highly successful from our point-of-view; most of the Aksumite kings are known to us only from the legends on their coins, all other evidence for their existence having perished or disappeared among the ruins of Aksum. The main features and significance of the coinage are dealt with in Ch. 9 below. From the evidence presented through study of the coinage (Munro-Hay 1978) it can be inferred that Endubis employed the Roman monetary system as a model, but used his own selected designs to maximise the impact of his coinage as a vehicle to convey the official propaganda. The subsequent kings added or removed motifs and other elements of the design as the current situation recommended.

A new title, not met with before in Aksumite records, first appears in the coin-legends of the pagan rulers. This consists of the word 'Bisi', from 'be'esya', 'man of..' in Ge'ez, followed by a name. It could be perhaps a tribal or clan designation, or perhaps a military title, and it remained in use until the sixth century AD (see Ch. 7: 5), and possibly even on into the eleventh and later centuries (Conti Rossini 1901).

Endubis and his successors all included the pre-Christian disc and crescent symbol on their coins, until, with Ezana's conversion in c. 333 AD it was replaced by the cross. This enables us to group the five kings Endubis, Aphilas, Wazeba, Ousanas and Ezana at the head of the coinage sequence. Although the first four of these pre-Christian kings are not mentioned anywhere else, the archaeological record, in so far as it can be interpreted, almost certainly leads to the conclusion that at least some of them were responsible for the erection of the series of large decorated stelae in the central necropolis of the capital (Ch. 5: 5). Some of the tombs marked by these stelae must also be theirs, but in most cases the tombs belonging to the various stelae have not yet been identified. Very little political information can be extracted from the coins for this period, but it may be that Wazeba and Ousanas ruled for a time conjointly (see Ch. 7: 3), since there is one issue which combines obverse dies of Wazeba with reverse dies of Ousanas. The scarcity of Wazeba's coins may hint at a short reign. His unique use (at this period) of Ge'ez for his coinage, instead of the usual Greek, may betray an interest in encouraging the use of the coinage in Ethiopia itself, rather than mainly for external trade.

It may have been during the reigns of Endubis or Aphilas that the last events we know of during the first Abyssinian involvement in Yemen

11. A gold coin (diameter c. 18mm) of king Ousanas of Aksum with the pre-Christian disc and crescent symbol above his head.

occurred. By the 270s Yasir Yuhan'im of Himyar and his son and co-ruler Shamir Yuhar'ish seem to have ended the Abyssinian danger, and, in addition, to have triumphed to such an extent that they could annex Saba itself. About 290AD Hadhramawt fell in its turn, and Shamir Yuhar'ish adopted, by 295, the longer title of king of Saba, Dhu-Raydan, Hadhramawt, and Yamanat. If the Ethiopians retained territory on the east side of the Red Sea, it must have been at most some minor coastal districts; at any rate, the inscriptions of Shamir no longer mention them.

In the fourth century, after the reign of Shamir Yuhar'ish, another South Arabian inscription alludes to Karibil Watar Yuhan'im, king of Saba, Dhu-Raydan, Hadhramawt and Yamanat, sending ambassadors to the *"land of Habashat and Aksuman, to the nagashi...and he (the nagashi?) sent with him as emissaries 'HQM and ZLNS"*.

Ousanas seems very likely to have been the king to whom the two captive Tyrian boys, Frumentius and Aedesius (see Ch. 10: 2), were brought after the killing of their shipboard companions. This king is called Ella Allada or Ella A'eda in the traditional account, and Budge (1928: 1164-5) interpreted this name as Alameda, Ella Amida; a reasonable enough suggestion, since from the numismatic point of view Ezana, the king who adopted Christianity, seems to follow Ousanas, while the tradition relating the circumstances of Ethiopia's conversion states that the converted king was the son and successor of Ella Allada/A'eda, though under the regency of his mother (but see also Dombrowski and Dombrowski 1984: 131-3). The name is testified later as Alla Amidas (Ch. 4: 7); Ousanas may have adopted it as his throne-name, and it is not impossible that one of the inscriptions published by the Deutsche Aksum-Expedition (Littmann 1913: IV, DAE 8) actually belongs to Ousanas rather than Ezana; its 'Bisi' title certainly includes the letter 's' and whatever identity, such as 'Ousanas Bisi Gisene', is accepted, 'Ezana Bisi Alene' is definitely precluded (Munro-Hay 1984ii: 108).

Ezana is the most famous of the Aksumite kings before Kaleb. Several inscriptions of his are known, which tell a good deal about his military exploits and furnish many other details about fourth century Aksum. His most significant contribution to Ethiopian history was his official adoption

11a. Drawings of two silver and three bronze issues (d. c. 10-16mm) of king Ezana of Aksum, some with the disc and crescent symbol, and some with no religious symbol at all.

of Christianity around 333AD, which he signalised by putting the cross on his coins (it also appears on one of his inscriptions; Schneider 1976ii: fig. 4), and by dropping the claim to be the son of the god Mahrem.

In Ezana's time intercourse with the Roman empire continued, but even if the conversion to Christianity (Ch. 10: 2) was designed to bring Aksum closer to Rome or Constantinople, it was not a policy which he followed slavishly. There seems to have been little response to Constantius II's suggestion (c 356AD) that Frumentius, by now bishop of Aksum (to whom Mommsen (1886: 284, n. 2) referred in his phrase 'an Axomitic clergyman'), should be sent for examination for doctrinal errors to the emperor's bishop at Alexandria (Szymusiak 1958). Constantius, leaning towards the Arian heresy, was currently at loggerheads with patriarch Athanasius of Alexandria, who had consecrated Frumentius for his new see probably around 330AD. Athanasius had been sent into exile, and an Arian bishop installed in his stead. It was to this man, George of Cappadocia, that Constantius, declaring himself fearful for the Christian faith in Aksum, wanted Ezana and his brother to send Frumentius. But since Frumentius remains revered as the founder of the Ethiopian church, which does not follow Arianism, it may be assumed that the request was ignored, and that, as the Ethiopian Synaxarium says, he '*died in peace*' (Budge 1928). In any event, the Arian emperor and bishop did not last much longer, and delaying tactics might have avoided the necessity to give a definite response to the request before the emperor's death in 361.

Ezana's titles (see Ch. 11: 5) show that he considered himself to be at least theoretically the ruler of very large areas of present-day Yemen, Ethiopia and the Sudan. Interestingly enough, his use of the title 'king of Saba (Salhen) and Himyar (Dhu-Raydan)' is similar to only the most modest of those used in the Yemen itself; around 300AD the title 'king of Saba and Dhu-Raydan and Hadhramawt and Yamanat' came into existence, and was used by rulers such as Shamir Yuhar'ish and Karibil Watar Yuhan'im, whilst by the end of the fourth century, under Abukarib As'ad, it developed into 'king of Saba and Dhu-Raydan and Hadramawt and Yamanat and the Arabs in the Tawd (highlands) and the Tihamat (coastal plain)'. It seems certain that Ezana did not actually control any of the the Arabian kingdoms, but his use of only the attenuated Arabian title and the apparent circulation of some of his coins in Yemen perhaps indicate that some sort of arrangement was reached between the two regions, or even that a coastal foothold was still retained by Aksum on the other side of the Red Sea. If predecessors of Ezana, like the 'king of kings' Sembrouthes, had claimed the Arabian titles, they might simply have remained in the least expanded form by tradition; the Arabian kings themselves never used the parallelism Saba/Salhen, Himyar/Raydan in their own titles, though Shamir Yuhahmid was referred to as 'of Dhu-Raydan and Himyar'.

In Africa, though most of Ezana's military expeditions were more or less tribute-gathering rounds in his own kingdom, pacifying any unrest in transit, he mounted at least one large-scale campaign against the Sudanese Noba and Kasu which his inscriptions (see Ch. 11: 5) claim as a major victory. Two fragmentary Aksumite inscriptions found at Meroë itself may be traced to this campaign, or perhaps to a similar one by a predecessor (Sayce 1909, 1912; Hägg 1984; Burstein 1980; Bersina 1984). It appears that Ezana's campaign was celebrated by Christian inscriptions, while some of the interpreters of the Meroë inscriptions believe that they were dedicated to the pagan Ares/Mahrem; if so, they probably belong either to an early campaign of Ezana, or to some predecessor.

At some uncertain point in our Periods 2 and 3, comes one of the best known of all Aksumite inscriptions; the *'Monumentum Adulitanum'* (Ch. 11: 5). The inscription itself has been lost, but its Greek text detailing the campaigns of an unnamed Aksumite king was preserved by the merchant Kosmas in the sixth century when he copied it for king Kaleb at the behest of Asbas, archon or governor of Adulis (Wolska-Conus 1968: 364ff). It was inscribed on a stone throne, behind which lay a fallen and broken inscription of king Ptolemy III of Egypt, who reigned in the third century BC. Unfortunately, Kosmas, copying the two inscriptions, simply carried on from the end of Ptolemy's inscription to the Aksumite one without including the section (if it still existed) with the Aksumite ruler's name and titles.

Certain details put the inscription broadly into context. It is of a pre-Christian ruler, whose campaigns took him from the Nabataean port of Leuke Kome ('White Village' – the exact position of which is still uncertain, Gatier and Salles 1988) at the limits of the Roman possessions on the east coast of the Red Sea, to the country of the Sabaeans in South Arabia, and to extensive African territories, apparently ranging from the lands bordering Egypt to the Danakil desert. Huntingford (1989) gives the latest of many attempts to outline the historical geography of the text. The author refers to himself as the first and only king of his line to subdue so many peoples, but this could be mere hyperbole. The gods he mentions, and the ritual of setting up a victory throne, are also known from Ezana's inscriptions. In short, he could be situated chronologically almost anywhere between Gadarat and Ezana. His inscription is of immense value, since it supplies a sort of gazetteer for the limits of the contemporary Aksumite empire; or at least the limits of the sphere of influence, since it is not very likely that some of the more far-flung areas could ever have been retained as Aksumite possessions. It is notable that this inscription has a year-date 27, while Sembrouthes' inscription has 24 years and one of the inscriptions from Meroë has the date of year 21 or 24. Sembrouthes or Ezana (whose reign spanned at least a quarter century) are therefore both candidates for the *Monumentum Adulitanum* and Ezana (who campaigned in the Meroitic region) may, as mentioned above, be responsible for the Meroë 1 inscription. But Sembrouthes, if he really fits as we have suggested in the mid-third century, would have reigned at a time when just such activities in Arabia as are detailed in the *Monumentum Adulitanum* are to be expected. He also gives himself the titles of Great King and king of kings, perhaps suitable to one who had campaigned, like the unknown author of the Adulis inscription, so vigorously to establish his kingdom's power in new regions. It now seems very unlikely that Ezana could have set up an inscription dedicated to pagan deities so late as his 27th year. It is not beyond hope that future excavations may actually find the famous *Monumentum Adulitanum*, which Kosmas saw set up outside the port-city on the Aksum road.

6. Period 4: Ezana after his Conversion, to Kaleb.

Owing to the lack of inscriptions and other sources of information, this period is very inadequately documented. A regulation of Constantius II of the late 350s, in the legal text called the *Codex Theodosianus* (Pharr 1952: 380, 12.12.2) speaks of persons travelling (presumably on official business) to the Aksumites and Himyarites. It reads;

> *The same Augusti and Julianus Caesar to Musonianus, Praetorian Prefect; No person who has been instructed to go to the tribe of the Aksumites or the Homerites shall henceforth tarry at Alexandria beyond the space of the time-limit of one year, and after a year he shall not receive subsistence allowance.*

This gives the impression that contact was relatively frequent between the empire and Aksum in the later fourth and early fifth century. The law was issued at about the same time as the letter of Constantius II to Ezana and Sazana was written.

AV I

EBANA AR I

11b. Drawings of a gold and silver issue (d. c. 16mm and c. 14mm) of king Ebana. The obverse of the gold issue bears a legend which may read 'king of the Habashat', and the reverse of the silver shows a cross-crosslet with a gold-inlaid diamond-shaped centre.

The Aksumite coins continue to provide a sequence of rulers, and from their designs and legends some conclusions can be drawn (see Ch. 9). One remarkable feature of these coins, is that the gold (in one case in a hoard with some late Roman solidi – Munro-Hay 1989ii) has often been found in South Arabia, and that much of the gold and some of the silver bears a legend which may read 'king of Habashat' or 'king of the Habashites'. Could this be a hint that the Aksumites still managed to maintain some kind of legal (or even actual?) footing there, as asserted by Ezana's title 'king of Saba and Salhen, Himyar and Dhu-Raydan'? Only one silver Aksumite coin, probably of the fifth century, has so far been reported from South Arabia, from Shabwa, capital of Hadhramawt (Munro-Hay, *Syria*, forthcoming.)

Other interesting features of the coinage of this period are the appearance of the cross, often gilded, on the coins, and the issue of coins with no royal name in all three metals. One king only, Mehadeyis (MHDYS on the unvowelled coin legends), issued copper/bronze coins with a Ge'ez legend, interestingly enough almost an exact translation of the Roman emperor Constantine's famous motto 'In hoc signo vinces' (by this sign (the cross) you will conquer). He is also the last king to specifically mention Aksum or the Aksumites in his coinage legends until the post-Kaleb period.

Christian mottoes on the late fourth and fifth century coins abound, and it is evident that the climate was right, from the point-of-view of official sanction, for the missionary efforts of the Nine Saints whom the Ethiopian hagiographies attribute to the latter part of this period (Ch. 10: 4). There is no sign on the coinage of a lapse into paganism again (Pirenne 1975; Shahid

11c. Drawing of a bronze coin (d. 14mm) of king MHDYS of Aksum, with a gold-inlaid cross on the reverse, and a legend which reads 'By this cross he will conquer'.

11d. Drawings of Aksumite anonymous coin issues in gold (d. c. 17mm), two types of silver (d. c. 13mm), and two types of bronze (d. c. 13mm and 15mm). The cross on the reverse of the lower examples of the silver and bronze is inlaid with gold. The bronze issues are the commonest of all Aksumite coins.

1979), but rather of an increasing emphasis on the rulers' Christian faith. The names of the kings whose coins situate them in this phase of Aksumite history are; Ezana, MHDYS, Ouazebas, Eon, Ebana, Nezana, Nezool, Ousas and/or Ousana(s). Specific coinage questions are dealt with in Ch. 9 below.

Since coins of king Ouazebas were found in the occupation debris of a room buried under which were some of the broken fragments of the largest of the stelae at Aksum (de Contenson 1959; Munro-Hay, forthcoming) , this, Aksum's largest monolithic monument, could have fallen as early as the reign of Ouazebas himself, very likely in the late fourth or early fifth century. The stele seems to have been the last of such monumental funerary memorials and possibly they went out of favour as Christianity spread, bringing with it new ideas about burial (see Chs. 5: 4-5, and 14)

The story of a *skholastikos*, or lawyer, of Thebes in Egypt who travelled to India after a stay at Aksum is preserved in a letter written by a certain Palladius, probably the bishop of Helenopolis by that name who lived from 368-431AD (Derrett 1960; Desanges 1969). Palladius travelled to India to investigate Brahmin philosophy in the company of Moses, bishop of Adulis. Palladius' journey seems to have been undertaken sometime in the first quarter of the fifth century, and it was after that that he wrote his letter to some personage of high rank to inform him about the Brahmins, using the *skholastikos*' information. The latter had spent some time in Ethiopia, entering the country at Adulis and going on to Aksum. He eventually was able to go on an 'Indian' ship to India. His comments have been thought to indicate that the reputation of Aksum had declined rather in this period: the

11e. Drawings of gold issues (d. c. 18mm) of the kings Ousas/Ousanas/Ousana, possibly different spellings for one name. The reverse dies all bear the Greek legend 'Theou Eukharistia' – By the Grace of God – under a cross.

king of Aksum is apparently referred to rather scathingly as an Indian minor kinglet (*basiliskos mikros*). Although this title could simply result from the attitude of a Roman subject to almost any ruler in comparison to the Roman and Persian emperors, it may also reflect a certain dimunition of Aksumite power at the time. The exact meaning of the title 'basiliskos', however, is still the subject of discussion (Donadoni 1959; Hansen 1986), and may actually

11f. Drawing of a bronze issue (d. c. 17mm) of king Ouazebas of Aksum; the reverse bears the Greek legend 'Touto aresē tē khōra' – May this please the people – and the area around the royal bust is gilded.

11g. Drawing of a gold coin (d. 16mm) of king Kaleb of Aksum, with, on the reverse, the king's monogram followed by the Greek words 'Uios Thezena' – Son of Thezena.

be a superior title to *basileus* in certain circumstances. A significant point is that *basiliskos* appears to be used otherwise particularly for Nubian rulers. It is the title used by the Blemmye king Kharakhin, a certain Pakutimne refers to himself as 'epiph(ylarkhos) of the basiliskos', the six Blemmye/Beja kings captured by Ezana's brothers (DAE 4, 6 & 7) are called *basiliskoi*, and king Silko of the Nobatae is also *basiliskos* (Munro-Hay 1982-3: 93, n. 23). It may be that Palladius or the *skholastikos* confused the titles of the Aksumite king and a Nubian ruler; but *mikros* is still not very complimentary.

Kaleb, first ruler in our next period (see below), calls himself the 'son of Tazena' on his inscription found at Aksum (Schneider 1972) and on his gold coins (where it is written in Greek as Thezena or variants; Munro-Hay 1984: 116-123). Tazena is also known from the Ge'ez stories about the Nine Saints, where he is identified as a king (Sergew Hable Sellassie, 1972: 115ff). Kaleb's own inscription from Aksum refers to *'the throne of my fathers'* which may not actually confirm that his father Tazena was king but at least means that Kaleb regarded himself as belonging to the legitimate dynasty. Tazena, if he actually ruled as a king of Aksum, may be identified with one or other of the names known from the coinage, since Aksumite rulers used several names; Ousas/Ousana(s) being perhaps the most likely identification from the numismatic point-of-view (Munro-Hay 1987). The sequence given by the king-lists (Conti Rossini 1909) and hagiographies is usually Sa'aldoba, Ella Amida, Tazena, Kaleb, but apart from Tazena's name on Kaleb's coinage, so far only Kaleb himself can be accurately identified from other sources. There exists a Syriac work, the *Book of the Himyarites* (Moberg 1928), about the war in Himyar which Kaleb waged against the Jewish king Yusuf. The surviving leaves of this book were found, remarkably enough, acting as padding for the covers of another much later book and through this safe concealment survived to our day. In the *Book of the Himyarites* mention is made of a previous expedition conducted by the Aksumites to Arabia, led by a certain Hiuna. This name unquestionably resembles the royal name Eon (EWN) as it is written in Greek on the coins of Eon Bisi Anaaph (Munro-Hay 1984: 88-9). The difference in the spelling is no more than would result from transposing the name into the two languages concerned. However, the coins in question, apparently of the beginning or early part of the fifth century,

12. Drawing of a gold coin (d. 17mm) of king Eon, with, on the obverse, the legend +CAC+ACA+XAC+CAC, which, with its variants, may mean 'King of Habashat'.

seem to be of too early a style to admit this identification. Accordingly, it has to be assumed that Eon and Hiuna are different people, unless, as is also possible, there is some distortion in the apparent chronology of the *Book of the Himyarites* at this point. The book only mentions Hiuna in its contents list, the particular chapter concerned having disappeared; *'On the first coming of Hiuna and the Abyssinians'*. The chapter, then, could refer to a previous expedition at some remove in time. However, the possibility that Hiuna might be a contemporary of Kaleb is enhanced by the latter's inscription (Schneider 1974: Drewes 1978), which apparently declares 'I sent HYN ..BN ZSMR with my troops and I founded a church in Himyar'.

Eon, interestingly enough, appears to be the first of the Aksumite rulers to use the mysterious title + BAC + CIN + BAX + ABA, on his gold coins. This is of uncertain meaning but has been interpreted to include the phrase 'Basileus Habasinōn', or king of Habashat/the Habash, one of the titles used by the South Arabians in their inscriptions when referring to the Aksumite rulers (Doresse 1957: I, 278ff). Further, Eon's gold coins have been found in South Arabia, as have those of almost all his successors until the reign of Kaleb (Anzani 1928, Munro-Hay 1978, Munro-Hay forthcoming). It is possible, then, that the Aksumites continued to struggle to preserve some sort of foothold or official presence in South Arabia during the fifth century, in spite of the consolidation and expansion there of the power of local rulers such as Abukarib As'ad. We cannot know for certain how much truth there might be in this suggestion until inscriptions of one or other of the Ethiopian kings of the period or their Arabian contemporaries come to light.

7. Period 5: Kaleb to the End of the Coinage.

The events of the time of Kaleb swell the sources available for Aksumite history to a disproportionate degree, and have resulted in the assumption that Kaleb was Aksum's greatest and most powerful ruler. However, the majority of the sources merely consist of more or less repetitious accounts by ecclesiastical historians full of praise for Kaleb's incursion into the Yemen to crush the anti-Christian persecutor, and often add little or nothing to the information of more reliable sources.

Kaleb invaded the Yemen around 520, in order to oust the Jewish Himyarite king Yusuf Asar Yathar, who was persecuting the Christian population.

12a. Drawings of two gold coins (d. c. 18mm) and a bronze coin (d. 15mm) of king Kaleb.

This ostensible reason for mounting the expedition across the Red Sea probably covers a number of other causes, since it seems that Yusuf may have also acted against Aksumite interests, and those of her Roman allies, in the political and commercial spheres.

One later source (the historian known as Pseudo-Zacharias of Mitylene; Brooks, ed. 1953) claims that Yusuf had acceded to power in Himyar because an Aksumite appointee to the throne had died, and, it being winter, the Aksumites could not cross the Red Sea to install another king. However, the source is not a contemporary one, though the very fact that he makes such a statement is interesting. King Ma'adkarib Ya'fur, who left an inscription of year 631 of the Himyarite era (c. 516AD), may have been the deceased ruler, but his titulature is the very long one including *'Hadramawt, Yamanat, and their bedouins of the high plateau and coastal plain'*, and it seems very unlikely that he was actually an Aksumite appointee (Rodinson 1969: 28, 31).

The various Latin, Greek, Syriac and Ge'ez sources (admirably summarised in Shahid 1971) have left a complicated set of names for the two protagonists in this war. Kaleb Ella Atsbeha is usually referred to by variants of his throne-name (such as Ellesbaas, Hellesthaeos, etc), though John of Ephesus calls him Aidog. Yusuf is called Dhu-Nuwas in the Arab accounts, and a variety of names in other sources (Damianus, Dunaas, Dimnus, Masruq, Finehas, etc) which seem to be based on this epithet or nickname or are derived from other epithets.

The chronology of the rulers of the Yemen in Kaleb's time is tentative, and one inscription which refers to the death of a king of Himyar, dated to 640HE/c525AD, has been taken as announcing the death of king Yusuf, thus situating Kaleb's invasion in 525. But it may well refer to the death of his successor, the viceroy Sumyafa' Ashwa'. With the useful assistance of dated inscriptions the chronology can be reconstructed as follows;

Ma'adkarib Ya'fur – c.517/8AD;

Yusuf Asar Yathar 517/8 – 520;

Sumyafa' Ashwa' 520 – c.525;

Abreha 525 – at least 547.

The Arab historians Ibn Hisham, Ibn Ishaq and Tabari, each of whom has a slightly different version of events (Guillaume 1955; Zotenberg 1958), tell of rivalry between Abreha and another of the *najashi*'s generals in the Yemen, Aryat. This would seem to have occurred around 525.

When Kaleb's forces arrived in Yemen, there was a certain amount of fighting, celebrated by various inscriptions. One (Rodinson 1969), of some *qayl*s or princes of 'Yusuf Asar Yathar, king of all the Tribes', is dated to year 633 of the Himyarite era/c518AD, and mentions that the king destroyed the church and killed the Abyssinians at Zafar, the Himyarite capital, demonstrating clearly that there were already Abyssinians in the country at the time; this rather speaks in favour of Pseudo-Zacharias' statement noted above. In the end, Kaleb's invading force was able to rout and eventually kill Yusuf. Another, Christian, ruler, Sumyafa' Ashwa', was appointed, whose inscription (Philby 1950; Ryckmans 1946; Ryckmans 1976) refers to him by the title of king, but also as viceroy for the kings (in the plural) of Aksum; this inscription actually names Kaleb by his 'Ella'-title, as Ella A(ts)bahah. Another inscription, possibly part of this one or a close parallel, appears to name the town of Aksum itself (Beeston 1980ii).

The Ethiopian viceroyalty lasted for perhaps four or five years, until c525, when the viceroy, Sumyafa' Ashwa', was deposed, and Abreha became king in his stead. The contemporary Byzantine historian Procopius mentions that Sumyafa', whose name he graecises as Esimiphaios, was a Himyarite by birth. The deposition of Sumyafa' was, apparently, accomplished with the support of Ethiopians who had remained in the Yemen, and Kaleb attempted to punish them and Abreha by sending a force of three thousand men under a relative of his. But this force defected, killing their leader and joining Abreha. The infuriated Kaleb sent yet another army, but this was defeated and accordingly Abreha was left on his throne (Procopius; ed. Dewing 1914: 189-191).

Abreha in later years used the titles of 'king of Saba, Himyar, Hadramawt, Yamanat, and all their Arabs of the Coastal Plain and the Highlands' (Ryckmans 1966; Smith 1964; Sergew Hable Sellassie 1972: 148, 153). This title, apparently last used by Ma'adkarib Ya'fur, seems to have lapsed during Yusuf's usurpation (Rodinson 1969) and Sumyafa' Ashwa''s viceroyalty, and it is interesting to observe that although Kaleb of Aksum used these same titles, his son Wa'zeb abandoned the longer title and contented himself with the old claim of Ezana's time to overlordship of Saba and Himyar only (Schneider 1972). This seems to reflect exactly the position as Procopius, writing after the death of Kaleb, related it, and seems to indicate that the titulature of the Aksumite kings did have some real significance in relation to events, rather than consisting of a merely traditional listing of both actual possessions and former claims (Ch. 7: 5). The essential of the situation is, that while the Aksumites may have been palliated by a formal submission and tribute, in actual terms they had permanently lost the control of the Yemen. A poem recorded by one of the Arab authors (Guillaume 1955: 34) sums up the history of Dhimar (Yemen) in this period, (as seen through anti-Ethiopian eyes);

'To whom belongs the kingdom of Dhimar? to Himyar the righteous;
to whom belongs the kingdom of Dhimar? to the wicked Abyssinians;
to whom belongs the kingdom of Dhimar? to the noble Persians;
to whom belongs the kingdom of Dhimar? to the Qoreysh, the merchants".

Glorious though Kaleb's re-establishment of the Christian faith in the Yemen seemed to contemporary (and later) ecclesiastical historians, it was Aksum's swan-song as a great power in the region. The real result may well have been quite the opposite; a weakening of Aksumite authority, over-expenditure in money and man-power, and a loss of prestige. The venture was, it seems, too ambitious for the times, and did Aksum nothing but harm in the long run. Nevertheless, for a while we still hear of embassies arriving from the Byzantine empire with trade proposals, and others going to Abreha in the Yemen (recorded on his Marib Dam inscription of 658HE/c543AD) and to the Persian king to persuade him to release certain bishops jailed at Nisibis (according to John of Ephesus' life of Simeon, bishop, of Beth Arsham – Brooks 1923; Doresse 1971: 102). Evidently Aksum still remained in the main stream of international affairs for a while.

Kaleb's inscription and coins, the hagiographical tales (and the king-lists, rather surprisingly, as well), confirm that Kaleb Ella Atsbeha's father was a certain Tazena. He is not represented on the coins, but could be included under some other name; one of the great difficulties of Aksumite numismatics. The gold coins which most closely resemble those of Kaleb come from a group bearing the royal names Ousas/Ousana/Ousanas, which may all belong to only one king. Perhaps he is to be identified with Tazena, as noted above (Ch. 4: 6). On the other hand, the emphasis on naming Kaleb's father on all his son's surviving official documents, and his use of the phrase '*throne of my fathers*' in his inscription (see above) might lead us to suppose that some political need was felt for this assertion of legitimacy; perhaps Tazena's kingship was somehow in dispute, or perhaps he was not an Aksumite king, but a claimant in the line of succession? The late compilations of the tales of the Nine Saints mention a king Tazena as the father of Kaleb, but their evidence is not necessarily reliable.

The Ethiopian traditions say that Kaleb eventually abdicated the throne,

13. Drawings of coins (d. 17 mm) of king Alla Amidas of Aksum.

sent his crown to be hung on the Holy Sepulchre at Jerusalem, and retired to a monastery. Since there are actual die-links between the coins of Kaleb and a king Alla Amidas (Munro-Hay, Oddy and Cowell, 1988), it is possible that he and Kaleb may have ruled together, Kaleb perhaps later retiring, thus explaining the plural term 'the neguses (*nagast*) of Aksum' in the inscription of Sumyafa' Ashwa' (Ryckmans 1946: line 3). Another line (8) in this inscription mentions that 'they submitted to the kings (*amlak*) of Aksum'; however, these locutions might apply to a concept of 'the crown of Aksum', since a further phrase (line 14) alludes to the *ngsy* in the singular form.

Kaleb's son Wa'zeb (W'ZB) is known from an inscription (Schneider 1974), where he is actually called *'son of Ella Atsbeha'* using his father's throne-name. He is presumably represented on the coins by another name, possibly Ella Gabaz (Munro-Hay 1984ii). Wa'zeb has left only this inscription, in Ge'ez, written in South Arabian script like Kaleb's, but so damaged that it is very difficult to decipher (but see Ch. 11.5). The story of Abba Libanos, the 'Apostle of Eritrea', mentions a king called 'Za-Gabaza Aksum', perhaps another version of the name Ella Gabaz (*Dictionary of Ethiopian Biography* 1975: I, 103); a suggestion confirmed very recently by Sergew Hable Sellassie (1989) who notes a homily of the Metropolitan Elias of Aksum about Abba Mat'e, Libanos, in which it is stated that the contemporary king was Ella Gabaz. Ella Gabaz and Za-Gabaza Aksum may be epithets indicating that Wa'zeb (if the identity is admitted) did some important building work at Maryam Tseyon cathedral.

The coinage of this period is extremely difficult to put in order. There are often only single surviving specimens of issues, or a bewildering array of mutually exclusive factors to take into account when attempting to classify them into a sequence. However, among names known from the coinage, apart from those already noted above, are Wazena (tentatively identified with Alla Amidas), Ioel, Iathlia/Hataz, and Israel. If the identity of Alla Amidas with Wazena is correct (Munro- Hay 1984ii), and this ruler was a colleague or immediate successor of Kaleb, it may be that Wazena is the name found

14. Drawings of a gold coin (d. 18mm) of king Iathlia/Hataz, with two issues each of Hataz in silver and bronze.

in the opening phrases of Abreha's 543AD Marib inscription; *'viceroy of the king Ella 'ZYN'* (see Schnieder 1984: 162-3). This would be a somewhat bizarre rendering of a supposed name 'Wazena Ella Amida' with, in addition, the *waw* written as *'ain*.

King Israel bears the name of one of Kaleb's sons in the legendary histories (Conti Rossini 1909; Sergew Hable Sellassie 1972: 161), but seems too far removed from him from a numismatic point-of-view to be so identified (Munro-Hay 1984ii). Two more kings, Armah and Gersem, close the sequence of the coinage. The coins of the later kings are very degenerate in appearance in comparison to the earlier issues, and their gold content is much debased. It would seem that Aksumite prosperity was on the decline through a combination of reasons, but that coins continued to be issued until the disruption of the Red Sea trade which had brought the experiment with a monetary economy into being finally removed the need for it. Some features of the design of the later coins are extremely reminiscent of Byzantine models.

There are certain factors which favour suggesting that king Gersem

15. The obverse of a gold coin (d. 18mm) of king Israel of Aksum. Photo British Museum.

belongs at the end of the coinage sequence, but a number of alternative points might favour Armah as the last king of Aksum to issue coins (Munro-Hay 1984ii; Hahn 1983). Armah's name could conceivably be related to that of Ashama ibn Abjar, or his son Arha, known from the accounts of some early Islamic historians, through the common process of Arab mis-spellings or inversions by copyists (Hartmann 1895). Armah produced (so far as we know to date) no gold coins, which might suggest that he had accepted that there was no purpose in producing them, as his kingdom was by now at least in part cut off from the Byzantine trade network. His silver has an unusual reverse, depicting apparently a structure with three crosses, the central one gilded; Hahn (1983) suggested that this could represent the Holy Sepulchre, and have been placed on the coins in reference to the Persians' seizure of Jerusalem and the holy places in 614. On the obverse the king's crown is gilded as well. Armah's bronze coins are the largest produced by the Aksumites, and unusually show the king full-length, seated on a throne; these and the elaborate gilded silver coins may have been designed to compensate for the lack of gold. Unfortunately there are neither archaeological contexts, nor

16. Drawing of a silver coin (d. 16mm) of king Armah, depicting, on the reverse, a gateway adorned with three crosses, possibly representing the Holy Sepulchre in Jerusalem.

overstrikings among the coinage, which can confirm which of these kings actually issued the last coins of the Aksumite series.

Structures have been found at Adulis, Aksum and Matara which contain the coins of all these later kings, showing that these towns were probably functioning at least until the end of the coinage, and were still under Aksumite control. Considerable quantities of pottery, often decorated with elaborate crosses, and other material including imported amphorae, provide evidence of still flourishing trade and local industries during the time of at least some of the later rulers. It is interesting to note, however, that the mottoes on the coins seem to grow increasingly less interested in royal and religious themes, but in the reigns of the later kings begin to ask for 'Mercy and Peace to the Peoples'. Perhaps it is pure imagination to see in this a response to the current situation of Aksum, but it can be suggested that gradually things were getting worse in both the condition of the kingdom in general and in the capital itself. Aksum may possibly have suffered from the plague which reached Egypt in 541 (Procopius, ed. Dewing 1914: 451ff; see also Pankhurst 1961 for more notes on diseases in Ethiopia), and had spread all over the eastern part of the Roman empire a year or two later; some claimed that it had originated in 'Ethiopia', but the term could refer to the Sudan or even other parts of Africa. If, however, Aksum was the victim of an epidemic, it might be an additional reason for the failure of the attempt to control king Abreha in the Yemen, and for the gradual decline of Aksum from that time onwards.

An interesting, but very tentative, source for Aksumite history in the later sixth century takes us much further afield for sources, to China. In 1779 the *T'ien-fang Chih-sheng shih-lu*, written between 1721 and 1724 by Liu Chih, was published. This was a life of Muhammad, the 'True Annals of the Prophet of Arabia', written using an older book of records about the prophet in Arabic found at Ts'eng Liu. It has been translated into English by Mason (1921). According to Leslie (1989) the original used by Liu Chih is very likely to have been a Persian translation of a biography of the prophet written by Sa'id al-Din Muhammad b. Mas'ud b. Muhammad al-Kazaruni, who died in AH758/1357AD, but at the time of writing the sources used by the latter have not yet been traced. However, it is interesting to note that the book contains a number of mentions of Abyssinia. The reigning *najashi* was said (Mason 1921: 35) to have sent an ambassador with gifts on sighting a star which marked the birth of the prophet (c570), and later (c577) when Muhammad was seven, the text (Mason 1921: 47) tells that the *najashi* Saifu ascended the throne. Abd al-Muttalib went to congratulate Saifu on his accession, and a speech of the former is quoted. He declared that

> *"The great king, your grandfather, was a benevolent king, and his grandson is a holy sovereign, who breaks off with flatterers and follows what is right, avenges the oppressed and, acting upon right principles, administers the law equitably. Your servant is the superintendant of the*

> *sacrifices in the sacred precincts of the True God, a son of the Koreish, who, hearing that your Majesty has newly recieved the great precious throne, has come to present congratulations".*

Saifu recognised Muhammad's greatness from portents he had found in the books, but prophesied that he would have troubles.

However much the Chinese translation may colour the narrative, there remain very interesting points in this account. If a king 'Saifu' came to the Aksumite throne in c. 577, and was the grandson of a particularly eminent Aksumite monarch, could that monarch have been Kaleb, so well-known to the Arabs as the conqueror of the Yemen? The text also adds (Mason 1921: 102) that Saifu's own grandson was the *najashi* who received the Muslim emigrants in the fifth year of Muhammad's prophetship, 615-6AD (Ch. 15: 4). If this very late and very much second-hand account deserves any credit we may postulate that Kaleb's son(s) ruled until c. 577, to be succeeded then by his grandson, followed by other members of the same family until Ashama ibn Abjar. Ibn Ishaq (Guillaume 1955: 153ff) says that Ashama only succeeded after the reign of an uncle who had usurped the throne from Ashama's father (Ch. 7: 5). The coins and inscriptions offer, as we have seen, Alla Amidas/Wazena, and Ella Gabaz/W'ZB (Kaleb's sons?), followed by Ioel, Hataz, Israel, Armah and Gersem, for this period. It seems that this comes close to the number of rulers recorded in the later sources; two sons of Kaleb according to the Ge'ez texts, a grandson Saifu succeeding in c. 577 after the Chinese text, another ruler and his usurping brother according to Ibn Ishaq, and finally Ashama, who died in 630, according to the Muslim chroniclers.

The situation at the ancient capital at this period was not what it had been in former times. Overuse of the land around a city which had supported a substantial population for some six hundred years was doubtless beginning to result in food-supply deficiencies, and in addition the Nile-levels recorded in Egypt indicate that the rainfall was not so constant as before (Ch. 1–2). The clearance of the wooded hills around the city, whether for charcoal or planting of crops, allowed the rains to carry off the topsoil, exacerbating the agricultural problems (Butzer 1981). The very grave dimunition of the Red Sea trade, and the loss of revenue from that source may have combined with internal troubles, such as a resurgence of independence among the northern Beja tribes, or even dynastic difficulties, to hasten the abandonment of Aksum as the capital of the kingdom. Whatever the case (for the situation under Ashama ibn Abjar and the wars of the *hatseni* Danael see Ch. 15: 4–5) it seems that possibly before the middle of the seventh century AD, Aksum, though it continued to exist in a reduced way until the present as an ecclesiastical centre, and even ritual centre for the kingship, had ceased to be viable as Ethiopia's capital city.

A famous Ethiopian of this last period of Aksum was one of the early converts to Islam, Bilal ibn Rabah. He was a freed slave of Ethiopian origin born in Mecca who became the first *muadhdhin* – muezzin – or chanter of the call to prayer. He also bore the prophet's spear, which was a gift of the *najashi* Ashama to the prophet's cousin al- Zubayr, and was used from 624AD to point the direction of prayer. Bilal died about 640AD (*Dictionary of Ethiopian Biography* 1975: I, 41).

8. The Post-Aksumite Period.

The period from the seventh to the twelfth century, though recognised here as post-Aksumite in the sense that Aksum was no longer the political centre of the kingdom, has generally been included by previous writers on Ethiopian history as Aksumite; accordingly, a brief sketch of the few known events occurring during this time may be useful. Aksum's name seems to have no longer been applied to the Ethiopian people, but 'Habash' remained, as usual, the Arab name for them, and the country was called 'Habashat' (Irvine 1965; but see Beeston 1987). The period concerned includes the greater part of the seventh century, and terminates with the advent of the Zagwé dynasty in about 1137 (another long-disputed date, see Munro-Hay, *The Metropolitan Episcopate of Ethiopia and the Patriarchate of Alexandria 4th–14th centuries*, forthcoming).

1. Realignment.

The reign of Ashama ibn Abjar, and the inscriptions of the *hatsani* Danael, are discussed in Ch. 15: 4–5, and are suggested to represent the end of the Aksumite period in Ethiopia. An entirely different picture of the kingdom now emerges. The coinage, and with it the use of Greek and the trade connections into the Red Sea and the Roman Christian world gave way to a different economic and political orientation. Such commodities as cloth (al-Muqaddasi, in Vantini 1975: 176) and probably the ever-needed salt were used in barter, but now trade was, it seems, limited only to neigbouring countries in Africa and Arabia. The kingdom, though almost always regarded by Arab writers during this period as a powerful and extensive state, eventually lost the use of the coast, and other areas formerly under a tribute relationship to the Ethiopian state became completely independent.

As Connah (1987: 71–2, 95) has pointed out, the new condition of relative isolation had both advantages and disadvantages, the greatest benefit being that Ethiopia could safely withdraw itself into the mountains and take up a strong defensive stance. This was, of course, offset by the loss of its international position, but, as we have said, the decline of the Red Sea trade was the result of great events in the outside world which Ethiopia could only accept by its own realignment. The country's political connexions were nearly all with Muslim states from this time onwards, though a few brief mentions are made of the Christian Nubian kingdoms (see below). Al-Mas'udi speaks of a treaty between Abyssinia and Ibrahim, ruler of Zabid in the Yemen, by which the latter's ships continually moved between the two countries with merchants and merchandise (de Meynard and de Courteille 1864: 34), and relations apparently remained intact with the Yemeni rulers after the country's conquest by a neighbouring queen (see below). Ethiopia's metropolitan bishops still came from the patriarchate of Alexandria, but were now obtained by application to the Muslim governor of Egypt (Munro-Hay, *The Metropolitan Episocopate of Ethiopia and the Patriarchate of Alexandria, 4th–14th centuries*, forthcoming). Muslim states arose in the Dahlak islands and on the coasts, and in later times became a grave danger to the Christian state.

But the Ethiopian kingdom itself did not remain static; as it lost in the north and east, it gained in the south, and the dynastic capitals of the later Zagwé (c. 1137) and Solomonic (c. 1270) dynasties were successively situated further in that direction. Trading objectives changed too; but still Arab traders continued to come to Ethiopia. The country still possessed excellent agricultural resources, gold, ivory, hides, and many other products, and doubtless the expansion southwards allowed the Ethiopians of the post-Aksumite era to develop certain aspects of their export trade in luxuries as much in demand in the Arab world as they had been in the Roman; we hear of merchants of Oman, Hejaz, Bahrein, and the Yemen trading there (see below). Ethiopia may have found itself increasingly outside the main stream, but was certainly not finished as a polity. The brief reports of the next few hundred years speak of a large and powerful Habash realm, and, as far as we can tell, only in the later tenth century did disaster strike.

2. Successor Capitals.

The immediate successor capitals to Aksum are mentioned mainly by Arab authors, illustrating well the new alignment of trade and therefore knowledge about the country. In many cases these repeat the information of preceding writers, sometimes anachronistically. The astronomer Al-Battani, for example, who died in 929AD, repeats information from Ptolemy, and names 'Ksumi, the town (or, land) of the king of Kush' (Nallino 1907:II, 47). This obviously refers to Aksum; but most other Arab writers provide completely different names. The earliest is Jarmi or Jarma, followed by Ku'bar or Ka'bar.

Abu Ja'far al-Khuwarizmi, writing before 833AD, seems to be the first to cite a town called *'Jarma, the town of the kingdom of Habash'*, as well as *'Jarmi, the great town'*, in company with such other towns as Dunqula (Dongola), capital of the Nubian kingdom of Muqurra (Vantini 1975: 50). Al-Farghani, writing before 861AD, mentions *'the towns of the kingdom of the Habasha, which are called Jarmi (Jarma), Dunqula and the town of the Nuba'* (Vantini 1975: 53). Ibn Rusta, who died before 913AD, wrote of *'Jarmi, the capital of the Habasha and Dunqula, the capital of the Nuba'* (Vantini 1975: 87), and around 950AD Ishaq ibn al-Husain wrote that *"The main town in the country of the Habashat is (the town of) Jarmi, (which is) the capital (dar) of the kingdom of the Habasha. This kingdom is ruled by the najashi"*. Interestingly, this author repeats Kosmas' old tale about silent trade in the lands of the Habasha (Vantini 1975: 122-3), as do others even later (eg. al-Zuhri, Vantini 1975: 262).

About 966AD al-Maqdisi simply confirms the previous information, writing that *"One of the towns of the First Climate is..Jarmi, a town of the king of the Habasha, another is Dunqula, the town of the Nuba"* (Vantini 1975: 147), and a little later Ibn Yunus (d. 1009AD) listed both Jarmi and Madinat al-Habash (here Dongola/Dunqala?) with their latitudes and longitudes (Vantini 1975: 223). Al-Tusi, an astronomer who died in 1273AD, also mentions these two towns with their latitude and longitude (Vantini 1975: 380).

Al-Biruni (d. 1048), though a pupil of al-Mas'udi, does not mention Ku'bar (see below), but in his list of towns, he includes *"Jarma (Jarmi), a town of the Habasha"* and Aydhab as a Habasha town, the frontier between Beja and Habasha (Vantini 1975: 231–2), while al-Marwazi (d. after 1120AD) mentions that the First Climate *"passes through a country called Jarma, which is the residence of the king of the Habasha, and through Dunqala, which is the capital of the Nuba"* (Vantini 1975: 250). Yaqut (d.1229) mentions among the towns of the First Climate *'Jarma, the town of the king of the Habasha; Dumqula, the town of the Nuba'* (Vantini 1975: 341). Abu'-l-Fida' (1273–1331AD) wrote that *"Jarmi is the capital of the Habasha. It is mentioned by the majority of the travellers in the books of routes"* (Vantini 1975: 463), and Ibn al-Shatir (1304–1379AD) still notes the latitudes and longitudes of *"Jarmi of the Habasha"* and *"Dongola of the Nuba"* (Vantini 1975: 525). Finally, it may be that the name Tambra or Tarma, used by al-Wardi (d. 1457AD) is a last memory of Jarmi or Jarma; he describes the town as *"a big town on a lake in which the Nile waters collect"* (Vantini 1975: 724).

Al-Ya'qubi (fl. c. 872–891) is the first of the Arab authors to mention Ku'bar or Ka'bar. His report is interesting in that it names five Beja kingdoms bordering on the *najashi*'s realms and on Alwa (the Arab name for the Nubian Christian state of Alodia, with its capital at Soba). They each had their own king, and there is no mention of dependence on the *najashi*'s kingdom; the last known Aksumite claim to control Beja and Noba is in W'ZB's titulature (Schneider 1974). Al-Ya'qubi describes

> *"a vast and powerful country. Its royal town is Ku'bar. The Arabs go thither to trade. They have big towns and their sea coast is called Dahlak. All the kings of the habasha country are subject to the Great King (al-malik al-a'zam) and are careful to obey him and pay tribute"* (Vantini 1975: 73).

This information, well over two hundred years after the time of Ashama ibn Abjar, indicates that the Ethiopian kingdom had maintained itself relatively well, and was still in control of some of the coastal area.

Al-Mas'udi, who died in 956 AD, gives rather similar information in his geographical work *Muruj al-Dhahab*, the 'Meadows of Gold'.

"The chief town of the Habasha is called Ku'bar, which is a large town and the residence of the najashi, whose empire extends to the coasts opposite the Yemen, and possesses such towns as Zayla', Dahlak and Nasi' (Vantini 1975: 131).

He repeated this in his *Akhbar al-Zaman*;

"..the Habasha are the descendants of Habash b. Kush. b. Ham. The largest of their kingdoms is the kingdom of the najashi, who follows Christianity; their capital is called Kafar (Ka'bar). The Arabs used since the earliest times to come to this kingdom for trade' (Vantini 1975: 143).

Al-Harrani, writing about 1295AD, mentions that

"one of the greatest and best-known towns is Ka'bar, which is the royal town of the najashi...Zayla', a town on the coast of the Red Sea, is a very populous commercial centre...Opposite al-Yaman there is also a big town, which is the sea-port from which the Habasha crossed the sea to al-Yaman, and nearby is the island of 'Aql" (Vantini 1975: 448).

Ibn Khaldun (1332–1406) also knew that Ka'bar was formerly the capital of Abyssinia (Trimingham 1952: 59).

Conti Rossini proposed that Ku'bar originated in a mistaken rendering of [A]Ksum in Arabic (1909: 263, n.1). He says that *"Aksum was the political capital still in the tenth century..I call..kings of Aksum the kings anterior to the Zagwé, who went down into Lasta"*. Vantini (1975: 131), whose extremely useful compendium of translations from Arab authors we have used extensively in this section, also thought Ku'bar was Aksum, suggesting a distortion from an epithet, 'kabur', The Noble, or the name of some place near Aksum. Paul (1954: 71) identified Ku'bar with Adulis. The editors of Mas'udi's book *The Meadows of Gold*, where he mentions Ku'bar, identified it with Ankober in Shewa, influenced by the current name for the Shewan capital (de Meynard and de Courteille 1844: 34). Taddesse Tamrat (1970: 87–8; 1972: 37) thought Ku'bar might be in southern Tigray or Angot; an Ethiopian legendary account (Kur 1965: 18) says that the (ninth- century?) king Dil Na'od moved the capital *"from Aksum to the country of the east"* in the seventh year of his reign, and since the same phrase elsewhere in the text describes the Lake Hayq region, Tamrat suggested Ku'bar was in that general direction. In fact, little reliance can be placed on the names and dates (Tamrat 1972: 36, n. 3) in these legends, and it seems that Ku'bar's position must remain a mystery for the time being. It is almost certainly not Aksum, but could conceivably be some other major Aksumite town which, for various reasons, was considered to be a more suitable spot for the capital; possibly in the eastern region where many towns were built along the north-south route west of the escarpment.

We thus have Arab authors writing of Jarmi from before 833AD to well into the fourteenth or even fifteenth century, and of Ku'bar from the later ninth century until c. 1259AD. There seem to be three possibilities here.

One is that the two cities were in fact one and the same. It is very unlikely that any of the later writers did anything more significant than simply copying the older works, and one might propose that this town, wherever it was, lasted as capital of Ethiopia only from the transfer from Aksum (between c. 616–630?), or later if there was another capital between this time and the first mention of the new one in Arab sources, until the fall of the kingdom to the Queen of the Bani al-Hamwiyya in the mid-tenth century (see below). This would credit the work of al-Ya'qubi and al-Mas'udi, who generally seem well informed.

The second possibility is that there are two cities in question. If the name Jarma were an epithet for the capital, perhaps from the Ethiopic word *girma*, which means something like venerable or revered, it would seem likely that Jarmi was Aksum, to which this epithet was well-suited. Some authors would have simply repeated the outdated information that it was still the capital, and continued to do so even after Ku'bar had taken over that status, in spite of the more up-to-date reports of the better informed writers such as al-Ya'qubi and al-Mas'udi. In support of this theory, according to Vantini (1975: 380, n. 1) it appears from al- Tusi's own map that Jarmi corresponds to Aksum. However, the version of the map in Yusuf Kamal (1930–35: III, 1045r) as reconstructed by Lelewel, shows 'Dziarmi' considerably south of Aden following al-Tusi's longitude, and Kammerer (1929: 48) noted that *"la carte de Ahmad el-Tusi est un croquis élémentaire"*.

The third possibility seems the most likely; that Jarmi has nothing to do with Abyssinian Ethiopia, but is in fact Ptolemy's town of Garami, metropolis of the Garamantes in Libya. Arab geographers would have taken Garami in 'Ethiopia' (the broad term used of all the area occupied by dark-skinned peoples) as the capital of the 'Habash', used as a similarly general term. Jarmi is thus no longer a rival to Ku'bar as the post-Aksumite capital.

Other names for capitals are mentioned in the sources. An anonymous treatise of 982/3AD, written in Persian, the *Hudud al-Alam*, notes about the country of the Habash that

> *"This country has a very mild climate. The inhabitants are of a black complexion. They are very lazy and possess many resources. They obey their own king. Merchants from Oman, Hejaz and Bahrain often go to that country for trade purposes. Rasun, a town on the sea coast, is the residence of their king, while the army dwell in the town of Suwar: the Commandant-in-Chief resides at Rin, with (another?) army. In this province gold is abundant"*.

Rasun, it has been proposed, could stand for Jarmi through miscopied Arabic, though the coastal setting is unusual, and Minorsky proposed Aydhab and Zayla' for the other two (Minorsky 1937: 164, 473–4; Vantini 1975: 173).

An Ethiopian legend mentions that king Degnajan, who is supposed to have lived at the period just before Gudit's attack, left Tigray and made

Weyna Dega his capital, apparently a place in Begemder east of Gondar (Sergew Hable Sellassie 1972: 203, n. 115; 231, n. 98). Al-Idrisi, the famous geographer at the court of the Norman king Roger II of Sicily, writing before 1150AD, called the greatest of all the towns of the Habasha 'Junbaitah' (and variants), which seems likely to come from the Ethiopic phrase 'jan-biet', or king's house (Vantini 1975: 278; Conti Rossini 1928: 324). Another interpretation identified the three Ethiopian towns mentioned by al-Idrisi (which Kammerer (1929: 54) thought were *'toutes trois fantaisistes'*) with present-day villages; Miller (1927) decided that Gunbaita (Junbaitah) was Genbita near Kassala, Markata was Hanhita near Gondar, and Kalgun was Aganiti about half-way between Aksum and Ankober.

Al-'Umari (1300–1348AD) was aware of the antiquity, and even the (more or less) correct name of Aksum. He was employed in the chancery of the Egyptian sultan, and knew the protocol to observe when writing to the *haty* or king (Munro-Hay, *The Metropolitan Episcopate of Ethiopia and the Patriarchate of Alexandria 4th–14th centuries,* forthcoming), and perhaps had access to rather better archival material than many other writers. He states that a certain wadi

> *"leads to a region called Sahart, formerly called Tigray. Here there was the ancient capital of the kingdom, called Akshum, in one of their languages, or Zarfarta, which was another name for it. It was the residence of the earliest najashi, who was the king of the entire country. Next is the kingdom of Amhara, where is the capital of the kingdom nowadays, called Mar'adi; next is the territory of Shewa...'* (Vantini 1975: 509).

Amda-Tseyon's (1314–1344) chronicler confirms that his court was located at Mar'adé, apparently in Shewa (Taddesse Tamrat 1972: 274).

Finally, we have the town of 'Arafa or Adafa. This is mentioned in the *History of the Patriarchs* as the 'city of the king' of Ethiopia in 1210, with the additional note that the king was called Lalibela (Atiya et al: III, iii, 192). The town is called Adafa in the *Gedle Yimrha-Kristos* (Taddesse Tamrat 1972: 59), and was the capital of the Zagwé dynasty. This presumably means that those Arab writers who continue to mention Ku'bar after about 1200AD are simply repeating earlier information without updating.

3. The History of the Patriarchs and Ethiopia.

Beyond the brief descriptions of the country in Arabic historical or geographical works, we have almost no other information about events in Ethiopia except from the *History of the Patriarchs of Alexandria* (Evetts 1904 and Atiya 1948) and the Ethiopian *Synaxarium* (Budge 1928). The biographies of the Coptic patriarchs of Alexandria, spiritual heads of the Ethiopian Orthodox church, were careful to include references to the patriarchate's dealings with the kingdoms of the south, Nubia and the Habash, since the authority of the patriarchs there was a useful counter to their subordination to the Muslim government in Egypt. From this source we have a few glimpses of conditions in Ethiopia, though the majority of references concern purely church matters and are not very informative on other questions. A detailed analysis of all the notes about Ethiopia in the ecclesiastical records can be found in Munro-Hay (*The Metropolitan Episcopate of Ethiopia and the Patriarchate at Alexandria, 4th–14th centuries*, forthcoming).

During the patriarchate of James (819-830) the metropolitan John was ordained for Ethiopia (Evetts 1904: 508ff). During his metropolitanate, military defeats, compounded by plague which killed both men and cattle, and lack of rain, are mentioned. The metropolitan had been driven to return to Egypt by the opposition of the queen and people while the king was occupied at war, and he was only able to return in the patriarchate of Joseph (831–849). Dates around c. 820–30 have been suggested for these events, and it is interesting to note that during that decade the king of Abyssinia was involved in unsuccessful military engagements. At just this time, in northern Abyssinia, the Beja tribes were growing stronger, and in 831 a treaty between the caliph al-Mu'tasim and Kannun ibn Abd al-Aziz, 'king' of the Beja (Hasan 1973: 49-51), seems to recognise his power even as far south as Dahlak. This may well indicate that there had been disputes between the Beja and the Ethiopians, with the Ethiopians, at least temporarily, coming off rather the worse in the conflict.

It is also noted in his biography that Joseph had problems over his Abyssinian pages, presented to the church as gifts by the Ethiopian king (Evetts 1904: 528–31).

Nothing more is noted until the patriarchate of Kosmas III (923–934), when Ethiopian questions again came to the fore (Atiya 1948: 118–21; Budge 1928: III, 666–8). Interestingly, the eleventh century biographer, when he introduces al-Habasha (Abyssinia), adds the gloss that it is *"the kingdom of Saba, from which the queen of the South came to Solomon, the son of David the king"*, showing that this identification was current even then. The Ethiopian king, Tabtahadj (or Yabtahadj, Babtahadj- a name not recorded elsewhere- Perruchon 1894: 84; it is, in fact, a misreading of *bi-ibtihaj* 'with joy'), received a new metropolitan, Peter, and is said to have given him authority to choose his successor on his death-bed. Peter selected the youngest of the late king's two sons, but soon a monk, Minas, arrived with forged letters which declared that he himself was the rightful metropolitan, and Peter an imposter. This naturally found favour with the rejected brother, and Peter and the king he had chosen were deposed. Eventually the new king learned from Kosmas that Minas was actually the imposter, and he was executed, but meanwhile Peter had died in exile, and patriarch Kosmas refused to consecrate another metropolitan. The king therefore forced Peter's assistant to take up the post, uncanonically, thereby instituting a quarrel between monarchy and patriarchate which lasted for the unconsecrated metropolitan's lifetime, through four succeeding patriarchates and into a fifth. Eventually, during the patriarchate of Philotheos (979–1003), the quarrel was resolved, but only after Ethiopia had suffered terrible devastation.

The story is preserved in the *History of the Patriarchs* (Atiya 1948: 171–2) and in the Ethiopian *Synaxarium* (Budge 1928: I, 233–4), as well as in the accounts of certain Arab historians (see below). The first two refer to enemies who attacked Ethiopia, driving the king out and destroying his cities and many churches. In the *History of the Patriarchs* the enemy is named as the queen of the Bani al-Hamwiyya; a title which has not much assisted in identifying her. These ecclesiastical sources claim that the troubles were all due to the fact that metropolitan Peter had been deposed illegally, and when patriarch Philotheos, responding to the pleas of the king of Ethiopia sent through the agency of king Girgis II of Nubia, appointed a new metropolitan, Daniel, to Ethiopia, the troubles ceased.

The Arab historians add considerably to the history of Ethiopia at this point. Ibn Hawqal (Kramer and Wiet 1964: 16, 56) mentions that the country had been ruled for thirty years by a woman, who had killed the king, or *hadani*, and now ruled the *hadani*'s territory as well as her own lands in the south. This was written in the 970s or 980s, and so the queen's advent was probably in the 950s. A confirmatory note occurs in a reference which states that the king of the Yemen sent a zebra, received as a gift from the female ruler of al-Habasha, to the ruler of Iraq in 969–70 (el-Chennafi 1976). It seems more than likely that this queen is identical with the queen enshrined in Ethiopian legend as the destructive Gudit, Yodit, or Esato, who invaded the kingdom and drove the legitimate kings into hiding, in spite of her legendary association with the establishment of the Zagwé kings. In fact, it seems likely that a period of well over a hundred years yet had to elapse before this new dynasty came to the throne, and that the Ge'ez chronicles have become hopelessly muddled at this stage.

Between 1073 and 1077 more trouble occurred because of a false metropolitan (Atiya 1948: 328–330; Budge 1928: IV, 995). A certain Cyril arrived with forged letters to claim the metropolitanate, and actually managed to bribe the ruling *amir* of Egypt to force the patriarch to ratify the appointment. The problem was only solved in the patriarchate of Cyril II (1078–92), who consecrated a new metropolitan, Severus; Cyril fled to Dahlak, where he was arrested by the sultan, and sent to Egypt, where he was duly executed.

Metropolitan Severus wrote to the patriarch in Egypt that the country was in good order but for the practice of polygamy by the Ethiopian ruler and some of his subjects. He was, however, soon in trouble. He apparently tried to please the Egyptian *amir* by building mosques in Ethiopia, for which he was arrested. Letters with threats from the *amir* to demolish churches in Egypt were despatched to Ethiopia, but the king's reply was uncompromising and unimpressed; *"If you demolish a single stone of the churches, I will carry to you all the bricks and stones of Mecca....and if a single stone is missing I will send its weight to you in gold"* (Atiya 1948: 347–51).

The patriarchal biographies continue, without much useful information about Ethiopian affairs, to relate the history of the metropolitan George (Atiya 1948: 394–5), consecrated by patriarch Michael IV (1092–1102). This prelate behaved so badly that he was arrested and sent back to Egypt. A successor, consecrated by Macarius II (1102–28), was the metropolitan Michael (Sergew Hable Sellassie 1972: 203). He was at the centre of a dispute in the time of patriarch Gabriel II (1131–45) with the reigning king of Ethiopia, who wanted him to consecrate more bishops than was allowed by custom (Atiya 1950: 56–7; Budge 1928: 800–1). This would have allowed the king to elect his own metropolitan, since ten bishops could constitute the synod necessary to do so, and Ethiopia and Nubia were therefore limited to seven. The Egyptian caliph was at first supportive of the king, but when the patriarch, anxious not to lose his influence in Ethiopia, pointed out that the Ethiopian king, absolved from his obedience to the patriarch, could attack Muslim lands with impunity, he seems to have changed his mind. In any event, famine in Ethiopia is supposed to have persuaded the king that he was wrong, and the attempt to gain independence for the Ethiopian church was over.

Michael's metropolitanate had one more trial to go through (Atiya 1950: 90–1). In 1152, when he was very old, a messenger arrived in Egypt from an Ethiopian king to the vizir with a request that patriarch John V (1146–67) replace Michael with a new metropolitan. Michael had apparently quarrelled with this king, who was a usurper. Possibly this usurping ruler may be identified with an early king of the Zagwé dynasty of Lasta, who seem to have come to power around 1137. The fact that he did not write to the patriarch until 1152 may mean that the king had not found Michael too troublesome until then, or that the affair took some time to build up, and does not really militate against his identification as a Zagwé ruler; alternatively, the 1152 incident might have been the culmination of the old quarrel of the time of patriarch Gabriel, with the Ethiopian ruler taking revenge against Michael for thwarting him previously. In any event, John V declined to replace the metropolitan, who had done no wrong and could not therefore be legally deposed, and for this refusal was himself imprisoned; he was eventually released on the death of the vizir.

While limited in scope, the biographies of the patriarchs do allow glimpses of Ethiopia, which, combined with those from the Arab historians and geographers, are not uninformative. We learn that the kingdom was, if erratically, in touch with Egypt, and that the monarchy and ecclesiastical structure remained intact until around the 950's. At some time before 1003 the foreign queen's rule was terminated, the Ethiopian kingdom restored and the church hierarchy reinstated with metropolitan Daniel; but one might imagine that the destruction of cities and churches, and the death or captivity of part of the population, left the country in a weaker condition than before. In the reconstruction, foreign influences were not lacking; in patriarch Zacharias' time (1004–32), Coptic Christians were allowed to emigrate to Abyssinia, Nubia, and Byzantine lands (Atiya 1948: 196), while near the town of Qwiha, in Enderta, funerary inscriptions of Muslims, perhaps a trading community, have been found dating from 1001– 1154AD (Schneider, M. 1967); it may have been for such communities that some of Severus' mosques were built.

From the *History of the Patriarchs* we learn that in the ninth century the country suffered from war, plague, and insufficient rainfall, that it suffered a major disaster in the tenth century with the depredations of the queen of the Bani al-Hamwiyya. The remainder of the information from the eleventh and early twelfth centuries deals mainly with ecclesiastical questions, or in the case of the Arab geographers of repetitive and more or less inaccurate travellers tales. But the story about the attempt to increase the number of bishops in metropolitan Michael's time has some interesting facets. It mentions, unless this is mere rhetoric to emphasise the contrast with the later state of affairs after the patriarch blessed the land, that between 1131 and 1145 Ethiopia suffered several disasters. The king's palace was struck by lightning, and the land suffered from pestilence, famine and drought. Although the country recovered in due course, it must have been at about this time that the change of dynasty actually occurred, and Zagwé rule was established until c. 1270.

V

The Capital City

1. The Site

Aksum was built on gently sloping land which rose, north and east of the city, to two flat-topped hills, now called Beta Giyorgis and Mai Qoho respectively. The hills around the town are formed from a granitic rock, nepheline syenite (Littmann 1913: II, 6; Butzer 1981). Between Beta Giyorgis and Mai Qoho runs the course of a stream, the Mai Hejja or Mai Malahso in its upper reaches, which rises on the eastern slopes of Beta Giyorgis. Further west another stream bed, that of the Mai Lahlaha, also descends from the top of Beta Giyorgis. Run-off from the Mai Hejja and down the flanks of Mai Qoho above the town is caught in a large excavated basin, officially called *Mai Shum*, but often referred locally to as the 'Queen of Sheba's bath'. This is said to have been dug by one of the later metropolitan bishops of Aksum, Samuel, in the reign of king Yeshaq in about 1473 (Salt 1812; Monneret de Villard 1938: 49), but may very well be of Aksumite origin, enlarged or cleared by Samuel, just as it has been again enlarged and cleared recently. The basin lies directly below the north-west side of Mai Qoho, and access to it from above is aided by a series of steps cut into the rock, which may also date back to Aksumite times. Butzer thought that there was evidence for an earth dam some 50 m. below the Mai Shum reservoir (Butzer 1981: 479), and it is possible that much more water was caught or diverted in Aksumite times than today. Water was probably a very important element in the development of Aksum as the capital city of ancient Ethiopia. The name of the town itself is thought to be composed of two words, *ak* and *shum*, the first of Cushitic and the second of Semitic origin, meaning water and chieftain respectively (Sergew Hable Sellassie 1972: 68; Tubiana 1958). This name 'Chieftain's Water' seems to suggest that Aksum could have been the site of a spring or at least a good water supply, and perhaps it early became the seat of an important local ruler.

The two streams run south, that of the Mai Hejja skirting Mai Qoho hill (in its lower course it takes on different names, such as the Mai Barea, or the Mai Matare), and the Mai Lahlaha running directly through the town. Both lose themselves in the broad plain of Hasabo facing the town to the south and east. The two hills, both reaching to around the 2200 m mark above sea level,

17. A view of Aksum taken from below Mai Qoho hill looking over the Stele Park towards Beta Giyorgis hill.

18. The reservoir *Mai Shum* in its present enlarged state. Photos BIEA.

rise about 100 m above the town area, enclosing and sheltering it on two sides. Nowadays they are almost bare of trees, except where recent eucalyptus planting has occurred, but in Aksumite times there is reason to believe that they were probably forested to some extent. The geomorphologist Karl Butzer, exploring the area around Aksum, found that in the plateau of Shire, of which the Aksum region is part, were remnant stands of trees favouring a more moist climate, whilst the present montane savanna vegetation is the result of intensive human activity (Butzer 1981: 474–6). Only a few great sycomores still stand, some of which appear on Salt's aquatint of 1809, which also shows a fair scattering of other trees around the stelae and on the slopes of Beta Giyorgis.

The streams, which are seasonal, may either have run more continually in ancient times, when the rainfall was more constant, or have been supplemented by permanent springs. Possibly such springs helped to keep the Aksumite Mai Shum filled. In any event, travellers like Bruce (1790: III, 460–1) noted that there were springs functioning relatively recently and that the town was able to maintain gardens, though this was of course in its less populous days. Nathaniel Pearce, who lived in Ethiopia from 1810–1819, declared

> *"There is no river within two miles of Axum, but the inhabitants have good well water; there are many wells hidden, and even in the plain have been found, but the people are too lazy to clear them from rubbish. It appears probable that, in ancient times, almost every house had its well, as I have been at the clearing of four, situated at not more than ten yards from each other. The stone of which they are constructed is the same kind of granite of which the obelisks are formed"* (Pearce 1831: 162–3).

A well was found near the Tomb of the False Door, probably sunk to serve one of the houses built over the Stele Park in later times (Chittick 1974: fig. 2). Such wells would have been essential for those who lived at a distance from the streams, and also would have helped to make the inhabitants more independent of the behaviour of the natural springs and streams available.

Alvares (Beckingham and Huntingford 1961: 155) mentions a *"very handsome tank [or lake of spring water] of masonry [at the foot of a hillock where is now a market"]* behind the cathedral, *"and upon this masonry are as many other chairs of stone such as those in the enclosure of the church"*. Since there are thrones along the rock wall (thought by the DAE, who called it Mehsab Dejazmach Wolde Gabre'el, to be a natural formation (Littmann 1913: I, 31) , but illustrated by Kobishchanov (1979: 118) as 'cross-section of fortification embankment') on the west side of Mai Qoho, Alvares' description could possibly refer to this. The rock-wall, whether natural or man-made, could have acted as a retaining wall to waters overflowing from the Mai Hejja, or down the slopes of Mai Qoho, (or even from Mai Shum itself), and thus formed a lake of sorts along the foot of Mai Qoho. The word 'mehsab' means something like 'washing-place', which seems to confirm this idea.

2. The Town Plan.

By the time that the *Periplus Maris Erythraei* was written, the town of Aksum, together with Meroë, capital of the Kushitic kingdom (though here the text is corrupt – Huntingford 1980: 19), was prominent enough to be called by the anonymous author of that work a 'metropolis', a word reserved for relatively few places. It seems as if the main part of the town lay on either side of the Mai Lahlaha in the areas now known as Dungur and Addi Kilte. Here were all the élite dwellings found by the various archaeological expeditions (Littmann 1913; Puglisi 1941; Anfray 1972; Munro-Hay 1989). The Deutsche Aksum-Expedition traced the approximate ground plans of three very substantial buildings, which they called Ta'akha Maryam, Enda Sem'on and Enda Mikael after local identifications based on the *Book of Aksum* (Conti Rossini 1910), and they found traces of many others in the immediate neighbourhood. Subsequently, Puglisi, an Italian archaeologist, and Anfray, working on behalf of the Ethiopian Department of Antiquities, established that to the west were many more such structures. The whole area is scattered with the debris of the ruined buildings of this ancient quarter of the town. These large residences were basically, it seems, of one plan; a central lodge or pavilion, raised on a high podium approached by broad staircases, surrounded and enclosed by ranges of buildings on all four sides. The central pavilion was thus flanked by open courtyards. The plan shows a taste for the symmetrical, and the buildings are square or rectangular, with a strong central focus on the main pavilion. Ta'akha Maryam was furnished with an extra wing, and is the largest of such structures to have been excavated and planned so far.

How widespread the central part of the town was formerly is not yet known, but it may be assumed that the less permanent habitations of the poorer sections of the population were constructed all round the more substantial dwellings, and on the slopes of the Beta Giyorgis hill. Nothing of these has survived, but in time archaeologists may find evidence for the sort of dwellings we would expect; rough stone and mud, or wood, matting and thatch. One or two house models in clay found during the excavations give an impression of the smaller houses of Aksumite times (Ch. 5:4).

Interest in fortification seems to have been minimal. The country itself was a natural fortress, enclosed within its tremendous rock walls and defended by its mountainous and remote position, as well as by the military superiority of its armies. Within the town, the pavilion style of dwelling, enclosed by inner courts and outer ranges of buildings, were in some measure given privacy, and if necessary defence, by their very layout. Kobishchanov writes of fortified bastions around the sacred area, but these were in fact only the outer walls of the large structure of typical Aksumite plan which now lies beneath the cathedral, not walls for specific defence reasons (Kobishchanov 1979: 141; de Contenson 1963). Nothing is known about the street plan of the suburbs where these mansions lay, and whether they too partook of the

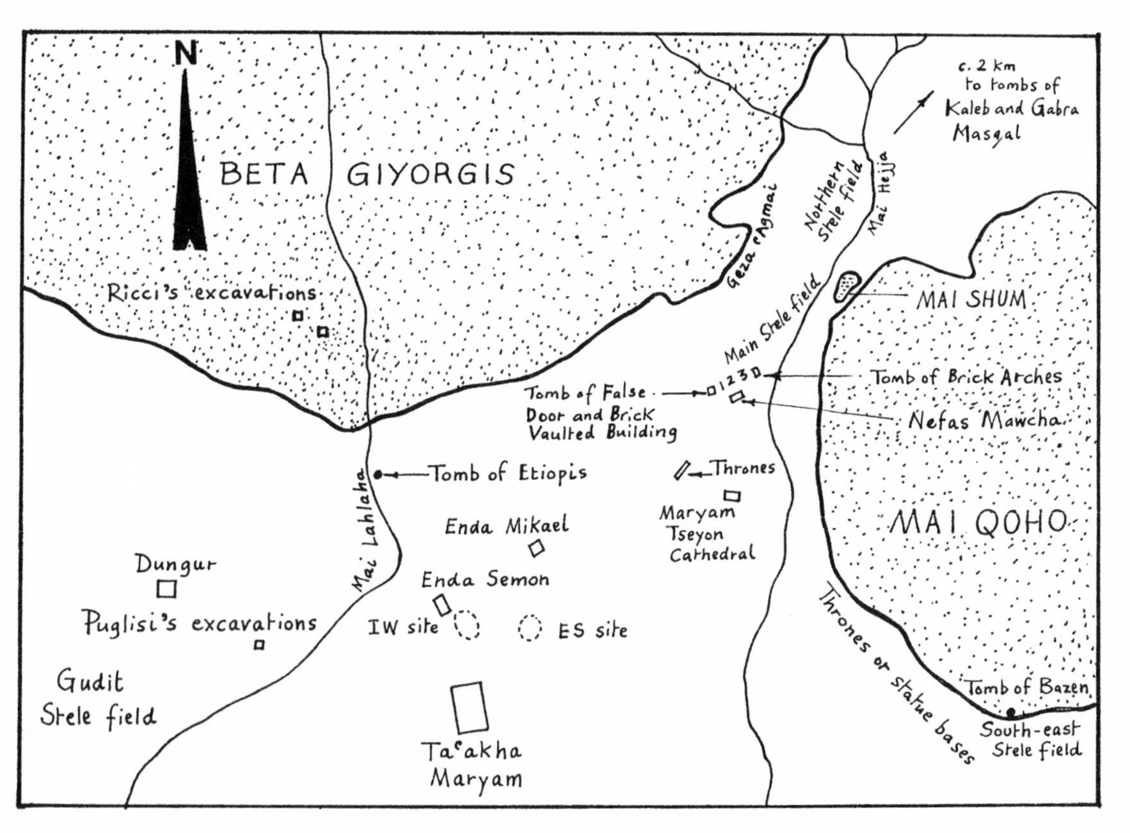

C. Plan of the ancient city of Aksum.

prevailing liking for symmetry by using a grid-pattern. The outer parts of the town very likely developed organically in a piecemeal fashion, and were in a constant state of alteration, enlargement, or rebuilding as structures decayed or developed. Such a development can be seen on the plan (Anfray 1974) of the excavated structures at Matara.

Flanking the town in various directions were the necropoleis or cemeteries. These are marked today by the numerous granite stelae, standing stone monuments which vary from rough and simple marker-stones to some of the largest single stones ever employed in human constructions. Fields of such stelae are found in the following locations;

to the south of Dungur (called the 'Gudit' field, after the legendary queen who sacked Aksum in the tenth century);

to the east of the town below the south side of Mai Qoho;

on the top of Beta Giyorgis to the north of the two church buildings there excavated by Lanfranco Ricci (1976);

and above all in the main stelae field running along the north side of the Mai Hejja. This latter can be divided into two, a northern group in the area known as Geza 'Agmai, and the main, southern group, ending almost opposite the cathedral and embracing the recently-made 'Stele Park', which includes all the decorated monoliths, and some enormous granite-built tombs (Littmann 1913; Munro-Hay 1989).

Rock-cut or built tombs are also to be found on the slopes of Mai Qoho hill, in the courtyard of the church of the Four Animals (Arbate Ensessa) in Aksum, and in the region of the so-called tombs of Kaleb and Gabra Masqal some 2km. north of the present town (Littmann 1913; Munro-Hay 1989). It is evident that there are many other structures in this region and to the north; an idea of the density of occupation can be gained from the survey work of Michels quoted in Kobishchanov (1979: Map 4).

The southern group of stelae in the main stelae field marks what was evidently the chief necropolis of the city, and the royal burial place. Directly facing it was a religious and ceremonial area now occupied by the sacred enclosure called Dabtera where the two cathedrals, old and new Maryam Tseyon, stand. The base of the podium of the old cathedral is an Aksumite structure, and other very substantial buildings have been traced in the area (de Contenson 1963i); if the custom of building churches on former sacred spots was followed here also, these may be traces of earlier cathedrals or pre-Christian temples. The architectural ensemble of this part of the town, of cathedral/temple, thrones, and stelae, shows an arrangement which may owe something to intentional design, but which was evidently also an extended process. The earlier examples among the great decorated stelae may well have been situated one after the other following a deliberate design; this impression is much stronger for the last three, which, dominating the terrace of lesser stelae, must have offered a sight which for dramatic quality was rarely equalled in the ancient world.

Near to and facing the old cathedral, is a cluster of granite thrones (Littmann 1913: II, 45ff) of which now only pedestals remain. Most of them are in a row running approximately north-north-east to south-south west. There are eleven in the row, two being double, with another two immediately in front of the main row. At least six of the thrones had some sort of pillared canopy, as emplacements for pillars can be seen in the stonework of the pedestals. Slots for their backs and sides show that the original design was for closed chairs like the picture (Wolska-Conus 1968) of the Adulis throne in Kosmas' book, and very likely at least some of these now-missing slabs bore inscriptions as did the Adulis monument. Some way to the southeast, between the row of thrones and the inner enclosure of the church, stand two other throne-pedestals, one with four columns still erect, and another set on a massive plinth. The throne-bases are noted in the *Book of Aksum* (Conti Rossini 1910) as the thrones of the Nine Saints, with others for Kaleb, Gabra Masqal and so on, or are attributed to the twelve judges of Aksum. In later times they served in the ceremony of the coronation. They may well have been the thrones which inscriptions tell us were set up as memorials of victories or other great events, like the one which still existed at Adulis in the sixth century, when Kosmas copied its anonymous Aksumite inscription. One of Ezana's inscriptions, DAE 10, (see Ch. 11: 5) mentions a throne set up 'here in Shado', possibly the ancient name of one of the two places at Aksum still marked by rows of thrones.

The second set of pedestals led in a row from beside the eastern stelae field towards the ceremonial centre of the town, and some of these still show traces which indicate that they once held statues. Plinths for statues are known from other parts of the town also, one having sockets for feet 92 cm long (Littmann 1913: II, 44, provided a photograph of this now-vanished monument). Perhaps this sort of monument gave rise to the legend that when Christ descended to earth to perform the miracle of filling up the lake where Abreha and Atsbeha later built the cathedral, he left his footprints in the rock; they were, according to the *Book of Aksum*, still visible in the fifteenth century. Some of the Aksumite inscriptions mention the erection of metal statues as victory memorials, but as yet only stone statues have been found in Ethiopia. These, of which the finest examples come from Hawelti, near Aksum, date to some centuries before Aksumite times, but there may have been a continuity of tradition from one period to the next (de Contenson 1963).

The town-plan of Aksum is thus fairly simple; it may be envisaged as commencing with a ceremonial approach from the east, lined with granite victory-thrones and statues of bronze and precious metals dedicated to the gods, leading to the religious centre with the royal cemetery lying to the north and east. The focus for this region seems to have been the temple/cathedral area, with another row of thrones. The main residential suburb with its huge palaces was situated to the west; and the whole was flanked with lesser cemeteries and more humble residential suburbs. It is probable that there was

19. One of the stone thrones or statue-bases which lined the entrance avenue leading to Aksum's main Stele Field. Photo BIEA.

at least one open square, a market-place perhaps, somewhere in the town centre. Since inscriptions and a statue base are reported to have come from the area between Ta'akha Maryam and Enda Sem'on (Littmann 1913: Schneider 1974), it may have been situated there, as such monuments may well have been set up in a public place. Civic building has not been identified; nothing has yet been excavated which can be categorised as public architecture, such as the structures housing town administrations, law-courts, covered markets or shopping arcades, baths, and the like so common in Roman town centres. As we have noted above, there is no hint that the Aksumite rulers needed to dominate their towns with citadels, or surround them with defensive walls, and the town must have simply petered out in the plain and on the slopes of the hills.

3. Portuguese Records of Aksum.

The most significant of the Portuguese accounts of Aksum is undoubtedly that of Francisco Alvares (or Alvarez), who came to Aksum in 1520. He was a careful and sympathetic observer who noted a good deal about the town, including details of many of the then extant monuments. His account has the special significance that it was the only one made before the sack of the city by the Muslim leader Ahmad Gragn. Several of the buildings which he mentions now do not exist (at least on the surface), but from the accuracy of those descriptions which can be checked, it is evident that his statements are worthy of respect. His description of Aksum was as follows (from Beckingham and Huntingford 1961); the square brackets indicate additions in Ramusio's Italian edition, apparently made from a different manuscript than that published in Lisbon in 1540.

Chapter XXXVIII.

(After the description of the church of Maryam Tseyon; see Ch. 10: 5));

> *Inside the large enclosure* (the outer enclosure around Maryam Tseyon) *there is a large ruin built in a square, which in other times was a house and has at each corner a big stone pillar, square and worked [very tall with various carvings. Letters can be seen cut in them but they are not understood and it is not known in what language they are. Many such epitaphs are found.] This house is called Ambaçabet, which means house of lions.*

It is not known what this structure, which has now disappeared, was.

> *Before the gate of the great enclosure there is a large court, and in it a large tree which they call Pharaoh's fig tree, and at the end of it there are some very new-looking pedestals of masonry, well worked, laid down. Only when they reach near the foot of the fig tree they are injured by the roots which raise them up. There are on the top of these pedestals twelve stone chairs [arranged in order one after the other] as well made with stone as though they were of wood. They are not made out of a block, but each one from its own stone and separate piece. They say these belong to the twelve judges who at this time serve in the court of Prester John.*

These are the thrones, of which only the pedestals now exist.

> *Outside this enclosure there is a large town with very good houses... and very good wells of water of [very beautiful] worked masonry, and also in most of the houses...ancient figures of lions and dogs and birds, all well made in [very hard, fine] stone. At the back of this great church is a very handsome tank [or lake of spring water] of masonry, [at the foot of a hillock where is now a market] and upon this masonry are as many other chairs of stone such as those in the enclosure of the church.*

This seems to refer to the row of thrones set on what seems to be a natural rock wall at the base of Mai Qoho; possibly in the sixteenth century this wall acted as a retaining wall for water, perhaps overspill from Mai Shum?

> *This town is situated at the head of a beautiful plain, and almost between two hills, and the rest of this plain is almost as full of these old buildings, and among them many of these chairs, and high pillars of inscriptions [;it is not known in what language, but they are very well carved].*
>
> *Above this town, there are very many stones standing up, and others on the ground, very large and beautiful, and worked with beautiful designs, among which is one raised upon another, and worked like an altar stone, except that it is of very great size and it is set in the other as if enchased* (the

standing stele and its base-plate). *This raised stone is 64 covados in length, and six wide; and the sides are 3 covados wide. It is very straight and well worked, made with arcades below, as far as a head made like a half moon; and the side which has this half moon is towards the south. There appear in it five nails which do not show more on account of the rust; and they are arranged like a quinas* (the five dots on dice). *And that it may not be asked how so high a stone could be measured, I have already said how it was all in arcades as far as the foot of the half moon, and these are all of one size; and we measured those we could reach to, and by those reckoned up the others, and we found 60 covados, and we gave 4 to the half moon, although it would be more, and so made 64 covados* (thus making it about twice too great, the covado being apparently 27 inches). *This very long stone, on its south side, where the nails in the half moon are, has, at the height of man, the form of a portal carved in the stone itself, with a bolt and a lock, as if it were shut up. The stone on which it is set up is a covado thick and is well worked; it is placed on other large stones, and surrounded by other smaller stones, and no man can tell how much of it enters the other stone, or if it reaches to the ground. [Near these] there are endless other stones raised above the ground [, very beautiful] and very well worked [;it seemed as if they had been brought there to be put to use, like the others that are so big and are standing up]; some of them will be quite forty covados long, and others thirty. There are more than thirty of these stones, and they have no patterns on them; most of them have large inscriptions, which the people of the country cannot read, neither could we read them; according to their appearance, these characters must be Hebrew* (perhaps actually Epigraphic South Arabian; does this mean that originally there were some inscriptions in the Stele Park?). *There are two of these stones, very large and beautiful, with designs of large arcades, and tracery of good size, which are lying on the ground entire, and one of them is broken into three pieces, and each of these equal eighty covados, and is ten covados in width. Close to them are stones, in which these had been intended to be, or had been enchased, which were bored and very well worked.*

These are the two largest stelae, but now the base-plate of the largest is missing.

Chapter XXXIX.

Above this town which overlooks much distant country [on every side], and which is about a mile, that is the third of a league, from the town, there are two houses under the ground into which men do not enter without a lamp (the 'Tombs of Kaleb and Gabra Masqal'). *These houses are not vaulted, but of a very good straight masonry, both the walls and the roof. The blocks are free on the outside. The walls may be 12 covados high; the blocks are set in the walls so close one to the other, that it all looks like one stone [for the joins are not seen]. One of these houses is much divided into chambers and granaries. In the doorways are holes for the bars and for the*

> *sockets for the doors. In one of these chambers are two very large chests* (the sarcophagi), *each one 4 covados in length, and one and a half broad, and as much in overall height, and in the upper part of the inner side they are hollowed at the edge, as though they had lids of stone, as the chests are also of stone (they say that these were the treasure chests of the Queen Saba). The other house, which is broader, has only got a portico and one room. From the entrance of one house to that of the other will be a distance of a game of Manqual* (a type of skittles) *and above them is a field... In this town and in its countryside...when there come thunderstorms...there are no women or men, boys or children...left in the town who do not come out to look for gold among the tillage, for they say the rains lay it bare, and that they find a good deal.*

This remark was taken by the editors of Alvares' book to mean that gold was actually washed out of the soil; it is, however, much more likely to refer to the finding of gold coins and other items in the earth, something still not infrequent at Aksum after the rains. Alvares also describes the now-disappeared western church of St. Michael with a 'tower of very fine masonry' and the two shrines of Abba Liqanos and Abba Pantelewon.

About one hundred years later, after Ethiopia had passed through the great convulsions of Gragn's wars, Manoel de Almeida described the town in his chapter XXI, *Acçum and its Antiquities* (Beckingham and Huntingford 1954: 90ff);

> *It is situated on the edge of very broad meadows in a gap where they come in between two hills. Today it is a place of about a hundred inhabitants. Everywhere there ruins are to be seen, not of walls, towers, and splendid palaces, but of many houses of stone and mud which show that the town was formerly very large.*

Much of this was presumably the remains of the early sixteenth century town.

> *A church of stone and mud, thatched, is to be seen there built among the ruins and walls of another, ancient, one, the walls of which are still visible and were of stone and mud to (for in no part of Ethiopia is there any sign or trace that lime has ever at any time been seen there, or any building, large or small, constructed with it) but very wide apart. From what is visible, the church seems to have had five aisles. It was 220 spans long and 100 wide, it has a big enclosure wall of stone and mud and inside it a very handsome courtyard paved with large, well cut stones, ending, on the side the church is, in a flight of 8 or 9 steps, also made of well cut stones. At the top is a platform of 10 or 12 covados in the space before the façade and principal door of the church.*
>
> *Outside this church's enclosure is another in which five or six big pedestals of black stone are to be seen. Near at hand are four columns of the same stone 10 or 12 spans high. Among them is a seat on which the Emperors sit to be crowned after first having taken his seat on the pedestals I mentioned and after various ceremonies have been performed on them*

(see Ch. 7: 6 for an account of the coronation).

What is most worth seeing here, a display of presumptuous grandeur, is many tall stones like obelisks, needles and pyramids. They are in a meadow lying behind the church. I counted some twenty that were standing and seven or eight that have been thrown to the ground and broken in many fragments. The tallest of those standing, if measured by its shadow, is 104 spans. Its width at the base is ten spans, it becomes thinner as it goes up, like a pyramid, but it is not square; it has two sides broader and two narrower than the other two. It is carved as though in small panels each of which is like a square of two spans. This is the style of all those which have this carving, which are the taller ones. The rest are rough and unshaped slabs without any carving at all. The shortest are from 30 to 40 spans; the rest are all taller. It can be seen from the fragments of three or four of those that have been overthrown, that they were much bigger than the tallest of those now standing, which I said was a hundred and four spans, and some can be seen to have been over two hundred. The old men of this country say that a few years ago, in the time of King Malaac Cegued, and the Viceroy Isaac who rebelled and brought in the Turks to help him against the Emperor, they overthrew the six or seven that lie on the ground in fragments.

No one can say what was the object of the former kings who raised them up. It may well be thought that they were like mausoleums erected near their tombs, since this was the object of the Egyptians. It was no doubt from them, through their proximity and the constant communication there was between them, that they learnt about, and that the workmen came to make, these barbarous and monstrous structures. A bombard shot away from this spot is a broad stone not much higher than a man on which a long inscription can be seen. Many Greek and some Latin letters are recognisable, but when joined together, they do not make words in Greek, Latin, Hebrew, or any other known language, and so the meaning of the writing is not discoverable.

Balthasar Tellez also added a little to the picture of Aksum in the seventeenth century, in his book published in Portugal in 1660, and later translated into English (1710); much of his information repeats de Almeida's.

"At this time there is no settled city in all Ethiopia; formerly the town of Aczum was very famous among the Abyssinians, and still preserves somewhat of its renown; and this place seems to have been a city, at least they look upon it as most certain, that the Queen of Sheba kept her court there, and that it was the residence of the emperors for many ages after, and they are crown'd there to this day....this is the city Aczum, or Auxum....at present it is only a village of about 100 houses. There are to be seen many ancient ruins, particularly those of a spacious church...The most magnificent thing that appears here, are certain very tall stones, in the nature of obelisks, or pyramids, the biggest of them 78 foot in length, the

19a. The title page of Telles' 1660 Historia de Ethiopia a alta after d'Almeida; some attempt has been made to 'Ethiopianise' the figure of the king and his courtiers.

breadth at the foot seven foot six inches. It is cut as it were in small cushions, each of them about half a yard square; the smallest of them being between 25 and 30 foot high are rude misshapen stones. Some of those which seem to have been tallest are thrown down, and they say, the Turks entering Ethiopia overthrew them. The end of erecting them may reasonably suppos'd to have been for monuments, near their graves; which was the design of the Egyptians in their so famous pyramids. Here is also a stone set up with a large inscription, in Greek and Latin characters, but they do not make any sense.

20. View of part of the central pavilion at Dungur, showing the granite corner-blocks, one of the re-entrants, and the rebates in the walls.

4. Aksumite Domestic Architecture.

The general style of the élite domestic buildings of Aksum has been described above (Ch. 5: 2), and reconstructions have been attempted (in Littmann 1913; and, more modestly, by Buxton and Matthews 1974). The pavilions in their domestic enclosures are the most typical examples of the unique Aksumite form of construction, and embody most of the characteristics of Aksumite architecture. The podia (the only parts of these buildings which survive, except in very rare cases) were built according to a style whereby the walls exhibited no long straight stretches, but instead were indented, so that any long walls were formed by a series of recesses or re-entrants and salients. These, considering that the building material was mostly random rubble (coursed stonework is rarely found), bound only with mud mortar, must have been designed to strengthen walls with low cohesion inclined to sag, and to deal with expansion and contraction caused by widely-ranging temperatures. Later structures, such as the Lalibela churches, show that the indentations were not used only on the podia, but extended to roof level.

At intervals of a little less than 50 centimeters as the podium walls rose they were rebated, each rebate setting the wall back about 5 centimetres. These rebates or *gradins*, sometimes up to seven, were often topped with flat slate-like stones forming a shelf or string-course. This design was perhaps inspired by the same architectural tradition illustrated in the pre-Aksumite period at the Grat-Beal-Guebri and the temple at Yeha (Anfray 1972ii: 58). It not only narrowed the walls as they rose higher, but assisted the run-off of rain from the surfaces of the walls, and thus protected the mud-mortar to some extent. The rebated walls with re-entrants and salients are one of the chief distinguishing marks of Aksumite architecture, and apart from their reinforcing function they would have enhanced the appearance of the massive podia of the palaces and mansions by breaking up the solidity of their mass with light and shadow. A wall at the structure called Enda Sem'on was remarkable in that it had not only five surviving rebates, but the wall above was preserved for a further 1.80m and including a blocked-up window with a stone lintel (Munro-Hay 1989).

Most of the surviving podium walls of these Aksumite structures were furnished at all corners with large and carefully cut granite corner blocks, which protected, linked, and supported the weaker parts of the walls. Occasionally a podium might be strengthened by a complete row of cut granite blocks, as still visible at Dungur and in the Aksumite part of the Maryam Tseyon cathedral podium. Granite was also used for architectural features such as columns, bases and capitals, doors, windows, paving, and the like, and particularly for the massive flights of steps which sometimes flanked two or three sides of the pavilions. A good deal of this stonework consisted of undecorated but well-dressed blocks, but some of the doorway blocks, or the columns and their bases and capitals, were decorated with a variety of designs.

A thick lime plaster was noted on the walls of one room in the large tomb called the Mausoleum at Aksum (Munro-Hay 1989), and similarly appears on a chamfered column at Maryam Nazret. Lime mortar has also been observed fixing stones on the podium of the Aksumite church at Agula, but it does not appear to have been regularly used.

At Adulis the main construction material was porous basalt (the same material was used for the stele at Adulis which Kosmas saw behind the marble throne there, lying broken into two pieces – Wolska-Conus 1968: 364) or sandstone. Polygonal blocks of basalt were used for walls, and cut cubes were assembled to form square columns. During the excavations at Adulis, Paribeni (1907: 464) was puzzled by the lack of doors and windows in walls he was able to clear up to a height of 3.40m. He concluded that they must only represent foundations, and this was in a measure true, since the buildings rose on podia as indicated by the excavations at Matara and Aksum. Among the structures which Paribeni cleared was one which he called the Ara del Sole, Altar of the Sun, because of a number of designs which he interpreted as hills and sun-discs carved on bluish marble plaques destined for fixing to the walls. A church had been built on top of the original podium, but the latter conformed in all other ways to the usual Aksumite style.

A second type of architecture, though similar in most essentials to that already described, employed wooden beams as a strengthening element within the walls. A square horizontal beam set in the wall supported rounded cross-members embedded in the stonework and forming ties across the width of the walls. The ends of these cross-members projected from the external wall (and were sometimes visible internally as well) in rows, forming the characteristic 'monkey-heads' often seen fossilised in stone in other examples of Ethiopian architecture. Doors and windows were constructed by a similar method, the openings being framed on all four sides and linked by cross members through the thickness of the walls; but the 'monkey-heads' are square. Most of these features were carved in granite on the decorated stelae, and some can still be seen in the surviving ancient rock-cut or built churches of Tigray and Lalibela (Buxton and Matthews 1974; Plant 1985; Gerster 1970). The framed doors and windows appear as a repeated motif in some of these later structures, and have been dubbed the 'Aksumite frieze', since they appear on the decorated stelae there (Plant 1985: 17, 20). However, the simple lintel was also known and employed, for example over the doorway of the East Tomb at Aksum and over a window at Enda Sem'on (Munro-Hay 1989).

It is possible that the original inspiration for the design of the decorated stelae came from the South Arabian mud-brick multi-storey palaces familiar to the Aksumites from their involments in that country, rather than from Ethiopian examples. On some of the Aksumite podia there could conceivably have been erected high tower-like structures of mud-brick around a wooden

21. The lower part of the still-standing decorated stele at Aksum, showing the imitation in stone of wooden architectural elements.

frame, such as that found at Mashgha in the Hadhramawt (Breton et al. 1980: pls. VIII, X) looking rather like the great stelae. But no evidence for such Yemeni-style buildings actually survives in Ethiopia, nor is there any archaeological indication there for mud-brick architecture. Alternatively, and more probably, the stelae could have been exaggerated designs based on the Aksumite palaces; and here there is archaeological support, since the struc-

22. Apparently created long after the Aksumite period, the churches of Lalibela still employed the same general style of architecture, including imitation beam-ends in stone.

ture called the 'IW Building' partly cleared by the excavations of Neville Chittick (Munro-Hay 1989), included just such wood-reinforced walls. Though the load-bearing strength of the rough stone and mud mortared walls is apparently very considerable, it seems most likely that these buildings would have been in reality limited to only two storeys above the podia. Evidence that the pavilions and some of these outer ranges were more than one storey high is provided by the occasional staircases which have been found. The central pavilions of Aksumite palaces were completely surrounded by ranges of subsidiary structures, pierced here and there by gateways and doors. Each ensemble must have formed very much the sort of thing mentioned by the sixth-century merchant Kosmas, who speaks of the 'four-towered palace of the king of Ethiopia' (Wolska-Conus 1973). The recessed central parts of each facade may have reached a storey less in height than the corner salients, giving the impression of towers (as shown on the reconstructions). Kobishchanov's eight-storied palace (1979: 141) of Ta'akha Maryam is probably an error for the number of stepped shelves which constituted the building's podium (Schneider 1984: 165).

Some of these structures were of very considerable size; Ta'akha Maryam measured 120 x 80 m, and its pavilion, at c. 24 x 24 m was the smallest of the three the German expedition cleared; if the other two were in proportion their overall size must have been very large indeed. Ta'akha Maryam thus covered around six times the total area of the more-or-less contemporary palace and

23. A column base from Aksum, possibly originally from the peristyle in the centre of the south wing of Ta'akha Maryam palace.

24. At the mansion of Dungur, some of the basement rooms contained rough stone supports, perhaps for wooden columns.

portico of the kings of the Hadramawt recently excavated (Breton 1987) at their capital of Shabwa, and, as a single architectural concept rather than an agglomeration of buildings, was larger than many European palaces (excluding such monumental constructions as the Roman and Byzantine Great Palaces) until the erection of such buildings as Hampton Court. Kosmas, when speaking of Kaleb's palace, sometimes simply refers to it as the royal dwelling, but on other occasions uses the latin word *palatium*, surely in recognition of its particular splendour (Wolska-Conus 1973: 321, n. 4.3).

The central pavilion at Ta'akha Maryam contained nine rooms, two of which were probably simply staircase-wells for access to the upper storey. The largest room was 7 x 6 m, and others measured 5 x 5 m, 7 x 4 m and 6 x 5 m. All had their roofs supported by two, three or four columns, and some had carefully flagged floors. In the south wing was a central peristyle with octagonal column-bases, and leading to the north corner-buildings were four-columned porticoes with elaborate floral column bases. The central pavilion of Enda Mikael measured 27 x 27 m with 10 rooms, following the same pattern as Ta'akha Maryam but with the central room divided into two. Room sizes were 6 x 6 m, 4 x 10 m, 5 x 9 m, and 3 x 9 m, with emplacements for four, eight or nine columns. The most substantial pavilion found to date was that in Enda Sem'on, 35 m square, with two enormous halls, each with twenty-eight column emplacements and measuring some 19 x 10 m; impressive dimensions, but needing more and more roof-support as the room sizes grew more ambitious, which must have resulted in a rather crowded effect. The lack of stone columns, commoner in the eastern Aksumite sites (Anfray 1974: 747), suggests that carved wooden ones were used, perhaps resting on rough stone pedestals as at Dungur, in some of the Matara buildings, and in some rooms excavated at Adulis (where they were capped with discs of basalt). These descriptions rest mainly on the published plans of the Deutsche Aksum-Expedition, which depend in parts on their assumption, probably correct as far as subsequent excavation has shown, that most buildings were more or less symmetrically arranged (see for example the plans in Littmann 1913: II, taf. XVII-XIX).

Anfray (1974: 762) suggested that the idea for such buildings ultimately derived from north Syria, and thought that *'un certain caractère de sobriété, de rigidité, de rationalité même dans cette architecture axoumite...paraît d'inspiration romaine*'. Whilst this may be partly true, a good deal of the inspiration might equally be derived from earlier local examples; the Yeha temple could hardly be plainer or more simple.

The architecture of the Aksumite élite residences should tell us something about the intentions and the character of the people who had them built, but this is in reality hard to interpret. The massiveness and solidity of the structures, and their simplicity and plainness, do indeed impress at first, but here we may well be missing such decorative elements as carved wooden columns, capitals and screens, and interior painting on plaster. Though in most Aksumite sites very few fragments of anything like elaborate carved stone or plaster-work have come to light as yet, churches in Tigray and Lalibela exhibit a rich selection of (albeit somewhat later) decorative elements (Plant 1985; Gerster 1970). These include painting on walls and ceilings, imaginative designs for windows, carved friezes, and carved wooden roof panels – some decorative woodwork survives at Dabra Damo, of uncertain date, and conceivably coming originally from a palace (Gerster 1970: 73). Some of this may well have been of Aksumite origin.

At Adulis, where perhaps more foreign influences might be expected, Paribeni (1907, loc. var.) found several examples of carved marble or basalt panels and decorative elements for affixing to walls, and carved architectural features such as acanthus or lotus capitals, or alabaster or limestone reliefs with formal floral designs or intertwined (vine?) leaves and branches; one also depicted a bird, possibly a peacock. Paribeni also found decorative marble colonnettes for framing screens – though these seem to have been imported ready-made from the eastern Mediterranean region, like those from an Adulite church excavated by the British in 1868 (Munro-Hay 1989i). He even found traces of lines, bands and leaves painted in red and brown on plaster in one house at Adulis. Most unusual among Paribeni's discoveries were plaques of a black schist, carved with shapes resembling oak leaves, which were cut in such a way as to accommodate metal inlay. At Aksum, the largest stele makes one concession to decoration with its filigree window-screens of superimposed stepped crosses under arches on the top storeys, perhaps modelled on something like the alabaster screens found until today in Yemeni houses. Constructional details like the beam-ends seem to have been left plain and visible. The churches of Lalibela, and others in Tigray, are nevertheless quite restrained where the architecture in concerned, however elaborate their interior paintings might be. As noted above, in the pavilions, smallish rooms, or larger halls thronged with columns, were a necessity given the limited means of spanning spaces, but the inevitable rather cramped feeling may have been largely offset by the use of open porticoes and wide courtyards.

A taste for the dramatic and the exclusive can perhaps be read into the appearance of the central pavilions in these courts, raised high on their podia, isolated by the courtyards surrounding them, and approached by massive flights of usually about seven steps. Such a design may be an expression of the special position of the rulers translated into architectural terms. There may have been an intention to isolate the pavilions as a convenience for security, but although the whole ensemble of pavilion, courtyards, and outer ranges was evidently to some extent defensible, that does not seem to have been a primary consideration. The Aksumites could surely, had they wished, have made stronger fortresses than these.

Some clay models of houses survive which illustrate the architectural style of the smaller Aksumite dwellings. A round hut, with a conical roof thatched in layers, and a rectangular doorway, is one type from Hawelti (de Contenson

1963ii: pl. XXXVII, b-c). A second type from Hawelti is rectangular, the doors and windows also rectangular, with a roof supported by beams whose 'monkey-head' ends can be seen below the eaves. The roof has a small parapet and there is a waterspout to drain it (de Contenson 1963ii: pl. XXXVIII-XXXIX). A third type (de Contenson 1959: fig. 8) from Aksum shows only the remains of the bases of typical Aksumite window-apertures with square beam-ends at the corners; this may also represent a rectangular or square dwelling. In the BIEA Aksum excavations fragments of a fourth type of house, also rectangular, but with a roof consisting of sloping layers of what appears to be thatch of some sort, were found (Chittick 1974: fig. 21a). Its doorway seems to be surmounted by a dentilled lintel, like that of the largest stelae and the Tomb of the False Door (see below).

The last of these house-types is particularly interesting, in that it shows a pitched roof on a rectangular building. Such a roof was evidently of advantage in the rains, and may have been used on larger structures as well. Possibly the palaces themselves were roofed with thatch; the columns would have supported cross beams, perhaps with carved panels like those from Dabra Damo inset between them, and above some sort of layered thatch could have completed the weather-proofing (for some discussion of roofing in Ethiopian structures, see Buxton and Matthews, 1974). No trace of Roman-style tiles has yet been reported from Aksumite sites, not even from Adulis, nor do the brick vaults known to have been used in tombs (see below) appear to have been employed in domestic architecture as far as present evidence reveals. Paribeni does note (1907: 545) a report that some buildings at Tekondo were roofed with slabs of slate. He also made a few comments about domestic housing in Adulis, noting that open areas, perhaps for sleeping, would be useful in the hot climate of Adulis, and suggesting that some of the structures found without doorways could perhaps represent partially underground dwellings with wood or straw upper parts. These would have been entered from above by ladders, and perhaps were occupied by some of the 'Cave-dwellers' mentioned by the texts.

5. The Funerary Architecture.

Apart from rock-cut tombs of various types, and others constructed by walling excavated pits, the Aksumites built some much more elaborate tombs. The chronology of these is uncertain, but some idea has been gained from the stratigraphical evidence provided by recent excavations (Munro-Hay 1989). The tombs show that the Aksumites were deeply concerned with the well-being of their kings and other citizens after death, and from the finds in one partially-cleared tomb, called the Tomb of the Brick Arches, we can see that rich funerary goods were buried with them.

Perhaps the most extraordinary of all the funerary structures at Aksum is the tomb called (at least since the time of the German visit in 1906) *Nefas Mawcha*, or 'the place of the going forth of the winds'. This name may be

25. Part of the great top-stone of the tomb called *Nefas Mawcha.*

26. View of the great stele and the *Nefas Mawcha*, showing how the stele, in falling, struck the corner of the roof and destroyed the equilibrium of the tomb. Photos BIEA.

derived from a legend, related in the *Book of Aksum* (Conti Rossini 1910), that at the foot of the largest stele lay tunnels where winds blew out any lights. The tomb is (cautiously) dated to the third century AD (Munro-Hay 1989). It consists of a gigantic single roofing block, measuring about 17 x 7 x 1 m, placed over a paved chamber surrounded by ambulatories on all four sides. These passages were also roofed with granite blocks, those of the inner ambulatory (perhaps actually a rubble-filled supporting wall) fitting under both the great roofing block and the outer ambulatory roof blocks. The stones were trimmed to fit at either end, and linked together with metal clamps, the holes for which are still visible. This huge structure was almost certainly intended to be covered over by earth as an underground tomb. No entrance survives since the largest of the stelae, in falling, destroyed the west end of the building and caused the rest to settle as a result of the shock.

An unexpected find was the Tomb of the Brick Arches. The tomb itself lay beneath a rough-stone and mud-mortared superstructure, most of which has now disappeared, and whose original form cannot be reconstructed. Between two parallel walls a staircase roofed with rough granite slabs descended until the tomb's entrance was reached. The first sign of anything unusual was the discovery of a granite lintel, and then, underneath it, the upper part of an arch of baked bricks. As the excavations progressed, it became apparent that this was a horse-shoe shaped arch, forming about three-quarters of a perfect circle, which rested at each side on slate-like stones forming plinths supported by the usual Aksumite rough stone and mud-mortared walls. The entrance led to an antechamber, from which two further horse-shoe shaped arches led into the tomb-chambers proper. All had been blocked with stones, and all had been broken open in ancient times when the tomb was partially robbed.

The entrance-arch had an internal measurement of 1.3 m across the widest point, and the bricks were square. One of the internal arches resembled this, but the second was rather different, with oblong bricks arranged so that the long and short sides followed each other alternately. The square bricks measured 27 x 28 x 7 cm.

The contents of the tomb have been tentatively dated by various methods to the early/mid fourth century AD. To find horse-shoe shaped baked brick arches of this early date in Ethiopia was very surprising, and of great interest for the history of architecture. Horse-shoe shaped arches are known from an earlier period in India, a country with which Aksum had vigorous trading relations from probably the first century AD, but these arches were carved from the rock and not built. More or less contemporary built examples are reported from Syria, and so the Ethiopian examples have a pedigree as old as any others, at least for the time being (Munro-Hay, *Rassegna di Studi Etiopici*, forthcoming).

Some distance away was found the so-called Brick Vaulted Structure, presumed to be a tomb of the same date as the Tomb of the Brick Arches, since it was also situated in the main necropolis and similarly employed brick

27. The Tomb of the Brick Arches. View from inside the vestibule, looking through the horseshoe arch towards the staircase. Photo BIEA.

28. Drawing of the granite entrance doorway to the tomb called the 'Mausoleum'. Photo BIEA.

horse-shoe shaped arches. But it also included relieving arches and lintels, and the rooms were barrel-vaulted with brick. These bricks were mortared together, and it is evident that the Aksumites knew the use of mortar (nb. de Almeida's statement above, Ch. 5: 3), but rarely felt the need to employ it, preferring their drystone walling with simple mud-bonding.

The Brick Vaulted Structure first appeared during the excavations (Munro-Hay 1989) as a stone wall of Aksumite style, built parallel to the courtyard in front of the Tomb of the False Door to the west. In due course, a number of bricks began to appear, soon proving to be the remains of collapsed brick vaults. These consisted of double rows of square baked bricks forming radial barrel vaults resting on string- courses of slate-like stone on top of the usual Aksumite stone and mud-mortared walls. The chambers covered by the vaulting seem to have been approximately 1 x 2 m in size, and one retained traces of the stone-paved floor of a superstructure over the barrel vaulting. The height of the vaulted rooms was about 4 m, and a tentative reconstruction seems to indicate that they flanked a central passage.

The vaults themselves were not horse-shoe shaped. But the entrance to one of the vaults (the only entrance found) was formed by a horse-shoe shaped arch, also 1.3 m wide across the centre, sealed with a stone blocking, and surmounted by a granite relieving lintel above which the bricks of the vault rose. This revealed a new and more complex combination of architectural features, which, as far as our present knowledge goes, is entirely unique. It seems as if the structure originally had a number of these vaulted rooms opening off a central corridor, but the complete plan has not yet been completely recovered.

A further tomb, probably the largest yet known at Aksum, was entered by a monumental granite doorway in typical Aksumite style, with carved granite square-headed beam ends protruding at the corners. This tomb was dubbed the 'Mausoleum', as a testimony to its size and elaborate construction, both totally unexpected by the excavators. Its plan consists of a long corridor behind the stone doorway, also entered from above by three shafts, and flanked by ten rooms, five on each side. It has not yet been cleared, only planned by crawling through the narrow gap left between the mud fill and the roof. The tomb is about 15 m square and lies to the west of the foot of the largest stele. The entrance to another tomb was found on the east side of the stele with a simpler doorway of rough stone topped by a granite lintel. Both of these tombs opened onto a courtyard at the foot of the stele, which must have been filled in before the collapse of the stele. The 'Mausoleum' was built largely of rough stone walling roofed with granite blocks, and was covered with huge quantities of dry stone fill. It may belong to the person for whom the giant stele was raised. At the west end of its central corridor can be seen the top of another brick arch, leading into a passage not yet entered; but whether it was of the horse-shoe type is as yet unknown, as it was never cleared. It is possible that the arch gives access to further chambers, but it seems unlikely that there will be any connection with the Brick Vaulted Structure to the west, since over 20 metres lie between them.

By the time this arch was found it was scarcely a notable discovery (see above). But earlier in the same season (1974), the very appearance of baked brick in Aksumite Ethiopian architecture would have been remarkable, since it had been previously noted only in a few special circumstances (Anfray 1974), and an arch in the same material was completely unheard of. It is certain that our ideas about the architectural limitations of the ancient Aksumites will require yet more revision when excavations can be resumed.

These baked brick features, horseshoe shaped arches and vaults, in Aksumite buildings of the fourth century AD, may mean that our ideas about the routes of dissemination of architectural ideas in Africa, the Near East, and Spain (where the horse-shoe arch was later familiar) also need some revision. Wherever the style originated, it was certainly not expected to turn up in Aksumite Ethiopia. Without being able to assert the idea too strongly until we have more evidence, there may even be a case for proposing the brick horse-shoe arch as another Aksumite innovation, perhaps based on ideas which arrived through the trade-routes with India.

29. The Tomb of the False Door; the door block during excavation. It is very similar in detail to the doorways carved on the three largest of the decorated stelae at Aksum. Photo BIEA.

It may be presumed that attached to all the stelae are as yet unrevealed tombs like those just described. The latest excavations confirmed that the whole area of the central 'Stele Park', apart from the tombs already mentioned, was honeycombed with shaft tombs and tunnels (Chittick 1974; Munro-Hay 1989). These consisted of chambers and passages cut into the rock, sometimes irregularly, sometimes following a more orderly plan. Some may be a combination of smaller tombs linked by robber tunnels cut later. Very little could be done to clear them and investigate their plan and content in the short time available, but the remains of tomb-furniture were found in some.

The most westerly of all the tombs found so far, excluding one small shaft tomb, was the Tomb of the False Door. This possibly late-fourth or fifth century tomb (Munro-Hay 1989) has a false-door facade with a dentilled lintel exactly like those on some of the decorated stelae, but instead set into

30. The ruined superstructure of the Tombs of Kaleb and Gabra Masqal, just outside Aksum. Photo BIEA.

a granite-built square structure exhibiting the typical Aksumite plan of symmetrical recessed facades. It faced onto a carefully paved court and was doubtless open to view. Below, however, was an underground tomb-chamber with a vestibule and a surrounding corridor, with two staircases descending from the court to the substructure. The staircases had been blocked by massive capping stones, only one of which now survives. The tomb now contains nothing but a smashed granite coffin.

The tombs customarily attributed to the sixth century Aksumite kings Kaleb and Gabra Masqal could conceivably be of that period or of the fifth century. The building-complex consisted of two underground granite-built tombs with a double superstructure which seems to have consisted chiefly of two columned halls set on a platform approached by a staircase. The façade was about 40 m long, and the two halls were not exactly the same size, that attributed to Gabra Masqal being a little larger. The eight- or ten-columned hall above the 'Kaleb' tomb measured c. 10 x 11 m, and that above the 'Gabra Masqal' tomb c. 10 x 13 m, though both also had niches to the east adding an extra 2 m. The Gabra Masqal hall contained some sort of architectural feature, possibly a cupola or baldaquin, perhaps for a statue of the deceased (see the illustration in Littmann 1913: II, 133). Each side of the superstructure also contained entrance halls and staircase-wells, and these side-buildings were linked by a broad main entrance-stair 23 m wide. This was surmounted by a terrace with two porticoes, each with a column in the centre supporting the roof; the base of the column on the Kaleb side was

31. Detail showing the entrance to the Tomb of Kaleb.

square and stepped, while the column (which survived) and base on the Gabra Masqal side were octagonal. The building may represent a memorial chapel or shrine to the deceased, perhaps a 'Christianised' development of the principle which gave rise to the decorated stelae and the Tomb of the False Door. The *Book of Aksum* claims that these tombs were filled with gold and pearls.

32. The white capping over a fill of stones on one of the platforms at Aksum. Photo BIEA.

The main southern stele field, particularly the area set aside in modern times as a 'Stele Park', is also characterised by the terracing achieved by erecting walls or platforms. The earliest of these platforms are the oldest architectural works yet found at Aksum (Chittick 1974; Munro-Hay 1989), and may date to the first century AD or possibly even a little earlier in some cases. Platform-building seems to have continued for some time, the typical examples being simple stepped or rebated revetting walls acting as facing to enormous quantites of freshly-quarried rock fill. They appear to have been carefully topped with layers of white and red soils, doubtless specially chosen for some religious purpose, and there are signs that sacrifices or sacrificial meals took place on or around them. They seem to precede some of the stelae and to be contemporary with others. At some time, possibly in the fourth century, major work was undertaken to raise the height of the stele field, the whole being faced with a long rebated terrace wall at least three metres high. It is on this terrace that the largest of all the stelae were raised.

6. The Stelae.

These are the most famous of all the monuments of Aksum. They range from very rough and simple stones erected to mark grave-pits, to massive sculpted towers which represent soaring multi-storeyed palaces. Such huge monuments represent an enormous outlay of labour and skill, particularly in the most elaborate specimens. There are six carved and decorated monuments, the largest, now fallen and broken, formerly exceeding 33 m in height, with a measurement at the base of about 3 x 2 m. It is carved on all

33. View from the *Nefas Mawcha* looking towards the restored terrace wall, showing the still standing decorated stele; to the left of it originally stood the two largest stelae.

34. The largest of all the stelae, lying as it fell over the terrace wall. (Photo D. Phillipson).

four sides and shows 12 storeys. It seems that the kings each tried to outdo the achievements of their predecessors; this largest of all the stelae exceeds by far even its nearest companion, which was only about 24 m high, and c. 2 x 1 m at the base. It was only ten storeys high and, though also carved on all four faces, was not so elaborate. One wonders if the giant stele ever actually stood, or whether it immediately plunged down to smash its (variously estimated) 400–750 tons to pieces on the terrace wall below, destroying the great tomb, Nefas Mawcha, as it fell. The stelae very often have only about one-twelfth of their length buried, very inadequate support when the total height began to grow, let alone when it exceeded 33 m.; the third tallest, also probably about 24 m long but only 21 m above the ground, still (rather surprisingly) stands dominating the terrace of stelae, in spite of the abraded surface of the Stele Park, which leaves it somewhat less support than it originally had. Only very few stones in the ancient world exceeded the Aksum stelae in bulk, notably those forming the *trilithon* at Baalbek, constructed in the first half of the first century AD, where the largest stone measures something in the order of 20 x 4 x 4 m.

The great monolithic towers unquestionably mark the sites of the tombs of the Aksumite kings, although only two tombs which can be directly associated with them have so far come to light. All six of the carved stelae are embellished with the elaborate doors, windows, beam ends and other features typical of Aksumite architecture. At their summits are emplacements for what seem to have been either one or two metal plaques, which we may perhaps imagine as gilded bronze embossed with the sign of the disc and

35. The top of one of the decorated stelae (no. 4) showing the emplacements presumably for fixing decorative plaques.

crescent or some other emblem of the kings or gods. All that now remains are the traces of the fixing nails, arranged in positions which could even represent the cross; conceivably those which bore pagan symbols were later 'Christianised' (van Beek 1967). At the base of the decorated stelae were granite base-plates, carved in the case of all but the second largest (those of the

36. The base-plate of one of the decorated stelae at Aksum (no. 4), showing the kylix carved in the raised central portion, and three others around it; in the background can be seen the fallen stele.

largest have never been found) with the kylix, or Greek-style wine-cup with two handles. Some show several of these carved cups, with surrounds of decorative carving to the base-plates. The missing front base-plate for Stele 6 was found by Chittick (1974: pl. VIa). It is supposed that the cups were for offerings; since there is a similar cup carved in the base of a fruit-press cut from the solid rock at Atshafi near Aksum, it may indeed have been for wine-offerings that these altar-like base-plates were prepared. Perhaps the wine-offerings were poured out during memorial ceremonies for the deceased.

The stelae appear to have been extracted several kilometres away at the quarries of Wuchate Golo to the west of Aksum, and dragged from there into the city. At the quarry the rows of holes cut into the rock to delineate the line of the desired cut can still be seen; wooden wedges, rammed into these holes and swollen with water would have eventually caused the rock to split. In some cases, traces of these wedge-holes remain on the stelae themselves.

The stelae were probably erected with the aid of earthen ramps and tremendous human effort. Very likely each stele was hauled into position, perhaps using wooden rollers, until its base lay beside a pit dug ready to receive it (or possibly sometimes a tomb shaft, only partly refilled, was utilised). Then it was slowly levered up, and as it rose, stones and earth were placed as a ramp beneath it. Eventually, when it had slid into the pit and been levered completely upright, the pit, after being sometimes lined with larger stones, was packed with rubble and the base-plates installed. It must have been a tense moment when the stele reached the point of perpendicularity,

37. View (from below) of part of the Ionic capital and shrine on stele no. 7; the plain stele no. 36 now lies beneath it.

and also when, once erect, the first steps were taken to remove the supporting ramp. Whether the rather unreliable African elephant could have been utilised in helping to manoeuvre these giant stones is not known, but makes an interesting speculation.

No Egyptian obelisks could equal the size of the largest of the Aksumite stelae (though the unfinished one in the quarry at Aswan comes quite close). This enormous stone must surely represent the apogee of the manifestation of personal power in monumental structures in the ancient world. The five others are more modest in size, but are still very large. We have no accounts of these stelae from ancient visitors to the city, but they must have been an awe-inspiring sight rising in a row on their terraces overlooking the capital. Now all but one lie smashed or partly buried in the stream-bed, save for the second largest, which, transported to Italy as loot during the period of the Italian occupation of Ethiopia, now rises, repaired and restored but deteriorating in the polluted air, near the site of the Circus Maximus in Rome.

38. Two of the plain round-topped stelae at Aksum. (Photo R. Brereton).

Prior to these very few stelae were decorated. There is one roughly-shaped specimen with very rudimentary representations of beams and 'monkey-heads', and another with an Ionic pillar and some sort of shrine rather elegantly depicted on it. A third has a circular object, perhaps a shield, topped with an angled and pointed line, carved on it. Finally, one has, carved near its base, the ancient Egyptian symbol of life, the 'ankh' (Anfray 1974).

A common type of stelae comprises those plain dressed ones with rounded tops. In some cases these preceded the great carved monuments, but in others the differentiation was probably caused by respective wealth; they were probably erected by contemporaries who could not hope to raise anything of the order of the decorated monoliths. These plain dressed stelae range in size from very large (more or less equal in height to all the decorated ones save the very largest examples) to comparatively modest dimensions. From the archaeological evidence, it can be said that in broad terms the development

39. In the eucalyptus groves now planted over the northern Stele Field at Aksum, two of the smaller unworked stelae. Photo BIEA.

was from the smaller and rougher completely undressed type to the dressed and then decorated types. Some allowance, however, must be made for the relative prosperity of those who erected stelae, and their social grouping. Even after the development of the dressed stelae, some people could doubtless still only aspire to a rough-hewn memorial for their tombs; very likely the larger plain dressed stelae belonged to persons of very high rank, and the decorated ones only to the rulers.

However, we remain completely uninformed as to who was buried beneath or near these memorials, though it is a natural inference that only the kings could have mobilised the necessary labour and skill to quarry, carve, decorate, and erect the giant stelae or build the larger tombs. At the other end of the scale a simple rough-cut tomb marked by a rough stele proved to contain sets of glass goblets and beakers, large numbers of iron tools, around eighty pottery vessels of excellent quality and many shapes (some certainly not for basic domestic use). This tomb, in the 'Gudit' stelae field, probably dates to the third century AD and in spite of its unimpressive appearance it clearly belonged to a person of some affluence (Chittick 1974: 192 and pls. XII, XIIIa, XIVa).

Some of the burials found in the Stele Park were of a different nature. In one shaft (Chittick 1974: pl. VIIIa) bodies were found in layers, with few grave goods beside personal ornaments. These, from coins found among them, seem to have been later Christian-period burials of simple type, and there seems to be no stele associated with the tomb.

One or two bodies found may have been human sacrifices, offered as dedications or on celebratory occasions. King Ezana, for example, mentions offering 100 bulls and 50 captives in an inscription (see Ch. 11: 5); these captives may, of course, have only been dedicated to the gods as slaves. The stelae base-plates furnished with carved goblets resembling the Greek kylix could have acted as offering bowls; but these may rather have been used for wine or the like instead of blood, as noted above. A Yeha stele has a similar offering-cup in its base-plate (Littmann 1913: II, 2), and perhaps the custom was an old one. However, one rough stele (no. 137) was found to have the bones of perhaps two individuals seemingly thrown down into the pit in which it was erected, and there are other examples of human and animal bones, often burnt, among the fill and capping material of the platform complex (Munro-Hay 1989). Such rituals in pre-Christian Aksum call to mind contemporary sacrifices in the neighbouring Meroitic kingdom, where the kings are often depicted slaughtering captives *en masse* in an imagery which descends from the pharaonic art of very early times. In the vast and rich graves found under the mounds at Ballana and Qustul in Nubia, the so-called X-Group rulers contemporary with the later Aksumite kings were buried with human and animal sacrifices, and, though not in Africa, there is also the example of the Romans, who sometimes sacrificed victims at their triumphs.

A few stelae have been noted placed beside structures which have been firmly dated to the Christian period, such as the Dungur villa, the building at Wuchate Golo, and Matara, Tertre D; at the latter place Anfrày suggests the stele might denote a sacred edifice (Anfray and Annequin 1965: p. 68 and pl. XLIX, fig. 4). This might well apply also to Wuchate Golo, but does not seem to be the case at Dungur.

The origins of the stelae are very difficult to disentangle. Attributions of stelae in Ethiopia to the pre-Aksumite period, though customarily acccepted (Munro-Hay 1989: 150), are not necessarily correct (Fattovich 1987: 47–8). A stele tradition appears nevertheless to have existed in the Sudanese-Ethiopian borderlands, and in parts of northern Ethiopia and Eritrea in pre-Aksumite times. Fattovich suggests, plausibly enough, that stelae belong to an ancient African tradition. In the case of the stelae at Kassala and at Aksum – despite the difference in time and the difference in the societies which erected them – he sees a similarity in several features. These include the suggestion that *'the monoliths are not directly connected with specific burials'* (Fattovich 1987: 63). However, this is questionable as far as the Aksum stelae are concerned, now that it has been possible to analyse the results of Chittick's work. Though it is not yet easy to identify tombs for all the stelae, it does seem that, at the Aksum cemeteries, wherever archaeological investigations have been possible there is a case for suggesting that stelae and tombs are directly associated.

VI

The Civil Administration

1. The Rulers.

The government of Aksum, as far as can be discerned, was administered through a pyramid of authority expanding as it passed from the king to the lower echelons. There is some slight evidence that at times there may have been two kings reigning comtemporaneously (Ch. 7: 3), but in such a case one of them would have presumably been recognised as pre-eminent. The structure of power appears to have been that of an absolute monarchy, with a form of kingship implying a semi-divine ruler, and with the king's immediate family retaining important supportive military and administrative posts. At the next level were provincial governors or chiefs and sub-kings.

What information we have concerning the theory of government, and the working of the administration and other government functions is episodic, and we may assume that over the centuries the machinery of government did not remain static, but was subject to gradual changes as situations altered. One of the more important changes must have occurred with the acceptance of Christianity. The pre-Christian kings whose inscriptions have come down to us called themselves 'son of the invincible god Mahrem', the royal tutelary deity, and thus asserted their own claim to divine honours; they may also have been high-priests of the state cult. This semi-divine status, though implicitly abandoned by the Christian kings – or at least transformed by the anointing and coronation rituals – seems to have lost them little if any authority, since they remained the *de facto* heads of their own church; one of the advantages of having the titular head of the church in far-away Alexandria (Ch. 10: 2). Ezana, the first Christian king, in order to keep the customary protocol intact in an inscription (Ch. 11: 5, DAE 11) simply replaced the divine filiation with his own real filiation 'son of Ella Amida, never defeated by the enemy'.

Various stratagems were employed to keep power vested in the royal family. This appears to have also included female members of the ruling dynasty, since Rufinus (ed. Migne 1849) tells us that the dowager queen acted as regent during Ezana's minority. If the theory suggested by de Blois (1984) is valid, the royal wives may have been chosen from the chief clans of the country, thus encouraging their support for the regime. Those royal wives who became the mothers of future kings, would pass on to their sons the clan-names used by the kings in their 'Bisi'-titles (see below).

Sons of the *nagashis*, like Baygat and Garmat (Ch. 4: 4), led military campaigns in South Arabia, and Ezana later employed two of his brothers on similar tasks. Sometimes things may not have worked out so well; the story of the rebellion of Abreha, who is said by Tabari (ed. Zotenberg 1919: 184) to have conquered the Yemen after a previous general, Aryat, had failed, illustrates this. Tabari thought that Abreha belonged to Kaleb's family, and was accused of trying to take power in the Yemen; the *najashi* sent Aryat back to the Yemen to take control, but Abreha killed him and then later managed to make an accommodation with the *najashi*. However, Tabari was writing some centuries after the event, and is not necessarily reliable; his source, Ibn Ishaq, does not mention any relationship between the *najashi* and Abreha (Guillaume 1955). Procopius, a contemporary of these events, says rather that after Abreha's coup, another army was sent to punish him, under a relative of Kaleb Ella Atsbeha, and that this army defected to Abreha's camp, killing their royal general (Procopius: ed. Dewing 1914). Abreha's assumption of command of the army, or at least of those parts of it which had remained in Arabia, far from the supervision of Aksum, was almost inevitable if the local leader (at that time Sumyafa' Ashwa', apparently a Himyarite by birth) was incompetent or for some reason disliked by the army, and the same thing often happened among generals in charge of the Roman legions. It is interesting to note, however, that Tabari gives various reasons for Abreha's eventual submission to his overlord, including the fact that the army would not have supported him against the *najashi* himself (Zotenberg 1919: 187). Whilst military power in the hands of any subject must have been a possible threat, the reserving of it in the royal family, though impossible to guarantee, must usually have seemed the safest course.

Delegation of authority was an evident necessity as the state expanded, and royal resposibilities for defence and administration became strained. The custom of confirming local rulers was one way of responding to this. Kirwan saw the 'archons' known from a sixth century account of Aksum as indicating an organised civilian administration on the Byzantine model, in contrast to the regime of petty kings under a supreme monarch (Kirwan 1972: 171). They may, in fact, be those same kings under a new title, and it is, after all, only the Byzantine subject Kosmas who gives them the Byzantine title 'archon'. Malalas' use of the title, as a comparative term when describing the chariot of king Kaleb, seems to refer to the Byzantine archons, rather than to Ethiopian ones (Kobishchanov 1979: 220; Munro-Hay 1980: 151). It is not known whether Aksumite soldiers formed garrisons in the provincial towns, but in cases where there was some uncertainty it would seem a likely form of check on the local rulers' loyalty.

Kosmas Indikopleustes mentions two archons or governors in his comments about Aksum during the reign of Kaleb Ella Atsbeha (Wolska-Conus 1968: 360, 368). These rulers both held extremely important posts in the political structure of the state, since they controlled vital links in the country's trade-system. The archon of Adulis, Asbas, was in charge of the port city, and the archon of the Agaw region controlled the gold trade of Sasu (perhaps Fazugli in modern Sudan) and was responsible for forwarding the caravans. These officials, if not members of his own family, or hereditary local 'kings', were certainly highly-trusted administrators in Kaleb's government. It may even be that Aksumite officials of this rank were appointed to supervise specifically 'Aksumite' interests in the regions alongside the hereditary local rulers themselves.

In general, then, the Aksumites arranged for the administration of the lands under their hegemony by appointing or confirming local rulers, and exacting tribute as a sign of dependence. Failure to pay this was an act of rebellion and a declaration of war against the *negusa nagast*. One inscription bluntly outlines the Aksumites' political philosophy on the matter; *"those who obeyed, he spared; those who resisted, he killed"* (Ch. 11: 5).

In the titulature of the Aksumite monarchs, the king is called the 'king of kings' (*negusa nagast* in Ge'ez, and *basileus basileon* in Greek). He claims authority over many other regions, some of which were not only far distant but evidently under strong governments of their own controlled by their own kings. These can scarcely have been under the authority of the 'king of kings' to any great degree. These kingdoms, such as Saba, Himyar, the Hadramawt in South Arabia, and African states such as that of the Noba, may have submitted in theory to Aksum, but very little, if any, real control can have been exerted except during actual campaigns, or where garrisons were left. This actually was the case in some South Arabian districts at times (a certain Sabqalum was possibly the resident of the *nagashi* in Najran; Jamme: 1962, 79, 319) but certainly not in all the three Arabian kingdoms mentioned.

The lesser chiefdoms or kingdoms nearer to the core of the Aksumite empire were controlled by the king's peripatetic expeditions. These seem to have been designed as tribute-collecting tours combined with a parade of the king's military might to overawe anyone inclined to withhold their dues. Oddly enough, 'rebellions' seem to have been quite a frequent feature (see Ch. 11: 5 for the texts of the inscriptions which mention these), but the Aksumite cities and towns show no apparent concern with defence. Possibly these rebellions were extremely localised, and for a good part of the time were easy to deal with. Aksumite military organisation seems to have been mobile and efficient, and very likely the occupants of the Aksumite heartland had little to fear from these rebels against the state. Some, like the Agwezat, appear in the fourth century as dutiful subjects under their king SWSWT, bearing gifts to the Aksumite king Ousanas (? DAE 8), then as rebels against Ezana (? DAE 9) under king Abba 'Alkeo, and later in the sixth century needed to be 'pacified' by Kaleb as well in a campaign which he undertook against both them and the Hasat people (Schneider 1974). The inscription of Kaleb, later revered as both a Christian king and saint, proudly details the numbers of men, women and children captured or killed. Ezana is supposed to have boasted – if the inscription is correctly translated (see Ch. 11: 5, DAE 9)- that he seized the Agwezat king and chained him, naked, with his 'throne-bearer'. In many cases these rebellions are recorded as being led by the local kings, who, of course, failed in their bid for independence in all the instances recorded by the pro-Aksumite writers of the inscriptions. The Tsarane tribe of Afan was among those who were the object of one of Ezana's campaigns, ostensibly as a punishment for interfering with a trade caravan. Their ruler was captured with his children and his people were severely dealt with. Punishment for rebellion could be death, captivity (resulting possibly in sacrifice -or presentation to the gods as a gift- or slavery), and sometimes transportation to another area. Ezana transported six Beja kings and their tribes, but the numbers given (a total of 4400) show that these tribes were relatively small units (DAE 4, 6 & 7 and Geza 'Agmai). The many lesser chiefdoms or kingdoms mentioned in the inscriptions were not considered to be of sufficient importance to warrant inclusion in the king of kings' titulature.The Aksumite system of ruling through existing tribal authorities must, in its way, have simply encouraged the spirit of independence among the subject peoples. Since their identity as separate peoples was not lost, weaknesses in the Aksumite state, or difficult moments such as the death of an Aksumite king and a disputed succession could always give rise to attempts to shake off the yoke. The inscription DAE 8, with its preamble referring to the king's 're-establishment' of his empire, may have resulted from a new king's need to demonstrate visibly his assumption of power. Possibly the regency of Ezana's mother explains why Ezana had to spend some time in re-integrating his kingdom after attaining his majority; regencies for child-rulers were often dangerous periods in the life of a kingdom. Nevertheless, eventually the smaller population groups lost their former separate identities, became absorbed in the larger polity, and with this assimilation disappear from Ethiopian history.

2. Officials of the Government.

High officials with 'ministerial' rank are almost unknown. One most unusual example was Frumentius, the future bishop of Aksum. After his capture he rose by his intelligence and application to the rank of controller of the royal exchequer and correspondence; a sort of finance minister and secretary. Nevertheless, he remained a prisoner, if not actually a slave, in the royal household. Only when the king died, did he and his relative Aedesius gain their freedom to leave if they wished, and he himself remained in Aksum to become more or less prime-minister to the queen-regent, according to the historian Rufinus (ed. Migne 1849). Rufinus got his information from Aedesius, who was with Frumentius at Aksum; but it is of course not impossible that he exaggerated Frumentius' importance. Frumentius is the only known figure who approaches the position occupied by the freedmen of the Roman Imperial government, who so often reached very high rank under certain emperors; but there may well have been other such men in the Aksumite administration.

Frumentius' position had been resigned when he eventually left the country, and must have been completely transformed when he returned as bishop or metropolitan of Aksum. In later times the church hierarchy may have included other bishops (such as Moses of Adulis, Ch. 10: 4) and a number of local appointees to ecclesiastical posts. Doubtless these ecclesiastics represented the real power of the church, since its head, the metropolitan or *abun*, was traditionally a Copt from Egypt, and they may have been able to use the organisation of the church in helping the civil administration to function. However, we have no information save the lists of metropolitans, and a few isolated details from the hagiographies, about the progress and influence of the church in Ethiopia in Aksumite times (see Ch. 10).

Nothing is known of the other organs of government, except for inferences drawn from inscriptions and later literary references. For example, there seems to have been a body of traditional law, of which a few sections only survive. These are concerned with regulating the provisions due to the king on visits, according to the Safra inscription (Drewes 1962). This seems to date to the third century AD, and could refer to the *negusa nagast* or to a local king. It does at least indicate that there was some sort of written legal code available. Some references allude to nobles and ecclesiastics surrounding or advising the king (Malalas: ed. Migne 1860; Guillaume 1955: 151–2), and a council of notables would not be at all unexpected. Ibn Hisham, mentioning the visits by representatives of the Quraysh tribe to Aksum, says that officials surrounding the *najashi* bore the title *shuyum*, with a gloss to explain the equivalent in Arabic, *al-aminuna*; minor chiefs called *shum*s have been concerned with the local administration of the country even into the twentieth century; the descendants of the Zagwé kings bore the title *Wagshum*.

Other glimpses of the administration of law and justice may perhaps be inferred from various oblique references or archaeological finds. Kosmas, describing the Adulis throne, comments that those condemned to death were, up to his day, executed in front of the throne; perhaps it was considered the symbol of the royal presence there (Wolska-Conus 1968: 378). The discovery of chained prisoners in dungeon-like rooms at Matara indicates punishment by imprisonment (Anfray 1963: 100, pls. LXI, LXXXI, LXXXII) and there is a note in Kosmas' work that the Semien mountains were a place of exile for those subjects condemned to banishment by the Aksumite king (Wolska-Conus 1968: 378).

There were certainly ambassadors, messengers and interpreters or translators to regulate the royal business, and they are mentioned by Malalas (ed. Migne 1860: 670; English translation in Sergew Hable Sellassie 1972: 138, after Smith 1954: 449–50). In addition, there must have been a corps of administrators, clerks, assessors and collectors of taxes, regulators of trade and market business such as weights and measures, and so forth, both at Aksum and other towns; but we know nothing about them as yet. From the extraordinary precision of the booty counts and prisoner tallies related in the inscriptions (Ch. 11: 5), the accounts clerks were evidently very efficient, and the inscriptions themselves reveal that some considerable pains were taken over recording precise details of chronology and events. The chronological details reveal that the Ethiopian calendar was in use by Ezana's time (Ch. 11: 5; Anfray, Caquot and Nautin 1970), and its use indicates that the inscriptions were meant to be very precise. Possibly, as in later times, there were official chroniclers for each reign.

There must presumably have been some sort of information system, perhaps a corps of messengers who were sent out to the peoples of the kingdom as required. The preparation of inscriptions in three scripts seems to reflect a desire to disseminate the official versions of the royal achievements to both native and foreign readers. However, the inclusion amongst the inscriptions of a version in Ge'ez written in an elaborated form of the South Arabian script with, sometimes, quite inappropriate use of the 'm'-ending (mimation) to the words to add an 'Arabian' touch, seems to show that these inscriptions were rendered into this script solely for prestige reasons, perhaps in imitation of the trilingual (Greek, Parthian and Sassanian) inscriptions in use in Persia. It can be imagined that an official with very much the same status as Frumentius, supervising the royal correspondence, might have had the task of drafting these inscriptions and preparing the Greek translations.

The coins were also part of the state propaganda. At first they were produced in all metals with Greek legends and were primarily aimed at foreigners who understood Greek. Later they became part of the bilingual efforts to disseminate information, many issues in silver and bronze being devoted to the Ge'ez-speaking *ahzab* (the peoples). By the fourth century the coins were used to convey messages from the central government in the form of mottoes, generally a different one for each issue (see Ch. 9). Once again, some high official must have decided the policy to follow with each new issue, and have approved the text and design before instructing the mint officials and die-engravers accordingly

Later Ethiopian tradition supplied a whole administrative hierarchy for the Aksumite rulers from Menelik onwards, starting with those sons of the elders of Israel who came with the first emperor to Aksum. Their titles and functions are detailed by the *Kebra Nagast* (Glory of Kings; Budge 1922: 62) and include generals (of troops, foot-soldiers, cavalry, the sea, and recruits), scribes (a recorder, scribe of the cattle, assessor of taxes), various priests, household and administrative officials (chief of the house, keeper of the decorations, bearer of the royal umbrella, administrator of the palace, chief of the royal workmen), and the judges of the palace and the assembly. A number of other titles occur in documents or copies of documents from the Zagwé and later periods (Ch. 7: 2). Whilst a good deal of this reflects the later administrative structure of the kingdom, such officials are to be expected earlier, though we have no actual proof of their existence from the Aksumite period.

VII

The Monarchy

1. The King and the State

It appears that to all intents and purposes, the Aksumite king was himself the embodiment of the state. This is emphasised on the coinage (see Ch. 9) where the image of the king appears on both the obverse and the reverse of the gold coins accompanied by his name and the title 'king of the Aksumites'. This sort of concentration on the king is most unusual, other coinages generally showing some symbolic representation of the state such as the image of Roma or specially chosen gods and goddesses, national symbols, or certain heraldic animals or birds. The only symbols permitted by the Aksumite kings to share their prominent position on the coins were the disc and crescent in pre-Christian times, and the cross after the conversion, unless the wheat or barley-stalks which appear on all gold coins and on some bronzes (Munro-Hay 1984i) may be regarded as some sort of badge representing the state.

In the pre-Christian period the king was considered to be the son of Mahrem, who was identified with Ares, the Greek god of battles. He was probably the special dynastic or tribal god of the Aksumites. This relationship would have enhanced the kings' position in the eyes of his subjects, raising him to a quasi-divinity which set him in a special category, apart from and above all other men. The Aksumite royal inscriptions emphasise the king as a dynamic figure, son of a deity, member of one of the Aksumite clans (see below, the 'Bisi'-title), the leader of his people as war-hero and conqueror, but also as judge and lawgiver.

It has been suggested that the title *negus* or *nagashi* originally denoted an official who was little more than a tax-gatherer for Sabaean colonial rulers. However, the whole concept of the Sabaean period in Ethiopia is now generally altered (Ch. 4: 1), and it seems that there was a true Ethiopian kingship as early as the time of the *mukarrib*s of D'MT and Saba (Drewes 1962; Schneider 1976i). The connecting links between these early rulers and the Aksumite kings are unfortunately missing from the archaeological record.

The pivotal position of the Aksumite king in the machinery of government must have meant that the personality of each individual who occupied the office had a strong influence on the character of the reign. There are very few

OUSANAS AV I

40. The Aksumite tiara and other items of regalia as seen on a drawing of a gold coin (d. 17mm) of king Ousanas.

glimpses of anything so personal; but we may perhaps suggest that Zoskales' interest in commercial profit and Greek literature, Ezana's predilection for military exercises and his qualities as a leader in war, and Kaleb's religious bent, do at least give some hints as to individual rulers' concerns.

2. The Regalia.

The kingship was thus of a sacred or semi-sacred character (for a study of this aspect in later times see Caquot 1957). On the coins the reigning monarch is depicted equipped with a regalia formed from various insignia whose significance is in some cases obvious, and in others obscure. The majority of the gold coins show the king wearing a magnificent tiara or arcaded crown on the obverse, and what seems to be a headcloth tied with a ribbon at the back on the reverse. From the presence of the same ribbon on the obverse as well, it may be inferred that this headcloth was also worn under the tiara. The headcloth (if it is so to be identified) is always shown with three gently curving lines radiating from a point at the king's forehead, possibly stretch-lines of the cloth, or possibly some sort of decoration, like an aigrette. It could be that the headcloth owes something to Meroitic antecedents, as some of the Meroitic kings are represented wearing a similar head-covering in their temple or tomb reliefs.

The tiara was not shown by king Endubis on his coins, which have only the headcloth on both obverse and reverse; but it does appear on the coins of Aphilas. Possibly, then, Aphilas was the first king for whom this elaborate tiara was made, though it may well have been in use considerably earlier. The earliest representations show it as consisting of an arcade of three arches separated by columns with bases and capitals (see drawings in Munro-Hay 1984). Surmounting this are four slender oval elements capped with discs, alternating with thin spikes. Such a crown is unique in contemporary iconography, and was doubtless an Aksumite invention based on a number of combined influences. The Roman radiate crown, the variety of complex headdresses of Egyptian type worn by the Meroitic kings, the Indian Kushan dynasty's crowns, or the tiaras and mural crowns of more or less contemporary Sassanian rulers of Persia like Ardashir I or Shapur I may have contributed to both the design and, more important, the idea of using such crowns.

41. A silver coin (d. 12mm) of king Aphilas of Aksum, showing the inlaid halo of gold around the king's head.

Perhaps most interesting of all, the style of the neighbouring Meroitic rulers' crowns was bequeathed to the so-called X-group rulers of Nubia, probably the same Noba who were in close proximity to, and sometimes vassals of, the Aksumite kingdom; and some of their crowns, in silver richly studded with carnelians, have actually been found on the skeletons of the rulers at their tombs at Ballana (Kirwan 1963: 62). We can thus show that the idea of these ornate crowns has very strong contemporary African parallels. It may yet be possible that one or more of the tombs at Aksum, whose excavation has only been briefly commenced, contains an example of the Aksumite tiara. A recent article by Bent Juel-Jensen (1989) notes some survivals of Aksumite royal headgear in illustrations in much later Ethiopian manuscripts.

As the Aksumite dynasty continued, the depiction of the crown grew simpler; the oval elements were reduced to three, and an arcade-less version appears, sometimes with a cross in the centre. Presumably the crown was at least partially made of metal, perhaps gold, or silver like the 'X-Group' crowns noted above. The crown and royal robes Kaleb is said to have sent to Jerusalem are supposed to have been valuable items; but the story only survives in a late record (Budge 1928: III, 914).

The idea has been advanced that the tiara was worn by the Aksumite king in his capacity of 'king of kings', whilst the headcloth would indicate his position as the 'king of the Aksumites' only. Alternatively, the two representations might indicate the rôle of the king in the different capacities of warlord or giver of peace (Munro-Hay 1978: 44; Anzani 1926: 22). An inlaid halo of gold surrounds the royal portrait on some silver and bronze coins, even in the Christian period, giving the portrait special prominence; on other coins the king's crown is gilded, but otherwise this honour is only shared by the cross.

In his hands the king holds a sword (rarely) or, more usually, a spear, sceptre, or short baton. In the fifth century the characteristic hand-cross appears. On the reverse of many gold coins the king carries an unusual object, possibly a fly-whisk or alternatively (or still as a fly-whisk) some sort of branch with berries. Some of the best examples show five branches or filaments, each with a little dot at the end. In a land-grant of the Zagwé king Lalibela's time (1225) the title of *aqabe tsentsen*, keeper of the fly-whisks, occurs (*Dictionary of Ethiopian Biography* 1975: 36), and in the later account of Zara Ya'qob's coronation, the *nebura-ed* of Aksum and the Tigray *makonnen* are mentioned as standing to left and right on the king's entry into Aksum waving olive-branches as fly-whisks; very evocative of this item of Aksumite regalia.

The kings are shown on their coins elaborately robed, at first in what seems to be a round-necked overgarment covering an under-robe, leaving the arms free. Sometimes what appear to be fringes are shown. Later, with the more frequent depiction of the facing bust, the robes are shown in different ways; most often with a central panel of horizontal lines on the chest flanked by vertical lines over the shoulders, or in two or three panels containing the king's arm, a hand-cross held in front of the chest, or the lines of the drapery.

A Byzantine ambassador's report (see below) mentions that the ruler of Aksum wore much gold jewellery, and this is confirmed by the coins. The king appears lavishly bejewelled, almost always wearing earrings, bracelets and armlets on which the jewels are depicted by dots, sometimes necklaces, and very probably finger-rings (too small to appear on the coinage designs).

There is only one eye-witness description of an Aksumite king, that of Kaleb Ella Atsbeha as related by one of Justinian's ambassadors, whose words are preserved by the historian John Malalas (ed. Migne 1860: 670). The report – for what it is worth; some commentators see it as a more or less imaginary description (Schneider 1984: 162) – shows the kind of pomp with which these ancient rulers supported their position, and details a barbaric magnificence and ostentation. Kaleb appeared in a high car, decorated with golden wreaths, supported on a wheeled platform drawn by four elephants. These were doubtless the smaller African elephant, and just such an elephant quadriga is shown on gold staters of king Ptolemy I of Egypt long before; they are also mentioned in accounts describing some of the elaborate religious processions in Ptolemaic Alexandria, and were employed in Roman symbolism as well, appearing for example on coins commemorating the deified emperor Claudius, and on joint consular gold medals of the Roman emperors Diocletian and Maximian (Williams 1985: pl. 3). Kaleb was dressed in a linen garment, embellished with goldwork, apparently a kind of kilt, and his body was decorated with straps sewn with pearls, and much jewellery; more than five armlets, golden rings on his fingers, and a golden collar or necklace. His head was bound around with a 'phakhiolin' or little bandage, and this headgear was also decorated with gold; four streamers or pendants hung down from it on each side. He held gilded spears and a shield, and moved amongst armed nobles to the sound of flutes and chanting. This description has features in common with the 'portraits' (actually fossilised

'ARMAḤ AEI and IA

42. Drawing of two bronze coins (d. c. 2cm) of king Armah of Aksum, showing, on the obverse, the king seated on his throne.

representations which do not alter much from the time of the first issues) on the reverse of the gold coins.

The picture at Qusayr Amra (Almagro et al 1975), painted some 200 years later in the hunting-lodge of an Umayyad caliph, shows an Ethiopian *najashi* dating probably from the period after the abandonment of Aksum as the capital. He is part of a group including the most prominent of the rulers of the known world, often called the 'Enemies of Islam' fresco. The figure seems (the wall-painting is badly damaged) to be in the stiff, hieratic pose of a Byzantine emperor, and to be dressed in Byzantine-style jewelled robes. It is probably just the conventionalised idea of the *najashi* by an artist who had never seen him, but the figure does appear to wear the typical Aksumite headcloth, just as the neighbouring picture of the Persian king depicts him wearing the characteristic Persian tiara.

The throne is only shown on the coins of the late Aksumite king Armah. It appears to have been a tall-backed chair, with probably carved legs and rail supporting a seat. The back is sometimes shown doubled, with a design of dots perhaps showing a cushion; and often the whole chair is indicated by dots, giving a rather Jacobean turned-wood impression.

There is no record of the sort of ceremonial with which the Aksumite kings surrounded themselves, apart from the sixth-century description quoted above from Malalas, and some later descriptions of a royal audience from Arab accounts of the court of the *najashi* Ashama ibn Abjar (Guillaume 1955). The Byzantine ambassador knelt before Kaleb when he presented the *sacra* or rescript from Justinian, and the king kissed the seal before having the document read by the translator. Possibly the status of the rulers, already enhanced by the regalia and the impressive setting supplied by the palaces, was further emphasised by the requirement of the prostration from Aksumite subjects, as had become the custom in the newly recast Roman monarchy of

Diocletian and Maximian (Williams 1985: 111) and had long prevailed in Persia.

It may be expected that already in Aksumite times some of the familiar trappings of African kingship (and indeed of kingship in other places) may have been in use in Aksum as they were in later times in Ethiopia. The umbrella is actually mentioned quite early, in the time of the Zagwé king Lalibela, though not as an attribute of the king but of the metropolitan bishop. Michael of Fuwa, newly arrived in Ethiopia, entered the royal city under an umbrella of cloth-of-gold with a jewelled top; five years later a brother of the Ethiopian queen usurped this privilege and began to go about under the umbrella of state (Atiya et al. 1950: 184ff). It may be valid to assume that this privilege was originally a royal one, perhaps dating even from Aksumite times. Another feature of later Ethiopian kingship was the use of drums; local rulers had the right to have drums beaten before them when travelling, and the royal drum 'Hyena and Lion' was beaten at the coronation (Ch. 7: 6). Again, we may imagine that this custom had earlier origins, and may have originated in Aksumite royal ceremonial.

3. Dual kingship

The suggestion that some Aksumite kings took colleagues on the throne has already been mentioned. The examples of this practise, frequent in the Roman and South Arabian ruling dynasties, might have encouraged the kings to hope that such a system could help overcome succession crises and make the king's day to day tasks in ruling an ever-expanding empire somewhat easier.

However, the evidence for this theory is very tenuous indeed. In some ways, the idea of dual kingship seems alien to the spirit of Aksumite monarchy as far as we know anything about it. Were both monarchs regarded as 'sons of Mahrem', for example, or was the duality, if it existed, really only the recognition of a successor during a senior ruler's lifetime, and purely an arrangement for the legitimate transmission of power? In this case, would only the senior partner be represented on the coins and use the titulature?

The first occasion when dual monarchy can be suggested is in the third century in the inscription mentioning Datawnas and Zaqarnas from al-Mis'al (Robin 1981). The idea is based on the use of the dual term, 'the two kings of Aksum'. The inscription remains unpublished and is therefore not yet available for study; and so the question must rest as to whether these kings actually ruled contemporaneously or in succession.

The second possibility for dual kingship is that raised by the bi-regnal issue of a silver coin of Wazeba and Ousanas (Anzani 1941: Munro-Hay 1978 and 1984ii; Hahn 1983). The production of such an issue could have been an accident, but this seems unlikely since the three known specimens are all from different dies, and such accidents are otherwise unknown. It could have been a deliberate issue of two jointly reigning kings, Wazeba presumably the senior, since the obverse die is his. Or it could have been produced by confusion in the mint where the dies of two jointly-reigning kings were being used simultaneously. There may be some political problem concealed in this issue; Wazeba presumably did not last for long, since he is otherwise known from only a single gold coin and a not-very-common silver issue, whereas all the other kings of the period are much better represented by the types of coins they issued and the numbers so far recorded.

An interesting conundrum, also touched on above, is posed by the status of Sazana, Ezana's brother. The numismatist Wolfgang Hahn, the chief proponent of the dual-kingship theory, has suggested (1983) that Sazana was a co-ruler of Ezana, and identifies some of the coins bearing the name Ousana as his. However, the sole documents which might justify this are the address of the Roman emperor Constantius II's letter to the two princes of Aksum (Szymusiak 1958), and the much later tradition whereby two brothers, Abreha and Atsbeha, were on the throne at the time of the conversion of Ethiopia to Christianity. The first of these documents is only a copy of the letter preserved in the writings of Athanasius of Alexandria; and even if the letter is an accurate copy, we have no means of knowing how well-informed the Roman chancery was about the Ethiopian sovereign and his family. The second is so late a tradition that it is of very dubious value, and another explanation has been given for the names Abreha and Atsbeha (see Ch. 10: 3). Ezana alludes to his brother Sazana in his inscriptions, but he neither accords him any special titles, nor does he differentiate him from the other brother, Hadefan, who is also mentioned. Finally, it is not considered that the numismatic suggestion has sufficient value to strengthen the proposal (Munro-Hay 1984ii).

Another possible dual reign is again suggested by the coinage. The kings Nezana and Nezool both have gold issues, which are, in terms of modern recovery figures, commoner for Nezool than for Nezana. On the other hand Nezana has a silver issue while Nezool does not (so far). On Nezana's silver appears a monogram, NZWL, or Nezool. The tentative interpretation of this is that Nezool was the chief partner in a dual reign, issuing gold in his own name, whilst his partner Nezana issued the lesser metal but also added his senior's monogram. On Nezool's death, Nezana issued his own gold, even employing one of Nezool's obverse dies with his own reverse (Munro-Hay 1984ii). However, the much enlarged selection of these coins supplied by the al-Madhariba hoard (Munro-Hay 1989ii) shows the condition of the die as worsening from Nezana to Nezool, and the situation could well be reversed.

The inscription of Sumyafa' Ashwa', appointed by Kaleb as king of Himyar, refers to 'the kings of Aksum', using the plural forms *nagast* and *amlak* (Ch. 4: 7; Ryckmans 1946). Since coins of Kaleb and Alla Amidas are die-linked (Munro-Hay 1984ii), it seems possible that the latter was co-opted

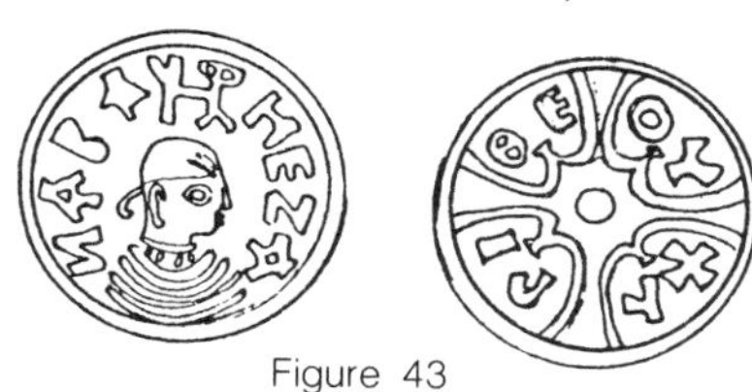

Figure 43

43. The obverse of a silver coin of king Nezana of Aksum shows the monogramme of Nezool above his head.

by Kaleb, (conceivably when Kaleb began to turn his attention to South Arabia), and that it is to these joint monarchs that Sumyafa' Ashwa' refers. However, the inscription, which is much damaged, mentions only Ella Atsbeha by name, and may simply refer to the Aksumite crown in general terms. The question is interesting in that Kaleb is the only one of the coin-issuing Aksumite monarchs who is thought to have left Africa for some considerable time, if we can believe the various accounts of the Himyarite war (Shahid 1979), and, under such circumstances, he would surely have needed to arrange a regency in his absence to deal with the day-to-day running of the kingdom.

Finally, again on numismatic grounds, Dr. Hahn has suggested that the kings Ioel, Gersem and Hataz all reigned together. Once again, the numismatic evidence, though interesting, is not conclusive enough to show beyond doubt that these three were joint rulers.

To sum up, the suggestion of dual kingship, plausible enough as a theory, seems conceivable for Wazeba/Ousanas, Nezana/Nezool, and Kaleb/Alla Amidas, but is not very convincing otherwise.

4. Succession.

Determining the nature of the succession is difficult. Though it might be expected that the monarchy was hereditary in a particular family following the system of primogeniture in the male line, this is not absolutely certain. Nor do we know if, as seems likely in so long a period, there were changes of dynasty. We know the names of sons of the third-century *nagashi*s Gadarat and 'Adhebah, respectively Baygat and Garmat, but they do not appear under those names elsewhere. Ezana's father was Ella Amida; but nowhere in the inscriptions is it stated that he was a king, although the 'Ella' element allows us to suppose that he was, and Rufinus (ed. Migne 1849: 479) confirms that the child-king who was later converted to Christianity, and who is usually identified as Ezana, succeeded his father. A ring of truth is given to this supposition by the fact that Ezana had to undertake a series of campaigns in Ethiopia and neighbouring countries in his early years, perhaps the result of neglect during a long minority under a regency in a system of tributary control such as the Aksumite. Ezana's assumption of his majority under such difficult circumstances, when he needed to set out immediately on campaigns to secure his kingdom, may also partly explain his continued use of pagan phraseology in his inscriptions; the result of a delay from practical causes in announcing his new religion.

The sequence Tazena-Kaleb-Wa'zeb follows from father to son, but in fact only the later hagiographies and king lists call Tazena a king, naming his father as another Ella Amida. Only for Wa'zeb, therefore, do we have primary evidence from Aksumite documents for hereditary succession on the throne. In spite of this paucity of evidence, the flourishing urban society of Aksum, with its prosperous trade and lack of defensive installations seems to indicate that the transmission of power was relatively stable over a considerable period.

The basic idea of the hereditary succession in Ethiopia is confirmed by Ibn Ishaq's biography of the prophet Muhammad, as preserved, though sometimes altered, abbreviated, and annotated, in the works of such later historians as Ibn Hisham and Tabari (Guillaume 1955: Introduction). The story as given in this source is very interesting from the point-of-view of late Aksumite history (Guillaume 1955: 153ff). It is reputed to have been told by 'Aisha, one of the prophet's wives. The future *najashi* was apparently the only son of his father and predecessor, who was murdered by certain Abyssinians in order to give the throne to his brother, who had twelve sons to guarantee the succession. He grew up and found favour with his uncle the new king, but the Abyssinians, frightened that he might yet become the next *najashi*, insisted on his exile. At this point the story becomes a little more embroidered; the future *najashi* is said to have been sold to a merchant, the reigning king to have been struck by lightning, and the twelve sons to have turned out to be too foolish to succeed. Inevitably, the *najashi* had to be brought back and finally triumphed. However unlikely some parts of this tale might seem, the assumption that the succession must rest in a certain family is interesting. The Chinese account of the life of Muhammad (Mason 1921) noted above (Ch. 4: 7), claims that the ruler whose accession to the Ethiopian throne occurred in c577 was the grandson of a certain 'great king', and that he was in due course succeeded by his own grandson, thus suggesting a descent in the same family for five generations without excluding the possible succession of brothers.

5. The Royal Titles.

The formal protocol of the Aksumite kings on their inscriptions is interesting both as an indication of which titles the Aksumite rulers decided, for one reason or another, to adopt, and as a guide to the official version of the kingdom's status at different periods. However, so far we only know the form of the titulary from widely separated instances, in the inscriptions of Ezana, Kaleb and Wa'zeb (see Ch. 11: 5). Ezana's titles are, on his pagan inscription in Greek, (DAE 4), *'Aeizanas, king of the Aksumites, the Himyarites, Raeidan, the Ethiopians, the Sabaeans, Silei (Salhen), Tiyamo, the Beja, and Kasou, king of kings, son of the unconquered Ares'*. The version written in the

Epigraphic South Arabian script (DAE 6) reads in the order *Aksum, Himyar, Raydan, Habashat, Saba, Salhen, Tsiyamo, Kasu, and the Beja*, and the Ge'ez version (DAE 7) reads *Aksum, Himyar, Kasu, Saba, Habashat, Raydan, Salhen, Siyamo, Beja*; both of these add the phrase *'king of kings, son of the unconquered Mahrem'*. There does not seem to be any particular anxiety over the order of the states mentioned, nor is precedence always given to Arabian or African names; however, the general outline of the majority of the inscriptional titularies seems to prescribe Aksum, Arabia and Africa in that order. On Ezana's other inscriptions he gives the filiation *Ella Amida*, and the title *Bisi Halen*, or *Alene*, and mentions that he is the son of Ares/Mahrem or, in the case of his Christian inscription, the servant of Christ. The inscription DAE 8 may not be of Ezana (to whom it was attributed by Littmann) but of his predecessor, possibly Ousanas. It appears to read '[Ousanas?] Ella Amida, Bisi [Gi]sene...' but this reading cannot at present be checked; the order of the countries following is the same as in DAE 4 but omits Habashat.

The next inscriptions preserved date from over 150 years later. Kaleb's inscription gives the protocol *'Kaleb Ella Atsbeha, son of Tazena, Bisi Lazen, king of Aksum, Himyar, Dhu Raydan, Saba, Salhen, the High Country and Yamanat, the Coastal Plain, Hadramawt, and all their Arabs, the Beja, Noba, Kasu, Siyamo, DRBT...and the land of ATFY(?)', servant of Christ'*. The South Arabian section of this is exactly that expanded form adopted in the later fourth century by Abukarib As'ad and employed by his successors in the region, including the Ethiopian usurper Abreha himself. The inscription of Wa'zeb more modestly only names *Aksum, Himyar, Dhu Raydan, Saba, Salaf (Salhen), Beja, Kasu, Tsiyamo, WYTG*. Wa'zeb also calls himself *'son of Ella Atsbeha, Bisi Hadefan'*, and *'servant of Christ'*. His titulary thus reverts to the older form employed by Ezana (and out of use in Arabia even at that time) for the overseas section, abandoning his father's more elaborate Arabian claims.

The titulary of an Aksumite king therefore consisted of several separate elements; the personal name, the 'Ella'-name, the 'Bisi'- name, a real or divine filiation, certain epithets, and then the enumeration of territories.

The personal name is often, in the case of the Christian kings, a biblical name. Apart from Kaleb, these are only known from the coinage.

The name preceded by 'Ella', meaning 'he who...' is an epithet, probably employed after the king's accession or coronation as his reign title or throne name. Kaleb's name Ella Atsbeha, for example, means 'he who brought forth the dawn'. Ezana's 'Ella'-name is unknown; possibly he could have used one or more, giving rise to the legend of 'Abreha and Atsbeha' as the rulers of Ethiopia in Frumentius' time. Such throne names might have been changed at times by kings anxious to commemorate some special feature of their reign.The 'Bisi' element, meaning 'man of...' may refer to a clan division in the royal family, or possibly to a military regiment with which he was especially connected. Among regimental names mentioned in the inscriptions there are a few which resemble the 'Bisi' names of one or other of the kings. The 'Bisi'-title is not available for all the kings, but is attested from Endubis to Wa'zeb, a period of over two hundred and fifty years, and later for Lalibela. These are the known examples;

Endubis Bisi Dakhu.
Aphilas Bisi Dimele.
WZB B'SY ZGLY (Zagalay?)
Ousanas Bisi Gisene.
Ezana Bisi Alene, Alen, or Halen.
Eon Bisi Anaaph.
KLB...B'S LZN (Lazen?).
W'ZB B'S HDFN (Hadefan?).
Lalibela be'esi 'azzal (but see below).

François de Blois has recently (1984) proposed a credible solution to the problem of the 'Bisi'-title. He suggests that the clan system in ancient Aksum was matrilineal, and thus each succesive ruler bore his mother's clan-name. These clans were also the basis of the military organisation, hence the coincidence of certain 'Bisi' names with certain regiment names.

All the kings known from inscriptions give their patronymic or filiation, and Kaleb does so on his coins as well. The custom was probably a usual one in Ethiopian society of the time, and is found also used in the inscriptions of the *hatseni* Danael, son of Dabra Ferem (see Ch. 15). In the twelfth-thirteenth century we have some of the elements of a titulary from the reign of Lalibela, the great Zagwé king. The *History of the Patriarchs*, which usually just refers to the kings anonymously, calls him Lalibala son of Shanuda ('the Lion') of the race of al-Nakba. Other sources add his throne-name, Gabra Masqal, and an epithet, *be'esi 'azzal*, 'the strong man', which resembles one of the earlier 'Bisi'-titles (Atiya et al 1950: III, III, 184ff; Conti Rossini 1901:188).

Given the nature of the Aksumite 'imperial' hegemony, with independent states bound in a loose federation only by their more or less theoretical subordination to the Aksumite *negusa nagast*, the territorial elements of the titulary do seem to represent fact rather than fiction. One hint in support of this assertion is that while Wa'zeb abandoned his father Kaleb's reference to the Hadramawt and the highland and coastal areas of the Yemen, the contemporary king in South Arabia, Abreha, continued to employ them in his own titulary. Procopius (ed. Dewing 1914: 191) tells us that Abreha agreed to pay tribute to Kaleb's successor and was thus recognised as tributary king, and perhaps some adjustment of the titulary was effected at the same time. The Aksumite version of the title was always different from that used in Arabia, naming both Raydan and Salhen, which refer to the chief castles or citadels of the two states Himyar and Saba respectively. Though the names of the castles or palaces are used in a treaty preserved in the inscription CIH 308 (Jamme 1962: 294) where Salhen and Zararan (Gadarat's palace) are both mentioned, presumably as the two seats of government of the signatories, the Arabian inscriptions never use the parallelism of country and palace in the Aksumite way.

An example of alterations in the titulary to suit events, but sometimes with the retention of traditional phraseology, occurs after Ezana's conversion to Christianity. It has already been noted (Ch. 6: 1) that Ezana abandoned the claim to be the 'son of the invincible Mahrem/Ares', replacing it on the inscription DAE 11 (Ch. 11: 5) with the very similar phrase 'son of Ella Amida, never defeated by the enemy', using his father's name to replace that of Mahrem although he had already used the phrase 'son of Ella Amida' a line or two earlier. The Greek version of this text reads 'son of Ella Amida, servant of Christ', an epithet also used much later by Wa'zeb 'son of Ella Atsbeha, servant of Christ', while Kaleb's inscription puts his filiation earlier, but still uses the old locution, completing the titles with 'servant of Christ, who is not defeated by the enemy'.

Among the African territories included in the titulary, Siyamo (Tsiyamo, Tiamo) seems to have comprised the eastern part of the Ethiopian plateau; perhaps the Enderta region of Tigray. The name may be a derivative of D'MT, the old kingdom which existed there in the middle of the first millenium BC. It is probably the same as the Tiamaa of the *Monumentum Adulitanum*, associated with Gambela, "a valley in the neighbourhood of Makale, in the province of Enderta" by Kirwan 1972: 173. The lands of WYTG, DRBT, and ATFY are districts (presumably African) whose whereabouts are as yet unknown. Schneider (1988: 115) notes a region called SRD, mentioned only on the Geza 'Agmai versions of DAE 6 and 7 (Ch. 11: 5). The Beja are the tribes of the Red Sea hills, the Noba the peoples of the Nubian kingdoms, and the Kasu the Kushites or Meroites. Finally, the term Ethiopia, employed as a translation for Habashat among the known inscriptions only by Ezana on DAE 4, appears for the first time in a Ge'ez manuscript (accompanied by the first such mention of Aksum itself) only in the twelfth century; though the text can only be tentatively dated (Sergew Hable Sellassie, 1989).

6. The Coronation.

Whilst there are no contemporary accounts of the Aksumite coronation ritual, it is interesting to learn how the later 'Solomonic' kings exploited the religious and historical prestige of the ancient site, by making it their ceremonial coronation place. Information can be assembled from different accounts of the coronations, such as those of Zara Ya'qob (1434-68) and Sartsa Dengel (1563-97), preserved in the royal chronicles (Perruchon 1893). The coronation of Susenyos on 18th March 1608 was described by the Spaniard Pedro Paez from the eye-witness account of João Gabriel, the Portuguese captain (Pais 1945-6: 115ff). The ceremony was accompanied by great pageantry, the king arriving with some 25,000 infantry and 1500 cavalry, riding a richly caparisoned steed, himself garbed in crimson damask with a golden chain around his neck.

Zara Ya'qob is the first king who is known to have resurrected the ancient coronation ceremony at Aksum – or, at least, who is known to have employed the sacred precincts as his coronation place, and who accordingly may be suggested to have exploited ancient rituals of Aksumite origin. The king would first of all distribute largesse by flinging gold amongst the crowd as he processed over rich carpets laid out on the streets from the entrance of the town to the cathedral area. Then, he would be seated on the coronation throne (one of the Aksumite stone thrones) for the actual ceremony. On other occasions he would take his place on a different throne for the blessing ritual; this one was flanked by the thrones of the twelve judges in the main group of thrones. There was also one destined for the metropolitan.

The ritual itself was as follows. As the king approached the cathedral, the priests, singing the chants composed by the legendary sixth-century musician-priest Yared, declared 'May you be blessed, O king of Israel'. The 'daughters of Zion' (the young women of Aksum) gathered in two rows on either side of the pathway near one of the Aksumite inscriptions to the east of the cathedral. The women stood to the left and right of the road holding a cord, with two older women holding swords. As the king's horse approached, the women questioned arrogantly 'Who are you, and of what tribe and family?' The king answered, 'I am the son of David, the son of Solomon, the son of Ibn Hakim (Menelik)'. A second and third time the king was questioned, and on these occasions replied with his real genealogy. He then used his sword to cut the cord, while the older women declaimed ' Truly, you are the king of Zion, the son of David, the son of Solomon'. Then the king was seated on the coronation throne, spread with precious cloths for the occasion; the throne was called 'the throne of David'. During the ceremonies the king also took on a new name, the throne-name, which, like the Aksumite 'Ella'-name, was an epithet often with a religious implication. Apparently they were chosen randomly from tablets inscribed with a selection of different names. Very probably the Aksumite rulers adopted their throne-names in the course of similar coronation ceremonies.

In addition, certain other ceremonies are mentioned, such as the leading in of a lion and a buffalo for the king to kill (Zara Ya'qob set his lion free, and his son Baeda Maryam did the same – though not at Aksum, but at Jejeno in Amhara, during a tonsuring ceremony – getting someone else to kill the buffalo). This doubtless theoretically served as a test of the strength of the king, harking back to beliefs in the identity of ruler and state; a strong ruler could protect his country against outside foes. Another ceremony involved the use of milk, mead, wine and water in an anointing ritual.

Among the Portuguese visitors to Ethiopia, both Paez and de Almeida devoted some space to the coronation ceremonies, using information derived not only from contemporary coronations, but also from the *Kebra Nagast*, the 'Glory of Kings', the oldest surviving collection of traditions in Ethiopia, probably codified at the end of the thirteenth century. The following description comes from Chapter XXII of de Almeida's book (Beckingham and Huntingford 1954: 92ff);

> *"How the Emperors are crowned in this place.*
>
> *This is the way in which the Emperor is crowned here. He arrives at Acçum and encamps in a very big meadow there. When the coronation day arrives he orders his army to be arrayed so that everyone should accompany him with the proper ceremony. The infantry goes in front, divided into different squadrons, the cavalry comes behind them, and the Emperor at the end, accompanied by the greatest lords...in their richest and best clothes...He approaches this place on the eastern side, and reaches the stone which..has an inscription"*

(according to the chronicle of Sartsa Dengel, *"the name of this place is Mebtaka Fatl, cutting of the cord"*; (Conti Rossini 1907: 89; also de Villard 1938: 63)

> *"Here the Abuna and all the clergy were awaiting him....the grandees dismount and range themselves in two rows...leaving a wide path between which is covered with large, rich carpets. The Emperor too dismounts and walks over the carpets but is met and stopped by three maidens whom they call maidens of Zion"*

(here follows the ritual of the challenges to the emperor and the final cutting of the cord, and, according to Sartsa Dengel's chronicle, musical instruments were sounded, above all the royal drum *Deb Anbasa*, 'Hyena and Lion'.)

> *"The Emperor scatters on the carpets many grains of gold which are picked up by those to whom this privilege belongs by ancient custom.*
>
> *The first enclosure of the church is the one in which...are some seats which were formerly, and still at the time when Father Alvares came to this country, twelve very well-made stone chairs, as he recounts in his book. Today there are no chairs and the bases or pedestals on which they stood are not as many. The four columns that I mentioned above (see Ch. 5: 3) seem formerly to have supported a vault. In the centre of them they decorate two pedestals with rich cloths and handsome chairs and the ground at the foot is carpeted. The Emperor sits here on one of the two chairs, the Abuna on the other. At the sides twelve dignitaries, some ecclesiastical, some secular, take their places, six on the right, six on the left. I shall describe them in the exact words of the book of these ceremonies that is kept in the same church at Acçum".*

(here follows an account from the *Kebra Nagast* of the officials bringing oil in a gold box for the anointing, holy water, a stick with a silk cord for keeping the people at a distance, the state umbrella, *'wild and domestic animals that can be eaten'*, fruits and edible seeds, milk, wine, water, mead, herbs, and perfumes, as well as the altar stone, the royal horse, and the royal mule. There were also brought in varieties of antelopes, a buffalo, a wild goat, and a lion, offerings from various districts. Songs, some in praise of the king, were chanted – apparently an innovation which Yared recommended to king

Gabra Masqal in the sixth century - and readings from the Old and New Testaments followed.)

> *"Then the people present go once round the place where the royal chair is, and throw flowers and perfumes upon it.....a lion and a buffalo are at hand, tied to columns; the king strikes the lion with his lance; then they release the other animals, tame and wild, and all the birds. The people of the camp kill all those they can catch for a feast.*
>
> *As the king comes to the place where his chair is he throws gold on the carpets. When he sits down they bring two plates of gold and two of silver. On the gold plates are milk and honey wine, on the silver water and grape wine. Then they anoint the king in accordance with custom, sprinkle all the ceremonial objects with water they have from the river Jordan, and cut the hair of the king's head as for clergy in the first tonsure. The clergy take up the hairs, the deacons continue to sing at the altar stone with lighted candles and the clergy cense with their thuribles. After going once round the place where the royal chair is, as though in procession, they go towards a stone which stands at the door of the church of Sion, called Meidanita Neguestat, i.e. protector of the Kings. They put the hairs on it and light them from the thuribles..".*

(Finally the ecclesiastics and the *abun* blessed the king after he had been into the church, and the ceremony was at an end).

This description of the mediaeval ritual of coronation in Ethiopia shows that a number of different strands were woven into the fabric of the ceremony. Doubtless some of these hark back to Aksumite times and pre-Christian observances. Some of these rituals may have originated in fertility rites, or were designed to affirm the king's strength, often traditionally connected with the well-being of the country he rules. The killing of wild beasts may be a survival from a royal hunt in which the king's courage and force could be demonstrated; if so, it appears to have been much watered-down in later times. Certain aspects of the ceremonies do have a Christian flavour, but others, like the burning of the hair, seem designed as protective rites. The scattering of gold shows the king as a dispenser of wealth, and the presentation of various wild animals not only gives the king the chance to release them in a merciful gesture (also benefitting the people who catch and eat them), but affirms his control of the different provinces whose special tribute they are. The donation to the king of agricultural products perhaps symbolises the tribute due to him, and also reinforces his position as ruler and dispenser, and alludes to his rôle in ensuring the land's fertility. The ritual of cutting the cord affirms his legitimate descent through the recent kings right back to the very founders of the kingdom, while the presence of the *abun* and church hierarchy, the army and nobles, confirms their acceptance of his right to rule. Some elements, familiar in the panoply of African monarchy, like the parasol and the state drum, can easily be imagined as heirlooms from the Aksumite tradition, though no contemporary reference to them survives; in some monarchical traditions the royal umbrella, and the laying of carpets when the king walks, are used to protect the king from the sun and the earth, contact with either being presumed to dissipate his essential force to the detriment of the land he rules.

The Ethiopian mediaeval coronation ritual as a whole, the last trace of Aksum's former function as the capital of the country, allows us to see the ruins of the city's monuments, through the eyes of the Portuguese and the native chroniclers, as a living and vital part of the mediaeval Ethiopian monarchy's most important ceremony.

VIII

The Economy

1. Population

An important factor in the economic development of the Aksumite state would have been its demographic history. Kobishchanov (1979: 122-5), in his discussion about Aksumite population, somewhat adventurously concluded that the largest towns, including Aksum, were, *'judging by the area they occupied'* to be *'numbered in thousands or a few tens of thousands of persons'*, and that the population of the whole Aksumite kingdom without Arabia and Nubia, was *'at the outside half a million'*. This was presumably based on available archaeological evidence. It has been mentioned above that a survey conducted by Joseph Michels in 1974 revealed a concentration of population in the immediate area around Aksum, where he identified eight 'culture historical phases' (Ch. 3: 3). His plans (Kobishchanov 1979: 24; Michels 1988) show many large and small élite residences, which he identified as belonging to the phases within the Aksumite period, but the entire city plan for any one period is not available. Accordingly, no valid population estimates can be made.

There is in reality little evidence which allows us to even try to estimate Aksumite urban populations. We cannot really judge population from the size of the towns, since their peripheral areas, where we may suppose a considerable number of people would be concentrated in contrast to the probably more sparsely-populated élite areas, were doubtless occupied by impermanent dwellings untraceable without excavation. Though such areas can be partially identified archaeologically by surface collection of sherds and so forth, this has only been done for Aksum, with the results shown on Michels' survey plan. From the chronological point of view, Michels (1986) considered that some of the élite residences behind Enda Kaleb dated from a late period in Aksumite history when the capital had been *'reduced to a loose cluster of villages'*. In earlier times the town would not have extended so far, and only after much more concentrated archaeological investigation can we expect to assemble an accurate picture of the town's various expansion phases over the centuries. Nevertheless, the general impression of the capital resulting from Michels' survey is of a town of considerable size, containing a corresponding population.

Doubtless the same applies to Adulis and Matara, where excavations have revealed sizeable areas of settlement (Paribeni 1907; Anfray 1963; Anfray and Annequin 1965). We have no real information about the extent of the other Aksumite towns and villages known so far only by their few surviving stone monuments (Ch. 3: 4), but their very number seems to hint at a substantial population in certain areas of the country. A few foreigners' descriptions of Aksumite towns imply that they were of a fair size, an interesting observation when such visitors were, like Nonnosus (Photius, ed. Freese 1920), familiar with towns of the importance of Rome, Constantinople, Antioch or Alexandria. When the number of known Aksumite town or village centres is taken into account, without considering the supporting rural population whose local centres these were, the estimate of half a million at the outside for the whole kingdom seems perhaps too cautious, since whole regions of the former Aksumite kingdom have only been cursorily surveyed for archaeological sites, if at all. Manpower, particularly in the military and agricultural sectors, must ultimately have been one of the most important bases of Aksumite power, and perhaps it was with this in mind that Ezana took such pains over moving troublesome Beja groups from their traditional lands to Matlia, instead of simply destroying them (see Ch. 11: 5).

The rather better climatic conditions deduced by Butzer (1981) may indicate that the carrying capacity of the land was greater in earlier Aksumite times, especially if the methods of agriculture were reasonably sophisticated, and therefore sizable town populations could have been supported by the work of fewer food-producers than might be expected. But as yet our knowledge about such questions as agricultural methods and possibilities, or about the area of cultivated or cultivable land, and the availability of easy transport to enlarge each town's food-catchment area, is completely inadequate. The land-charters of later ages, and some which claim to be of Aksumite or just post-Aksumite date, give the impression that adequate records about the land had been compiled (Huntingford 1965), but unfortunately information which might lead to the preparation of population estimates based on statistics of hearths or families per village is lacking.

It is not beyond imagination that Aksumite government officials maintained some records about the numbers of the population. Some sort of census would have helped in estimating such matters as taxation returns, available labour for large projects, or the size of military musters, and the accounting machinery was certainly available. The inscriptions DAE 4, 6 & 7 (Ch. 11: 5), for example, detail the exact numbers of the Beja tribes being moved to Matlia, and record precise amounts of food supplied to them. The establishment of a church organisation in the country might further have encouraged population survey to some extent, as boundaries between parishes or dioceses were fixed. No extensive cemeteries, with their useful information on the people's diet, diseases and mortality, have been excavated, although the bones collected by Leclant (1959i) and de Contenson

44. Drawing of a bronze coin (d. c. 15mm) of king Aphilas of Aksum, showing a wheat stalk in the reverse field; on all the gold coins of Aksum two such stalks frame the king's head on the obverse.

(1959i) and Chittick (Munro-Hay 1989) may eventually supply some information on the people of Aksum through the centuries. The first two found bones conjectured to date from the seventeenth to the twentieth century, while Chittick cleared a few tombs, notably that called Shaft Tomb A, in the main cemetery, and a tomb near the Kaleb/Gabra Masqal building, which contained a number of bodies.

2. Agriculture, Husbandry and Animal Resources. Aksumite Ethiopia possessed a mainly agricultural and pastoral economy, and its geographical situation gave it access to an unusual variety of environments which could be seasonally exploited for crop growing or grazing (Connah 1987; Phillipson 1989). The agricultural resource base, depending on rainfall and soil quality, seems to have been of far richer potential in Aksumite times than today, according to the work of Butzer (1981). Although the decline of the Red Sea trade links removed Ethiopia from the Roman/Byzantine orbit, it still remained a relatively rich and powerful state, according to the Arab authors who occasionally mention the kingdom of the *najashi* (Ch. 4: 8). Much of this prosperity must have been due to the considerable agricultural and domestic and wild animal resources of the country, amplified by a certain amount of trade with the Arabs. The soils in the Aksum region may have suffered from excessive exploitation and erosion (though there are still some good farmlands in the area), but the rich lands to the south which were the heartland of the later Ethiopian kingdom were very fertile. Famine is apparently first noted in Ethiopia in the ninth century (Pankhurst 1961: 236 after Budge 1928: I, 275); the story of the metropolitan John of Ethiopia (Ch. 4: 8.3) in the patriarchates of James (819–830) and Joseph (830-849) of Alexandria, attributes Ethiopia's condition to war, plague, and inadequate rains (Evetts 1904: 508ff).

The existence of the dam at Qohayto (Littmann 1913: II, 149–52), and the basin Mai Shum at Aksum (Littmann 1913: II, 70–73) indicates that water conservation was practised (as was inevitable in a country linked so closely to South Arabia both culturally and in the nature of the environment). However, so far no excavations have been undertaken at these sites, and neither the dam nor the basin can be securely dated. Butzer (1981) suggested that there had been an earth dam set across the Mai Hejja in Aksum, perhaps to augment the flow of water into the Mai Shum basin, and there may have been another pond for water conservation at the foot of Mai Qoho hill (Ch. 5:3; Alvares, ed. Beckingham and Huntingford 1961: 155), but again neither have yet been investigated. In short, though control of water for agricultural and drinking purposes can almost certainly be posited for Aksumite times, we have no contemporary reports or archaeological evidence to indicate the level to which irrigation or water-conservation were actually employed in the Aksumite kingdom.

The importance with which at least one of the agricultural staples was regarded can be inferred by the depiction on all Aksumite gold coins of ears of bearded wheat or primitive two-row barley (both identifications have been proposed), acting as a frame for the head of the king. On some bronze coins, the wheat or barley-head is the sole motif on the reverse, and the important place accorded to it seems to indicate that it was the specially selected symbol of Aksum or its rulers. The inscription of Ezana about his Beja war (see Ch. 11: 5; DAE 4, 6 & 7 and Geza 'Agmai) shows that the kings had access to stores of food and were able to issue food rations on a substantial scale when necessary. The Safra inscription (Drewes 1962: pp. 30ff) appears to deal with special allotments of food for specific purposes, possibly on the occasion of the residence of the king in the area. Meat, bread and beer are the basic subsistence foods mentioned.

At the Gobedra rock-shelter very near Aksum, David Phillipson (1977) found evidence of finger millet apparently from pre-Aksumite times; but this has since turned out to be intrusive (Phillipson 1989). The Safra inscription appears to be the earliest mention of grain products such as beer, flour, and bread. Ethiopia's special native cereal, *eragrostis teff*, is not attested from Aksumite times, but, like wheat, barley and spelt, it is very likely to have been cultivated on the Ethiopian plateau where numerous ancient forms of these crops are found. So far no evidence from oven or platter types has been adduced from excavated material which might lead one to assume that the characteristic *injera*-bread made from teff, now a staple of the Tigray diet, was known in Aksumite times.

The Russian scientist N. I. Vavilov investigated Ethiopian wheat and barley, and found that the majority was grown on the high plateaux between 2000 and 2800m, while the late Ruth Plant added a note in an unpublished article that the distribution of wheat and barley-growing regions in the north of Ethiopia closely follows that of the distribution map of Aksumite sites. Vavilov considered that Ethiopia was the centre of origin for cultivated barley (but see Fattovich 1989ii: 85). However, it is also possible that cultivated wheat and barley entered the region long ago from perhaps Egypt, where they have been found in contexts dating to around the fifth millenium BC. In any event, the existence of these crops in Ethiopia from an early period supports the possibility that settled farming communities had long lived on the plateaux of Ethiopia, prior to the South Arabian influences in the country. The crops they farmed were bequeathed to their Aksumite successors, though, as noted above, the identity of the grain ears depicted on the coins is still disputed. It has been identifed as a primitive two-row barley (Munro-Hay 1978), and Vavilov (1931: 10), from coins brought from Ethiopia, identified it as a wheat, *triticum turgidum*, subspecies *abyssinicum Vavilov*. But the two coins he illustrates as 'Abyssinian coins' in his fig. 4 are, oddly enough, not Aksumite, but are bronze issues of early to mid 1st century Judaea, one dating to the time of Coponius (6-6AD) or Ambibulus (9-12AD), the other to the time of Agrippa I, c. 42AD. Such coins have not otherwise been found in Ethiopia.

A number of different animals are attested from the Aksumite period in Ethiopia. Inscriptions and literary references to Aksum mention cattle, sheep, camels, and elephants. The latter were apparently not usually trained by the Ethiopians, according to Kosmas (Wolska-Conus 1973: 354; see Pankhurst 1974: 219-220). When the king wanted some for show he had young ones taken to be brought up in captivity. Elephant tusks, adds Kosmas, were sent by ship to India, Persia, Himyar and the Roman empire. The 'pack animals' captured from the Tsarane of Afan (Ch. 11: 5; DAE 10) may have been donkeys or camels; camel bones and teeth were found at Adulis (Paribeni 1907: 451). Yoked (humpless) oxen are modelled in clay standing in the base of bowls found in some of the tombs at Aksum, possibly fashioned for some sort of religious purpose; humped cattle (zebu) figures come from Matara (Anfray 1967: 44–45), from the excavator's second Aksumite period (which he dates to the sixth-eighth centuries). Cattle on the hoof, with iron and salt, were used to barter with western neighbours for gold, according to Kosmas (Wolska-Conus 1968: 360), and most inscriptions tell of the seizure of large numbers of animals as plunder from defeated enemies (Ch. 11: 5). Inscriptions also note that some animals were used for sacrificial purposes, or at least presented to the gods (Ch. 11: 5; DAE 10). One or two pottery figures of birds exist from Aksumite times, and (with a little imagination) we can perhaps identify chickens and pigeons or doves (Chittick 1974: pl. XIIc; Paribeni 1907: fig. 48; Wilding in Munro-Hay 1989). Among wild animals the giraffe, taurelaphus (buffalo) and rhinoceros are mentioned by Kosmas (Wolska-Conus 1973: 314–321), the former being sometimes tamed and kept in the palace to amuse the king. The Ethiopian buffalo was wild, in contrast to that of India, where it was used as a beast of burden and supplier of milk. The rhinoceros was called the *aroue harisi*, apparently from Ethiopian words meaning wild beast and plough (Wolska-Conus 1973: 317 n. 2.1). The latter designation apparently referred both to the shape of its snout and the use to which its thick skin was put. Kosmas saw a wild one at a distance, and the stuffed skin of another in the royal palace. The monoceros or unicorn Kosmas admitted not having actually seen, but he did see four brass figures of him set up in the king's palace. The ibex, lion, and perhaps some species of deer or gazelle are depicted in Aksumite art forms (Ch. 13:

3). Two small bronze figures from Aksum are possibly dogs (Chittick 1974: fig. 23). A number of agricultural tools, notably a sickle, also came from tomb finds (Munro-Hay 1989). The pottery and glass beakers and goblets found in the tombs might have been used for the local beer, *sewa*, or the honey wine, *mes* or *tej*, which are mentioned in the ancient inscriptions dealing with the issue of rations. Oil (vegetable) and butter are also mentioned and wines and oils were noted in the lists of imports (see below). Local oils were probably derived from linseed and *nug*, and olive oil was imported. Wine or oil presses, with basins, channels and spouts carved in the rock, are known, which date to Aksumite times (Littmann 1913), but vines are only mentioned by the Portuguese in later centuries (Pankhurst 1961: 213).

3. Metal Resources.

Local exploitation of mineral resources is not well documented, but gold seems to have come from the Sudan (Sasu), some southern Ethiopian regions and possibly Gojjam, Eritrea, and the Beja country, and iron ore, silver, lead and tin are also mentioned, though mostly from Portuguese sources (Connah 1987: 72; Pankhurst 1961: 224–9).

The gold trade from the south is known from the sixth century (Kosmas, ed. Wolska-Conus 1968: 360–1), and reports about Ethiopia's wealth in gold reached ludicrous heights in later times (Pankhurst 1961: 224–7). Kosmas' story about the exchange of gold for iron, salt and cattle is supported by de Almeida's account (Beckingham and Huntingford 1954: 149) of gold obtained in his day from Cafraria (a general name for the lands extending from the southern kingdom of Enarya east to Malindi and west to Angola), where the Cafres exchanged it for clothing, cows, salt and other goods. Even when Bruce was in Ethiopia, gold from the south was exchanged for similar products, iron and copper, skins and hides, and beads (Pankhurst 1961: 227). Alvares (Beckingham and Huntingford 1961: 159–60, 457) was tempted to try his own experiments at gold-washing in Aksum, inspired by reports that much gold was found after storms. His attempts may have been doomed to failure through a misunderstanding; doubtless his informants referred to the finding of small gold objects, such as coins, rather than actual gold in the soil as occurred in Damot or Enarya far to the southwest (Pankhurst 1961: 224–7). Even now the people of Aksum find considerable quantities of ancient coins after the rains have washed the soil away. Some gold has also been reported from Gojjam, much closer to Aksum (Pankhurst 1961: 224; Kirwan 1972: 171; Crawford 1958) and ancient gold workings are claimed in Eritrea (Tringali 1965: 151–2; see also the brief note on material from the Museum of Mankind appended to the account of the Adulis excavations of 1868, Munro-Hay 1989i) and in the Beja territory (Kobishchanov 1979: 134), where there was much activity from the ninth century when the Arabs became interested (Hasan 1973: 50). The greater part of the gold, that from the south, was found by panning or by searching river beds, and was not from mines.

Silver seems not to have been common, but some reports of mines exist from the Portuguese period (Pankhurst 1961: 227–8). Possibly the considerable issues of silver coins, over some 300 years, depended on imported silver, but this seems very unlikely in view of the amounts used and the fact that many silver issues were adorned with gold overlay, scarcely necessary if the metal itself were already a rarity. It seems probable that the Aksumites had local silver sources, possibly including some of those mentioned by the Portuguese in later centuries. Doubtless the exploitation of precious metals was kept as much as possible under state control.

Sources of iron ore were apparently fairly common in Tigray (Pankhurst 1961: 228–9; Fr. Raffaello Francescano in Monneret de Villard 1938: 60). Copper and bronze do not seem to be noted except as an import in the *Periplus* (Huntingford 1980: 21–2), though tin was apparently available in later times (Pankhurst 1961; 229).

4. Trade, Imports and Exports.

The vigorous trade which Aksum undertook was an important element in the acquisition of its power and position in the early centuries AD, and was probably the origin of a good part of its wealth. Policing of the trade-routes was therefore of vital importance, and it is mentioned in the anonymous *Monumentum Adulitanum* inscription (Ch. 11: 5) that the land route to Egypt, and the defence of the Red Sea coasts on both the African and the Arabian sides, were objects of vigilance to the Aksumite monarchy. Apart from long-distance land and sea routes, internal transport must have depended on some sort of state maintenance of at least the main roads in reasonable condition for porters or pack-animals; a practical move also useful for military purposes. We have no reports about Aksumite bridges, though the Portuguese later built some of which vestiges are still visible today. Ethiopian rivers are scarcely navigable, though some of the lakes are. Lake Tsana, which the Aksumites must have reached, is well-known for its reed boats, which rather resemble ancient Egyptian types. However, the river valleys, when dry, can also supply relatively easy passage from place to place. We have several accounts of the trade of the Aksumite kingdom, both internal and external, and archaeological work has confirmed many of the chief categories of goods being handled. The earliest account of the trade of Ethiopia, that of Pliny, (ed. Rackham 1948: 467) mentions the goods brought to Adulis by the 'Trogodites and Ethiopians'. These exports were all animal (or human) products of the region and are listed as ivory, rhinoceros horn, hippopotamus hides, tortoise shell, monkeys, and slaves.

The *Periplus of the Erythraean Sea* includes a brief chapter on Aksum, and as this information is of the first importance for any analysis of Aksumite economic affairs it is here quoted in full (Huntingford 1980: 20–21; for a more recent translation see Casson 1989: 51ff);

> *"After Ptolemais of the Huntings, at a distance of about 3000 stades, there is the customary mart of Adouli, lying in a deep bay that runs southwards;*

in front of it is an island called Oreine, which is about 200 stades out in the sea from the inmost part of the bay, lying along the mainland on both sides, where ships entering anchor on account of attacks from the mainland. For at one time they used to anchor right inside the bay at the Island called Of Didoros along the mainland where there was a crossing on foot, by means of which the Barbaroi living there attacked the island. And opposite Oreine on the mainland, twenty stades from the sea, is Adouli, a village of moderate size, from which to Koloe, an inland city and the first ivory market, it is a journey of three days; and from this, another five days to the metropolis called the Axomite, to which is brought all the ivory from beyond the Nile through the district called Kueneion, and thence to Adouli. For the whole quantity of elephant and rhinoceros which is killed grazes in the interior, though occasionally they are seen by the sea round about Adouli. Out to sea beyond this mart, on the right, lie several small sandy islands called Alalaiou, where there is tortoiseshell, which is brought to the mart by the Ikhthuophagoi.

And at a distance of nearly 800 stades there is another very deep bay, at the mouth of which on the right hand is a great sandbank, in the depths of which is found deposited the opsian stone, which occurs in this place only. Zoskales rules these parts, from the Moskhophagoi to the other Barbaria, mean [in his way] of life and with an eye on the main chance, but otherwise high-minded, and skilled in Greek letters.

To these places are imported:

Barbaric unfulled cloth made in Egypt, Arsinoitic robes, spurious coloured cloaks, linen, fringed mantles, several sorts of glassware, imitation murrhine ware made in Diospolis, orokhalkos, which they use for ornaments and for cutting [to serve] as money, material called 'copper cooked in honey' for cooking-pots and for cutting into armlets and anklets for women, iron used for spears both for hunting elephants and other animals and for war, axes, adzes, swords, big round drinking cups of bronze, a little money for foreigners who live there, Ladikean and Italian wine, but not much. For the king are imported: silver and gold objects made in the design of the country, cloaks of cloth, unlined garments, not of much value.

Likewise from the inner parts of Ariake: Indian iron and steel, the broader Indian cloth called monakhe, *cloth called* sagmatogenai, *belts, garments called* gaunakai, *mallow-cloth, a little muslin, coloured lac. The exports from these places are: ivory, tortoiseshell, rhinoceros horn. The greater part is brought from Egypt to the mart between the month of January and the month of September, that is, from Tubi to Thoth. The best time for the trade from Egypt is about the month of September"*

The exports of Aksum came from all over its area of hegemony. Along the route Adulis-Koloe-Aksum-Kueneion, starting from the latter (suggested to be the Sinaar region of the modern Sudan, Schoff 1912: 61, but possibly meaning the somewhat closer regions over the Takaze/Atbara river), came, according to the *Periplus* (Huntingford 1980), ivory from the country beyond the Nile. A tusk was found at Adulis (Sergew Hable Sellassie 1972: 74/5), eloquent witness to this part of Aksum's trade network. From the Blemmyes (Beja), says Kosmas, came emeralds (beryls), taken into India by Ethiopian merchants (Wolska-Conus 1973: 352–3); Olympiodorus (Kirwan 1966: 123) notes that the Beja/Blemmyes controlled the emerald supply by the early fifth century, when he was permitted to visit them, and Epiphanius (ed. Blake, de Vis 1934), writing at the end of the century, confirmed that the Ethiopians obtained emeralds from the Blemmye country. From islands in the Red Sea came tortoise-shell, and obsidian from near the shore (see above), and from Sasu (perhaps the gold-bearing Fazugli region some 200km. south-south-west of Lake Tsana, in modern Sudan) came gold, which was exchanged for salt, iron and meat (Wolska-Conus 1968: 360). Products from the animal life of the Ethiopian region figure high, as in Pliny's account, and include monkeys and other live animals, ivory and rhinoceros horn and hippopotamus hides. Aromatics, spices and other vegetable products either local or transhipped, such as incense resins, cassia, and sugar-cane (Kosmas, ed. Wolska-Conus 1968: 358), also formed part of the Aksumite trade in the exotic. Frankincense trees even now grow in the region to the south-east of Aksum, and Strabo, in the first century BC already notes that the Sabaeans engaged in the traffic of aromatics, *'both the local kinds and those from Aethiopia; to get the latter they sail across the straits in leathern boats'* (Page 1930: 349). Human life was also part of the trading wealth of the state, and slaves, noted by both Pliny and Kosmas, may have figured prominently among the exports (Connah 1987: 72, 89).

Salt, which was of sufficient importance to figure in sixth-century internal trade (Kosmas, ed. Wolska-Conus 1968), later became one of Ethiopia's currency goods; most of it probably came from the low-lying Danakil region east of the highlands. In later times it was transported in blocks called *amole* (or *gayla* in Tigrinya). The products of local industries or of agriculture and stock-raising, do not seem to have figured among the exported goods, though in later times hides and leather became an important export. The Muslim *hadith* mention that leather goods from Mecca were much in demand in Ethiopia (Guillaume 1955: 150-51). The local manufactured goods would most likely have been solely for the internal markets, and probably not of the necessary quality to be taken on long trade voyages. The contrary was true of the products of the Roman empire and India, which were much desired and appreciated by the élite of Aksum, if we can interpret from the lists of imports, and the finds in tombs and domestic buildings. Iron, though long known in Ethiopia and neighbouring Sudan, was still an important import, both as raw material and in the form of tools and weapons. Articles specially made to order in precious metals, a varied selection of glass vessels, various fabrics and made-up garments, and some wines, oils, and spices are mentioned as imports by the *Periplus*, Kosmas, and others. Even some coin, in the form of either brass pieces or Roman coined money, was imported for trading purposes, apparently long before the decision was taken to facilitate trading exchanges by the issue of the local coinage.

A good deal of the imported material mentioned in the sources has turned up at Aksumite sites, particularly in such tomb deposits as that found in the Tomb of the Brick Arches at Aksum itself. Here was found glass in quantity, of high quality (more was found in a tomb in the Gudit Stelae Field, including two sets of goblets and beakers), iron, bronze, gold, silver, bone and ivory, ceramics, wood and leather. A good deal of this was probably of local manufacture, but some of the metalwork and the glass was certainly imported. From other parts of Aksum and from other Aksumite sites came amphorae in which wine or oils were imported, some of the luxury glass vessels from the Roman world, foreign glazed wares, perhaps from the region of the Persian Gulf, and occasional gold Roman or Indian coins. The presence of such items is testimony to the success of the Aksumites in developing the potential of their trade from both the interior and overseas trans-shipments into a rich source of revenue. Agriculture, however, probably remained the dominant form of economic activity almost everywhere in the country, except in a few special circumstances, and more or less uniform farming would have reduced the need for much internal traffic in bulky agricultural products (even if there had been the roads and transport facilities to carry them on any but the main routes). Cattle, of course, could be driven for sale as required, as illustrated by the Sasu gold trade where cattle on the hoof formed part of the trade-goods (Kosmas, ed. Wolska-Conus 1968). Certain locally manufactured goods, like pottery, may have been partly made by specialists in certain places where there was a large demand, but in country areas were perhaps not the work of such specialists. Most towns were probably rather regional markets than trade centres, importing local agricultural produce for their maintenance and distributing some craft products, and acting as local administrative or religious centres. But a few may have been financed to some extent by trade, such as Koloe, the ivory market, and of course Adulis itself. Apart from limited inter-regional movement of goods, the foreign trade, though rich, seems to have been chiefly in luxuries for the few, and it is unlikely that the metalwork, glass, cloth and so on brought to Adulis found a mass-market in Aksumite Ethiopia, any more than the ivory and so forth from Africa met with a very wide distribution outside.

No information is available about the system of taxation employed by the Aksumite rulers, but doubtless a good deal of the state's income depended on the categories noted above; population, land and its yield, livestock and trade. Land and population would have formed two basic and permanent taxable factors, relatively easy to administer, and later land-charters show that there was a well-kept record of land ownership (Huntingford 1965) which may well date back to Aksumite times. Foreign trade passed through a customs-post at Gabaza near Adulis, and probably on certain routes, or in the markets themselves, tolls were levied on the movement of trade or manufactured goods. It seems likely that relatively few taxes were paid in money, though such taxes would have stimulated money use and enhanced its profitability for the state. Taxes in kind were probably the norm save in the larger towns or on particularly important trade goods, and very possibly there were state granaries or supply depots where cereals, livestock and other foodstuffs collected as tax were held. From such repositiories may have come the materials for the food supplies issued during the forcible transportation of Beja tribes described by Ezana's inscriptions (Ch. 11: 5), and doubtless there would have been state help available to the population in times of shortage. Possibly also there may have been dues such as unpaid labour contributions, and supplies for royal progresses, officials travelling on state business, and soldiers in time of war.

5. Local Industries.

The economy of Aksum in the days of its prosperity was flourishing enough to support a selection of specialised local industries. Perhaps the most impressive was the pottery (Anfray 1966; Wilding in Munro-Hay 1989), large numbers of both luxury and utilitarian wares being produced in very varied, sometimes elegant shapes. Pottery could be finished in a number of ways; elaborately decorated with incised or stamped patterns, slipped, painted, or burnished. There may have been a local glass industry (see also below), and the discovery of faience vessels in typical Aksumite shapes leads to the impression that it too was locally made (Chittick 1974).

Skins and hides were presumably used for clothing and bedding in the colder months. Woven fabrics may have been produced, but there is no actual evidence except for the loom-weights excavated (Wilding in Munro-Hay 1989), and Kosmas' (Wolska-Conus 1968) allusion to Aksumites wearing white cloth kilts or loin-cloths. The draperies, sometimes apparently fringed, shown covering the kings' shoulders on the coins were possibly among the imported garments mentioned by the *Periplus* (Huntingford 1980), as was also perhaps the gold-worked linen kilt worn by Kaleb in Malalas' description (ed. Migne 1860; see Ch. 7: 2 above). Cotton may have come from Meroë (see p. 228), or perhaps from other areas within Aksumite control.

The many stone implements found at Aksum were probably made for leather-working or for ivory and bone carving; ivory, bone, or wood handles have been found in certain tombs (Munro-Hay 1989). An interesting ethnographic parallel for the use of obsidian tools, apparently limited to the scraping of animal hides among the Gurage, Sidamo, and Arussi peoples of present-day Southern Ethiopia, is supplied by Gallagher (1974).

There must also have been local workshops for metal objects, many examples of which have been found during excavations in Ethiopia. Some

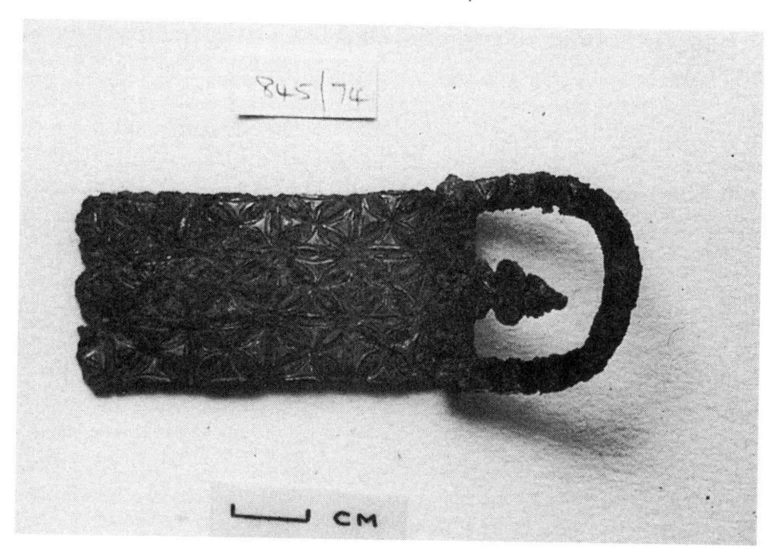

45. A bronze belt buckle decorated with silver crosses and inlay of dark-blue glass, from the Tomb of the Brick Arches at Aksum. Photo BIEA.

objects might have been imported. But such items as the statues of gold, silver, and bronze which inscriptions mention as raised to the gods in celebration of victories (Ch. 11: 5; DAE 4, 6 & 7, Geza 'Agmai) would very likely have been of Aksumite manufacture and style. A bronze belt, with inlaid glass and silver decoration including crosses of typical Aksumite style as seen on the coins, may also have been a local product (Chittick 1974); if so, this confirms that there was probably a local glass industry as well. Helen Morrison, who catalogued and studied the glass from Aksum (Morrison in Munro-Hay 1989), found that a considerable number of unusual colours of glass came from the Aksum excavations, and that some painted designs on glass were, so far, unattested elsewhere; features which may go towards confirming that the Aksumites set up their own glass workshops. A glass-kiln has in fact been reported from Aksum, but the find has not yet been confirmed or published.

If local workers succeeded to imported mint-masters in the making of dies for the coinage, as seems probable, this may account for the gradual decline of standards of die-cutting; but the Aksumites compensated to some extent for the less skilled work by the inlaying of gold on the bronze and silver using mercury-gilding.

Stone-working was very highly developed, as the stelae and other carved objects show, and the mason's yards must have been continually busy shaping the blocks needed for corners, doorways, paving and so on. Carved stone capitals, bases and water-spouts were among the more common categories of decorated stonework found during excavations (see Ch. 13: 3). Bricks, too, used in tombs and certain special installations, were surely made and fired nearby.

6. Food.

The Aksumites would doubtless have served their food in some of their large range of pottery vessels, after preparing it in the coarse-ware cooking vessels on open fires, in ovens or on charcoal-fed stoves. Much of their diet would have consisted of products of the local environment. Beef or mutton, bread, beer (*sewa*), honey wine or mead (*tej*), with various sorts of vegetables and fruits are to be expected locally, while imported wines of Laodicea and Italy, spices, and olive oil added to the luxury of the tables of the richer citizens. Archaeological evidence for the importation of wines and oils is supplied by the amphorae used to transport them; Paribeni even suggested that tar found in one amphora may have been used as a preservative, as in Greek resinated wines. It is unknown whether the Aksumites themselves cultivated the vine. Honey may have been used as a sweetener as well as a drink. Many of these foodstuffs are mentioned by the Safra inscription (Drewes 1962: 41, 48-9) or by the *Periplus* (Huntingford 1980: 22)

From the numerous medium-sized bowls found, it may be deduced that a part of the diet consisted of something like a cereal porridge or gruel. Wheat or barley-cakes and bread were also probably made, and the importance of the grain is illustrated by its depiction in a prominent position as a frame for the king's head on many Aksumite coins. Large numbers of grindstones testify to the preparation of flour for bread at, for example, Matara and Adulis. Anfray (1974: 752) noted that they are of the round, turning, type at Adulis, but oblong on the plateau sites. Anfray (1963: pl. CXLVI and 1965: pl. LXXIII, 4) also mentions small mortars from the pre-Aksumite period, perhaps for use in the preparation of cosmetics rather than food. Dairy products would certainly have been part of the diet, and doubtless eggs were eaten. For meat, there was beef or mutton, and also any wild animals which might have been considered edible. By one hearth in Adulis, the French excavator Francis Anfray found a cooking-pot still containing the mutton bones of a meal never cleared away (Anfray 1974: 753). Pork was not eaten in later times and possibly this abstention, observed by the Jews and Muslims as well as the Orthodox Ethiopians for practical health reasons, was of early origin as domestic pigs are not attested. Dietary prohibitions are later reiterated in the *Kebra Nagast* (Budge 1922: 159). Fishing may have been practised. The turtles which produced the 'tortoise-shell' may also have added to the coastal Aksumites' diet, though creatures without fins and scales are among those included in the later list of prohibited foods. Those who brought the tortoise-shell to the market are referred to by the author of the *Periplus* as Ikhthuophagoi, or fish-eaters. The excavations at Adulis produced both fish-bones and bronze fish-hooks (Paribeni 1907: 483, 540). Shell-fish were also later prohibited, again possibly an old custom. No early visitor has said whether the Aksumites liked raw beef, cut from the living animal, as Bruce (1790) reported (to the horrified disbelief of his eighteenth century English readers) about the Ethiopians of his day.

Almost certainly some foodstuffs would have been eaten from wooden or basketwork vessels (the typical Ethiopian 'table' today, the *mesob*, is of basketwork). Wooden cooking or eating utensils, and basketwork storage bins can also be presumed with some likelihood. In the lowest building level at the Maryam Tseyon site in Aksum, an exceptional find was a row of large *pithoi* or storage pots, probably for bulk storage of some sort of dry grain (de Contenson 1963i: pl. XII).

IX

The Coinage

1. Origins

Aksum was the only African state in ancient times, outside the Roman dependencies, to issue its own national coinage (for references on coinage questions see Anzani: 1926, 1928, 1941; Munro-Hay, loc. var: Hahn 1983; much of the following chapter is based on Munro-Hay 1984iv). The Aksumite coinage lasted from about 270 AD, or a little later, into the early seventh century, and seems to have been used in both external trade and internal market transactions. How far the whole kingdom was able to employ a monetarised economy is still a matter for conjecture, but so far coin-finds have been reported from all excavated Aksumite sites.

By the time of Aksum's first recorded military ventures to the Yemen, the coinage of the South Arabian kingdoms would seem to have been nearing the end of its use, if it was not already discontinued. This coinage, chiefly of silver in Saba and Himyar, and bronze in Hadhramawt, only very rarely seems to have included electrum or gold pieces. It is much more likely that the immediate origins of the coinage of Aksum were influenced by Roman trading in the Red Sea, though perhaps the awareness of Kushaṅa and Persian coinages also inspired the Aksumites to emulation. The Aksumite coinage followed the Roman/Byzantine weight system, and this and certain other factors add probability to the suggestion that Rome was the primary region to which Aksum looked when the issue of a coinage was planned. At any rate, adoption of a coinage would have immensely facilitated exchange of products and all other public and private business in which it was employed, and must have given considerable impetus to the economy.

Whilst there is no actual proof, except for the tentative identification of a pottery object from the excavations as a coin-mould (Wilding in Munro-Hay 1989), it would seem very likely that it was at Aksum itself that the coins were minted. No other African state south of the Sahara issued coins until the sultanate of Kilwa began coinage-production possibly in the mid-tenth century.

2. Introduction and Spread of the Coinage.

Few African societies possessed a market or exchange system so evolved as to require a universally accepted form of currency; the need for such a currency stands in a direct ratio to the complexity of the society which has developed, and the ultimate expression of the requirement for currency in the ancient world was a coinage system. Use of a general purpose money evidently simplifies the system in representing the medium of exchange, the standard of value-measurement, a means of holding wealth at discretion, and a means of payment for services, all in one form. As Plato commented , *'money reduces the inequalities and immeasurabilities of goods to equality and measure'*. A coinage, fashioned from a precious metal, and of convenient size for representing large sums with little weight and bulk, was also much more broadly recognised than other types of currency in the international framework in which Aksum's trade became involved. Coinage gave the economy a central emphasis from which every aspect of the state's functions could spring. Wealth could pass easily in both local and external transactions, so long as the standard conformed, and Aksum accordingly linked its coinage with the Romano-Byzantine monetary system.

Within the area of Aksum's control, circulation of the coinage could have been encouraged by the demanding of coinage payments for certain taxes, by state payments for military and other services in coinage, and by the gradual increase in the number of merchants in the markets using it as the standardised medium of exchange. Commodities formerly expressed in different values could be exchanged with this single easily-controlled factor, and the rate of trade speeded up considerably. The traditional value of each object in relation to a complex variety of others was thus centralised, and inevitably the simpler system would gain, as long as the ultimate guarantor, the Aksumite ruler, was visibly apparent to support it. Gold and silver in the pure state are intrinsically valuable, but in a debased currency, or a currency where the value in spending power is above the real value of the metal it is of course only viable while the issuer represents the ultimate redeemer. With token currencies, like the bronze, (though in Aksum the gilding might have adjusted this to some extent) the real value of the coins was representative and not actual.

Aksum's coinage was a successful experiment to judge from its continuance reign after reign for at least three hundred years. The combined factors of the power of the kings in a military context, improving and increasing the possible routings for goods and providing for their greater security, and the centralising of the spheres of commerce in a monetised economy, must have supplied to trade a steady climate of increase. It has been observed that the issue of a coinage generally stimulates an economy, and Aksum was no exception. The increasingly complex trade would have been much more easily dealt with after Aksum had entered the world of its trading neighbours with a monetary system on a par with theirs.

At the time of the *Periplus*, the Aksumite state imported *orokhalkos* or brass *"which they use for ornaments and for cutting as money"*, and *"a little money (denarion) for foreigners who live there"* (Huntingford 1980: 21–2).

The use of metal as money before the issue of a minted coinage certainly hints that the Aksumites were aware even at that time of the advantages of a currency which did not require special care or maintenance and was divisible at need. Neither Zoskales, the ruler of the region at the time, nor his successors for well over a century, issued their own coins and it would seem as if the kingdom was only beginning to orient itself towards the use of coinage. The use of Roman money among foreign residents and merchants is not surprising, but the Aksumites' or Adulites' use of cut brass is; possibly brass was a relatively costly item in Ethiopia at the time. This comment in the *Periplus*, seeming to imply that Aksum was already using metal pieces as money, was one of the points which made Jacqueline Pirenne's suggestion (1961) that the *Periplus* was of third-century date seem plausible. Now, however, the accumulation of evidence for an earlier date seems conclusive, and it must be accepted that the conditions preparatory for Aksum's move to production of their own coinage existed long before they were put into action. Eventually, however, Aksum, with its outlet to the Red Sea at the port of Adulis, decided to produce its own coinage instead of importing it; both Roman (Anfray and Annequin 1965: 68–71) and Indian (Mordini 1960, 1967) gold reached the country, as attested by archaeological evidence. The Indian material consisted of a hoard of Kushana gold coins of kings Vima Kadphises II, Kaniska, Huviska, and Vasudeva I found at the monastery of Dabra Damo, and dated to around 220AD, while the most dramatic find of Roman gold consisted of coins and jewellery of the time of the Antonines found at Matara. A number of Himyarite coins have also been found at Aksum (Munro-Hay 1978). Archaeological finds of this sort are rare, and the amount of foreign money circulating was probably relatively restricted.

Prior to the introduction of the coinage, the primitive economy doubtless worked on the barter system, which remained the customary method of dealing with trade in certain areas of the Aksumite trade network, even during the existence of the coinage. It is almost inconceivable to imagine that money was used very much in the remoter countryside, or that money taxation could have been levied outside limited urban areas or at special toll points. The archaeological evidence is meagre, owing to lack of exploration, but coins finds have been reported from Arato to Lalibela (Munro-Hay 1978), and they are plentiful on all excavated town sites (see below). Much of the population doubtless lived in a more or less self-sufficient rural setting, where contacts with foreign trade were minimal, and money was scarcely needed in day to day exchange. Aksum continued to deal with non-monetised economies in, for example, the gold trade with Sasu in the Sudan (Wolska-Conus 1968: 360), and doubtless also in other African regions.

In the reign of Kaleb the Sasu gold trade was conducted through the medium of salt blocks (later known as *amole*), iron, and cattle (imported on the hoof, and killed on arrival). Whether other products were employed as a standard for measuring relative values, as the *amole* or salt block was until comparatively recent times (Pankhurst 1961: 260–5), is not known. The *amole*, though used as a currency, in later times varied in value as one travelled further from the centres of production in the eastern lowlands, but its transport to Sasu shows that even in ancient times it was an important element in the trade of Aksum. Other goods were directed towards the more sophisticated trade of the Red Sea, with its outlets to the Graeco-Roman world and the East. These valuable exports, whose trade routes fell under Aksumite control, helped the original development of the state towards the more evolved market system which eventually induced it to issue its own coinage.

The Aksumite coinage-province is very little known. At the cities on the route from the coast to the capital, as expected, there have been archaeological finds of coins. The excavations at the port of Adulis, the inland town of Matara and Aksum itself have yielded coins, and others have come from lesser sites in Tigray and Eritrea, but in very small numbers. Coins, including one of king Armah, were found at Arato in Eritrea, and a coin of Ouazebas came from Lalibela (but not from an archaeologically attested context). Other coinage finds from South Arabia (by far the richest source for the gold coins of Aksum so far) consist of gold coins dating only from the time of Ezana to Kaleb. This has been construed as indicating a certain Aksumite control in the area, and such a theory may indeed be valid. But it may also be that some of the coins represent hoards deposited at the time of Kaleb's Arabian war; to this category may belong the coins now in the Kunsthistorisches Museum in Vienna, and the extremely important al-Mudhariba hoard (Munro-Hay 1989ii). If this is so, the theory that the Aksumites retained some control in South Arabia must depend more on the mention of South Arabian kingdoms in the Aksumite royal titularies, the Epigraphic South Arabian inscriptions, and the hint in a Greek text that the Aksumite kings appointed the Himyarite rulers (Ch. 4), than on coinage evidence. Such information is only available in and before Ezana's time, and later in the reign of Kaleb. Taxes in sixth-century Himyar were, interestingly, computed according to weights of gold coins which were last used at the time of Ezana (Boissonade 1833; Munro-Hay 1978).

It would seem not unlikely that Aksum's armies in South Arabia would have been paid in coin from the military chest, and it is therefore notable that the king whose wars with South Arabia are best documented, Kaleb, has many more gold issues than other kings, perhaps reflecting an increase in production to pay his armies. The provenance of the majority of these issues is South Arabia. Possibly the hoards mentioned above represent coin gathered in Kaleb's time from all the issues still current in Aksum, and taken over with the armies. Alternatively they could have been collections of foreign coins belonging to Himyarites deposited during the advance of Kaleb's forces or in subsequent disturbances, or simply capital sums buried for security by Aksumites or Arabs who were never able to disinter them.

Since the Aksumites claimed control over parts of South Arabia for a very long time (from perhaps the early 200's to the second quarter of the sixth century, whether intermittently or not), finds of coins there are not surprising. It is surprising, however, that neither the silver nor the bronze fractions are found there – save for one silver coin of Ebana found at the Hadhrami capital, Shabwa – and also that many of the gold issues have as yet no reported find spots from Ethiopia itself. Apart from the South Arabian gold finds, Aksumite coins are rarely met with elsewhere; only a few bronze coins have come to light outside Ethiopia, in Israel (Caesarea, Beth Shan and Jerusalem), Meroë and at Qaw and Hawara in Egypt (Barkay 1981; Meshorer 1965–6; Munro-Hay 1978: 81ff). So, by and large, the coinage in silver and bronze, with its unique addition of gilding, appears to have been designed for use within the borders of Ethiopia. The gold was primarily aimed, as its Greek legend specifying 'king of the Aksumites' indicates, towards the outside world, and seems to have been used either for specialised purposes such as paying soldiers in Arabia, or for general trading capital in relatively large sums. In contrast, given its local use, much of the silver and bronze coinage mentions only the king's name with the word 'king', and does not need to specify 'of Aksum'.

3. Internal Aspects of the Coinage.

In producing their own coinage the Aksumite rulers would have had all sorts of considerations before them. The coinage must be, first of all, acceptable both externally and internally, to foreign traders and the Ethiopian population at large. Endubis, apparently the first of the kings to try the experiment of superseding the imported coinage of the time of Zoskales by one guaranteed with his own name, issued in all three metals; a good quality gold, silver and bronze. The value-relationships of the metals among themselves is not known; state control of the gold resources is indicated by the story of Kosmas, noted above, and doubtless the supplies of other metals were also closely monitored. Endubis appears to have decided upon the half-aureus as the suitable weight for his gold issue, probably to provide a supplement to the Roman aurei already in current use. The weight of these coins, around 2.70 grammes, indicates that they were issued at some time in the latter half of the third century AD.

At first, the language selected for the coinage legends was Greek rather than the native Ge'ez. This is an obvious reminder that the purpose of the coins was to participate in the trade with the Graecised Orient. It is possible that the first coiners for Aksum came from the Roman world, perhaps Alexandria, where coins of a similar flan (though quite different design), were produced until 297AD (Hahn 1983).

The design of the coins was of primary importance, and must have been very carefully chosen. The coinage for Endubis concentrated almost entirely on the king himself, as the representative of the state. The coins, with raised

46. The first of the Aksumite coin issues; drawings of gold (d. c. 16mm), silver (d. c. 15mm) and bronze (d. 15mm) coins of king Endubis.

relief in all three metals, depict the king wearing the Aksumite helmet or headcloth on both obverse and reverse. The headcloth has rays, pleats, or perhaps a sunburst indicated at the front, rather like the aigrette at the front of the turban of some Indian prince. There is always a triangular ribbon, representing perhaps the ends of a fillet holding the headcloth in position, or the ends of the cloth itself after it was knotted into place, shown falling at the rear behind the king's neck. The legend, in Greek, gives Endubis' name, and the title 'ΒΑΣΙΛΕΥΣ ΑΞΩΜΙΤΩΝ' (always actually written ΒΑCΙΛΕΥC ΑΞWMITW); basileus Aksomitō(n), king of the Aksumites. There is also another title, 'bisi Dakhu', BICI ΔΑΧΥ, meaning apparently 'man of Dakhu' which is sometimes referred to as the 'ethnicon' in the assumption that it represents some sort of tribal affiliation, every Aksumite king bearing a different version of it (Ch. 7: 5).

As well as the unusual emphasis on the king, there are one or two other indications as to those elements which Endubis deemed important enough to emphasise on this excellent propaganda medium for his kingdom. First of all, his religion. This is represented by a disc and crescent symbol set at 12.00 on both faces of the coins, in continuation of the earlier Himyarite custom. It is suggested that these symbols represent deities of the sun and moon, or perhaps the royal tutelary deity Mahrem. It could be that, given the importance of this latter deity in the royal myth (see Ch. 10), it was he whom Endubis chose to put symbolically on his coins.

A second specifically Aksumite element of design was the depiction of two ears of wheat or barley framing the royal bust on the obverse and the reverse of the gold coins only. Its depiction on the coins could have been intended to show the king as the provider and source of bounty, under the gods. Ears of wheat as central heraldic motifs had centuries previously appeared in similar position in the field on issues such as those of Metapontum in Lucania, Sardinia, Morgantina in Sicily, Ilipense in Spain, and others, and

47. The augmented series of issues (excluding the bronze type already illustrated in fig. 44) of king Aphilas; three types of gold (d. c. 16mm, 12mm, and c. 7mm respectively), two of silver (d. 17mm and c. 12mm), and two of bronze (d. 18mm and c. 15mm)

later as a group on *cistophori* of the Roman emperor Nerva, but never in the form found on the Aksumite pieces. Possibly the grain stalks were actually a symbol of the Aksumite state itself, since its position on the gold coins is so prominent, and so closely related to the king.

The basic elements of design, established by Endubis, appear to have satisfied the Aksumite rulers ever afterwards, but for a few additions at different periods. Such changes doubtless result from specific intentions by the issuing authorites to achieve certain aims.

First of all, Endubis' successor Aphilas added an even more imposing appearance to the gold coins, by causing his image on the obverse to be altered to show him crowned with the splendid Aksumite tiara. This was a high crown, whose lower part consisted of a colonnade of arches supported by columns whose capitals and bases are visible even on the tiny images permitted by the flan size of the coins (diameter c. 17mm). Above the arches rose spikes, separated by elements of an elongated oval shape surmounted by discs. It appears that the tiara rested upon the headcloth (retained on the reverse design) as the fillet-tie is still visible behind. Other items of regalia (Ch 7:2) appear with Aphilas' issues. These include a spear, or sometimes a short stick, a branch with berries (?) – in later, less precise designs it looks rather like a flywhisk – tasselled fringes to the draperies, and, with the depiction of the arms, more jewellery in the form of armlets and bracelets. Aphilas, then, without abandoning any of the precedents set by Endubis, seems to have desired to show himself in the full magnificence of his state regalia, whilst retaining the simpler headcloth image as well. Several suggestions have been aired to explain this (Ch. 7: 2). Whatever the case, it was this design which fossilised as the traditional one for the Aksumite gold coinage until the last issues, with only a very few further alterations, such as the introduction of an inner beaded circle around the king's image by Ezana after his conversion to Christianity, and king Gersem's use of a frontal portrait.

Aphilas also instituted some less successful experiments. His quarter-aureus is only known from one specimen, and he also issued considerable numbers of very tiny gold coins whose weight seems to indicate one-sixth of the aureus. The weights of the surviving specimens are often, as might be expected, a little down on the theoretical weight; this is one of the means by which a coinage can be very profitable to an issuing authority. However, the Aksumites were reasonably careful over their gold weights, and sometimes a coin is found which is even a little over the theoretical weight. Perhaps due to archaeological accident at this stage, since very few coins have been available for analysis, but later very deliberately employed, is the very slight debasement with silver from the standard set by Endubis; the lowest gold content so far recorded for Aphilas has sunk to 90% (Oddy and Munro-Hay 1980; Munro-Hay, Oddy and Cowell 1988). The constant decline of the gold content, slow as it was at first, must eventually have been a severe blow to the credibility of the Aksumite coinage, and would have set it at a disadvantage against the Roman gold, which was of very high purity and very reliable.

A shifting inter-relationship of value with the Roman gold may have been the reason why the Aksumites retained the heavier 'tremissis' of c. 1.60g. when the Romans reduced the weight of their tremissis to the true third of a solidus, with a theoretical weight of about 1.51g. under Theodosius I in c.383. Only right at the end of the series, with Iathlia (=Hataz?) and Gersem are lesser weight coins issued, whilst Ella Gabaz, in the sixth century, issued some unusually heavy specimens. Weight variations could have emerged from a mint practice of striking a given number of coins from a given amount of metal – from Roman examples the weight of each individual coin could thus vary considerably, even at its emergence from the mint in pristine state. The element of seignorage, the mint profit, or at least coverage of expenses, could be arranged by the retention of a small part per pound of metal – this has a corollary in as much as it would help to guard the coinage from destruction since each coin would represent a theoretical purchasing power slightly in excess of its real value, fractionally reduced vis-à-vis the correct proportion of the pound of gold.

To return to Aphilas' innovations, it is apparent that, although the experimental fractions died out with him as far as the gold was concerned, he also experimented with fractions of silver and bronze. The silver half which he issued was retained as the norm for Aksum, the heavier silver being discontinued in the next reign or two. Presumably, the value it represented was too high for a single coin in the particular market situations to which it was exposed, and the half was instituted as a more convenient weight; Aphilas did the opposite with his bronze, issuing a very heavy (presumably double) type, weighing 4.83g. in the only known specimen. Like the quarter-aureus, it may have been soon withdrawn, resulting in its rarity today. Interestingly enough, both of these issues showed the king from a frontal position (as also on one of his normal weight bronze issues), a style abandoned afterwards until the sixth century, and used only by Gersem on the gold, as noted above.

The designs on Aphilas' issues introduced two other features, which also did not last long. The tiny gold fraction had nothing on the reverse but the words 'kin(g) Aphilas', the only time a purely epigraphic reverse appears in the entire series. On one of his bronze issues, he placed the ear of wheat alone in the centre. Only Ezana(s), in a pre-Christian issue, copied this design, which then died out.

All these innovatory issues were doubtless efforts by Aphilas to speed up acceptance of the use of the coinage within his kingdom, and to develop its use for trade, as well as to raise his own international prestige by the advertising medium which the coinage offered. Aphilas seems to have made further considerable efforts to encourage the use of his smaller silver fraction by recourse to a completely unique expedient. On the reverse of the coin, around the royal bust, the whole area delineated by the circle outside which the legend ran was covered with a thin layer of gilding. The result was both attractive, showing the king in a halo of gold, and impressive; it showed the wealth of the king of Aksum in an inescapable fashion.The work must have been costly, as well as difficult to execute, and indicates how earnestly the mint authorities viewed the need to impress a people unused to coinage with its real value. Whether the half-value silver coins were deliberately underweight to counteract the value of the added gold is unproven, but very likely, since the heaviest surviving examples of Aphilas' silver gilt issue weigh less than half of the lightest surviving specimens of the heavier issue without gilding.

Aksum seems to have had considerable supplies of gold available for its coinage. As the number of coins available for study increases, it is becoming evident that numerous dies were employed. Although we cannot even

48. The apogee of Aksumite coin production; a drawing of the sole known gold coin (d. 17mm) of king Wazeba of Aksum, the only gold coin issued with a Ge'ez legend.

estimate the numbers of coins which could have been struck from a single die before it became too worn for further use, it is evident that certain rulers at least issued gold pieces in impressive quantities.

The rulers who succeeded Aphilas, as well as abandoning gold fractions, appear to have slowly and very slightly reduced the weight of their half-aurei, but to have more or less retained the level of purity of the gold. Perhaps the Aksumite sovereigns were trying to adjust their coinage to agree with the reform of the Roman monetary system from 1/60th of a pound of gold (5.45g.) to 1/72nd of a pound before 312AD. The theoretical weight would have been 2.27g. for the Aksumite issues.

Wazeba, very possibly Aphilas' successor for a brief time only (one gold coin is known, and not too many silver), altered, for the first and only time on the gold issues, the language of the legend. His Ge'ez legend, and the monogram of South Arabian style which he employs on the same coin, make one think that perhaps he aimed his gold coinage more towards Ethiopian users, and also possibly to those South Arabian regions which some of his successors claimed as part of their kingdom. After Wazeba, the use of Greek remained permanent for the gold, but gradually, starting with Mehadeyis (MHDYS) for the bronze and with Wazeba himself for the silver, the native language came to supersede the Greek, doubtless a reflection of its local circulation area. Greek, however, still remained prominent on silver and bronze throughout the fifth and into the sixth centuries.

With Ezana/Ezanas (his name is written sometimes in Greek with the euphonic 's' ending) several important observations must be made with regard to the coinage. His reign embraces the period of the second quarter of the fourth century until at least 356 AD. His first issues, following his predecessors' example in most features, have only a very slight average weight reduction. The second phase is represented by his abandonment of the old disc and crescent symbol of the pagan period, and the adoption of the cross. The report of Ezana's conversion to Christianity is recorded also by his inscriptions (Ch. 11: 5), and this very vital change was signalled to a larger audience by his coins. Undoubtedly, whatever may have been the king's personal committment to the new religion, its political implications were very

ĒZANAS PAGAN AV I

ĒZANAS CHRISTIAN AV I

ĒZANA CHRISTIAN AV I

49. With the adoption of Christianity, king Ezana of Aksum abandoned the symbol of the disc and crescent on his coins, and replaced it with the cross; drawings of three gold coin types (d. c. 17mm) of Ezana, the first pre-Christian in date.

significant, aligning the kingdom with the Byzantine/Roman world by even stronger bonds. Reluctant though some authorities have been to accept it, it seems as if Ezana has very strong claims to be the first ruler anywhere to use the Christian cross on his coins, since some of his gold coins with the cross are of the weight used before Constantine the Great's reform of the currency in 324. Even if Aksum was a little tardy in following the Roman shift to the lighter weight, these coins seem unlikely to have been issued more than a decade or so after the change in the Roman system; perhaps in 333, the traditional date for the conversion of Ethiopia.

A second Christian gold issue of Ezana is known, in which the weight is indeed reduced to around 1.60g., evidently in response to this change in the Roman gold. Constantine's institution of the solidus, a pure gold coin weighing 4.54g., meant that the Aksumites followed with their 'tremissis' of a theoretical weight of 1.70g., basing their coinage system, as they did up to this point, on the Roman standard. It is this lighter 'tremissis' which has so far been found exclusively in South Arabia, while the gold types with the name Ezanas have so far been found solely in Ethiopia. Whether this is fortuitous, or reflects some real intention to issue a gold coin for South Arabian regions still under Aksumite control, is unknown, but it may be significant since Ezana employs the title of 'king of Saba and Himyar' on his inscriptions. There is no conspicuous debasement for Ezanas reign, though the quality of the workmanship begins to decline.

Ezana did issue a bronze coin in his Christian period, but only one example has been found. However, both he and his predecessor Ousanas appear to have issued coins on which they abandoned the disc and crescent, replacing it with no other symbol, though in one case a gold inlaid disc with four points

49a. Drawing of a silver coin (d. c. 13mm) of king Ousana(s) with no religious symbol.

or rays is used. It has been suggested, plausibly enough, by Bent Juel-Jensen, that this could be a depiction of a shield with crossed spears (1986). Could these coins represent the period mentioned by Rufinus (see Ch. 10: 2) when the converter of Ethiopia, Frumentius, was already beginning to bring Christians together in Ethiopia, possibly even influencing the king towards Christianity? This king, Ella Amida (=Ousanas?), in due course died and left his son under the regency of his queen; Frumentius eventually converted Ezana and probably the court as well, but it is not clear how quickly this was announced publicly by inscriptions and coins. It is possible that, in this period just before and during the conversion of the court and king, there was some uncertainty as to the best method of demonstrating the conversion to the people through the medium of the coinage, but the disc and crescent, were, as a start, suspended on some issues. Eventually, Christian symbolism appeared through the use of the cross.

50. Two gold-inlaid bronze coins (d. c. 17mm) of king Ouazebas of Aksum, bearing the Greek motto TOYTOAPECHTHXWPA, 'May this please the people'; the coins are gilded around the king's head in the centre.

50a. Drawing of a gold coin (d. c. 18mm) of king Nezool of Aksum, bearing a Greek motto reading 'By the Grace of God'.

4. The Mottoes.

There emerges at this stage yet another unusual feature of the Aksumite coinage. Large numbers of bronze coins were issued, perhaps by Ezana or perhaps by an immediate successor, with no royal name, just the word 'basileus', king. But on the reverse a prominent Greek cross appeared in the centre of the field, surrounded by the motto TOYTOAPECHTHXWPA, 'May this please the people'. A silver issue with a similar reverse design bore a cross with its centre and arms hollowed out and gilded. This is the first example of the typical Aksumite numismatic motto (or, in a rather unfortunate translation from Kobishchanov (1979), the 'demagogic slogan'). The mottoes are a rather attractive peculiarity of Aksumite coinage, giving a feeling of royal concern and responsibility towards the people's wishes and contentment, but they were also very practical; the Christian theme of the first of them shows how the kings exploited this useful propaganda instrument to proclaim their new faith throughout the country, or at least as far as the coinage itself spread. King Ouazebas, (c. late 4th – early 5th century) similarly used this motto, and also introduced the gilded halo on his bronze issue, whilst MHDYS employed the Constantinian phrase 'By this cross you shall conquer' and had a spot of gold placed in the centre of the cross itself.

The employment of these mottoes for political or religious themes continued until the collapse of the monetary system. Many fifth-century kings use the phrase 'By the grace of God', or 'Thanks be to God', and later rulers declared 'Christ is with us', or asked for 'Mercy and peace' and the like. Others emphasise certain aspects possibly of political importance. Kaleb (6th

51. Drawing of a bronze coin (d. c. 16mm) of king Wazena of Aksum; on the obverse the king holds a grain stalk and is surrounded by a motto, while on the reverse a gold-inlaid cross-crosslet is depicted.

51a. Drawing of a silver coin (d. c. 14mm) of king Kaleb bearing a Ge'ez motto which may read either 'He who is fitting for the city (country)' or 'May this please the city (country)'.

century) makes a point of the phrase 'Son of Tazena' perhaps to affirm legitimate succession. Kaleb's emphasis on his paternity might be connected with some dynastic disturbance. The coins of Wazena similarly announce, around the royal bust, 'He who is fitting for the people', which could also be

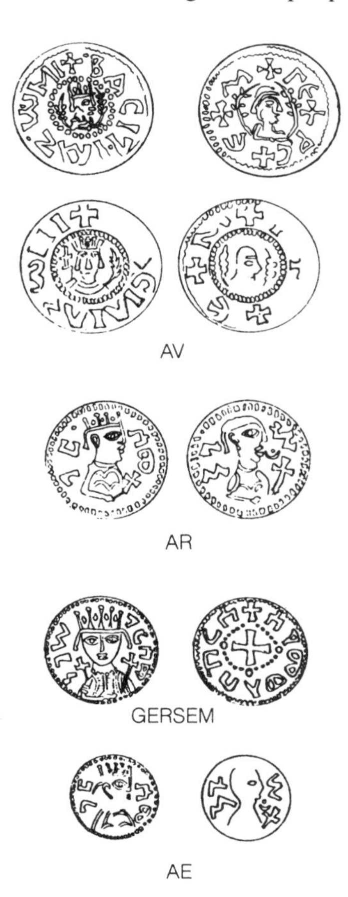

52. Drawings of the coinage of king Gersem of Aksum, consisting of two gold types (d. c. 17mm), a silver type (d. c. 16mm) which sometimes shows vowelling on some of the letters, and two bronze types (d. c. 16mm); the first of the bronze types bears the motto 'He conquers through Christ'.

53. Drawings of gold coins (d. c. 16mm) of kings Ella Gabaz and Ioel; the Greek legends are beginning to grow more barbarous at this period.

an indication of difficulties in the succession. On the other hand the legend could mean 'That which is fitting to the people', and would be a direct translation into Ge'ez of the old Greek motto still used on Kaleb's bronzes; 'May this please the people'. Kaleb's silver already employed this motto in Ge'ez, but instead of 'country' the word *hgr* or 'city' was used, possibly referring to Aksum itself as the capital city.

Much of the interpretation of these mottoes is subjective, but they were evidently chosen with a purpose, and it is of value to at least suggest possible motives for them. It may be, for example, that the change of emphasis in the mottoes towards the end of the coinage hints at unrest in the country. After the Christian mottoes which we interpret as part of the propaganda to spread Christianity, the kings Armah, Israel, and Hataz all use mottoes asking for mercy or peace for the people. Occasional references seems to indicate military activity; Gersem, perhaps the last or penultimate of the coin-issuers, employs the phrase 'He conquers (shall conquer) through Christ'.

5. The End of the Coinage.

From the introduction of the 'tremissis', the Aksumite coinage denominations seem to have changed very little. The gold continued into the seventh century, stable in weight but more and more debased with silver, and increasingly degenerate in appearance, with often badly-written Greek legends. Probably, by this period, the internal decline of the country represented by the debasement of the gold coins was supplemented by the closure of trade routes by Persian and then Muslim activity, marking the end of the old Red Sea commerce. How long money continued to be used in preference to other currency goods such as salt blocks or cloth (which al-Muqaddasi says was used as a medium of exchange in Ethiopia in the 10th century; Vantini 1975: 176) is not known. The end of the coinage may have been gradual, or resulted from an Aksumite military defeat. At any rate, severance of the trading links which had given the original impetus to the coinage, or instability in the country's internal affairs, seem to have ended Aksum's long experience of a monetary system not many decades after 600AD.

6. Modern Study of the Coinage.

The rediscovery of the Aksumite coinage has been a slow process. Nathaniel Pearce, who was in Ethiopia at the beginning of the nineteenth century, may have been the first to describe Aksumite coins (although parts of his descriptions are hard to reconcile with the Aksumite series, and may have referred to Roman coins found at Aksum instead). He says, speaking of the wells at Aksum, *"I was told...that in clearing out the rubbish of a well which,* (the Greek Apostella) *had discovered, he found some gold coins which he shewed me; and indeed, two of the same kind came into my possession several months afterwards, but, unfortunately, having forwarded them to Mr. Salt, they were lost upon the road. One of them had a bald man's head upon one side and apparently arms upon the reverse, the second had a woman's head, with a forked crown on it, and something imitating a balance or scales; the characters were Greek. The coin was as thick in the middle as an English half crown, though not thicker than a shilling round the edges, and in circumference about the size of a guinea"* (Pearce 1831: 163). The thicker central part of the flan sounds like a description of the coins of Endubis, as does the 'bald man's head', whilst the forked crown might be a description of the Aksumite tiara; but neither of the reverses sounds Aksumite.

As the nineteenth century progressed, as few scholars noted a coin here and there; Halévy in 1837, Rüppell in the 1840s, Langlois in 1859, Kenner, von Heuglin, Longperier and d'Abbadie in the 1860s, Friedländer in 1879, Drouin, Prideaux, von Sallet and Schlumberger in the 1880s. In 1913 Littmann published the DAE report, with a chapter on the coins. Much more significant were the publications of Arturo Anzani in 1926, 1928, and 1941, and of Carlo Conti Rossini in 1927. Since then there has been a steady, though sparse, appearance of publications gradually enlarging the known corpus of coins, and commenting on their historical and numismatic significance. A full bibliography is given in Munro-Hay (1984).

X

Religion

1. The Pre-Christian Period

We are fortunate in having translations into Greek of the names of some of the gods mentioned in the Aksumite inscriptions (Ch. 11: 5). These indicate the identifications the Aksumites themselves found for their gods among the deities of the Greek pantheon. Of these, Astar was associated with Zeus, and Mahrem was paralleled with Ares. Beher, if his name is cognate with the Arabic word *bahr*, the sea, may be Poseidon, who was certainly worshipped in some equivalent form in Aksum, as the *Monumentum Adulitanum* (Ch. 11: 5) indicates. This interpretation is uncertain, however, since the names of the two deities Beher and Meder seem to derive from words meaning land or country in Ge'ez (see the note in Ullendorff 1973: 94,1). It seems, therefore, that when they are joined with Astar (see below) the three form an Ethiopian trinity of either heaven, earth and sea, or one with a possibly agricultural significance. The trinity Heaven, Earth and Ares (in Greek), or Astar, Beher and Mahrem (Ge'ez) is also known from Ezana's Geza 'Agmai inscription (Ch. 11: 5).

The worship in Ethiopia of South Arabian gods (Ryckmans 1951: 19ff) like Astar (Venus), Ilmuqah (Sin, the moon, chief god and protector of the Sabaeans), Nuru (the luminous, the dawn), Habas (Hawbas, probably an aspect of the moon-god), Dhat Himyam (the incandescent) and Dhat Ba'adan (the distant) both female aspects of Shams, the sun, perhaps representing the summer and winter sun, is indicated by inscriptions on incense-altars and the like, and also by a number of rock inscriptions from the pre-Aksumite period. One block, found in the walls of the basilican church at Enda Cherqos near Melazo, doubtless came from one of the pre-Aksumite sanctuaries, and is dedicated to what is essentially a solar triad, consisting of Venus, the moon in two aspects, and the sun in two aspects; Astar, Habas and Ilmuqah, Dhat-Himyam and Dhat Ba'adan. It has been suggested that some of these gods were still worshipped in Aksum, according to an interpretation of the inscription of GDR *nagashi* of Aksum on a bronze implement found at Addi Galamo (Atsbi Dera) as a dedication to Ilmuqah (Jamme 1957); but this interpretation, which included an unknown deity called Erg or Arg – and various theories constructed on it (Kobishchanov 1979: 48–9, 226) – appears

54. A pre-Aksumite altar from Addi Grameten near Kaskase with a dedication in the South Arabian script to the goddess Dhat-Himyam.

to be wrong (Schneider 1984: 151). A number of other gods, of whom nothing further is known, are mentioned in pre-Aksumite inscriptions (Schneider 1973).

The Aksumite inscriptions do not mention Ilmuqah, but concentrate mainly on Astar, Beher, Meder and particularly Mahrem, identified with Ares. The latter was the Aksumite royal or dynastic god, who was regarded as the father of the king, and his invincible guard from danger. Possibly Mahrem had taken on some of Ilmuqah's attributes. If he was the god honoured on the coins, as is possible since he was the special royal patron, it may have been he who was represented by the disc and crescent formerly a characteristic of the old South Arabian coins and altars. Alternatively these could have been the symbols of other gods of the Aksumite pantheon, or of its chief god Astar. Astar (Athtar in South Arabia), though a god in this case, bears the same name as the northern Semitic goddess Ishtar, Astarte, Ashtaroth and so on, the fertility deity represented by the planet Venus. Where a triad is mentioned he is always the first of the three, and was probably therefore the head of the Aksumite pantheon, as his identification with Zeus would also imply. In the translation (supposedly done in 678AD; see Trimingham 1952: 48 n. 1; Cerulli 1968: 20, questions this date) of the Greek version of *Ecclesiasticus* into Ge'ez, the word for *theos* (god) which the translators selected was Astar; in the final analysis the Ethiopian's choice for a word to describe the Christian god was *egziabher*, 'Lord of the Land' (in the sense of the whole world), using a combination employing the same word as the old divine name Beher. Beher and Mahrem were also masculine divinites, whilst Meder appears to have been feminine.

Mahrem, the war-god of the Aksumites, was also the royal and dynastic patron. The expansionist state, under kings who were war-leaders, is proclaimed by the inscriptions, which are almost exclusively on the subject of war; and these inscriptions particularly mention Mahrem/Ares as the helper of the king and the recipient of the thank-offerings after the campaigns (Ch. 11: 5). He is mentioned with other gods, sometimes apparently as part of a trinity. He possessed lands, flocks and herds, and prisoner-slaves (unless these were actually sacrificed to him), and gold, silver and bronze statues which were the gifts of the king. Ezana dedicated to him also the inscriptions themselves on which he detailed his conquests, accompanying these monuments with curses against anyone who interfered with them. He also offered to Mahrem a SWT and a BDH (in Greek COY'ATE and BEΔIE); two words of unknown meaning (Bernand 1982; Geza 'Agmai inscription, see Ch. 11: 5).

Sanctuaries of the older gods are known in Ethiopia from Yeha and the Hawelti-Melazo region, which includes the sites of Gobochela and Enda Cherqos. These sites are of particular interest in that they furnish information about the paraphernalia of the temples, from which one can gain some idea of the pre-Christian observances of Ethiopia. Though much of this material is pre-Aksumite, it is worth noting here since the old religion still persisted to a certain degree into Aksumite times.

At Yeha there is of course the famous temple, dating from the period of strongest Sabaean influence. The very existence of this large and very well-constructed structure on Ethiopian soil testifies to the importance of the cult practised there. Later (and infinitely more humble) pre-Aksumite religious buildings are also known. At Gobochela was found a rectangular structure in an enclosure, with inscriptions on plaques and altars mentioning Ilmuqah (Leclant 1959ii). Incense-altars of South Arabian type still lay on a sort of raised bench in this 'temple', some bearing the disc and crescent symbol, or the club or mace also connected with Ilmuqah. Such altars testify to the use of aromatics in the worship of the gods in Ethiopia as well as Arabia. An inscription from Gobochela alluded to the dedication of an altar by a *mukarrib* of D'MT and Saba to Ilmuqah. Also found were the statue in white stone of an animal (probably a bull like the alabaster and schist examples found at Hawelti-see below), and two round altars on tripod legs, made of alabaster, comparable to two round altars with disc and crescent symbols and inscriptions found at Hawelti. At Enda Cherqos (de Contenson 1961ii) a rectangular basilican church dating to perhaps the fifth century was revealed, with, built into it, the remains of older inscriptions mentioning the gods Astar, Hawbas and Ilmuqah, Dhat-Himyam and Dhat-Ba'adan as well as the title '*mukarrib* of D'MT and Saba' (Schneider 1961).

At the site of Hawelti (de Contenson 1963ii) two more rectangular structures were found, surrounded with a sort of bench on which had been placed ex-voto pottery figures of bovids and other animals, including a leopard and a tusked boar, primitive models of steatopygous women (forming an interesting comparison with the female statuettes found at Adulis and Matara, see Ch. 12: 1 & 5), model houses, and miniature yokes. From here also came an elaborately-carved throne and a statue in white limestone (parts of others were found too) which has close stylistic connexions with another found at Addi Galamo near Atsbi Dera (Caquot and Drewes 1955). The latter is associated with a plinth bearing an inscription which has been interpreted as reading 'That he might grant a child to Yamanat (YMNT)' – (but see also Ryckmans 1958). Usually the Hawelti 'throne' and statue are thought of as ex-voto offerings to the lord of the temple by richer citizens (de Contenson 1962); but Jacqueline Pirenne (1967) proposed that the two statues and covered thrones represented the naos and the divinity of each of the temples. She also suggested, with some likelihood, that some of the objects found at Gobochela, Hawelti and Enda Cherqos were actually older than the structures involved. They had been taken from a now-destroyed temple of the 'Sabaean' period, either by descendants of the original dedicators of the altars, or by worshippers who still venerated the same gods but had lost the skill to produce such monuments. This would explain the juxtaposition of finely carved altar, inscriptions, thrones and statues with crude structures and

55. The interior of the great pre-Aksumite temple at Yeha; the best preserved of all the ancient structures in the country.

rough pottery ex-voto objects. Hawelti also produced some bronze objects, rings and openwork plaques, similar to others found with pottery deposits in small pits at Sabea in the Agame district (Leclant and Miquel 1959). Numerous other articles came from the stele area and some apparently ritual deposits at Hawelti. The general impression is that the objects were left at the temple as reminders to the gods about a number of human affairs; childbirth or fertility in the family, crops and domestic animals, protection against wild animals, safety and prosperity of the house, and other such cares. Further possible ex-voto objects consist of crescents and phallic or female figures from Sembel-Cuscet (Asmara) and Aksum (Tringali 1987).

Both the temple at Yeha and the throne from Hawelti depict the ibex, the sacred animal connected with the worship of Ilmuqah. Perhaps the bull (also sacred to Ilmuqah) succeeded the ibex in popularity as an ex-voto offering in Ethiopia, since several bull-figures have been found in Ilmuqah temples there, and one small schist image from Gobochela even has a dedication to Ilmuqah written on it (Leclant 1959: 50, pls. XXXIX-XL; Drewes 1959: 95–7). The bull was also the symbol of Sin, the moon-god particularly venerated in the South Arabian kingdom of Hadramawt, where the bull was depicted with the letters SYN on coins issued at the Hadrami royal castle called Shaqar in the capital, Shabwa. Most of these pre-Christian sites are marked by stelae, but it seems that they served as memorials or offering places rather than tomb-markers as later in Aksum. Apart from the disc and crescent symbols found on the altars, the later Matara and Anza stelae also bear these symbols, which may indicate that the great stelae at Aksum were similarly dedicated on the now-missing metal plaques at their summits. Pottery with the symbol has been found, and it appeared on the coins until the reign of Ezana, when the cross began to be used instead. The disc and crescent, however, presumably divested of its sacred character, continued to be used in Ethiopia as (apparently) a mint-mark on coins until the very end of the coinage (Munro-Hay 1984i: see Gersem, Armah).

Apart from the 'state' religions (if we may call them so) of the Sabaean or D'MT periods, there was probably an underlying stratum of more popular beliefs connected with animals, birds, and the various manifestations of nature, the weather, and so forth. It may be that some of these survived in magical rites connected with the kingship and enacted at the royal coronation, preserved by the continuance of that ceremony at Aksum in the time of the Solomonic restoration (see Ch. 7: 6).

A priesthood, presumably arranged in some sort of hierarchy, would have served the gods and made the offerings and sacrifices. It seems quite likely that the king, claiming divine descent, may have held a prominent place in it, perhaps as high-priest, at least of the dynastic deity Mahrem. However, there is no indication of this in the surviving texts, and nothing is known of the personnel of the pre-Aksumite temples. At the earliest period, the *mukarribs* of D'MT and Saba may have acted as both priest, offerer of sacrifices, and ruler, since these attributes are apparently represented in the meaning of the title (Ryckmans, J., 1951). Later, when the title *mlkn* (malik, king), and *nagashi* came into vogue, the greater part of the priestly side of the kingship may have been entrusted to one or several high-priests and their subordinates, but this is simply surmise.

Paribeni (1907: 469–70) found near his 'Ara del Sole', trenches with walls lined with stone (and in one case containing two rows of bricks), and filled with ashes. In the lower levels these contained no other material but ashes, and Paribeni suggested that they were dug to receive the material from animal cremations. He noted the care with which the pure ashes were deposited in the trenches, but added that there were no traces of carbonised bones. Around the Aksumite stelae, several deposits of carbonised bone were noted, and it seems very possible that dedicatory meals were prepared as part of the ceremonies of burial during the pagan period.

2. The Conversion to Christianity.

The primary evidence for the conversion of Ethiopia in the reign of Ezana in the fourth century is found in the king's own inscriptions and coins. In the former (Ch. 11: 5), the locutions used to express his devotion to the gods are altered to Christian forms. The coins also abandon the disc and crescent symbol and replace them with a cross or several crosses, and a cross is even found on one of Ezana's inscriptions written in the Epigraphic South Arabian script, on the reverse of a Greek text which opens with Christian phraseology (Schneider 1976ii). An important feature of the coinage, already briefly noted (Ch. 9: 3), is that Ezana's Christian issue in gold with the name written Ezanas, is of the weight in use before the reform of the Roman currency by Constantine the Great in 324AD. His next issue, on which the name is written as Ezana, followed the new pattern. This means that at some time relatively close to 324, Ezana had already decided to proclaim his new faith on his coinage. Even if we imagine that coins of the earlier weight might have been issued at Aksum for a few years after Constantine's reform, we still have a very early date for the conversion of Ezana and the appearance of the cross on Aksumite coinage (Munro-Hay 1990).

This 'official' conversion of the king is confirmed by Rufinus (ed. Migne 1849: 478–80), a contemporary Latin writer, who derived his information from Aedesius of Tyre, who had been a prisoner and servant in the royal household at Aksum with Frumentius, the future bishop. Since Rufinus' account is so important for the history of Christianity in Ethiopia, it is given here in full in translation;

One Metrodorus, a philosopher, is said to have penetrated to further India in order to view places and see the world. Inspired by his example, one Meropius, a philosopher of Tyre, wished to visit India with a similar object, taking with him two small boys who were related to him and whom he was educating in humane studies. The younger of these was called Aedesius, the other Frumentius. When, having seen and taken note of what his soul fed upon, the philosopher had begun to return, the ship, on which he travelled put in for water or some other necessary at a certain port. It is the custom of the barbarians of these parts that, if ever the neighbouring tribes should report that their treaty with the Romans is broken, all Romans found among them should be massacred. The philosopher's ship was boarded; all with himself were put to the sword. The boys were found studying under a tree and preparing their lessons, and, preserved by the mercy of the barbarians, were taken to the king. He made one of them, Aedesius, his cupbearer. Frumentius, whom he had perceived to be sagacious and prudent, he made his treasurer and secretary. Therefore they were held in great honour and affection by the king.

The king died, leaving his wife with an infant son as heir of the bereaved kingdom. He gave the young men liberty to do what they pleased but the queen besought them with tears, since she had no more faithful subjects in the whole kingdom, to share with her the cares of governing the kingdom until her son should grow up, especially Frumentius, whose ability was equal to guiding the kingdom - for the other, though loyal and honest of heart, was simple.

While they lived there and Frumentius held the reins of government in his hands, God stirred up his heart and he began to search out with care those of the Roman merchants who were Christians and to give them great influence and to urge them to establish in various places conventicles to which they might resort for prayer in the Roman manner. He himself, moreover, did the same and so encouraged the others, attracting them with his favour and his benefits, providing them with whatever was needed, supplying sites for buildings and other necessaries, and in every way promoting the seed of Christianity in the country.

When the prince for whom they exercised the regency had grown up, they completed and faithfully delivered over their trust, and, though the queen and her son sought greatly to detain them and begged them to remain, returned to the Roman Empire. Aedesius hastened to Tyre to revisit his parents and relatives. Frumentius went to Alexandria, saying that it was not right to hide the work of God. He laid the whole affair before the bishop and urged him to look for some worthy man to send as bishop over the many Christians already congregated and the churches built on barbarian soil. Then Athanasius (for he had recently assumed the episcopate) having carefully weighed and considered Frumentius' words and deeds, declared in a council of the priests: 'What other man shall we find in whom the Spirit of God is as in thee, who can accomplish these things?' And he consecrated him, and bade him return in the grace of God whence he had come. And when he arrived in India as bishop, such grace is said to have been given to him by God that apostolic miracles were wrought by him and a countless number of barbarians were converted by him to the faith. From which time Christian peoples and churches have been created in the parts of India, and the priesthood has begun. These facts I know not from vulgar report but from the mouth of Aedesius himself, who had been Frumentius' companion and was later made a priest in Tyre (Jones and Munroe 1955: 26–7).

Rufinus' story is simply told and involves no incredible miracles or impossible situations. The two youths, Frumentius and Aedesius, and their kinsman Meropius, were apparently all Tyrians with Greek names and education (Pétridès 1972). The lapsing of a Romano-Ethiopian treaty resulted in their captivity and servitude in the Aksumite royal household. On the death of the king (Ousanas Ella Amida?; see Ch. 4: 5) Aedesius and Frumentius were given freedom to leave if they wished, but chose to remain in the country. Frumentius being appointed to look after state matters by the queen regent, took the opportunity to encourage Christians in the country where he could. King Ezana, on attaining his majority, assumed control of the administration; he may already have been converted by Frumentius and Aedesius, but no mention of this is made. In any event, they departed for the Roman world to return home. However, when Frumentius went to Alexandria to report on the progress of Christianity in Ethiopia, and to ask for a bishop for Aksum from Athanasius, the patriarch, he was himself chosen and consecrated, in about 330AD, and so returned to Aksum again as its bishop. This founded the custom of receiving a bishop from the patriarchs of Alexandria which continued until our own time (Munro-Hay, *The Metropolitan Episcopate of Ethiopia, and the Patriarchate of Alexandria, 4th–14th centuries*, forthcoming).

The custom had its advantages. From the point of view of the Alexandrine patriarchs, it kept the Aksumite kingdom within the sphere of influence of the see of St. Mark, with the Nubian kingdoms of Nobatia, Alodia, and Makoria and the Libyan Pentapolis. The patriarch retained the right, established by Athanasius' consecration of Frumentius, to select a bishop for Ethiopia's metropolitan see. Eventually the system whereby the bishop chosen had to be a Coptic Egyptian monk, no native Ethiopian being eligible, became accepted. As far as the Ethiopian ruler was concerned, this meant that he had as local head of the church a foreigner, probably almost completely ignorant of the conditions prevailing in the country, and even of its language; in short, one whose interference in local politics was likely to be minimal, and who could offer little rivalry to the king's decrees. It is not certain when this arrangement became institutionalised, but it was later 'established' by an apocryphal canon attributed to the Council of Nicea. At times all did not work out so well. On one occasion a metropolitan or *abun* arrived with forged credentials and, since the distance to Alexandria was great and the journey difficult, it took time before the imposture was detected. Another problem arose when a king and metropolitan fell out, and the patriarch refused to send a new *abun*. It was the absence of *abun*s and the quarrel with the patriarchate which was piously believed to have caused the punishment delivered by the mysterious 'Queen of the Bani al-Hamwiyya' about whom an unnamed Ethiopian king wrote to king Girgis II of Nubia in the tenth century (Ch. 4: 8).

3. Abreha and Atsbeha.

According to the Ethiopian traditional accounts of the conversion, Frumentius was captured during the reign of Ella Alada (Amida?), who was succeeded by two brothers, Abreha and Atsbeha, who were the first Christian kings. It has been suggested (Hahn 1983) that these names were constituent parts of the titulary of Ezana and his brother Sazana, but, as mentioned above (Ch. 7: 3) there is no real proof for this joint reign. They could alternatively have been two successive 'Ella'-names adopted by Ezana. It may also be that, due to a confusion of legends, the conversion has become muddled with the other great Aksumite religious event, king Kaleb's invasion of the Yemen to end persecution of Christians there. As Kaleb's throne name was Ella Atsbeha, and the name of the rebellious general in the Yemen was Abreha, this theory could easily provide the explanation for the Ethiopian legend (Ullendorff 1949). Abreha built the great cathedral at San'a, and tried to turn it into a major pilgrimage centre, and so both he and Kaleb gained reputations as powerful champions of Christianity. Abreha is said to have written to the *najashi* saying 'I have built a church for you, O King, such as has not been built for any king before you. I shall not rest until I have diverted the Arab's pilgrimage to it' (Guillaume 1955: 21)

Some more ideas on the identity of Ezana and the date of his conversion have recently been aired. One theory (de Blois 1988) concluded that the Aksumite ruler Ezana of Constantius II's time was a different person from king Ezana, son of Ella Amida, known from his inscriptions. This latter would have been an uncle and direct predecessor of Kaleb, the brother of Kaleb's father Tazena, and the Andug of the Syriac sources; his reign would have concluded between 518 and 523. He would have been the first Ethiopian royal convert to Christianity, the earlier Ezana of the fourth century having retained his pagan beliefs; in spite of the presence of Frumentius, later consecrated bishop of Aksum, and in spite of Constantius II's communication with him on ecclesiastical affairs.This view of the position of Ezana, multiplied into two kings, once again takes little account of the concrete evidence from the coinage. The consistency of the gold content in all three gold issues bearing the names of Ezanas/Ezana, the heavier weight of Ezanas' pagan and Christian issues, and the fact that the Ezana issue reduces its weight to follow the contemporary Roman weight reduction, together with stylistic points, conclusively place Ezana in the fourth century, and indicate that the conversion took place as the Ethiopian traditions relate. The difference between the coins of Ezana Bisi Halen and Kaleb in terms of style, weight, gold content, and palaeography is radical, and the two cannot possibly have been successive rulers. Schneider (1988) also dismisses this new theory for other reasons.

Laszlo Török (1988) accepts that the king Ezana who was a contemporary of emperor Constantius II eventually converted to Christianity. But he holds that this could only have happened after 361, since he believes that the text of Constantius II's letter 'is unambiguous as to the paganism of the tyrants Aizanas and Sazanas'. He goes on to say that 'everything thus points to the probability that Ezana's conversion, and consequently, the campaign against the Noba and Meroe, cannot be dated earlier than the decade after 361, perhaps closer to 370 than 360'. Török also believes that the inscription published by Anfray, Caquot and Nautin (1970) does not belong to Ezana but to a brother and successor of his whose name he reads AG..AS.

The first of these ideas is evidently based on a subjective reading of the letter of Constantius II. It can as well be asserted that the emperor did not specifically address the Aksumite rulers as Christians since he knew perfectly well that they were Christians, and had been for some time. He simply began to discuss an ecclesiastical point important to him with people he regarded as fellow Christians, and nowhere is there any remark which seems 'unambiguously' to indicate their paganism.

The evidence for the postulated ruler AG..AS remains equally unconvincing. It seems far more probable that this king AG..AS never existed. There are no coins bearing his name, and the inscription almost certainly belongs to Ezana (exceptionally spelled AZANAS) as Anfray, Caquot and Nautin believed. Most importantly, it bears Ezana's well-known coinage and inscriptional title Bisi-Alēne as well as his patronymic Elle Amida; the Greek spelling of the Bisi-title is in this case also exceptional, being rendered as either Bisi Alene or Bisi Alēn on the coins. The inscription appears to be a version in Greek, with slight variations, of the 'monotheistic' vocalised Ge'ez inscription DAE 11 (Ch. 11: 5) of Ezana Ella Amida Bisi Halen. It is notable that in the case of the pagan inscriptions DAE 4, 6 and 7 of Aeizanas, and their parallels on the Geza 'Agmai inscription, there are also small variations between the different versions. The most interesting here is that whereas the former version writes Saiazana and Adefan in Greek for the king's brothers' names, the latter writes Sazanan and Adiphan, showing a similar variation in the spelling of proper names; we now have four different spellings of Ezana's name in Greek; (Ezana(s), Aeizanas, Aizanas, Azanas). In sum, neither of these two latest ideas about the chronology of Ezana, and the Ethiopian conversion, seem strong enough to alter the view generally accepted.

4. Ecclesiastical Development.

Not very much is known of the early centuries of church history in Ethiopia. After the royal adoption of Christianity, numbers of people may have simply followed the lead of the monarchy. Beyond this predictable guidance from a powerful ruler towards his subordinates, we have no idea which particular features of the new faith may have made it appeal to the Aksumites, but in time Christianity became a strong influence in Ethiopia. Constantius II's attempt (Ch. 4: 5) to subordinate Frumentius to his Arian appointee in Alexandria was unsuccessful, and Frumentius, under the names Feremnatos

Fig. 55a. A late 17th century picture from a Life of Aregawi, written and painted at Dabra Damo, showing the Nine Saints. Photo B. Juel-Jensen, MS Aeth. J-J 44.

or Abba Salama, is still revered in Ethiopia as the founder of the faith. The lists of the metropolitans (which do not always include the same names) show a continuous line of *abun*s of whom nothing at all is known (Guidi 1871; Zotenberg 1877; Chaine 1925; Ayele Teklahaymanot 1984; Munro-Hay, forthcoming). Other bishoprics were established, including Adulis. One incumbent of the latter see, Moses, is known from a travel account dated to the fifth century (Derrett 1960; Desanges 1969).

The main event of the period, and one which had a profound effect on Christian Ethiopia, was the arrival of missionaries, like the so-called 'Nine Saints'. They came largely, it seems, from the eastern Roman Empire, doubtless fleeing from persecutions there (Sergew Hable Sellassie 1972: 115ff). After 451 AD the Council of Chalcedon had condemned the monophysite belief, but Alexandria and its dependent churches continued, despite the persecution, to hold to the doctrine of Christ's single nature. The Ethiopian hagiographies refer to an influx of 'Roman' Christians at about this time as the *Tsadqan*, or 'Righteous Ones'. They, and the Nine Saints, and doubtless others like them, possibly including some Syriac-speaking Roman subjects, began or continued the spreading of Christianity into the Ethiopian countryside, and established their hermitages in places which are still local cult centres. Two of these missionaries, Abba Liqanos and Abba Pantelewon, are commemorated by churches in the environs of Aksum itself, on small hills which may have previously been pagan sanctuaries. Pantelewon's monastery is said to have been the place where king Kaleb retired after his abdication (Budge 1928: III, 914). The missionary Abba Afse went to Yeha, site of the largest and most important Sabaean temple in the region. A number of these wandering monks are said to have suffered persecution from the pagan inhabitants of the land, before their miracles, and some timely help from the royal armies in the case of the Balaw-Kalaw or Bur people near Matara (Sergew Hable Sellassie 1972: 125–6; Schneider 1963: 168) persuaded the populace of their virtue.

Monasteries like Dabra Damo were also founded by the sixth century (though the surviving church is thought to be rather later - Buxton 1970: 102). This particular monastery is supposed to have been founded by Kaleb's son Gabra Masqal on the site where another of the Nine Saints, Aregawi, settled. He was the founder of monasticism in Ethiopia, and it becomes frequent in the hagiographies to hear of people retiring to either hermitage or monastery. Both Kaleb and his son Wa'zeb followed Ezana's example in emphasising their faith by the epithet *Gabra Krestos*, servant of Christ, in their inscriptions (Ch. 11: 5).

Biblical quotations appearing in the inscriptions indicate that the translation into Ge'ez was well under way by the fifth to seventh centuries. The Aksumites received apocryphal books as well; the *Book of Henok* (Enoch) and others are only preserved in their entirety in their Ge'ez versions (Ullendorff 1968: 34). Some works dealing with the rules and regulations of monastic communities were also translated; these would have helped in the establishment and regulation of the Aksumite monasteries.

By the sixth century, if the Ethiopian legends are to be believed, the liturgical music attributed to Yared was being used (Ch. 13: 4). Ethiopian church ritual today contains many extraordinary features, which may well date even to pre-Aksumite times. There is also a strong Jewish element, owing to Jewish influences received, it seems, before the introduction of Christianity. The modern 'Ethiopian Jews' the Falashas, present, according to Ullendorff (1973: 106–7), a remarkable mixture of pagan, Jewish and Christian elements from Aksumite times. Their 'Judaism' would not be more than a reflection of those Jewish elements imported into Ethiopia from South Arabia, which have been added to both pre-Christian and Christian beliefs.

The distance and irregularity of patriarchal supervision must have allowed many things to be retained in, or adopted by, Ethiopian Christianity, which Alexandria might not have entirely condoned. Thus there is a very individual slant to Ethiopian church ceremony. Deacons (called *dabtara*) dance before the *tabot* or ark at festivals, whilst the music of drums and sistra, local violins and trumpets accompany the splendid chants of Yared. The sistrum was used in ancient Egypt and may have entered Ethiopia from there; though its use doubtless spread in later times through the worship of Isis in the Roman empire. Special festivals, like Timkat, a ceremonial re-baptism, and the keeping of the Jewish Sabbath, annoyed the Catholic Portuguese and contributed to their failure in Ethiopia. Circumcision is practised, priests marry, magical spells with a Christian overtone are employed for defence against demons, and innumerable fast and feast days swell the church calendar. Much of this must have existed already in the Aksumite kingdom, and from what evidence we have it seems that the Ethiopian church quickly became one of the great institutions in the country.

The Aksumites do not seem to have been plagued with many heresies, but there is an interesting account which does mention one. When the Byzantine bishop Longinus, in the 580s, was in the southern Nubian kingdom of Alodia, he came across persons who had been converted to the heretical belief of Julian of Halicarnassus (who held that Christ's body was incorruptible), by Aksumite missionaries (John of Ephesus, ed. Brooks 1952: versio 180; Vantini 1975: 20 for an English translation). Perhaps these had been sent in the days when Aksum still claimed suzerainty over the Noba; the last incidence of such claims is that of Wa'zeb in his inscriptional titulary. In any event Longinus persuaded those who advocated this heresy that they were wrong, and received their recantations. The account, preserved by John of Ephesus, is interesting in that it tells us that in the sixth century Aksumites were propagating the Christian faith in Africa and Arabia.

CHURCHES.

Abreha and Atsbeha are supposed, according to the *Book of Aksum* (Conti Rossini 1910: 3), to have constructed the cathedral at Aksum on land which Christ miraculously dried up from a former lake for the purpose. There were, in fact, certainly two earlier Aksumite buildings there already, the remains of which were excavated by MM. de Contenson and Anfray, and the podium of the present cathedral rests on another Aksumite structure, possibly an earlier church (de Contenson 1959, 1963: Anfray 1965). One or both of these earlier buildings may have been associated with a pre-Christian temple if, as elsewhere, the custom was to establish the church on an already sanctified site, though the excavated remains seem rather to show the usual type of 'mansion' style of structure for the buildings. The church of Abba Pantelewon, outside Aksum, for example, seems to have been built on a site already in use in pre-Christian times. There is said to be a stone staircase inside it, but this is inaccessible to all but the priests.

The cathedral of Aksum, 'Our Lady Mary of Zion', or Maryam Tseyon, was also known as Gabaza Aksum, *gabaz* referring to a church or holy place. Land charters, surviving only as later 'copies', detail lands purportedly given to the church by Abreha and Atsbeha, Gabra Masqal, and Anbessa Wedem (Huntingford 1965). An early account of the church's magnificence is said to have been related to the prophet Muhammad during his last illness by two

56. View of the east end of the old cathedral of Maryam Tseyon at Aksum, showing the podium built on the ruins of an earlier, Aksumite, structure.

of his wives, Umm Habiba and Umm Salama, both of whom had been in exile in Ethiopia with their former husbands in the 620s. The description mentions that the walls were covered with paintings, and, if so, is testimony to the early commencement of a type of decoration which later became standard for Ethiopian churches (Sergew Hable Sellassie 186, n. 30). The cathedral was destroyed or damaged several times, the last but one before the present structure being a large five-aisled edifice, which was eventually destroyed by the Muslim armies under Ahmad Gragn. Alvares' description of the church and its environs, extremely valuable as it is the only surviving eye-witness description of the ancient church, is as follows (Beckingham and Huntingford 1961: 151)

> *"a very noble church, the first there was in Ethiopia: it is named Mary of Syon. They say that it is so named because its altar stone came from Sion. In this country (as they say) they have the custom always to name the churches by the altar stone, because on it is written the name of the patron saint. This stone which they have in this church, they say that the apostles sent it from Mount Sion. This church is very large; it has five aisles of good width and of great length, vaulted above, and all the vaults closed, the ceiling and sides all painted. Below, the body of the church is well worked with handsome cut stone; it has seven chapels, all with their backs to the east, and their altars well ornamented. It has a choir after our fashion, except that it is low, and they reach the vaulted roof with their heads; and*

the choir is also over the vault, and they do not use it. This church has a very large circuit, paved with flagstones like the lids of tombs. This consists of a very high wall, and it is not covered over like those of the other churches, but is left open. This church has a large enclosure, and it is also surrounded with another larger enclosure, like the enclosing wall of a large town or city. Within this enclosure are handsome groups of one storey buildings, and all spout out their water by strong figures of lions and dogs of stone [of different colours]. Inside this large enclosure there are two mansions, one on the right hand and the other on the left, which belong to the two rectors of the church; and the other houses are of canons and monks."

Alvares as one might expect, records that this church, was supposed to have been built by queen Candace.

It is presumed that the church of Maryam Tseyon as Alvares saw it reflects the result of continual development from an original foundation in or after the fourth century, through a number of improvements and additions. A proposed restoration of the church has been attempted by Buxton and Matthews (1974), basing their ideas on Alvares' not always very clear description. They also embody certain details of architecture from the Lalibela churches, which were constructed or decorated according to something of the same architectural tradition.

The *Book of Aksum* (Conti Rossini 1910) lists a number of churches, some of whose names were bestowed, following local tradition, on the palaces which the DAE found in 1906. The early churches of Ethiopia seem to have been apsidal basilicas, apparently following the plan customarily used in Syria (Anfray 1974: 763ff). This contrasts sharply to the round churches of the present day, which may well be based on a local African architectural tradition, but the province of Tigray is still largely characterised by churches of the rectangular plan.

In Aksum, two basilicas were found on Beta Giyorgis hill, and one was excavated (Ricci 1976; Ricci and Fattovich 1987). The structure, designated 'Bieta Giyorgis Superiore' from its position, showed two main building-periods. The lower structure was of typical Aksumite construction, but showed a variation in plan as it had side wings flanking the north and south walls near the east, or apsidal, end. A later structure was built on the original, without the usual Aksumite recessed plan, and consisting of a rectangular room whose roof was supported by four stone columns arranged in pairs, and with pilasters built in with the main walls on three sides (Ricci and Fattovich 1987: fig. e). In many places tombs had been constructed under the paving, and the paving, doorsills and the like sometimes included re-used stelae, probably brought from the stele-field found by Ricci on top of the Beta Giyorgis hill. In addition, some decorative stonework was found, including a block carved in relief with a Greek cross, and various fragments apparently from stepped column bases, from a column which was cruciform in section,

57. The relatively modern rectangular church of Maryam Tehot at Edaga Hamus stands on the ruins of an Aksumite structure distinguished by the use of cut stones in the walling instead of the usual mud-bound rubble.

and from water-spouts. A capital was also found, carved with volutes in relief.

A further basilica was excavated at Enda Cherqos (de Contenson 1961). Others are known at Matara (Anfray 1974: 756ff), and several at Adulis (Paribeni 1907; Anfray 1974: 750; Munro-Hay 1989i). Further such churches have been found at Agula and Qwiha, and very likely the surviving structures at Tekondo and Qohayto include churches (Doresse 1957: 200–201). An early (sixth-century? – Doresse 1957: 231–2) church was also constructed inside the temple at Yeha. Doresse speculated as to whether the internal circular colonnade of one of the Adulis churches excavated by Paribeni (1907: fig. 50) might represent an early example of a tendency towards the circular plan. Paribeni himself thought that the circular pillared structure in the church was a later addition, perhaps the support for a wooden baldaquin over some now-removed object. It may be that during the centuries there were some changes in the church ritual which were felt to be better expressed by the round church plan, though, as the rectangular type also continued in use, it may rather be attributed to ease of construction, or perhaps to the move southward of the Christian Ethiopian kingdom, where it simply reflected the common house-type. Where rock-cut churches are concerned, this architectural consideration obviously did not apply; though in fact most rock-cut churches may be earlier in date than the period when round churches became common.

The most splendid surviving built church is that at the monastery of Dabra Damo which may even go back to the sixth century, and there are a few other old built churches surviving. Of the vast number of rock-hewn churches in Tigray (Plant 1985), some may date to Aksumite times, and certainly many have Aksumite architectural features. Some of the Aksumite peculiarities of design and structure are also apparent at the rock-cut churches of Lalibela, carved and completed at an uncertain date, but usually attributed to Zagwé times, long after the end of Aksum (for exceptional pictures of some of these, see Gerster 1970).

A feature of some Aksumite churches was the baptistery. What seems to have been a building including a baptistery or similar monument survives at Wuchate Golo, just west of Aksum (de Contenson 1961i). The Wuchate Golo structure consisted of a podium approached by steps, and surrounded by corridors, on which the main feature was a circular cistern paved with a large rounded stone. Small stelae, benches and basins lay around the main building, which was flanked by a lesser structure containing five rooms. The coins found at Wuchate Golo seem all to be of the sixth or even early seventh century, and pottery fragments with crosses were excavated, implying a late Aksumite date for this curious building. De Contenson suggested that it represents a Christian church of a special type (1961i: 6–7).

Other baptisteries, with access to the water provided by two staircases, are known from Yeha (Doresse 1957: 232, and fig. opposite p. 240), Adulis (Paribeni 1907: fig. 50) and Matara. This latter was fed by an ingenious pipe-system formed by the bodies of pottery amphorae, fitted one within the other, passing through the baptistery wall to the outside (Anfray 1974: 766–8).

It is interesting to note that Kaleb's inscription (Schneider 1974) says "*I founded a* maqdas *in Himyar.....I built his GBZ and consecrated it by the power of the Lord*". Other sources claim that Kaleb built several churches in Himyar (Shahid 1979). The text may employ the word *gabaz* to refer back to the newly-founded church in Himyar, but this sentence, dealing with Kaleb's last act recorded in the inscription, comes in the position usually reserved in earlier examples for the dedication of captives, thrones, statues or the inscription itself, and it might instead signify reconstruction work by Kaleb at Aksum's own cathedral as a gesture of gratitude for his victorious campaign.

XI

Warfare

1. The Inscriptional Record

An important aspect of the Aksumite kings' responsibilities was the conduct of military campaigns, the main theme of almost all the Aksumite royal inscriptions which have survived (see Ch. 11: 5). The significance of this element for the kings is emphasised by Ezana's identification in the pagan period as the son of Mahrem, whose parallel in Greek was the war-god Ares. In most of the inscriptions we are given a fair amount of detail about the campaigns which the Aksumite rulers conducted throughout the Aksumite sphere of influence. Similarly, the South Arabian inscriptions mentioning Habashat and Aksum deal with Ethiopian military activities on the east side of the Red Sea. We therefore have a considerable amount of information about the Aksumites' methods and tactics in warfare. It is very probable that the Aksumite system of controlling subject peoples through their own rulers had the effect of encouraging these to try the strength of their overlords at each succession or other crisis. This might explain the 'revolts' which occurred at places apparently quite near to the centre of the kingdom. The inscriptions and coins often use the word 'peace', but we gather that the 'Pax Aksumita' was, if not apparently seriously challenged, in need of continuous repair.

The Aksumite inscriptions are rather stereotyped in style and content, being the official records of the campaigns. In general, they commence with the reasons for the campaign; these included damage to a trading caravan, DAE 10; rebellion of vassal kings or tribes, DAE 4, 6 & 7, Geza 'Agmai; and a combination of rebellion and a plea for assistance from subjects under attack, DAE 11, Anfray, Caquot and Nautin 1970. Other reasons, implied in a general way by the *Monumentum Adulitanum* inscription, but certainly important, were the need to deal with such questions as frontier security, piracy in the Red Sea, and the security of land routes for trade.

After the justifications for war, the inscriptions next recount any diplomatic efforts towards achieving a peaceful settlement (DAE 11) and, these failing, there finally came the decision to make war.

The next stage in the inscriptions is the account of the campaign itself. Details are supplied as to the routes and encampments, provisioning, the strategy, the troops or regiments used at different phases of the campaign, and the eventual inevitable victory. Geographical information abounds, though it is often difficult to place on the modern map, and the enemies or allies and their environment are also sometimes the object of a brief description.

Finally, the results of the campaign are noted. Men, women, and children killed or captured, and plunder in the form of animals and goods, are all proudly recorded with meticulous figure and word accounting. Any settlements are noted, usually expressed as 'giving laws' to vassal kings and sending them back to their territories after payment of tribute. In some cases the settlement involved retaining land, property and prisoners or transporting tribes to new lands by force. Offerings to the gods, or later the construction of Christian sanctuaries, are the usual acts of gratitude to the deity after these campaigns. Accounts of these form the closing part of the inscriptions. The setting up and consecration of the inscription itself, apparently often as part of a throne, *manbar* – *Monumentum Adulitanum*, DAE 10, DAE 11 (two thrones, one in Shado in Aksum, the other at the confluence of the Seda (Blue Nile) and Takaze (Atbara)) – seems to have been a customary ceremonial act to mark the victory. The inscriptions often terminate with a formula which curses anyone who defaces them. The trilingual inscriptions, (actually written in two languages, Greek and Ge'ez, using three scripts, Greek, Ge'ez and Epigraphic South Arabian) were designed to present the kings' deeds to the local and foreign populace in the best possible light. Two different versions of the Beja campaign inscription of Ezana, in both cases 'trilingual', were set up in different parts of the capital; unless we are missing duplicate copies of other inscriptions as well, this presumably indicates that Ezana was particularly proud of his victory over these people, and also wanted to emphasise his subsequent treatment of them.

Kaleb's inscription (see below) in the South Arabian script alludes to events in Himyar. Another, Ge'ez, inscription carved in alabaster was found at Marib in the Yemen (Kamil 1964; Caquot 1965). This latter inscription was fragmentary but was of exceptional interest as being only the second Ge'ez inscription ever found there (the first was on an alabaster lamp, Grohmann 1911). The inscriptions may mention Kaleb's famous Himyar war against king Yusuf, but what details are known about this campaign come from outside reports.

2. The Military Structure

The military establishment was undoubtedly one of the key institutions of the Aksumite monarchy, and as such was closely associated with it. The king himself was the commander-in-chief, but royal brothers and sons, and perhaps other relatives, were frequently put in charge of campaigns when the king was occupied elsewhere. The semi-sacred character of the monarchy may have been one of the bases of its domination, but the control of its military arm by members of the ruling family must also have been a source of strength and security. It is possible that the brothers of Ezana who were in theoretical charge of the Beja campaign described in the inscription from Geza 'Agmai (Bernand 1982) and in DAE 4, 6 & 7 (Ch. 11: 5) were in fact very young at the time (Munro-Hay 1990), and that experienced military leaders accompanied them. Nevertheless, credit for the victory went to the royal brothers under the supreme authority of the king.

There seems to have been at least one remarkable war-leader king (Ezana), though the achievements of Gadarat earlier in the third century could hardly have been accomplished without some military skill. Kaleb, too, managed to organise a major overseas expedition, and to win an initial success even if the results were, in the long run, negative (see Ch. 4).

The Aksumite army was organised into *sarawit* (sing. *sarwe*), groups or 'regiments' of unknown numerical strength, each with a name (possibly a provincial district name, or a 'tribal' name, see Ch. 7: 5), under their own commanders or generals. The generals of these groups were referred to in the inscription DAE 9 by the title *nagast*, the plural of *negus* or king, exactly the same as the word used in the royal title *negusa nagast*, king of kings, in the same inscription. This indicates the importance of their office, and was possibly a reminiscence of the former sub-kingdoms now part of Aksum. The troops were presumably levied as needed, though there must surely have been some kind of 'Praetorian Guard' at the capital for ordinary guard duties about the palace, treasury and the king's person. In mediaeval times such troops were designated by the name of the part of the palace which they guarded. If the troop-names were related to provinces, perhaps the local rulers had to send contingents on demand to their overlord in Aksum. Sergew Hable Sellassie (1972: 95) suggested that the troop-names referred to function, identifying commando, elephant-fighter, and infantry units.

The inscriptions speak of specific troops being sent on certain missions, and thus have preserved several of these Aksumite troop or 'regiment' names. It may transpire that these names are reflected in the 'Bisi'- title of the kings, as one or two have a close resemblance to those of individual kings. The 'regiment' names known include Hara, Halen, Damawa, Sabarat, Hadefan, Sabaha, Dakuen, Laken, Falha, Sera, Metin, Mahaza; they have been referred to by different modern authors as detachments, *Truppe*, armies, *corpi di militzia, colonnes,* and *troupes*, all translations from the Ge'ez word *sarwe*. Unfortunately, as yet we do not have the Greek translation of this from any of the inscriptions. From the known 'Bisi'-titles of Aksumite rulers we can find parallels as follows: Halen for Halen; Hadefan for Hadefan; and Dakuen for Dakhu.

When on campaign, encampments were set up, possibly in some cases in recognised military stations or garrisons, or traditional muster-points. Certain provisions were requisitioned where necessary from the enemy's country. Others were brought on beasts of burden or by human portage.

Mention is made of the water-corvée, and the provision of water must have been particularly important when the campaigns reached the more arid areas. Camels were certainly used in transport, and are sometimes specified among the plunder taken.

There is no hint as to the size of the regiments or the armies, but in various inscriptions the dead and captured are noted as follows; DAE 11- killed 758, prisoners 629; DAE 10- killed 705, prisoners 205; Kaleb inscription; killed, more than 400 men (figure lost for women and children). Fifty of the captives in DAE 10 were given to Mahrem as an offering. In the sixth century Arabian war, the historian Procopius says that the Ethiopian army sent by Kaleb to the Yemen to punish the usurper Abreha and his supporters for the deposition of Sumyafa' Ashwa' consisted of three thousand men; a figure the more convincing for its relative modesty. This army in fact turned against Kaleb, and remained to support Abreha (Procopius, ed. Dewing 1914: 191). Later Arab writers elevate the numbers of men sent to the Yemen to 70,000 men under Aryat (Guillaume 1955: 20, after Ibn Ishaq). Tabari (Zotenberg 1958: 182) agrees with this figure, mentioning that Dhu Nuwas (Yusuf Asar) had 5000 men at San'a; he then says that the *najashi* sent another army with 100,000 men under Abreha. After Abreha's rebellion the *najashi* sent another 4000 with Aryat's second mission, and on its failure began to assemble yet another army to punish Abreha. The numbers of men in these armies, swelling as the story develops, are certainly highly exaggerated, and only Procopius' information seems credible; though of course there is always the standard explanation that the lower figures represent the real fighting strength, and the higher the whole mass of non-combatant dependents. The inscription of Yusuf Asar Yathar (Rodinson 1969) claims that he took 11, 000 prisoners, but even if the figure is a true one, many of these must have been from Arabs fighting against the king on the side of the *najashi*.

3. Weapons

Military equipment is shown on certain stelae at Aksum. The so-called 'Stele of the Lances' is now known to be part of Stele 4 (after the DAE notation), whose apex is to be found elsewhere in the town (Chittick 1974: 163); on it two spears, one with a long blade and one with a shorter blade, were depicted. The Ethiopian slave Wahsi, one of the first of his countrymen to embrace Islam, was famed for his skill with the spear. Ibn Ishaq's comment here is interesting, in that he specifically mentions that Wahsi could *"throw a javelin as the Abyssinians do, and seldom missed the mark"*. Wahsi himself, questioned later at his house in Homs, mentioned that at the time when he killed Hamza, the prophet Muhammad's uncle, in battle, he was *"a young Abyssinian, skilful like my countrymen in the use of the javelin"* (Guillaume 1955: 371, 376). He also killed the false prophet Musaylima with his javelin after Muhammad's death. It seems from the reports about Wahsi's career that spear-fighting was an Ethiopian speciality at the time.

58. The reverse of the so-called Stele of the Lances (part of no. 4), depicting a round shield.

On the reverse of the Stele of the Lances is depicted a round shield. What may be a round shield is also carved on the back of the still-standing Stele 3. The Arab author al-Maqrizi, who died in the mid-fifteenth century, mentions that the Beja still used shields of buffalo-hide called 'aksumiyya' and 'dahlakiyya' (Maqrizi,*al-Khitat* Ch. 32, in Vantini 1975: 621). The former were made of buffalo-skin, reversed or 'turned round the side'.

No personal armour has yet been found, nor are there any surviving representations of soldiers, except from one most unusual source. In the Musée des Tissus, Lyon, there is brightly coloured woven textile fragment, apparently of Egyptian manufacture of the sixth century, which, it has been suggested, is a copy of a Persian textile based on an original fresco (Browning 1971: 176). Grabar thought it might be either imported from Persia or made in a factory in the Roman empire after an Iranian model (1967: 326). It came from the excavations at Antinoë, and is thought to represent a battle scene from one of the Yemeni (or Aksumite – Grabar, 1967: fig. 382) wars of the time of Khusrau I. A seated potentate, possibly the Persian king himself or perhaps his viceroy, is enthroned, seated in a hieratic pose holding his sword, point downwards, watching a contest between Persian warriors and black and white troops. The Persians are shown mounted or on foot, fully clothed with tunic and trousers, and armed with bows. Their adversaries wear only a small kilt, and what seems to be a sword-belt diagonally across one shoulder; a black warrior, who seems to be a captive tied by a rope to a Persian horseman, has his broad-bladed, flat-ended sword slung behind his back. The white warriors are long-haired, like the Persians and earlier Yemenis as depicted on their coins and in sculpture, and one holds a small round shield. This textile may provide the only picture we have of an Aksumite soldier, albeit fighting in the Yemeni wars outside Aksumite control.

The *Periplus* (Huntingford 1980: 21-2) lists certain weapons among the imports into the Aksumite region. Iron (sideros) used for spears is specified, the spears being used for hunting elephants and other animals as well as for war. Swords are also in the list, and iron and steel figure as raw material.

Tomb finds at Aksum have revealed iron weapons, including tanged spear-heads which closely resemble those on the Stele of the Lances. Iron knives or poniards, probably originally with bone or wood handles, were also found, and, from Matara (Anfray and Annequin 1965: pl. LXIV, 1), came a handle of bronze decorated on each side with bosses formed by the heads of large nails. The Aksumite kings depicted on the coins sometimes hold a spear (or, in Aphilas' case – Munro-Hay 1984: 50 – what is apparently a sword), and spears and shields are mentioned in the description of the Byzantine embassy to Ethiopia by John Malalas (see Ch. 7: 2). A few arrow-heads, but no swords as yet, have been found during archaeological excavations in Ethiopia.

Although there is as yet no direct evidence, one would suppose that horses were known and used in warfare; some of the regiments could perhaps have been cavalry forces. That horses were valued possessions in at least one of the lands under Aksumite hegemony is shown by the burial of horses, in elaborate silver and jewelled harness, at the tombs of the 'X-Group' monarchs at Ballana (Kirwan 1973). In later times in Ethiopia favourite chargers were of such importance that a leader could be named after his horse; one suggestion even relates the 'Bisi'-title of the kings to their horses (Pankhurst 1961: 30, n. 68).

The use of elephants for Kaleb's state chariot, and the report (Photius, ed. Freese 1920: I, 17–19) of one of the Byzantine ambassadors, Nonnosus, that he saw some 5000 of them grazing near Aue (sometimes identified with Yeha (Bent 1896: 143–7), but probably further to the north-east; see Ch. 3: 1) on the Adulis-Aksum route, make it possible that they could have been used for military purposes, though Kosmas notes that the Ethiopians rarely trained them (Wolska-Conus 1973: 354). Camels would have been used in desert warfare, and two camel-riding spies were captured by Ezana during his Noba campaign. Camels, as well as donkeys or mules, may have been employed as transport animals.

4. The Fleet

There are numerous occasions when ships and shipping are mentioned in Aksumite contexts. The various expeditions and trading ventures overseas would suggest that Aksum was mistress of a fleet of some kind. Though there is no really clear statement to that effect in the local sources, a fleet is mentioned in the *Monumentum Adulitanum* inscription, and other inscriptions (DAE 2, Marib inscription; see Ch. 11: 5) also refer to expeditions by land and sea. In the case of the Adulis inscription, concern for the sea-lanes and the coastal defence of the country, as well as land routes, is manifested. The king cites the area from Leuke Kome to the Arabian kingdoms as one area of operations, then on the Ethiopian side he established the Solate people to guard the coasts. The *Periplus* (Huntingford 1980: 20) notes that ships anchored cautiously at the island of Oreine since, in the past, the anchorage which was to become Adulis' harbour, Gabaza, had proved dangerous because of raids from the local people. This could not have been tolerated later, when the port's function as a gateway to trade had grown more important, and the *Periplus* may indeed refer to a period when Aksum was still consolidating its position on the coast.

Some of the commentators on Kaleb's expedition to the Yemen allude to ships, and even to the shipyards of Adulis/Gabaza (Munro-Hay 1982: 117; Sergew Hable Sellassie 1972: 132–3). Perhaps the most interesting comment of all came from the sixth-century historian Procopius, who not only stated that Kaleb -whom he called Hellestheaios, his version of Elle Atsbeha- collected a fleet of ships, but also described Ethiopian and Indian ships. He mentions that

> *"all the boats which are found in India and on this sea* (the Red Sea) *are not made in the same manner as are other ships. For neither are they smeared with pitch, nor with any other substance, nor indeed are the planks fastened together by iron nails going through and through, but they are bound together by a kind of cording. The reason is not as most persons suppose, that there are certain rocks there which draw the iron to themselves (for witness the fact that when the Roman vessels sail from Aelas into this sea, although they are fitted with much iron, no such thing has ever happened to them), but rather because the Indians and the Aethiopians possesss neither iron nor any other thing suitable for such purposes.*

Furthermore they are not even able to buy any of these things from the Romans since this is explicitly forbidden to all by law' (Procopius, ed. Dewing 1914: 183–4).

The Aksumite technique whereby ships were made by binding with ropes, not by using nails, which is also mentioned by the *Periplus* as existing on the East African coast (Huntingford 1980: 29), lasted until recently in the Somali, Hadrami, and East African coastal regions, where such 'sewn boats' were common. Procopius information is a very good indication that when he speaks of Kaleb's fleet he was actually referring to Aksumite ships rather than others simply using Aksumite ports. It cannot be said what proportion of goods might have been shipped in Aksumite vessels, but as a trading nation with a maritime outlet of great importance, and later on an empire to administer overseas, it is certain that Aksum's merchant fleet or navy was a useful, even vital, part of the apparatus of commerce and government.

5. The Aksumite Inscriptions

Since a very large part of the information we have about the Aksumite rulers comes from their inscriptions, it seems useful to give English translations of the most important of these. The published versions are very varied; and it is admittedly not easy, given the damaged state of some of the inscriptions, and the uncertainty of meaning of certain words in others, to see what precisely is meant, or where a new train of thought has begun. These translations, then , cannot be thought of as in any way definitive. Even so, something of the mood of the Aksumite inscriptions still comes over in these translations, and there are many interesting details. A number of early Ethiopian inscriptions were published by Drewes (1962), and others by Schneider in various volumes of the *Annales d'Ethiopie*. These are not repeated in this section, but have been quoted where appropriate in other chapters. A *Recueil des textes antiques de l'Ethiopie*, a very much needed compendium, is also in preparation (Bernand 1982: 106). The label DAE indicates the number given to those inscriptions published by the Deutsche Aksum-Expedition (Littmann 1913, IV), and some of Ezana's inscriptions were also published by Littmann in 1950.

DAE 2.

This much-damaged inscription was found at Abba Pantelewon near Aksum. Greek. It has neither name nor titles preserved, but appears to be an Aksumite royal inscription of the pre-Christian period. The translation is from Sergew Hable Sellassie 1972: 69.

...in this space... and he orders(?) to be repaired...it and the other side of the sea...unconquerable (god) of the Aksumite...the first and only(?)...in

distant (and) big...an infantry...I have dedicated...to unconquered Ares of Aksumite...

Monumentum Adulitanum. Greek.

This anonymous inscription only survives in the copy made in the early sixth century AD by Kosmas Indikopleustes at Adulis (Wolska-Conus 1968: 372–8).

...and after I had commanded the peoples near my country to maintain the peace, I entered valiantly into battle and subdued the following peoples; I fought the Gaze, then the Agame and the Siguene, and, having conquered, I reserved for myself half of their lands and their peoples. The Aua and Singabene and Aggabe and Tiamaa and Athagaous and Kalaa and the Samene people who live beyond the Nile in inaccessible mountains covered with snow where tempests and cold are contiuous and the snow so deep that a man sinks up to the knees, I reduced to submission after having crossed the river; then the Lasine, and Zaa and Gabala, who inhabit very steep mountains where hot springs rise and flow; and the Atalmo and the Beja and all the people who erect their tents with them. Having defeated the Taggaiton who dwell up to the frontiers of Egypt I had a road constructed going from the lands of my empire to Egypt.

Then I fought the Annine and the Metine who live on precipitous mountains as well as the people of Sesea. They took refuge on an inaccessible peak, but I beseiged them on all sides and captured them, and chose among them young men and women, boys and virgins. I retained also their goods.

I defeated also the barbarian people of Rauso who live by the aromatics trade, in immense plains without water, and the Solate, whom I also defeated, imposing on them the task of guarding the sea-lanes.

After I had vanquished and conquered, in battles wherein I personally took part, all these peoples so well protected by their impenetrable mountains, I restricted myself to imposing tribute on them and voluntarily returning their lands. But most peoples submitted of their own free will and paid me tribute.

I sent an expedition by sea and land against the peoples living on the other side of the Erythraean Sea, that is the Arabitas and the Kinaidokolpitas, and after subjugating their kings I commanded them to pay me tribute and charged them with guaranteeing the security of communications on land and sea. I conducted war from Leuke Kome to the land of the Sabaeans.

I am the first and only of the kings my predecessors to have subdued all these peoples by the grace given me by my mighty god Ares, who also engendered me. It is through him that I have submitted to my power all the peoples neighbouring my empire, in the east to the Land of Aromatics, to the west to the land of Ethiopia and the Sasou; some I fought myself, against others I sent my armies.

When I had re-established peace in the world which is subject to me I came to Adulis to sacrifice for the safety of those who navigate on the sea, to Zeus, Ares and Poseidon. After uniting and reassembling my armies I set up here this throne and consecrated it to Ares, in the twenty-seventh year of my reign.

The 8th to 10th century manuscripts in which this inscription is preserved have some explanatory glosses about some of these names; thus Gaze apparently means the Aksumites, still called Agaze, the Siguene are the Suskinitai, the tribes near Adulis are called the Tigretes (the earliest mention of Tigray?), the Tiamaa are the Tziamo and Gambela, the Atalmo and Beja are the Blemmyes, the Taggaitai (Tangaitai) are also called Attabite.. and Adra..s, the Sesea are tribes of Barbaria, the Solate are those living by the sea in Barbaria, called the Tigretai of the coast in Barbaria, and Sasou is the furthest part of Ethiopia, beyond which lies the ocean and the Barbareotes who traffic in incense (Huntingford 1989: 43).

DAE 8. Ge'ez written in the South Arabian script.

Inscription attributed to Ezana, but possibly of his predecessor Ousanas (Ella Amida?) Bisi Gisene. For a note about the problems in attributing this text, see Schneider 1987: 615.

.....Ella Amida, Bisi ..s.m, king of Aksum, Himyar, Raydan, Saba, Salhen, Tsiyamo, Bega and of Kasu, king of kings, son of the invincible Mahrem. He departed on campaign to re-establish his empire and put it again in order. Those who obeyed him, he spared; those who resisted him, he put to death.

He came to 'LBH and there came with presents SWSWT king of the Agwezat with his people, and he received his submission and he was made subject. Then he sent him away to return to his country.

Then he arrived at FNSHT and there arrived with his people and presents the king of Gabaz, SBL and he received his submission and he was made subject. Then he sent him away so that he could return to his own country.

Next he came to HMS, and there came all the tribes of Metin, and he received his submission and let them return to their own country. And he improved the roads and subdued the country?

And he provided safe conduct on the road for the bringing of tribute together with provisions for men and women, and gave food to his four armies in enemy country? At the camp where he installed himself, he assured provisionment by requisitions imposed on the enemy. He fought with them, and held a muster (of his troops) in the field and completed their complement (?).

Then he came to ..mo, and he received its (his?) submission; he came also to MTT and fought it (him?) and he reduced MTT with spilling of blood.

Then he (came to) Samen...he extracted tribute.. and he received submission and sent them off so that they could re-establish order in their country. From there he crossed the rivers, and then came ..L the king of WYLQ who said 'Our people are come and with them....establish order with you...O our king.........

(the remaining lines are too fragmentary to be useful)

The Meroë Inscriptions.

Apart from an unvocalised Ge'ez graffito on one of the pyramids of group A (no. 19) at Meroë, reading ..*'son of Julius..all the world..'* (Lepsius, R., *Denkmäler aus Ägypten und Aethiopien* 1913, abth. VI, bl. 13,1), and another on a wall of temple T at Kawa (Laming-Macadam, M. F., *The Temples of Kawa*, I, The Inscriptions, London 1949: 117–8), these inscriptions are the only ones found on Meroitic territory. New versions have at last succeeded to those of Sayce (1909 and 1912).

Meroë I. Greek. Translation of Bersina (1984).

...king of the Aksumites and Himyarites...immediately attack those who rival...did not submit contrary... kingdoms(?) to them, and I destroyed the...the said ones, heading for this place...originating from another ten... with the king as far as... most of all in Sue...chiefs and all their children... I came immediately...to your homes... besides the fruit (tribute)... copper.. years 21 (or 24?)...

As a good example of the difficulties of these inscriptions in their broken and worn state, the interpretation by Hägg (1984: see also his forthcoming note in *Meroitic Newsletter*) is contrasted; it appears to fit well with the usual phraseology and content of Aksumite inscriptions.

*of Axum and Himyar...[son of the invincible god] Ares. When [the people of]... disputed...I conveyed from...(?) and I pillaged the...(?) having arrived here....is produced, and another (*or *(women) of noble birth and another)...together with the king as far as...most (things) in the...generals and children...I went against [the?] at once...I shall [?] to you...subject to pay tribute...a bronze [statue?]...21 (*or *24).*

Meroë II. Greek. Translation of Hägg (1984).

..of Ares.....having arrived here I sat down..giving [as a recompense?..]..[to Ares] this throne.

The Inscriptions of Ezana.

DAE 4. Greek, from the three-script versions DAE 4, 6 and 7.

The Campaign against the Beja; (I). *Aeizanas, king of the Aksumites, the Himyarites, Raeidan, the Ethiopians, the Sabaeans, Silei (Salhen), Tiyamo, the Beja and Kasou, king of kings, son of the unconquered god Ares. Since the people of the Beja rose up, we sent our brothers Saiazana and Adefan to fight them. When these had taken arms against the enemy, they made them submit and they brought them to us with their dependents, with 3112 head of cattle, 6224 sheep, and beasts of burden. My brothers gave them meat and wheat to eat, and beer, wine and water to drink, all to their satisfaction whatever their number. There were six chiefs with their peoples, to the number of 4400 and they received each day 22,000 loaves of wheat and wine for four months, until my brothers had brought them to me. After having given them all means of sustenance, and clothed them, we installed these prisoners by force in a place in our land called Matlia. And we commanded again that they be given supplies; and we accorded to each chief 25,140 head of cattle.*

In sign of recognition to he who engendered us, the unconquered Ares, we have raised statues to him, one of gold, one of silver, and three others of brass, to his glory.

DAE 6 and 7 are written respectively in the epigraphic South Arabian and unvocalised Ge'ez scripts, and are more or less the same as DAE 4 in content. The dedications at the end are to Astar, Beher and Mahrem (DAE 6), and Astar, Meder and Mahrem (DAE 7). The land of Matlia is referred to as Dawala-BYRN in these versions (according to Littmann; Schneider (1984: 155) reads the phrase as "*the land MD, a region of our country*", supported by the as yet unpublished new version noted below), and both also end with a curse formula against anyone damaging the inscription and the record of extra gifts to Mahrem.

The Geza 'Agmai inscription (DAE 4, 6 and 7 bis*).*

Three more versions of the same inscription as above (DAE 4,6 and 7), also in Greek, epigraphic South Arabian, and unvocalised Ge'ez scripts, translated by Bernand 1982.

Greek.

The Campaign against the Beja (II). *Aeizanas, king of the Aksumites, Himyarites and Raeidan, the Ethiopians, the Sabaeans and Silei, Tiamo and the Beja and Kasu, king of kings, son of the invincible god Ares. When once the Beja tribe revolted, we sent our brothers Sazanan and Adiphan to make war upon them, and when they came back, having made them submit, they led them to us with their entire horde and their animals, 3112 cattle, 6224 sheep and 677 beasts of burden, feeding them with cattle, wheat, wine, mead, beer and water to satiety, during four months, amounting to 4400 people, provisioned each day with 22,000 loaves, until I had changed their residence. These people who had been brought to us, after having granted them all that was necessary for them, having clothed them and changed their residence, we established them in a part of our territory called Matlia and ordered that they be further provided there, giving to each kinglet 4190 cattle, so that the six kinglets had 25,140 cattle. As a thank-offering to the invincible Ares who begat me, we consecrated to him a statue of gold, one of silver, and three of bronze. I have consecrated this stele, and dedicated it to Heaven, the Earth, and the invincible Ares who begat me. Should anyone wish to damage it, may the god of Heaven and Earth lead him to ruin, and his name cease to exist in the land of the living. In gratitude this has been consecrated for well-being. Furthermore we have consecrated to the invincible Are's a COY'ATE and a BEΔIE.*

The deities mentioned are named by the Ge'ez and South Arabian script versions as Astar, Beher and Mahrem; Beher here is definitely associated with the earth (Ch. 10: 1). These versions render the last but one line as a formula not dissimilar to the coin-mottoes which seem to have begun with Ezana's Christian issues (Schnieder 1984, 1987), and the Ge'ez version also adds the extra line found in the Greek version; *And as we have erected (this stele), let it be propitious for us and for our country forever. And we have offered to Mahrem a SWT and a BDH*; both terms of unknown meaning.

DAE 9. Vocalised Ge'ez.

The name and most of the titulary are restorations, and the inscription could be differently attributed; the pagan epithet and the vocalisation, however, make Ezana a likely candidate for it.

The Campaign against the Agwezat. *[Ezana, son of Ella Amida, Bisi Halen, king of Aksum, Himyar, Raydan, Saba, Salhin, Tsiyamo,] Beja and of Kasu, king of kings, son of the invincible Mahrem.*

The Agwezat took the field and arrived at Angabo. There came to meet us Aba'alkeo, king of the Agwezat, with his tribe, and he brought tribute. And, when later we arrived at 'Alya the camp in the land of Atagaw, we obtained camels and beasts of burden, men, women, and provisions for twenty days. But the third day after our arrival, since we recognised the perfidy of Aba'alkeo, we delivered the Agwezat who had come with their king to pillage; and those whom we plundered we bound, and as for Aba'alkeo, we left him naked, and chained him to the bearer of his throne (or, after Huntingford 1989: 53, *Aba'alkeo king of the Agwezat we did not leave, but we bound him (also) along with the bearer of his throne*; or, after Schneider 1984: 159, this passage means that only Aba'alkeo was *not* put in chains). *We then ordered the column Mahaza and the commanders of the columns to march night and day. Then they sent the column Mahaza and the column Metin, and they were ordered to go and fight the Agwezat. Then they went to...and arrived at Asala? and came to Ereg? and took what they found. And they left by the pass of Asal and... river Nadu* (or, Huntingford 1989: 53, *And they went to the place of assembly...and reached 'Asala (?); and they came to Ereg and... and went out by the slope of Asal and...river Nadu), and killed all those whom they met.*

From there they came to the territory of Agada where they killed and captured men and beasts. Then they sent the troop Daken and ordered it to go by Se'ezot and from the east...they retired...and the carriers of water brought water (or, Huntingford 1989, *and they turned by Tabenya and descended where the water falls). And the three columns Daken, Hara, and Metin rallied at Ad(ya)bo.. Then they sent the column Hara and ordered them to go towards Zawa..t.*

And from there for the third time they sent the column Laken and dispatched it and ordered it to proceed to Hasabo and it left for the pass (Huntingford 1989: 53, *slope)of Tuteho and descended.,.,the river, and reached Lawa and descended towards Asya.. And together they departed from Hezaba. and camped at .. and they entered and passed the night. And at dawn, they attacked...followed to the mustering place of Magaro and the three columns...to the river, with Falha and Sera.*

DAE 10. Vocalised Ge'ez.

The Afan Campaign. *[E]zana, son of Ella Amida, Bisi Halen, king of Aksum, Himyar, Raydan, Saba, Salhin, Tsiyamo, Beja and of Kasu, son of the invincible Mahrem.*

The Tsarane, whose country is Afan (Huntingford 1989: 55, suggests *Awan), attacked and annihilated a merchant caravan. And we went to war against them, and we sent columns, those of Mahaza, Daken and Hara and we ourself followed and camped at the place of encampment of the troops at 'Ala* (Huntingford 1989: 55, *Alaha) and from there we sent out our troops. And they killed some of the Tsarane, and captured others and took booty. We vanquished Sa'ene and Tsawante and Gema and Zahtan, four peoples, and we seized Alita* (Huntingford 1989: 55, *Alitaha) and his two children.*

And 503 men of Afan and 202 women were put to death, in all 705. Men and their women (Huntingford 1989: 55, *belonging to the baggage train) were made prisoner, 40 men and 165 women, total 205. The booty comprised 31,900* (Huntingford 1989: 55, *31,957) head of cattle and 827 beasts of burden.*

And he (the king) *returned in safety with his people and raised a throne here in Shado which he put under the protection of the gods Astar, Beher and Meder. And should anyone remove or displace it, let him and his race be exterminated; let him be extirpated from these lands. And he brought a thank-offering to Mahrem who begot him, 100 head of cattle and 50 captives.*

DAE 11. Vocalised Ge'ez.

The 'monotheistic' inscription; there have been many speculations about the form of the dedication of this inscription, some authors attributing it to a monotheism not specifically Christian. This complication seems unnecessary when what seem to be the Greek and South Arabian script versions (below) are considered. It may rather reflect an uncertainty as to how to refer to the Christian god in the earliest Christian period of the country.

The Noba and Kasu Campaign. *By the might of the Lord of Heaven who in the sky and on earth holds power over all beings, Ezana, son of Ella Amida, Bisi Halen, king of Aksum, Himyar, Raydan, Saba, Salhin, Tsiyamo, Beja and of Kasu, king of kings, son of Ella Amida, never defeated by the enemy.*

May the might of the Lord of Heaven, who has made me king, who reigns for all eternity, invincible, cause that no enemy can resist me, that no enemy may follow me!

By the might of the Lord of All I campaigned against the Noba when the Noba peoples revolted and boasted. 'They will not dare to cross the Takaze' said the Noba people. When they had oppressed the Mangurto, Hasa and Barya peoples, and when the blacks fought the red people and they broke their word for the second and third times and put their neighbours to death without mercy, and pillaged our messengers and the envoys whom I sent to them to admonish them, and they plundered them of what they had including their lances; when finally, having sent new messengers to whom they did not wish to listen but replied by refusals, scorn, and evil acts; then I took the field.

I set forth by the might of the Lord of the Land and I fought at the Takaze and the ford Kemalke. Here I put them to flight, and, not resting, I followed those who fled for twenty-three days during which I killed some everywhere they halted. I made prisoners of others and took booty from them. At the same time those of my people who were in the field brought back captives and booty.

At the same time I burnt their villages, both those with walls of stone and those of straw. My people took their cereals, bronze, iron and copper and overthrew the idols in their dwellings, as well as their corn and cotton, and threw them themselves into the river Seda (Blue Nile). Many lost their lives in the river, no-one knows the number. At the same time my people pierced and sank their boats which carried a crowd of men and women.

And I captured two notables who had come as spies, mounted on camels, by name Yesaka and Butala, and the chief Angabene. The following nobles were put to death: Danoko, Dagale, Anako, Haware. The soldiers had wounded Karkara, their priest, and took from him a necklace of silver and a golden box. Thus five nobles and a priest fell.

I arrived at the Kasu, fought them and took them prisoner at the confluence of the rivers Seda and Takaze. And the day after my arrival I sent into the field the columns Mahaza, Hara, Damawa? Falha? and Sera? along the Seda going up to their cities with walls of stone and of straw; their cities with walls of stone are Alwa and Daro. And my troops killed and took prisoners and threw them into the water and they returned home safe and sound after terrifying their enemies and vanquishing them thanks to the power of the Lord of the Land.

Next, I sent the columns of Halen, Laken? Sabarat, Falha and Sera along the Seda, going down towards the four towns of straw of the Noba and the town of Negus. The towns of the Kasu with walls of stone which the Noba had taken were Tabito(?), Fertoti; and the troops penetrated to the territory of the Red Noba and my peoples returned safe after taking prisoners and booty, and killing by the might of the Lord of Heaven.

And I erected a throne at the confluence of the rivers Seda and Takaze opposite the town with walls of stone which rises on this peninsula.

And behold what the Lord of Heaven has given me; prisoners, 214 men, 415 women, total 629; killed, 602 men, 156 women and children, total 758, and adding the prisoners and killed 1,387. The booty came to 10,560 head of cattle and 51,050 sheep.

And I set up a throne here in Shado by the might of the Lord of Heaven who has helped me and given me supremacy. May the Lord of Heaven reinforce my reign. And, as he has now defeated my enemies for me, may he continue to do so wherever I go. As he has now conquered for me, and has submitted my enemies to me, I wish to reign in justice and equity, without doing any injustice to my peoples. And I put this throne which I have raised under the protection of the Lord of Heaven, who has made me king, and that of the Earth (Meder) which bears it. And if anyone is found to root it up, deface it or displace it, let him and his race be rooted up and extirpated. They shall be cast out of the country. And I have raised this throne by the power of the Lord of Heaven.

Christian Inscription of Ezana. Greek. (Anfray, Caquot and Nautin 1970; Judge 1976).

This appears to be the beginning of the Greek version of the above inscription DAE 11. If these were somehow arranged on a stone throne, the rest may have continued on another part. On the reverse is the South Arabian script version (below).

In the faith of God and the power of the Father, son and Holy Spirit who saved for me the kingdom, by the faith of his son Jesus Christ, who has helped me and will always help me.

I Azanas king of the Aksumites, and Himyarites, and Reeidan and of the Sabaeans and of Sileel and of Khaso and of the Beja and of Tiamo, Bisi Alene, son of Ella Amida servant of Christ thank the Lord my God, and I am unable to state fully his favours because my mouth and my mind cannot (embrace) all the favours which he has given me, for he has given me strength and power and favoured me with a great name through his son in whom I believed. And he made me the guide of all my kingdom because of my faith in Christ by his will and in the power of Christ, for he has guided me. And I believe in him and he became to me a guide.I went out to fight the Noba because there cried out against them, the Mangartho and Khasa and Atiaditai and Bareotai saying that 'the Noba have ground us down; help us because they have troubled us by killing'. And I left by the power of Christ the God in whom I have believed and he has guided me and I departed from Aksum on the eighth day, a Saturday, of the Aksumite month of Magabit having faith in God and arrived in Mambarya and there I fed my army.

Inscription in South Arabian script.

This appears to be the third version of the DAE 11 text, and is important in that it ends (on one of the sides) with a cross, similar to that found on the coins attributed to this period just after the conversion of Ezana. It lacks a name, but the content and style allowed Schneider (1974, 1976) to suggest the attribution. His suggestion is backed up by the fact that this inscription is on the back and one side of the Greek version, which stops at a higher level, where it is supposed that the seat on the throne on which it was inscribed intervened.

Kaleb Inscription. Ge'ez in the South Arabian script.

This damaged inscription has been translated by Schneider (1974), who also translated what little was possible of the W'ZB inscription below. It chiefly relates a campaign against the Agwezat and Hasat.

The Lord strong and brave, the Lord mighty in battle. By the power of the Lord and by the grace of Jesus Christ, the son of the Lord, the victorious, in whom I believe, who has given me a strong kingdom by which I dominate my enemies and trample underfoot the head of my adversaries, who has guarded me since infancy and established me on the throne of my fathers....., I trust myself to Christ so that all my enterprises might succeed, and that I may be saved by him who pleases my soul? With the help of the Trinity, the Father, Son, and Holy Spirit.

Kaleb, Ella Atsbeha, son of Tazena, Be'ese LZN, king of Aksum, Himyar, Raydan, Saba, Salhen, and of the High Country and Yamanat, and the Coastal Plain and Hadramawt and of all their Arabs, and the Beja, Noba, Kasu, Siyamo and DRBT........ of the land ATFY(?), servant of Christ, who is not defeated by the enemy.

With the help of the Lord I fought the Agwezat and HST. I fought them, having divided my troops...(here follow some troop names) *my country and with... march day and night...kill..Agwezat...iniquity? and I sent the Atagaw and the* (more troop names?) *they killed the HST and I followed with... peace....refuge...by the might of the Lord....made captive...there, their country with their offerings...thousand...and the cattle which they had taken...-return...carry on the back...and the number killed of the Agwezat and the HST was men 400...women and children 1...the total...captives, men, women and children 4.. total of the killed and captives was... and the booty of cattle...hundreds, camels 200. This the Lord gave me...make war...Himyar...I sent HYN SLBN ZSMR with my troops and I founded a maqdas* (church) *in Himyar.. the name of the Son of God in whom I put my reliance.. I built his GBZ and consecrated it by the power of the Lord..and the Lord has revealed to me his holiness? and I shall remain on this throne..and I have set it under the tutelage of the Lord, creator of heaven and earth, against he who should destroy, pluck up, or break it. And he who would tear up or destroy it, let the Lord tear up...*

Drewes (1978) suggested that lines 34-7 of this inscription actually mention HYWN', or Hiuna, known from the *Book of the Himyarites*; his translation reads '*He (God) gave me a great name, that I might wage war against Himyar. I sent HYN (..)BN ZSMR with my troops and I founded a church in 'QN'L (...) the name of the Son of God, in Whom I believe. I constructed its* gabaz *and I consecrated it by the might of God..*'

Inscription on an alabaster lamp acquired at Aden (Grohmann 1911).
Ge'ez.

...Zadagan and has fallen...(s)ons and his two brothers a(nd)...? and their land...while...till the (sun) set....they return...

Marib Inscription.

Vocalised Ge'ez, attributed to Kaleb (Kamil 1964; Caquot 1965; Müller 1972).

'and he shall exalt you'...I passed through the port of Zala?...I fought with their army...as the Psalm says...'his enemies shall flee before your face'...making prisoners and taking booty...he chased the gentiles before...aboard ship....its coast which God had delivered to me....and half my army...my army descended by the opening..half of my army descended...

Pirenne and Tesfaye (1982) published some new ideas about this and another fragment from Marib – see also Müller 1972 -, and an inscription from the Himyarite capital Zafar in which the designation 'Angebenay' appears, which they conjecture to signify Kaleb. Igonetti (1973) has also published the Zafar Ge'ez inscription as follows;

and he authorized....the faith of the Father....'Angabenay....Christ....in Greece....and they arrived...

W'ZB Inscription. Ge'ez in the South Arabian script.

This inscription is very difficult to read (only Huntingford 1989: 65-6 seems to have attempted it – his translation is that used here – though Schneider (1974) published a preliminary analysis), but some useful phrases can be distinguished.

Wa'zeb, king of Aksum, and Himyar, and Dhu-Raydan, and Saba and Salaf (=Salhen) and of the Beja, and Kasu, and Siyamo and WYTG(?), Bisi Hadefan, son of Ella Atsbeha, servant of Christ.

and my troops fought....I fought.....with the army and soldiers....I will kill your enemies and I will fight against your enemies....my God... the troops under my orders... God will fight for you, and you shall keep you peaceful....by the power of the Lord I entered their country.... I found them fleeing, refugees in their fortress the name of which is DGM....I lived within the enclosure of the fortress....they occupied the entire camp and the fortress....all nations compassed me about, in the name of the Lord I have vanquished them....having been killed then? and for that? I sent.... the troops HDQN and S.RT and SBH and DMW and 'GW.... O Lord, fight against them who make war against me, take hold of shield and spear and stand up to help me; let them be dust before the wind, that the angel of the Lord chase them, and it is said in the Psalms, I will pursue my enemies, and capture them. You gird me with strength in battle, and You make all those fall who stand up against me and You make my enemies turn their backs on me, and it is also said, the right hand of the Lord doth valiantly, the right hand of the Lord has exalted me....and praise Your holy name....the troops which I had sent submitted and killed and prayed and took captives...safe and sound, by the power of the Lord, and I set up a throne in methm?...WYT(L); and I returned safe and sound with my troops, by the power of the Lord.; and I lived at ZWGS and they found refuge there in a place uninhabited by the combatants....our county? and a battle? en route and for that

I sent in expedition the troop Hara... and they killed, and took captives and booty, by the power of the Lord, and returned safe....and that which the Lord gave me at the time of the first expedition and at the time of the last expedition...prisoners, men....women and children...; killed, men....women and children...all the 'gd of the WYTL submitted in offering their presents..

The inscriptions of the hatseni *Danael.* Vocalised Ge'ez.
(Cerulli 1968; Kobishchanov 1979; for a cautionary note about these readings, see Schnieder 1984: 163).

DAE 12.

In the name of the Father and of the Son and of the Holy Spirit, I have written this, hatsani Danael, the son of Dabra Ferem. There came ...hatsani Karuray....attacked him...and I swore that...608 foals. And I captured 10.000 oxen and 130 steers...and our servants, who always..I summoned them..and there were none who did me good, except 30 people, all...they returned and went to KSL (Kassala?) and did not leave me?...the proclamation that they should go, and those who went for the giving of presents. And I surrounded those who came to Kassala...and they plundered? the Barya. Booty, 103 steers...and 200 sheep.......and curse them forever. And they said to me, 'Your land, woe'. As I heard these words, I marvelled, and ....they were doing; my translators advised them, and I went out. And as they showed themselves unfriendly to me, they attacked?... and I made a judgement against them...and I fought them and captured massive booty: 17,830 foals, 10,030 oxen, and I captured 30 tribes.

DAE 13.

In the name of the Father, and of the Son and of the Holy Spirit, I, hatseni Danael, son of Dabra Ferem. When the people of Wolqayt devastated the land of HSL, and came to Aksum, I expelled them and was harsh to them and killed them and captured 102 foals and 802 cattle. And I made the people go...and the equipment, and from here I made them enter the country of Ablas.....whose name is Maya Tsaltsal, and I plundered 10,000 sheep...3000 cattle...and I went while my people were raiding and taking captive. And they returned home when I entered, day....our entry before...booty..we waited in the enclosure...I plundered it...

DAE 14.

And the king came, and desired to rule over me, while I was in Aksum, in the manner of his father, like a poor man (?). When he had taken booty, he came to Aksum. But I came out, and my enemy was frightened (?), I took the newcomer captive: before blood was shed, I subjected the king of Aksum and dismissed him to administer Aksum as the land of my dominion; and he was released (?). And... I sent into the field...

XII

Material Culture; the Archaeological Record

From the very uneven choice of excavation areas at Aksum and other Aksumite cities, we have inevitably a view of Aksumite everyday life which favours the upper echelons of urban society. Palaces, mansions, large and important tombs, and churches contain the remains of objects from these élite groups, whilst the living equipment of their lesser urban contemporaries (not to mention country-dwellers) has not often been found. Exceptions are possibly Adulis, where the excavators seem to have found smaller houses, though it is possible that these too belong to the outer buildings of a mansion, and at the sites E2 and F (the latter near a church) at Matara. As yet, the results of these excavations are only known through the brief preliminary report of Francis Anfray (1974). The series of rooms found by Paribeni (1907: plan, fig. 37) at Adulis contained so many gold coins that they hardly seem to have been occupied by the humbler echelons of Adulite society.

However, in spite of this emphasis on the richer groups, certain elements of material culture cross the social boundaries to some extent. Pottery (excluding luxury types) is a good example of this, whilst glass and much of the decorative metalwork can be expected mainly from the élite contexts. To some extent coinage may have been universally used, though obviously gold would have been unlikely to reach the peasant or ordinary artisan in much quantity. By analogy with better-known ancient civilisations, it seems that the copper coinage would have been the common market-exchange medium where barter was not practised, and thus could move freely on many levels, whilst the more valuable coins moved less and were perhaps chiefly employed for major long-distance trade or storage of wealth.

I. Pottery.

Both fine and coarser ceramic wares have been found in very large numbers (see the various excavation reports in the *Annales d'Ethiopie*; Anfray 1966; Wilding in Munro-Hay 1989). These were made in a pottery tradition which seems to be particularly Aksumite and to owe relatively little to either the pre-Aksumite period or to foreign influences (but see below). The commonest types are fired to colours between orange and almost brick red, and there are also black or grey wares from different periods. Some less usual wares are brown, or red-brown. Chronologically, it seems that the red wares are typical of earlier Aksumite times, the brown coming later in perhaps the fifth century, while the black wares typify the post-Aksumite period (except for the black pottery with incised decoration which was found in the earliest excavated levels at Adulis, which seems to belong to an earlier tradition – Paribeni 1907: 448, 547). Aksumite grey wares vary in date, the finer specimens in earlier shapes being perhaps examples of the prevalent red wares which had not been correctly fired in the kiln, and the coarse large grey pots with rough geometric decoration being of late or post-Aksumite date. A much rarer type is called purple-painted ware, since areas of the surface are decorated with paint of an almost brownish-purple colour, and a mat-impressed ware has also been found which may owe its origin to influences from the Nile Valley, where such decoration was common.These various wares were often burnished, painted, incised or otherwise decorated. A very common and characteristic decorative style has been called the 'Classical Aksumite' style. This employs lightly impressed designs, mainly vertical corrugations, combined with small ovoid impressions arranged in a staggered fashion like footprints, sometimes filling diamond-shaped panels. The corrugations and certain of the shapes of the vessels may owe something to metalwork originals. Other decorative motifs included all sorts of appliqué designs; crosses, crescents, small ridges and the like, as well as more ambitious ones consisting of little pottery hands clinging to the rim of a bowl and linked by swags, or depicting modelled birds perched on frilled rims (de Contenson 1959: pl. XVIII; Wilding in Munro-Hay 1989). Some pots and bowls received stamped impressions on the bases or inside, often of very elaborate forms based on the cross and other motifs. Particularly common on the red-brown bowls were little incised or stamped crosses or palmettes (see for example Paribeni 1907; fig. 60). Other incised decoration was also common, lines and panels predominating, but including many different styles of cross and even sometimes roughly incised inscriptions.

It may be suggested that some of the shapes, mainly hole-mouth bowls and round-bodied flasks or jars, owe their origin to the 'African' side of Aksum, while the ledge-rimmed or ring-based bowls owe more to the pottery styles of the Roman world. Such a range of influences affecting Aksumite pottery is to be expected considering Aksum's particular position, but should not be over-emphasised; the overall style of decoration seems certainly to have been a local inspiration. Differences in the pottery found at such sites as Adulis, Matara, and Aksum, typifying three different regions of the country subject to different influences and developments, are not well understood, but for the time being a western and eastern 'provincial' style seem to be recognised (Anfray 1973i; Michels, in Kobishchanov 1979: 26).

Some tomb vessels, largely in the red wares, seem to have been created with some very specialised use in mind. Bowls containing modelled images of two oxen yoked together, 'foot-washer' bowls, with, in the centre, a kind of platform (occasionally two), sometimes with a runnel for water, conceivably for painting henna on to the feet, stem bowls, bird-shaped vessels, tripod jars, and strainer jars are among these (Chittick 1974: fig. 19k, pl. XIIIb, pl. XIIa, Pl. XIIc, pl. XIIb and fig. 19c, and pl. Xiib illustrates all these types). Another unusual pottery type is the human-headed ointment (?) jar. The necks of these round-bodied jars (Chittick 1974: pls. XII b-c, XIVb; Leclant 1959: pl. III-IV *bis*; de Contenson 1959: pls. XV-XVII), accessible from the top through a narrow opening, depict women with a hair-style in which the hair turns out sharply at about chin level. There are several differences in detail, some with zigzags representing the strands of (plaited?) hair, others with a sort of cap on the top of the head. Earrings are sometimes shown, and on the whole one gains the general impression of a coiffure somewhat like that of the women of Tigray even today. Plaited hair, lying close to the head at the top, but allowed at the base to frizz out freely, is a style which can still be seen in preparation by the hairdressers during market days in Aksum nowadays. On one example from the Tomb of the Brick Arches at Aksum, part of the globular body of the pot survived, and bore an arm painted in yellow paint on one side. Interestingly, pots of the same general type, though with different hairstyles, were collected relatively recently in the Azande country of south-western Sudan by Sir Harold MacMichael (Horniman Museum, London; 30.12.50/1–2).

Painted decoration on pottery might consist of crosses in various colours, plant motifs, or panels filled in in different ways. Red, black, and white were popular colours, and there was a purplish paint in use in later Aksumite times (Chittick 1974: pl. XIVc). The ordinary shapes included, very frequently, globular-bodied jars with more or less long and thin necks, sometimes very close to the typical coffee-pot used even now in Ethiopia and the Sudan, where their round bases rest on rings of plaited straw or other fibres. Bowls, either round or ring-based, were also very much used, together with beakers, and many types of handled jars, cauldrons, storage vessels and the like.

Imported amphorae are also not uncommon, and were employed for various purposes after their original contents had disappeared. Some were cleverly used to form a sort of water supply-pipe to a baptismal pool near a basilica at Matara (Anfray 1974: 757–8, and pl. IV, 2); others served as coffins for the burial of babies at both Adulis and Matara (Anfray 1974: pl. II, 1; Paribeni 1907: 452, 480); and a third use was as furnaces or ovens. At Adulis several examples of the latter were found, and also other types of vessel employed as ovens or for industrial purposes; Paribeni suggested that some examples from Adulis were employed in liquefying tar and in gold-working. His excavations at Adulis revealed what was apparently a gold-workshop, with amphorae and ashes in association with a collection of gold rods, earrings, and two elaborate bejewelled crosses with chains; in a different place a stone mould for making jewellery was found (Paribeni 1907: 453, 483–6 and figs. 20–21, 461, fig. 7). Many of the amphorae may have come from Alexan-

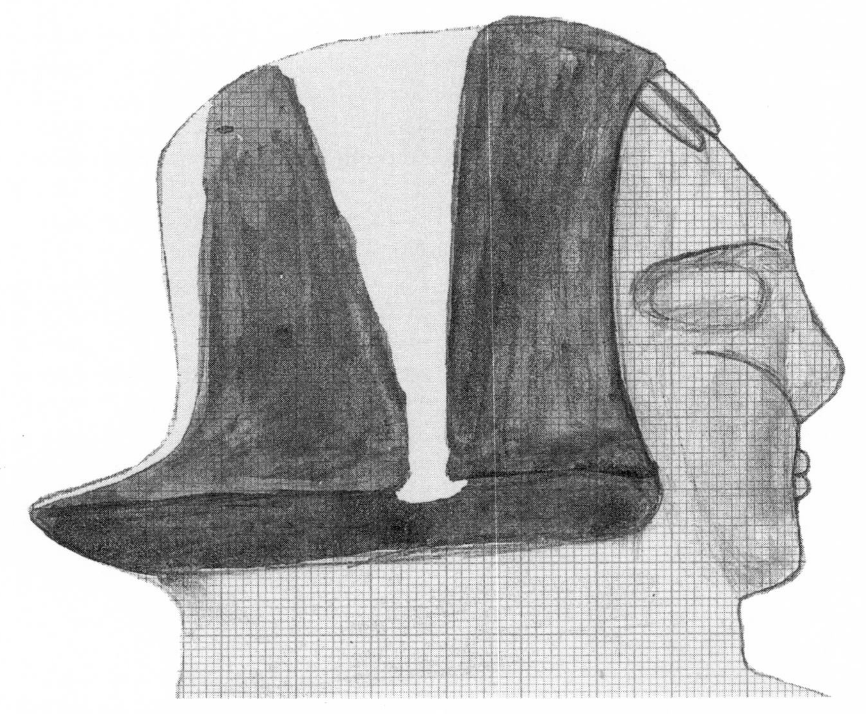

59. Profile view of a painted head from a jar from the Tomb of the Brick Arches at Aksum.

dria (Paribeni 1907: 455). Some bore incised or painted identification marks at shoulder level, and they were sometimes sealed with terracotta discs, plastered over, with an identification mark stamped or painted on top (Paribeni 1907: 456, 520, 522, 524, figs. 4, 39, 41, 43, 59).

One very specialised imported vessel found at Adulis was a flask stamped with a design showing the Egyptian St. Menas between two kneeling camels; such vessels are supposed to have held water from a spring near the saint's tomb in Egypt (Paribeni 1907: 538, fig. 54), and this one may have been brought to Adulis by a pilgrim.

Among imported pottery types were a number of lamps. While at Aksum lamps tended to be of a very simple open type, probably local, Adulis produced a wider varity including some closed lamps with moulded decoration which certainly came from the Roman empire, probably Egypt (Paribeni 1907: 499, fig. 28; 518, fig. 38). Others, perhaps local, consisted of small double or single spouted jars (Paribeni 1907: 460–1, fig. 5; 522–3, fig. 42; 526, fig. 45).

Most of the pottery shapes were evidently designed for eating, drinking, storage and cooking, but the more unusual ones perhaps served for special purposes like personal hygiene, cosmetics, or ceremonial occasions. Some

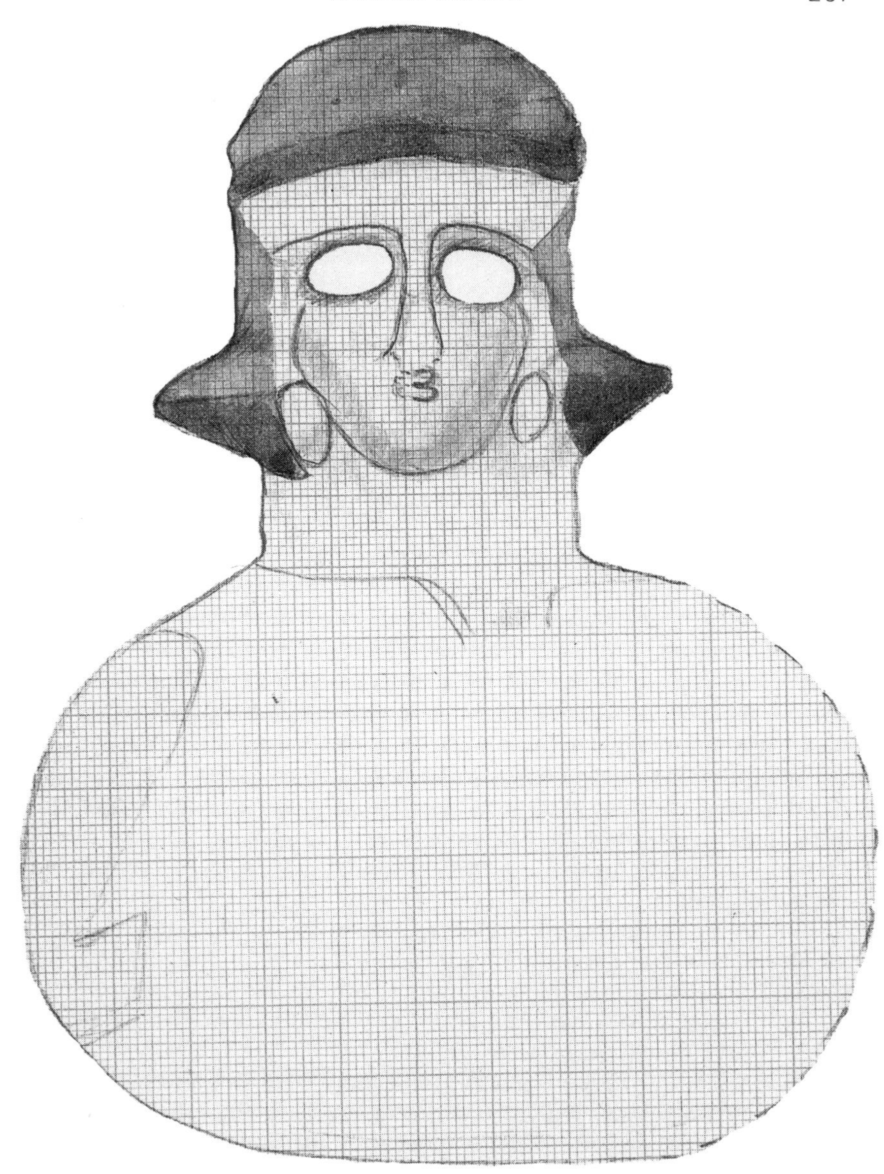

60. Only one of the human-headed jars found in the Tomb of the Brick Arches was still almost intact, and traces of one painted arm could still be seen.

may have been for ritual use, or made as specifically funerary goods to serve the dead in some way. This might account for the apparently long use of certain types; they could have been fossilised designs essential to some funerary purpose, though not in general outlasting the fourth/fifth-century change to Christianity.

One spherical pot from Adulis was closed completely except for a rectangular opening around which were impressed four crosses; it evidently served as a money box, since when found it contained thirty-three gold coins of king Israel of Aksum (Paribeni 1907: 501).

A row of very large 'pithoi', presumably for grain storage, was found in a building of Aksumite date whose ruins were found during excavation between the old and new cathedrals of Maryam Tseyon (de Contenson 1963: pls. VII, XII, XIIIa). Other pithoi came from Adulis, and one example was pierced with holes round the neck to attach it to the body; evidently these were unlikely to have carried liquids (Paribeni 1907: 462).

Aksumite pottery, with the exception of such imported categories as the amphorae for wine and other commodities, was mostly locally made, without the use of the potters' wheel – though Paribeni (1907: 548) thought that the rough locally-made pottery of Adulis was made on the wheel. The style and decoration evolved, although, as we have said, some basic outlines of shape can be paralleled from both Nubia and the Roman empire, was unique to the Aksumite region.

The coarser wares included two types of stoves (Chittick 1974: fig. 21), presumably for cooking with charcoal obtained from the local woodlands, now vanished. The remains of ovens or kilns have also been found at Aksum (Anfray 1968: fig. 22) and Matara, in the latter place together with pottery on a habitation floor (Anfray 1974: pl. V 2–3; 1963: 99 and pl. LXXX). Pottery groups left in place were not infrequent at Matara, and these and collections of pottery from tomb-groups should eventually allow us to date the different styles more precisely (Anfray 1963: pls. LXXV, LXXVIIa).

The Aksumites seem to have imported certain blue or green-glazed wares, which have been found at Aksum, Adulis and Matara, perhaps from the Persian Gulf region. At Aksum and Adulis only sherds were found, but at Matara a complete pot was preserved (Anfray 1965: 6; 1974: 759, fig. 6). The Aksumites also used faience vessels apparently of local manufacture, their friable sandy bodies covered with a turquoise-blue glaze. One example found was an exact imitation of the fluted pottery bowls with little handles, and this product in typical Aksumite style seems to confirm that the faience was from a local workshop (Chittick 1974: pl. XIVe).

Miscellaneous pottery objects have also been found. A few animal figures (aside from those which stood in the animal-figure bowls already mentioned) are known, and the figure of a dove impressed with a cross came from Adulis (Paribeni 1907: 528, fig. 48). Pottery discs, plain or pierced, which may be gaming pieces or loom-weights for weaving, are commonly found. Numbers of little pierced crosses and cones in pottery were excavated, most commonly at the Enda Sem'on site at Aksum, but also at Matara (Anfray and Annequin 1965: pls. LXV, 3; LXVI, 1). Their use is unknown. A few dice of pottery, marked with dots to indicate the numbers, came from Matara (Anfray and Annequin 1965: pl. LXVI, 4; Anfray 1968: pl. 5). From Matara also came the steatopygous figure of a woman, of seemingly prehistoric type, but found in an Aksumite level (Anfray 1968: fig. 13); another example came from Adulis (Paribeni 1907; 486).

2. Glassware.

It may be imagined that the more expensive imported wines and the better-quality local mead were consumed from some of the vessels included among the rich range of glassware found at Aksum (Morrison in Munro-Hay 1989) and Matara (Anfray 1968: fig. 16). This was probably mostly imported, though some types may have been made locally; as previously noted, there was an unusual incidence of exotically-coloured or decorated glass from the Aksum excavations, representing types unknown elsewhere at the moment. Glass from habitation sites is generally very fragmentary, but is naturally best preserved in tomb deposits. A set of stem goblets decorated with a swagged design, and smaller beakers with restricted necks were found together in one tomb, with the owner's best crockery and sets of iron tools (Chittick 1974: pl. XIVa). Since such glass seems to indicate a quite luxurious level of living, perhaps the tomb-owner was a prosperous merchant. In another tomb, much richer, possibly even royal, was found a large purple stem goblet, a purple flask with a long neck, and fragments of an engraved glass bowl with an inscription in Greek (Chittick 1974: fig. 22). Glass lamps, presumably oil-fed, together with the bronze chains which would have suspended them, came from one of the mansions. It is unlikely that glassware, at least imported glassware, percolated very far down the social ladder, as it was not only brought down the Red Sea from Egypt or Syria, or perhaps in some cases from Persia to the east, but then transported by land into the interior of the country by the merchant caravans. This troublesome journey must have made it an expensive commodity by the time it arrived at Aksum. The *Periplus* (Huntingford 1980: 21) mentions several sorts of glass as being imported into Aksum from the Roman world. One, imitating a type called *murrhine*, may have been coloured glass resembling agate or similar semi-precious stones (Schoff 1912: 24, 68), or perhaps *murrhine* describes a type of mosaic glass made by the so-called *millefiore* or mosaic-glass technique in which slices from rods of coloured glass, forming faces and other patterns, were fused together. Examples of this glass, apparently not made after about the end of the 1st century AD, have been found at Aksum (Morrison, in Munro-Hay 1989).

Some of the jewellery worn by the Aksumites was of glass, chiefly bangles and beads. One necklace, its beads found scattered across the chambers of the Tomb of the Brick Arches, consisted of glass globes overlaid with thin gold leaf, in turn covered with a thin layer of glass. Ear-plugs and possible gaming pieces have also been identified from among the large number of glass items excavated.

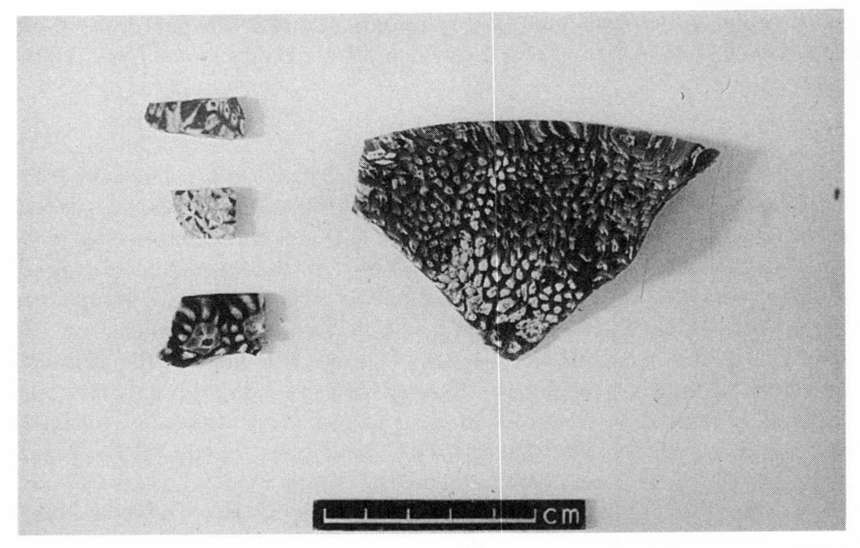

61. Mosaic or millefiore glass fragments, dating to a relatively early period (1st century BC- 1st century AD), came from the Aksum excavations. Photo BIEA.

Stone Bowls.

In what seem to be rooms belonging to one of the mansions excavated in the Addi Kilte district of Aksum the remains of many purplish breccia bowls were found (Chittick 1974: fig. 25), lathe-turned and finely made. They appear to have been smashed and incorporated in the rubble make-up for a plaster floor in a room later destroyed by an intense fire; none were recovered complete. The shapes ranged from a squat flat-based bowl to a stem cup. They were probably part of the luxurious equipment of some prosperous Aksumite. Nothing like them is known from elsewhere in Ethiopia (though a few fragments of marble plates were found at Matara; Anfray and Annequin 1965: pl. LXVII, 3), and they may have been imported. A number of basins of marble and alabaster were found at Adulis, some of impressive dimensions; a few were decorated with relief carving (Paribeni 1907: 458, 491).

Metalwork.

The metal equipment used by the Aksumites seems to fall into two categories. In the first, items of luxury, such as jewellery, costly boxes, small decorative objects, bowls, and figures in the round appear in gold, silver and bronze, or combinations of these metals. Appliqué plaques in bronze, decorated with enamelling, glass inlay, or gilding, for fixing onto wooden boxes or furniture, are especially notable. Among figures in bronze, two (of three) Graces, an ibex, lion figures, and two dogs (or leopards ?) have been found, all of small size (Chittick 1974: fig. 23; Anfray and Annequin 1965: pl. LXVIII; de Contenson 1959i: pl. XIX; 1963i: pl. XIVa-b). A lion-head figured on a bronze vase-handle at Adulis, and also on two examples of bronze door furniture found among the ruins of one of the churches there; on one of the latter the lion holds a ring in its mouth (Paribeni 1907: 462, 530, and fig. 53). The *Periplus* (Huntingford 1980: 21–22) mentions that brass and bronze were imported, the first for use as money, the second for drinking-cups, cooking-pots and armlets and anklets for women. Four bronze bowls or cups found at Addi Galamo seem to be of Meroitic origin (Caquot and Drewes 1955: 41, & pl. V). A low three-legged bronze vessel with a flat handle in the shape of an ivy-leaf, supported below by a ring handle, came from Adulis; though rather shallow, it may have been used for drinking wine (Paribeni 1907: 500–501, fig. 29).

Very little gold and silver has come to light at Aksum, in contrast to the treasure of Matara (Anfray and Annequin 1965: pl. LXIX and figs. 12–13), or the gold-worker's hoard from Adulis (Paribeni 1907: 483ff), but enough to show that some Aksumites could afford gilded bronze ornaments, silver bowls or silver-overlaid objects, and gold jewellery. One tiny gold nail was found in the Tomb of the Brick Arches, perhaps the remains of an attachment to a casket. Some silver and gold objects *'made in the design of the country'* are mentioned as imports by the *Periplus* (Huntingford 1980: 21) . In the Tomb of the Brick Arches a bullet-shaped silver amulet case was found lodged among the stones of a blocked doorway (Chittick 1974: fig. 24a). A number of gold beads, earrings and pendants of different types, from Aksum, Kaskase, and a few other sites, have been published by Giuseppe Tringali (1987).

Much of this material, not surprisingly considering Aksumite trade contacts, has a generally Eastern Mediterranean appearance. From earlier, pre-Aksumite sites such as Yeha, Sabea, and Hawelti came bronze 'identity-markers', open-work plaques sometimes in the shape of animals, and sometimes including letters, possibly forming the owner's names, in the Epigraphic South Arabian script (de Contenson 1963ii: pls. XLIIb, LIIIa). Such sites also produced bronze tools (axes, sickles, knives) of a type different to the later Aksumite ones, and including some curved tools (chisels?) resembling the bronze object bearing an inscription of king GDR from Addi Galamo (de Contenson 1963ii: pls. L, LI). A very interesting, but unfortunately very tiny, fragment of a bronze plaque from Adulis bore traces of two Sabaean letters.

Matara produced a bronze 'polycandilon' with four chains holding a circlet with six holes for candles, and a bronze pot which contained the Matara treasure of gold crosses, coins and chains (Anfray and Annequin 1965: pl. LXVIII, 7; LXIX, 2). From Adulis, appropriately, came parts of Roman bronze balances (Paribeni 1907: 539, fig. 55; Anfray 1974: pl. II, 2) and numerous different weights, some marked with Greek letters (Paribeni

1907: 562–3). Perhaps the most magnificent bronze object so far found in Ethiopia is a lamp from Matara (Anfray 1967: 46–8; 1968: pl. 5). The lamp seems to be formed from a bronze imitation of the lower jaw of some animal (a boar?) -though it has also been described as a conch- set on a circlet of arcaded pillars like those of the Aksumite royal crown. From the back rises a leaping dog, which is trying to seize a fleeing ibex.

In the second category of metal objects come the tools, weapons, and other objects in iron (Munro-Hay 1989). Sickles, knives, chisels, saws, axes, tweezers, hinges, spear and arrow heads, hooks or staples, and other unidentifiable objects have been found. Much of this represents the basic equipment of the artisan or soldier; the peasant might have had a spear or a knife or two, or an iron reaping hook (one was found in a tomb), and there are obvious examples of military equipment. Some iron rings found at Matara (Anfray 1963: pl. LXXXI) apparently binding a prisoner in his cell (his skeleton was also found), recall Ezana's boast that he had chained the king of the Agwezat with his throne-bearer (Ch. 11: 5, DAE 9). The *Periplus* (Huntingford 1980: 21–2) mentions a number of iron tools and weapons among the imported goods from the Roman world, while from India (Ariake) came iron and steel as a raw material.

Paribeni (1907: 461, 486, 492) noted small tesserae of lead, possibly for use as tokens in commercial transactions, and other formless fragments of the same material, from Adulis, and he also found traces of lead pins used for fixing metalwork to carved schist plaques (Paribeni 1907: 506–7. fig. 32).

5. Other Materials.

A very large number of stone tools are noted by various excavators at Aksum and other sites. They generally seem to be smallish scrapers, made of such materials as agate, chalcedony, and obsidian (Munro-Hay 1989; Anfray 1963: pl. CXIb). Probably they were used to treat some other material, such as skins, wood, or ivory. Paribeni (1907: 450) noted that the obsidian and other utensils found at Adulis did not mean that the levels from which they came were of great antiquity; he suggested that perhaps such implements continued in use among the poorer elements of the population long after metal tools were made or imported, and either this or some specialist use as suggested above doubtless explains their presence in a number of contexts at Aksum (Munro-Hay 1989; Puglisi 1941). Larger axes of polished stone were found also at Matara, one made of serpentine (Anfray and Annequin 1965: pl. LXIV, 4; LXV, 2).

All sorts of grind-stones or polishers, and a variety of stone mortars, come from Aksumite sites, doubtless used for grinding everything from grain to eye-paint and spices (Anfray 1963: pl. CXIIb-c; Anfray and Annequin 1965: pl. LXVII, 4). A lava specimen from Adulis was found complete, with an upper and lower stone, the former furnished with a pivot, the latter with a hole for the pivot and two lateral holes for wooden handles to assist in the rotation (Paribeni 1907: 498: fig. 26).

From Matara and Adulis came stone images of very plump females, a type which has also been found in pottery from the same places (Anfray 1968: fig. 13; Paribeni 1907: 498–9, fig. 27, 486). Two small stone objects have been found which may have served as seals, both being pierced for suspension. One, from Aksum, was of white stone with an indistinguishable design carved on one end, and another, from Adulis, in black and white variegated stone, was pierced longitudinally like a bead, and bore the image of two winged griffins, summarily carved (Munro-Hay 1989; Paribeni 1907: 493, fig. 23). The onyx bezel of a ring engraved with an eagle on a globe, an opal bezel bearing an image identified as Jupiter Ammon, and a carnelian inscribed with four letters in perhaps an Indian script, as yet unidentified, were also found at Adulis (Paribeni 1907: 521, 526, 529). Objects of this class may well have belonged to members of Adulis' international merchant community.

Only one little leather object, somewhat of the shape of the stelae-tops at Aksum (Chittick 1974: fig. 24c), and a few fragments of ivory, including possible gaming pieces from Adulis and part of a decorated ivory vase from Matara (Paribeni 1907: 454, 486; Anfray 1963: pl. CXIa), now remain to testify to these industries. Bone appears to have been used for knife-handles, in one case decorated with bronze nails (Paribeni 1907: 480). Tiny fragments of ostrich eggshell from Adulis (Paribeni 1907: 454, 458, 517) may hint at its use, perhaps in one of the forms still seen in Ethiopia – cut into discs and pierced as beads, or used entire to decorate roof-finials, particularly on churches. Shells were used as decoration, at least at Adulis, where they were easier to obtain. They were probably sewn, as in relatively recent times, onto cloth or skins (Paribeni 1907: 485–6), and one example even bore an inscribed word in Greek letters (Paribeni 1907: 490). Fragments of coral (and even sponge) were also found at Adulis, as well as a large piece of amber (Paribeni 1907: 517, 519, 524, 528).

Wood from Aksumite times is rare, but is known as a building material, and was also probably used for furniture. In the Tomb of the Brick Arches at Aksum traces of wood were found on glass-inlaid bronze plaques, which seem to have come from a wooden chest, and the coins of king Armah depict a tall-backed chair or throne, perhaps made of carved or turned wood. There must have been other Aksumite wooden furniture, as well as structural elements in buildings, such as pillar shafts, capitals, doors or shutters, or roof-panelling such as at Dabra Damo. Traces of some of this ancient work may still survive in some of the old churches of Tigray and other provinces of Ethiopia, but what little has been found is very hard to date.

XIII

Language, Literature, and the Arts

1. Language

The language of the Aksumite kingdom was Ge'ez (Ethiopic), a Semitic tongue assumed (but not proven) to have an ancestry in old South Arabian. Ge'ez, possibly deriving its name from the Agwezat or Agazi tribal group, is now a dead language except for its use in traditional Ethiopian Orthodox church rituals and in some specialised circumstances, such as poetry. It was written in characters descending from the same parentage as the script now called Epigraphic South Arabian, but more cursive in form; the modern Ethiopian alphabet is the only survivor of this script today. Its development required that certain letters employed in dialects of South Arabian were omitted and others added as necessary. A number of early texts and graffiti from Ethiopia are themselves in a cursive form of the old South Arabian script (Drewes 1962). Time and the influence of the Cushitic languages of Ethiopia (Agaw or Central Cushitic being the most important) both helped in the transference from the original language to Ge'ez.

The arguments advanced for the origins of the Ge'ez script would fill a small book (Ullendorff 1955; 1960: 112ff; Drewes 1962: Ch. V; Drewes and Schneider 1976). Some have seen it as a development from the monumental South Arabian script, others as related to the contemporary cursive scripts found in both Arabia and Ethiopia; the mechanics of the change, the experts have suggested, could have been through either intentional or accidental alteration. The script could have been inspired by an early importation, or even by a more recent inspiration subsequent to the period of the earlier inscriptions.

A fair number of inscriptions have been found dating from pre- Aksumite times and written in the epigraphic South Arabian script, at such places as Yeha, Kaskase and Hawelti-Melazo. Some of these employ a form of the language which is apparently more or less pure Sabaic, while others, though contemporary, show linguistic features perhaps indicating that they were carved by Ethiopians (Drewes 1962; Schneider 1976i). The use of the South Arabian script continued on into Aksumite times (or was revived then?) and as late as the reigns of Kaleb and W'ZB monumental inscriptions were still written in a version of this script, but using the Ge'ez language.

In the early fourth century, the purely consonontal script was found inadequate, and a system of vowelling was adopted, which greatly facilitated the reading of Ge'ez. The origins and history of the vowelling system are uncertain; it might have been influenced by some Indian scripts (Pankhurst 1974: 220–2; Chatterji 1967: 53), and it might in turn have influenced Armenian (Olderogge 1974: 195–203).

This innovation was employed on the inscriptions, and doubtless on whatever (not so far discovered) papyrus, parchment or other impermanent medium the Aksumites kept their records. It was not generally adopted on the coins, whose legends remained unvowelled, except for very rare and partial vowelling on the coins of one or two later kings, until the end of the series. However, even without the vowelling, the coins provide a very interesting sequence from which the changes in the styles of the letter-forms can be ascertained from the third to the seventh century (Munro-Hay 1984iii). This information, combined with inscriptional material, is one way of tentatively dating newly-discovered Ge'ez documents. However, such palaeographical work is still in its infancy, and lacks sufficient numbers of documents which can be reliably dated to make it an efficient tool at present. Early inscriptions closely resembling South Arabian ones have been dated according to the palaeographical studies of Pirenne (1956), but again there might be a case for readjustment (Schneider 1976i).

In a recent (unpublished) paper, Roger Schneider has commented on some fascinating anomalies in Ge'ez writing on Aksumite inscriptions and coins (see also Drewes 1955; Hahn 1987). The existence of one vocalised letter on certain silver coins of Wazeba, a predecessor of Ezana, may well indicate that the process of vocalisation was under way before Ezana, though the unvocalised Ge'ez inscription of Ezana (DAE 7) has made it commonly accepted that the development of vocalisation occurred during his reign. Littmann (1913, IV: 78), Drewes and Schneider all suggest deliberate archaising; some of the letters, apart from lacking vowels, are of forms very much more ancient than those current for Ezana's time. This is not just over-elaborate academic discussion. For whatever reasons Ezana had this done (and Drewes suggests perhaps a desire to emphasise the links with South Arabia, or perhaps to point to the ancient origins of Aksumite royal power), it is of interest that almost no kings of Aksum in the subsequent centuries introduced vowelling on their coins, or when they did, it was only on a letter or two; and this long after vocalisation must have been current on other media.

Preceding the common use of Ge'ez, Greek was the chosen official language of the inscriptions and coins. This was evidently largely orientated towards foreign residents and visitors, and can hardly have been understood by more than the smallest section of the ruling class and merchant community. There must also have been a body of more or less learned men who acted as scribes in preparing the drafts of the inscriptions, perhaps priests or a special corps of clerks. Greek remained the language of the coins, particularly the gold, until the end of the coinage, but its quality degenerated quickly. Coins datable to the fourth and fifth centuries already show errors in their Greek legends.

A few inscriptions were drafted in several versions; Greek, and in Ge'ez in two redactions, the first in the Ge'ez script, the second in the South Arabian script. Use of this 'pseudo Sabaean' seems to have been mere vanity, perhaps trying to equal the tri-lingual inscriptions set up by the Sassanian kings of Persia, since there can hardly have been any real reason for rendering a Ge'ez inscription into the South Arabian monumental script. Presumably a native speaker of Ge'ez would be able to recognise the gist of the text, the letters, though differently oriented and more rectilinear, being still recognisable; but a Ge'ez version was also supplied. A visiting South Arabian would have understood the script but not the language. The South Arabian script might might perhaps have retained something of a sacrosanct aura, as the ancient vehicle for dedicatory inscriptions, so that it was felt that a version in that script fulfilled the requirements of tradition; but that seems a little far-fetched as an explanation by the time of Kaleb and W'ZB.

When king Kaleb of Aksum received Greek-speaking ambassadors, he employed an interpreter to translate the letters from the emperor; but this may have been due to the formalities of court protocol rather than of necessity (Malalas, ed. Migne 1860: 670).

It can hardly be doubted, from the evidence of survivors such as the 'proto-Ge'ez' inscriptions of Matara, Safra, and Anza, and the series of royal inscriptions, that there was a fair body of written material in Ge'ez extant in Aksumite times, though examples found to date cannot in any way compare numerically with the sort of material surviving from most other ancient civilisations. Small inscriptions have been found on vessels of stone and pottery (Littmann 1913: IV; Drewes and Schneider 1967: 96ff; Schneider 1965: 91–2; Anfray 1972: pl. III). One, on a rock on Beta Giyorgis hill overlooking Aksum, seems to be a boundary-marker reading *'Boundary between (the land of) SMSMY and SBT'* – either the names of the owners, or of the parcels of land. Future archaeological missions will almost undoubtedly reveal more of these minor inscriptions. Abroad, Ge'ez inscriptions are known from Meroë, Socotra (Bent 1898), and South Arabia.

A later manifestation in the development of letters in Ethiopia was the translation of various literary works from other languages such as Greek, Arabic and Syriac into Ge'ez, with concomitant effects on the language itself.

2. Literature and Literacy

Of Aksumite literature we know virtually nothing except that between the fifth and seventh centuries the Bible and other works began to be translated into Ge'ez (in some cases by Syrian/Aramaic speakers, thus absorbing certain additions to the vocabulary of the Ge'ez language). Traces of the early biblical translation survive in the form of quotations in some of the inscriptions.

The Ge'ez royal inscriptions themselves show an accomplished use of the language, and well exploit the propaganda medium provided by them. The earlier use of Greek for monumental inscriptions may have been an important factor towards the 'stylistic confidence' shown by the Ge'ez inscriptions, and this may not in fact reflect a long literary tradition (Irvine 1977). Zoskales, an early Aksumite ruler, was an educated man who spoke Greek, and the royal example, as well as the influx of Greek-speaking merchants, doubtless encouraged the spread of learning which resulted in the use of Greek for even the national inscriptions and coinage. One feels that there must have been a certain amount of literacy in the country for the kings to take such care with the inscriptions and the coin legends with their mottoes (Ch. 9: 4). A ruler like Ezana, educated under the influence of Frumentius, who later returned to be installed as Ethiopia's first bishop, would surely have been able to speak and read Greek, and been well aware of the advantages of such propaganda media in both foreign and local circles.

Very occasionally, there are other indications of literacy, like the inscription left by a presumably Aksumite Ethiopian, Abreha, in the Wady Manih on the road to the Egyptian port of Berenice. Its interpretation is, as usual, not quite clear, partly from uncertainty as to the significance of certain words, partly due to its condition (the last three lines are almost completely illegible). Sergew Hable Sellasie's version reads *"I Abreha, man of Aksum, spent the night here [and] came believing in the might of the Lord of Heaven Aryam, with my son"*. Littmann read it as *"I am Abreha Takla Aksum and I stayed here. [I] came [protected] by the power [of the Lord of the Sublime] H[eaven] with my son"*. Ullendorff suggested *"I Abreha am the founder of Aksum"* (or, *"founder of the [Church of] Aksum"*) *"and have my domicile there"* (Sergew Hable Sellassie 1972: 109; Littmann 1954; Ullendorff 1955). Schneider (1984: 158), after discussing the state of the text as it is preserved now, concluded, perhaps wisely, that after "*I Abreha*" 'the rest is speculation'. However, the inscription is of interest since it is unvocalised and apparently of the early fourth century AD; it confirms that the name Abreha was in use in Ethiopia at the same period as the mysterious Abreha and Atsbeha of Aksumite legend. Another unvocalised inscription from Dabra Damo, associated with crosses, reads simply *"I prayed"* (Littmann 1913: IV, 61).

A more mundane inscription, on a pot found at Aksum, reads *"he who breaks it, pays!"* (Anfray 1972: pl. III).

In late Aksumite times the inscription of the *hatseni* Danael was carved on one of the statue bases in the city (Ch. 11: 5); this is, with the funerary inscription of Giho, daughter of Mangesha, from Ham (Conti Rossini 1939; Cerulli 1968: 18-19), one of the latest inscriptions we have. At Ham Conti Rossini also noted archaic Ethiopian inscriptions, probably simply names of travellers like those from a grotto at Qohayto, together with Aksumite pillars and other objects. The funerary inscription reads;

> *"Giho, daughter of Mangasha, died in the month of Tahsas, the 27th day, at dawn, the day before the vigil of the Nativity, a Wednesday, being the year...Ella Sahel. But as it is written 'Man born of woman is of few days' as it is written in the Gospel 'He who has eaten my flesh and drunk my blood shall not taste death, and I will raise him at the last day'; and as is written in the Prophet 'The dead shall be raised, and those who are in the tomb shall live'.*

Sergew Hable Sellassie (1972: 198), read the middle lines as *"on the eve of Christmas on the day of Wednesday. And died a year after we had (conquered?) our enemy Ella Sahel"*. Conti Rossini suggested a date of the 7th or 8th century for this inscription. Monneret de Villard (1940) noted that the shape of the tablet on which the inscription is carved resembles the typical Meroitic altar of offerings, and thought that Giho's name was also Meroitic in origin; since such a funerary inscription is so far unique in Ethiopia but not unknown in Nubia, perhaps it does show some influences from there. It has been suggested that 'Ella Sahel' refers to a king of that name who appears in the king-lists, but the reading of the sentence is obscure (Schneider 1984: 163).

The later Ethiopian love of stories of the miracle-filled lives of saints, and the wonderful tales of old, may have had some literary reflection as early as Aksumite times, helping to both develop and preserve them. The compilation of the chronicles of the kings, as in mediaeval times, may have been an Aksumite custom, as illustrated by the preserved inscriptions. But if so the only traces we have of them are the Ge'ez king lists repeated in later times, with a few glosses about exceptional events. The patent inaccuracy of the lists, and the non-appearance of most known Aksumite rulers, show that only a very little was transmitted to later ages about Aksumite history, and presumably any such ancient chronicles perished during one of the periods of unrest from late Aksumite times.

There can be little doubt that the art of making parchment and keeping records or literary works by the use of parchment scrolls (as in the Nubian kingdoms later), or larger flat pages (as in Ethiopia in the mediaeval period) could have been practised in Aksumite times, and one day we may hope to find something of the sort in, perhaps, one of the Aksumite tombs. Records of government business and commercial transactions, as well as religious and other works, were certainly kept from early times, but the climate of Ethiopia does not have the dryness which has preserved so much perishable material in Egypt and Nubia. Most of the surviving Ethiopian parchment books are of relatively recent date, but there remains the hope that some earlier works may one day be discovered.

3. The Arts

No Aksumite painting, beyond that on pottery, has survived, and much of the decorative material which has been found is of uncertain provenance.

62. The figure of a lioness carved on a rock at Gobedra, near Aksum.

Some of it may have originated in Egypt or Syria, or even South Arabia. Surviving metal-work objects, such as small images of an ibex, the Three Graces, and a pair of dogs, or glass-inlaid bronze box fragments (see Ch. 12), may have been foreign work imported into Aksum. No large statues have yet been found of the Aksumite period – though possibly one of the gold, silver and bronze statues mentioned in the inscriptions, to which some of the granite plinths still existing at Aksum probably once belonged, may have survived the desire to melt down its metal, and be still awaiting the excavator's pick. The only truly Aksumite art-form we yet know of (apart from some plastic modelling on pottery, and some carving on flat surfaces and in the round) is architecture (see Ch. 5: 4) and the limited imagery of the coinage (Ch. 9).

In view of the later liking for elaborately-painted walls in the churches, it may not be too surprising to find, one day, paintings on the plastered walls of one of the tombs, palaces, or churches, like that reported to Muhammad by his wives (Muir 1923: 490; Sergew Hable Sellassie 1972: 186, n. 30; Lepage

63. Drawing of a bronze coin (d. 17mm) of king Israel of Aksum showing a Greek cross in a ring of dots.

64. Drawing of a silver coin (d. 16mm) of king Wazena of Aksum, showing a Greek cross framed in an arch rather similar to the design on the silver coin of Armah, fig. 16.

1989: 52). Muhammad was apparently involved in a strange scene with some of his womenfolk, who had tried to help him as he lay dying by feeding him an Abyssinian remedy consisting of Indian wood, a little *wars* seed, and some olive oil. Muhammed then made them all swallow it as well. "*After this, the coversation turning upon Abyssinia, Um Selame and Um Habiba, who had both been exiles there, spoke of the beauty of the cathedral of Maria there, and of the wonderful pictures on its walls. Overhearing it, Mohammad was displeased and said 'These are the people who, when a saint among them dieth, build over his tomb a place of worship, and adorn it with their pictures; in the eyes of the Lord, the worst part of all creation"*...

Of uncertain date is the carved lioness, over 2 m long, on the rock of Gobedra, near Aksum (Littmann 1913: II, 73), but carved stone lion (or bull) heads (Anfray and Annequin 1965: pl. LXVII,5-6) were often used as waterspouts on Aksumite buildings, and were still so employed in Alvares' time (Ch. 10: 5). The much larger rock scuplture of a lion at Kombolcha in southern Wollo may be an Aksumite creation (Gerster 1970: 25, pls. 9-10), or perhaps dates from the post-Aksumite period. Carving on shell (an ibex from Aksum; Munro-Hay 1989) is attested as well, but not necessarily of local production. If, as suggested above, parchment or papyrus books or scrolls were used in Aksumite times, the art of calligraphy or even the beginnings of the illumination of such books may also have a long history.

We have a certain amount of evidence that the remarkable development of

65. Drawings of a silver coin (d. c. 17mm) bearing the monogramme AGD, showing a gold-inlaid cross under an arch, and two silver and two bronze issues of king Ioel (d. between c.12 and c. 14mm respectively), depicting the cross in various forms; in a circle, as a hand-cross, and in the Latin and Greek styles.

elaborate variations on the cross-motif, for which Ethiopia is even now very notable, was in full swing in Aksumite times. On the coins the cross is gradually expanded to a design with gold inlay, accompanied by additional features like crosslets on the arms, and various-shaped frames. Many pottery vessels have stamped crosses on their bases, possibly the result of carved wooden stamps now vanished. There are a number of these from Aksum, and a more elaborated type was commonly found at Matara (Wilding in Munro-Hay 1989; Anfray 1966). On other vessels the crosses are incised, and accompanied by monograms and other symbols. The long-footed Latin cross is uncommon, though it does appear, and the equal-armed Greek cross is the main type used.

4. Music and Liturgical Chant

The liturgical music used even today, preserved both by memory and a system of musical notation (Buxton 1970: 154ff), is attributed to the deacon Yared, who lived in the reign of Kaleb's son Gabra Masqal, in the sixth century. He is said to have so improved the dull chants of his time, that in a performance before Gabra Masqal both chanter and king were so absorbed that the king's spear, on which he was leaning, pierced Yared's foot without either noticing. There is much legendary material about Yared, but nothing yet preserved goes back further than the fifteenth century. The only early comment which mentions music is in Malalas' account of a Byzantine embassy, when he states that some of the Aksumites surrounding Kaleb when he appeared on his elephant-drawn car were playing the flute (ed. Migne 1860: 670). However, it is not unlikely that the Aksumites may have had some of the musical instruments which are familiar today in Ethiopia, such as the drum (beaten before kings and nobles, and a sign of rank, at least from mediaeval times), the tambourine, the sistrum (*tsanatsil*), the one-stringed violin (*masinqo*), or the *begena* and *krar*, the larger and smaller types of Ethiopian harp or lyre.

XIV

Society and Death

1. Social Classes

We have remarkably little information about the stratification of Aksumite society, but some suggestions can be made using indications from archaeological and other evidence. Mobility between classes, inheritance, marriage status or other family arrangements are all at present quite outside our knowledge. Polygamy can perhaps be assumed by analogy with later custom, but there is no actual evidence. Later Ethiopian law followed the *Fetha Nagast*, 'The Law of the Kings' written in Arabic by a Copt in the mid-thirteenth century, and translated into Ge'ez perhaps in the middle of the fifteenth century (Tzadua 1968), but inscriptions like that of Safra show that there were earlier legal codes in use (Drewes 1962).

We do not know if there was any prestige derived from being an 'Aksumite' (as in the case of the extra privileges bestowed on a Roman citizen), rather than a member of one of the other communities which made up the kingdom. A distinction between Ethiopia/Habashat and Aksum itself is implied when the kings are referred to by South Arabian inscriptions as '*nagashi* of Habashat (Abyssinia) and Aksum'. It has been noted elsewhere that the tribes such as the Agwezat, presumably part of Habashat but not Aksumites, retained their identity for a long while as a distinct people; but after a while any such Aksum/Habashat dichotomy may have blurred.

Social class may well have been based on the ownership of land, perhaps entraining more or less feudal committments down the scale, but there is little reliable evidence to affirm this from the Aksumite period. Copies of land-grants to individuals and institutions are preserved (Huntingford 1965), but no originals survive from Aksumite times. Huntingford notes, however, that there is a good possibility that the early charters might be genuine transmissions; they all include Christianised sanction clauses which resemble those on the Aksumite inscriptions (Ch. 11: 5, Geza 'Agmai, DAE 10, DAE 11, Kaleb inscr.). If this is true, although all the examples given are grants to Maryam Tseyon cathedral, we can imagine that individuals might have been similarly rewarded by the kings with estates and villages to support their rank, and that land-registers of some sort were maintained. The only actual 'land-grant' we know of from Aksumite times is that of king Ezana to the six Beja chieftains

(Ch. 11: 5, DAE 4, 6 & 7, Geza 'Agmai); and this is exceptional being a forcible removal of a population. However, it does illustrate that the king possessed land to bestow, as we might expect from the *Monumentum Adulitanum*'s statement about conquered peoples; *"I reserved for myself half of their lands and their peoples..."*

Slaves, perhaps largely prisoners of war or criminals, are alluded to occasionally. Kosmas seems to imply that the majority of those at home and in the hands of foreign merchants came from Sasu and Barbaria, roughly the western Sudan and south-eastern Ethiopia or Somalia (Wolska- Conus 1968: 378). Such unskilled basic tasks as field work and rough quarry work, hauling, and domestic work could be expected for them. Exceptions would be prisoners of some special quality, like Frumentius and Aedesius, destined for tasks of greater responsibility, who probably were not actually considered as slaves. Procopius speaks of 'slaves' (*δουλοι*) in the Aksumite army in Arabia, but these seem to have been allowed to remain in Arabia, and were included among those who later rebelled against Sumyafa' Ashwa' (Esimiphaios), which leaves their actual status unclear (Procopius, ed. Dewing 1914: 189).

Ultimately, life in Aksumite times, as today, was based on the work of the peasant toiling in the fields. Ploughing with oxen, sowing, clearing, reaping, and threshing would have occupied his day, and very likely the land he worked was part of another's estate from which he could take only basic subsistence products for himself. Shepherding the flocks and herds, and tending vegetable and fruit gardens, would have been other countryside occupations. We have no information about land-tenure systems in Aksumite times, though gifts of land by the king to the gods or to the church are mentioned, the former in inscriptions, and the latter in both inscriptions and land-charters. Those of the latter which claim to be of Aksumite times are all in reality much later, but may preserve some genuine information (Huntingford 1965). Possibly the prisoners offered to the gods were destined, if not as human sacrifices, to work on such lands? It is also not known whether the peasants were free, or tied to the land. Probably the houses of such people, as today, were constructed of perishable materials, and contained little besides essential tools, skins for clothing and bedding, a few storage vessels, (including wooden or basketwork ones?) and perhaps one or two extras for the richer peasant. Such houses may have been round, like a clay house-model from Hawelti, or perhaps, in more prosperous circumstances, of the type found by de Contenson at Mazaber in the Hawelti-Melazo region (de Contenson 1963ii, pl. XXXVIIb-c; 1961iii: 44). The latter was a stone dry-walled house with the typical Aksumite steps or rebates in the wall, consisting of two rooms only, altogether about 9 m in length by about 4 m wide. Its only remaining contents were sherds from a few pottery vessels and fragments of household objects in bronze (a pin-head and a hook).

The specialist potter, metalworker, leather-worker or other artisan, in the urban setting, may similarly have lived in a relatively humble house, and exchanged his work for food or money at one or other of the markets, or he may have travelled, doing work where needed. The only excavated urban areas which could give an idea about the dwellings of such people are at Matara, but they have not yet been fully published. However, a certain idea can be gained from published plans (Anfray 1974: 756 and fig. 7), which show a sharp contrast to the neighbouring mansions. The symmetrical arrangement of the former is replaced by an irregular series of square or rectangular rooms, entered by twisting streets and through courts. The impression given is of an organic process, the residents building, rebuilding, adding, or removing rooms and walls as their needs required. Hearths, ovens, and abandoned pottery indicate living floors in these simple two- or three-room dwellings. Complete publication of these quarters of Matara may eventually give us an idea as to the sort of people, and the way of life, to be found in the humbler echelons of an Aksumite urban population. Whether those peasants or artisans who lived and worked in defined areas were obliged to join the armies when required is not known, but seems very likely. Certain specialists, smiths and so on, must have been necessary to minister to the armies on campaign, and staff such as cooks, porters, and grooms or herdsmen to tend the animals would also have been taken along. The local trader in the market towns was probably not much better off. But the merchant in the larger centres, the larger independent farmer (if such existed), and the various civil officials may have constituted something of a middle class, dwelling in rather better houses, perhaps like those illustrated by the clay models found at Aksum. These were apparently equipped with wooden doorways and window surrounds, and layered thatch roofs (de Contenson 1959i: pl. XIX, fig. 8; Chittick 1974: fig. 21a). A greater quantity of tools and fittings, with some occasional luxuries, can be imagined among their possessions. Good quality pottery, some glassware and decorative metalwork, jewellery, perhaps an Indian or Egyptian cloth robe or cloak, and meat and wine on the table are the sort of extras to be expected. They may have employed artisans and servants, or been able to afford a few slaves. Possibly the burial goods found in a tomb in the Gudit Stele Field (see below) belonged to someone from this level of society.

In the central area of the towns, and in country mansions, the landowners and rulers of the dominant class would have led a rather more pleasant way of life, surrounded by households comprising slaves and servants living in the outer wings of their houses where the domestic offices probably were. The great distinction among the élite residences appears to have been one of size, and, as one might expect, the largest were the metropolitan palaces. We can approximately divide the buildings into two groups, the very large 'palaces' and the lesser 'villas' or 'mansions', and these may reflect two echelons of the Aksumite élite; the rulers themselves, and the nobility and great officials.

Those we may term palaces were at Aksum, with the length of the four sides of their central pavilions ranging from 24–35 m; the smallest of these, Ta'akha Maryam, was surrounded by outbuildings measuring 80 x 120. After an intermediate structure, the 21 m sq pavilion at Dungur (Anfray: 1972: pl. I), where the outbuildings measured c. 64 m sq, measurements of the pavilions of the next size of building down ('villa' or 'mansion') varied as follows;

17.50 m, Tertre B at Matara (Anfray and Annequin 1965); the outbuildings measured 59.50 x 49 m;

15.20 m, Tertre C at Matara (Anfray and Annequin 1965);

15 m 'Addi Kilte villa (Puglisi 1941);

12.60 x 11.20 m, Tertre A at Matara (Anfray 1963); the outbuildings, if symmetrically arranged, were about 17 × 15.50 m;

In the central pavilions of these structures we might expect to find the reception rooms, and, upstairs perhaps (Buxton and Matthews 1974), the main living quarters. The quality of the fittings would have varied with the rank of the owners, from the monarchs to perhaps different grades of noble or official. From tomb finds we can furnish these with gilded and decorated furniture, with vessels and other equipment of gold, silver, bronze, glass, and stoneware. To this we can probably add certain more costly furs and fabrics, perfumes and incense, carved wood and ivory work, and luxuries of the table both local and imported. Such establishments may have employed a number of specially-skilled retainers, such as musicians and singers, artisans of various sorts, clerks, accountants, bailiffs or stewards. We can imagine a fairly considerable population for the larger dwellings and dependencies; for example, Matara Tertre B had over thirty rooms in its outbuildings, the Dungur mansion, with its several courtyards, contained about fifty rooms, while Ta'akha Maryam had probably around eighty.

2. Funerary Practice

The Aksumites belonging to the last three categories above are those for whom we can envisage burial in the main cemeteries at Aksum. Tomb architecture, and the stelae, have already been discussed (Ch. 5: 5 & 6); it can be assumed that only the upper echelons of society could have had a built tomb or one of the larger rock-cut types. In the royal cemetery the dead were probably buried with considerable amounts of valuable gear, and with the full panoply of ceremony, sacrificial offerings, and the like. The dead of high rank were laid in stone coffins, and, surrounded with their equipment, were either sealed up forever, or to wait for the next member of the family to die if they were in multiple tombs. So far among the tombs dicovered, only that of the False Door seems to have been an individual tomb. Very likely the dead were dressed in their best clothing and decked with their jewellery, but no intact burial assemblage in one of the larger tombs has yet been found.

Stone coffins were visible in the partly-plundered Tomb of the Brick Arches, but no-one has yet penetrated into the inner chambers, where some of the burials still perhaps lie undisturbed since the robbery which scattered other occupants' possessions across the floor of the outer rooms.

The tomb excavated by the BIEA in the Gudit Stele Field, though it was only a simple excavated chamber marked by a rough stele, seems from its contents to have belonged to someone in the better-off social strata. However, it contained only pottery, glass and iron tools (though some valuable items may have been taken by robbers), whereas the only partially cleared Tomb of the Brick Arches, situated in the main cemetery but still a modest tomb in comparison to some of the really large ones, contained objects of every kind, including precious metals. Such a gap probably expresses the differences between the third and fourth categories discussed above, and indicates how the ruling class compared with even the next grade of their subjects in terms of material wealth.

Some tombs contained multiple burials with only a few personal items of jewellery, or the occasional pot or glass vessel (Shaft Tomb A at Aksum; Chittick 1974: 171). These seem to date to the Christian period, and probably the old customs requiring a mass of funerary equipment died away after the spread of Christianity. Tombs of persons of rank, such as the so-called Tombs of Kaleb and Gabra Masqal, and the tomb at Matara Tertre D (Anfray and Annequin 1965: pls. XLIV-XLV), were still very well-constructed, but contained less space for equipment. All these tombs, and that of the False Door, have been open for centuries or were so badly robbed in antiquity that nothing can now be said about their possible contents; only the stone sarcophagi remain in some of them, and even these are often smashed into fragments.

Rather lesser tombs were found in and around the building at Tertre A at Matara (Anfray 1963); they may be contemporary with the building, but are more likely to have been installed after its abandonment. There were six, either built of stones or simply dug into the earth, and roofed with stone slabs. Occasionally they yielded some pottery, and some contained three or four bodies. Information about the burial of newly-born or very young children comes from both Adulis and Matara. In these places, imported amphorae, formerly used for the conveyance of wine or oil from abroad, were used as miniature coffins to bury children in the houses of their parents. The necks of the amphorae having been broken off, the body was put inside, and the top closed by a stone lid (eg. Anfray and Annequin 1965: pl. L,1). The custom of burying children thus was not uncommon in the contemporary Roman world.

The discovery of two skeletons thrown into the pit at the base of Stele 137 at Aksum, and the fact that among the platforms and in some tombs were found animal bones, either burnt or not, may indicate that certain sacrificial ceremonies were enacted during funerals or dedications of stelae (Munro-

Hay 1989). Possibly the animal bones and charcoal were the remains of a funerary or celebratory meal. If Drewes (1962: 41) is correct in his interpretation of the Safra inscription A, we have there details of the offerings on the occasion of certain acts connected with death and burial. These seem to consist of the completion of an excavated tomb; the occasion of a funerary ceremony; the immolation of a cow; and a gathering at the tomb. The inscription is apparently of the third century, and the rites mentioned by it may have been the same as those enacted at the necropolis of Aksum, resulting in the occurrence of animal bones and their burnt remains in and around the tombs.

XV

The Decline of Aksum

1. The failure of resources

The long period of occupation of the city of Aksum evidently had a profound effect on the surrounding countryside, from which it drew the materials of subsistence. Some of the processes set in train can be inferred from the present state of the land, and consideration of the various factors involved. The local industries, including the manufacture of glass, faience, brick and pottery, and metal-working, all needed wood or charcoal for their furnaces. Charcoal was probably in further demand for cooking, and heating when necessary, and wood was used for furniture and other equipment as well as house-building. These activities slowly robbed the surrounding hills of their covering of trees – which, however, survived in a few enclaves on the Shire plateau to be noted by Butzer (1981), – and exposed their topsoil to degradation and erosion. The expansion of the population, probably adequately coped with at first by enlarging the food catchment areas by improved roads and transport facilities for goods into the city, and more intensive cultivation on the surrounding lands, eventually subjected these to overcropping. The pressure on the land would have shortened the rotation period of the crops, land which should have lain fallow for longer being pressed into use too soon. The subsequent lowering of the fertility level of the land again resulted in degredation and erosion, leaving an exhausted soil in the proximity of the city and the immediate countryside. Difficulties in maintaining the food-supplies may have been a significant factor in removing the capital elsewhere. A certain amount of recovery may have possible in some areas around the town, since the fertility of the hinterland of the much smaller town of later times was noted by travellers a thousand or so years later. Alvares simply mentioned that *'its countryside...is sown in their season with all kinds of seed'* (Beckingham and Huntingford 1961: 159). Others noted wheat, wine and vegetables growing at Aksum (Frate Rafaello Francescano, 1522; de Villard 1938: 60), a poor crop of fruit (Bruce 1790: III, 132), or, rather better, *'a vast plain richly cultivated with many sorts of grain and near the town grass-plots and meadows'* (Plowden 1868: 391–2).

We cannot be sure for the Aksumite period, but among the natural disasters which in later times reduced the agricultural and animal yield in

66. A scene near Aksum taken in 1974; a farmer ploughing in the Gudit Stele Field to the west of Aksum. Photo BIEA.

Ethiopia, cattle plague (Ch. 4: 8.3) and locusts are noted. For example, Alvares observed the desolation caused by the *'multitude of locusts... and the damage which they do'* (Beckingham and Huntingford 1961: 132). It is not inconceivable that, apart from the steady decline caused by overuse of the land, one or both of these may have occurred to emphasise the need to remove the capital to some better provided region.

2. THE CLIMATE

The work of the geomorphologist Karl Butzer (1981) has suggested that the climate of northern Ethiopia may have changed for the worse just after the Aksumite period. The measurement of the Nile flood levels, recorded in Egypt, indicates that after a long period of excellent rainfall, more erratic precipitation ensued; this seems to have been after the abandonment of the city. However, if the land had reached a state of advanced degradation during the late Aksumite period, even the heavier rains, though theoretically ideal for the growth of the crops, would have contributed to the erosion on the slopes above the city and in the surrounding fields. What had been an advantage before had become another element in the vicious circle of the decay of the resources. It was the material brought down by the run-off caused by the rains from the hillsides that began to cover the buildings in the town as they were abandoned and fell into ruin. Butzer's figures suggest that until about 750AD floods were high in Egypt, then poorer with very low levels from the mid-tenth to late eleventh centuries, the period when the kingdom, after the invasion of the queen of the Bani al-Hamwiyya, had decayed almost to the point when the Zagwé dynasty could take over (Ch. 4: 8.3). The low-water levels after 730, in part following the spring rains in the Aksumite region, were already averaging below normal. It may be going too far to say that insufficient 'little' rains (the March to May rains) combined with erosion caused by the action of strong June-September rains on the denuded land both to shorten the growing season and remove the topsoil. Nevertheless, climatic factors may have had their part to play in the abandonment of Aksum.

3. EXTERNAL AND INTERNAL POLITICAL TROUBLES

There are several hints that things began to go wrong in the Aksumite state in the later sixth and the early seventh century. Kaleb seems to have lost both prestige and an expensive war during his contretemps with Abreha, though after his death some sort of peace was patched up. The invasion may have been too costly a gesture for Aksum at the time, and the outlay in men and money must have had a deleterious effect on Aksumite power at home. Possibly the great plague of the 540s (Procopius; ed. Dewing 1914: 451ff), said to have emerged from Pelusium in Egypt, also had some effect on Aksum, as it did on the Roman world from the Mesopotamian provinces to Gaul, and across to Persia. The general political and commercial climate after first the Yemen and then Jerusalem and Alexandria fell to the Persians must have much damaged Ethiopia's trade in the Red Sea, and accordingly its prosperity.

To an unknown extent, troubles at the centre must have generated the hope in the outlying parts of the kingdom that it was time to essay another trial of strength with the Aksumite rulers, and revolts may have occurred which further weakened the kingdom by cutting off certain internal resources and routes (see below). For example, the Beja tribes, some of which had been crushed by Ezana long ago, later became independent of the *najashi*s (see al-Ya'qubi's comments; Vantini 1975: 71-3) and may have caused trouble to their theoretical overlords for some time before. The Agaw who later came to power with the Zagwé dynasty may also have been involved in the unrest.

Anfray, working at Adulis, found a thick layer of ashes over some structures, and deduced that the town's end had been brutal (1974: 753). Some historians have thought that the town was destroyed by a Muslim expedition in 640AD, but the Arab records regard this expedition as a disaster; and it seems unlikely that it was even aimed at the Ethiopian kingdom itself, but rather against Red Sea pirates (Munro-Hay 1982i). Increasing Ethiopian inability to keep the sea-lanes free may, however, have encouraged the Arabs to occupy the Dahlak Islands later on, probably in 702AD (Hasan 1967: 30). A certain Yazid b. al-Muhallab was exiled there by the *khalifa* 'Umar in 718/9AD. In spite of this, later Arab historians mention Dahlak as part of the dominions of the *najashi*s.

4. THE NAJASHI ASHAMA IBN ABJAR

For any ideas about the political situation in Ethiopia at the end of the Aksumite period, we rely on very tenuous information. One of the chief sources for the history of Ethiopia between 615-6 and 630AD are the recorded traditions about the life of Muhammad and his followers, the *hadith*. A note of caution must be sounded before accepting these tales, but Muslim historians were themselves very conscious that the *hadith* were sometimes suspect, and insisted as well as they could on accepting only those with an impeccable *isnad* or chain of reliable sources right back to the original teller of the story. Umm Salama's tale (see below) about a revolt in Abyssinia passed through two informants before it was written down by Ibn Ishaq.

If the compilers of the *hadith* are to be believed, the ruling *najashi* at the time of the prophet was a man of justice and equity, called Ashama ibn Abjar. Abu Talib composed a verse (Guillaume 1955) for this *najashi* to encourage his support for the Muslims against the Quraysh, who were preparing bribes for the king and his commanders (shums);

'Does the Negus still treat Ja'afar and his companions kindly,
Or has the mischief-maker prevented him?
Thou art noble and generous, mayst thou escape calamity;
No refugees are unhappy with thee.
Know that God has increased they happiness
And all prosperity cleaves to thee.
Thou art a river whose banks overflow with bounty
Which reaches both friend and foe'.

The *najashi* Ashama ibn Abjar died in 630 AD and was, according to Ethiopian tradition, buried at Weqro, about 65 miles to the southeast of Aksum (Taddesse Tamrat 1972: 34–5). If we can accept this tradition, the royal cemetery at Aksum may have been out of use by that date. Interestingly, but of uncertain significance, what seems to be a late tomb of someone of very high rank was found by Anfray and Annequin at Matara (1965; Tertre D). Both Ethiopian and Arab traditions mention the shift of the capital away from Aksum, assigning it to various reigns or periods (Sergew Hable Sellassie 1972: 203; Taddesse Tamrat 1972: 35ff).

The *najashi* Ashama, again according to the reports of the Arab writers (Guillaume 1955: 153) purportedly from the mouth of Umm Salama, one of the wives of Muhammad, had to face two revolts in his own country, which help to confirm the general feeling of unrest at this period also expressed by the coinage mottoes. The story, related by Ibn Ishaq, who died in the late 760s, is that Ashama had to fight a rebel leader across the Nile. This must have occurred sometime after the second *hijra* to Abyssinia in 615-6 (Muir 1923: 86), and before 628, when the exiles returned, since Umm Salama said that it happened while they were in the country. The Nile lay between to two parties, and the battle was fought apparently on the west side of the river, since the Muslim messenger, al-Zubayr, had to swim across on a water-skin to find out the outcome. The *najashi* was victorious, but later had to deal with another tentative at revolt, this time to do with his religion – perhaps in reality this episode is a piece of Muslim propaganda; (Guillaume 1955: 154–5). These stories, after that detailing the difficulties in the succession (Guillaume 1955: 153–4) indicate that the *najashi*'s reign was not an easy one. In 630 there was military activity against Abyssinians who had combined with the people of Jidda against the Muslims. Muir (1923: 436) noted that the nature of this combination was not clear, but suggested that the *najashi* might have been by now disappointed to find that Muhammad no longer supported Christianity; this is not likely, in view of the fact that the prophet is said to have prayed for the *najashi* after his death in 630, and presumably this incident, if of any official nature, is to be attributed to his successor in that year.

5. THE *hatsani* DANAEL

There is one internal clue to the end of Aksum as a power centre; the inscriptions of a certain *hatsani* (ruler, or perhaps at this time merely commander or general) Danael, found on one of the ancient granite pedestals at Aksum (Littmann 1913: IV, nos. 12–14). The title *hatsani* is that which became the usual one (with negus or *najashi*) for the kings of Ethiopia, sometimes rendered as hadani, hatse, atze etc. Apart from Danael's inscriptions, it first appears in Ethiopia as a royal title in the Zagwé king Lalibela's land-charters. From the inscriptions, it appears that Danael was engaged in military campaigns, and not only another *hatsani*, Karuray(?) but a 'king of Aksum' is mentioned. It appears that among other military activities the Wolqayt people had attacked the land of Hasla, and then gone on to Aksum. Danael claims to have expelled them and killed and captured a number of men and animals. Other campaigns may have led him to fight the Barya, and to the Kassala region – but the reading of the texts is very uncertain (Schneider 1984: 163). In the inscription DAE 14, which is better preserved than the others, it appears that Danael forced the king of Aksum himself into submission, making him in effect a tributary ruler. Whatever the exact political alignments of the time, Danael was able to set up his (badly carved) inscription on an Aksumite statue base.

Several explanations of the situation are possible. The inscriptions could even allude to the time of Ashama, with the people of Wolqayt from over the Takaze being repelled by Danael in support of the king of Aksum; if this is the case, the *najashi* must eventually have triumphed after almost successful tentatives by Danael to seize power. Later in the same reign, between 615 and 630, the old capital at Aksum would have been finally abandoned as the eponymous centre of the Ethiopian kingdom. If the tales about the splendours of Aksum's cathedral told to Muhammad by his wives (see Ch. 13: 3) are true, they may indicate that the exiled Muslims were actually at the court in Aksum after 615, during the city's last days as a capital. The next recorded

67. At the cathedral of Maryam Tseyon, a priest exhibits the crowns and other objects dedicated by former emperors.

permanent capital was that of the *najashi*s or *hadani*s who ruled from Ku'bar, the city mentioned in the ninth and tenth centuries by Arab writers (see Ch. 4: 8).

Whatever the case, with the Arab take-over of the routes and many of the destinations of Aksumite trade after the preliminary Persian incursions into Arabia and the eastern Roman world, the 'Aksumite' Christian kingdom changed its policies and bowed to events. The trade with the Mediterranean world had decayed and even the Red Sea route itself, when the Abbasid shift of the capital to Baghdad after 750AD had emphasised the role of the Persian Gulf, became much less important, not reviving until the Fatimids were able to police and develop it in the eleventh and twelfth centuries. The Aksumite cultural heritage (now bound firmly with Christianity), though no longer directed by a king of Aksum from Aksum itself, but by a *hadani* or *najashi* from elsewhere, continued its southward expansion, gradually retiring from the north and the coast over the centuries. The process seems to have been gradual, since Arab writers long refer to the size and wealth of the *najashi*'s realm, and certain regions, though occupied by Muslims, still remained tributary. In the later tenth century the state may have almost succumbed to 'Gudit', enabling the Agaw Zagwé eventually to seize control; but even then the churches of Lalibela, attributed to the Zagwé period, still indicate a strong continuity with the Aksumite cultural tradition.

By the mid-seventh century, then, Aksum had lost its political pre-eminence in the region of the Ethiopian plateau, the coastal plains, and the Red Sea. The Ethiopian monarchy had left Aksum and undoubtedly the nobility and the merchant community were also departing. The city's monuments were falling into ruin, and, the result of a slow process of attrition, the formerly rich agricultural land surrounding the city was now capable of only a reduced yield. These were troubled times, and neither invasion nor revolt can be ruled out; the undefended former capital would have been easy prey to invaders, as it was to Gudit and Ahmad Gragn later. Nevertheless, even the most miserable conditions did not deprive Aksum of its legendary heritage, and the departure of the king, the court, the *abun* and all the trappings of a capital still left it pre-eminent in the possession of its cathedral and religious tradition. The damage done to the cathedral, and the plunder of its riches, did not seem to diminish the reverence of the Ethiopians for the venerable structure; the church was rebuilt and coronation at Aksum was reinstituted as the symbol of legitimate kingship. Aksum managed to survive the hardships of its declining fortunes, and, a political backwater, it became enshrined in Ethiopian tradition as a sacred city, and the repository of the national religion and culture.

XVI

The British Institute in Eastern Africa's Excavations at Aksum

This final chapter is based on a talk given by the author to the Society of Antiquaries of London in October 1987, designed more or less to coincide with the publication of the report on the excavations undertaken for the BIEA by Dr. Neville Chittick at Aksum from 1972–1974. Chittick's untimely death in 1984 prevented him from writing a fuller account than his *Preliminary Report* of 1974, but this task was undertaken by the present author, and has now been published (Munro-Hay 1989). Since the last major book on Aksumite archaeology appeared before the First World War (Littmann 1913), new studies based on archaeological excavation are long overdue. In addition, the architectural, numismatic, chronological and general cultural information revealed by Chittick's excavations has radically changed the impression gained of Aksum and its civilisation through previously published material, and it is evidently useful to recapitulate some of the main points here. Some of this material has been mentioned in previous chapters, but is here described all together within the context of the two main archaeological campaigns of 1973 and 1974.

The BIEA excavations which Chittick directed were on a large scale, and there was a great deal of information to sift through. The result is that we have not only a much clearer picture of many facets of Aksumite life, but also valuable indications towards a chronology, one of the perennial problems in Aksumite studies. As usual, more information produces more problems; we cannot claim to have more than begun to solve them, but a good deal of progress has been made, and the general schema of Aksumite history presented by this book has greatly benefited from Chittick's work.

The excavations explored a large number of sites in and around present-day Aksum. The archaeology of these is fully described in Munro-Hay 1989. The location of the most important sites was as follows.

The easternmost sites excavated were those flanking or near to the superstructure covering the so-called Tombs of Kaleb and Gabra Masqal. Next to the west were a number of stele sites, called Geza 'Agmai (GA), 'Enda Yesus (EY), and Ghele Emmi (GE). In the eastern central part of the town the site DA revealed the Tomb of the Brick Arches, and many trenches were laid out around the Stele Park (ST) to investigate and to try to date the stelae. Among these trenches many tombs were discovered, including Shaft Tombs labelled A-C, and the Mausoleum and East Tomb near the largest stele. Certain other large tombs were also cleared; the Nefas Mawcha (NM) south of the great terrace wall above which the three largest stelae stood, and, to the west of the main stelae group, the Brick Vaulted Structure and the Tomb of the False Door (the THA and THC trenches). In the ancient residential centre of the city, two sites revealed what were almost certainly small parts of large mansions; they were labelled IW and ES. Finally, apart from a number of relatively unimportant exploratory trenches around the Stele Park (designated HAW, PW, WC, and ML), some trenches were laid out in a stelae field west of the modern town, opposite the Dungur villa excavated by Anfray (1972); these were called GT after the traditional identification of the area with the legendary queen Gudit.

An important, and previously unknown, feature found at Aksum, among the ST trenches, was a series of buried stone-revetted platforms, the earliest of which seem to have been constructed in the first century AD, according to radiocarbon readings. The latest seem to have been erected, or rather expanded, in the fourth century. Behind their facades, the platforms were filled with freshly-quarried stones with almost no admixture of earth, and topped, relatively carefully, with layers of white and red soils. These, and considerable deposits elsewhere, at such sites as GA, GE, and HAW, lay in levels which yielded no coins, and thus seem to precede the first issues in c. 270–90AD. But in some of the GA and ST early levels were glass fragments, including types such as the mosaic or *millefiori* glass generally dated to between the first century BC and AD 100. The *Periplus* and other accounts mention glass of several types among the items imported into Aksum from the Roman empire, and these finds not only confirm the *Periplus*' report, but help to date these platforms as the earliest yet known features at Aksum.

There are further indications that there was a considerable period of occupation at the site before the 'Classical Aksumite' period of the third and fourth centuries. Some stele, found standing upright in pits which had been dug into the earlier platforms, had been completely buried by subsequent deposits. All were of a rough undressed type which preceded the later carefully shaped and sometimes elaborately carved examples, some of which could be dated to the later third and the fourth century AD by accompanying material.

The stelae at Aksum have never been properly dated. During his excavations Chittick was surprised to find that, according to his estimate, *'the coins indicate that the deposits on which the stelae were erected accumulated in the Christian Aksumite period'*. This certainly seemed a little unlikely, in view of the mounting evidence as the excavations progressed that the stelae were closely connected to tombs and were probably memorials to the deceased Aksumite kings; but, as usual, the key to his dating was the coinage, which has since been radically re-dated (Munro-Hay 1978 et seq.). The particular coin-type which led Chittick to assume that he had found stelae of Christian date was an issue attributed by earlier numismatists (Anzani 1926) to the sixth century king Kaleb or his immediate successors. But the type can now be re-dated to a considerable time before Kaleb, on the basis of overstriking on coins of king MHDYS, probably a close successor of Ezana. Further, study of the stratigraphy in the trenches concerned has resulted in a different interpretation of the sequence of events, and no longer supports the idea that stelae were a late phenomenon at Aksum.

The French archaeologist Henri de Contenson, working at Aksum in the 1950's, found that fragments of the broken summit of the largest stele of all (no. 1) lay below an occupation level containing coins of the late fourth century king Ouazebas (de Contenson 1959: 29). The stele, according to the coin evidence, fell most probably in the late fourth or early fifth century; that is, after the official conversion of king Ezana in c. 330AD, but at a period sufficiently close to this event to make it likely that certain burial traditions such as the erection of stelae had not yet lapsed. Other structures in the Stele Park area are also dated to the later fourth century, and confirm that the cemetery was in use after the advent of Christianity, but probably for decades rather than centuries.

The stelae seem to have all been associated with tombs, but as yet the direct pairing of certain tombs with certain stelae remains difficult. Almost every trench opened in the central (ST) area of Aksum yielded either a fallen stele, broken fragments, buried upright stelae, or shafts leading to tombs and tunnels, and it is certainly premature to assume that we know the lay-out of the necropolis. Two of the tombs were of quite unforseen dimensions and sophisticated architecture. One, possibly associated with the largest stele, was dubbed the 'Mausoleum', and consisted of a 15 × 15 metre complex of rooms off a central passage. Included in its construction were drystone walling, a brick arch, three shafts, dressed or rough granite roof-blocks, and a magnificent granite doorway in typical Aksumite style. The second, called by the Tigrinya name 'Nefas Mawcha', a name meaning something like 'the place where the winds go out', consisted of two outer corridors roofed with dressed granite slabs, built around a central room which was covered with a single slab measuring some 17m × 7m × $1\frac{1}{2}$m. By a curious chance this tomb, roofed by the second largest stone known to have been employed in Aksumite construction work, was severely damaged when the largest stone of all, the great carved stele, crashed down and struck the tomb's north-west corner. This upset the complicated balance of roofing blocks and the entire tomb subsided. However, enough has remained intact for the excavators to be able to propose a restoration of its original design.

Though the stelae may not have been objected to for religious reasons (it has even been suggested that some of them bore crosses at the top, where nail-holes indicate some applied decoration; van Beek 1967), the collapse of the largest one, and possibly of the second largest too, may have been sufficient reason for the Aksumites to turn to a simpler but essentially similar memorial, the house-tomb.

The most accomplished monument of this type at Aksum, the Tomb of the False Door, was a surprising discovery. It is entirely made of dressed granite blocks, in the form of a house-superstructure with a magnificent carved granite door over a tomb chamber and a surrounding corridor, reached by a separate staircase from a paved courtyard. It was dated by Chittick to the pre-Christian period, since it was overlain by deposits containing glass attributed to the third century. However, it was later found that a stratum running beneath the stones of its courtyard abutted against an earlier stone wall, part of a building called the Brick Vaulted Structure. This latter, though incompletely excavated, appears to have consisted of a series of burnt-brick vaults, with horse-shoe shaped arches and granite relieving lintels, closely resembling the architecture of yet another tomb, the Tomb of the Brick Arches, so-called from its three horse-shoe shaped arches. This latter tomb contained material of probably mid-fourth century date. It therefore seems that the Tomb of the False Door is later than the arched structures, and probably of late fourth or early fifth century date. Very likely it was the next stage in the development of the necropolis architecture, since the fall of the great stele would probably have discouraged further such attempts, and the house-tomb type is a logical successor. A very close stylistic link between tomb and stelae is provided by the doorway and lintel of the tomb, carved in exactly the same manner as the doors depicted on the two largest, and latest, stelae. The early material found over the tomb, which was one reason for Chittick's assumption that it was of pre-Christian Aksumite date, appears to have been washed down from the higher slopes of the Beta Giyorgis hill which dominates the necropolis; it included a large number of stone scrapers also found in quantity on the top of the hill. Two other house-tombs, the double tomb building locally attributed to the sixth-century kings Kaleb and Gabra Masqal, and another found at the Eritrean site of Matara, are comparable.

The picture we have of the town is not all taken from the necropolis. At the same time the excavations cleared a number of domestic structures, particularly at two sites which were designated IW and ES. These revealed rough stone-built walls, strengthened by two techniques, wooden interlacing or the use of granite corner blocks. In addition the walls were arranged in a series of recesses, so that there were no long stretches of wall, and each wall rose in rebated steps, each lined with slate. This is, as we have noted (Ch. 5:4), typical Aksumite 'mansion' architecture. Only a few rooms were cleared in each place, but it was evident from the finds that these dwellings were the houses of prosperous Aksumites in possession of a high standard of living. Objects found included the fragments of many polished breccia bowls, glassware and elegant pottery, metalwork, coins, and other items. Temples or churches were not found by the BIEA expedition, nor were examples of the more humble dwellings which were probably built with perishable materials such as wood and mud plaster with thatched roofs.

The tombs, though only one was completely cleared, yielded rich grave-goods. The cleared one, marked by a rough stone stele, was not found in the main necropolis, but in the Gudit Stele Field west of the town (GT II). It appears to date from the mid-third century, and was merely a small chamber cut into the earth, with no built elements at all. It contained particularly fine pottery, two sets of glasses (stem goblets and beakers), and a large number of iron tools such as tweezers, saws, knives, and a sickle. The stele marking the grave, and the pottery, are 'Aksumite' elements; the glassware and tools could as well be from a Roman site as an African one.

Tombs in the main necropolis were evidently much richer, and the excavation of only one room in the 4th century Tomb of the Brick Arches revealed piles of grave-goods (mentioned above, Ch. 12), including glassware, pottery vessels in a multitude of shapes, some painted and decorated, all sorts of metalwork, including glass-inlaid bronze plaques, fittings for what was probably a wooden chest, gold fragments, a silver amulet-case, a bronze belt-buckle inlaid with silver and enamel crosses, iron knives with bone or ivory handles, and even leather and wood. In a number of small inner loculi, constructed by dividing the interior of the simply cut tomb by built stone walls, stone coffins could be seen behind a partly broken blocking wall. This tomb was also a surprise from the architectural point of view, since it was the first of those excavated which revealed the burnt brick horseshoe arches later found in even more elaborate styles in the Brick Vaulted Building. These must be among the earliest horse-shoe arches known, and were quite unexpected elements in Aksumite architecture, not being repeated in the later rock-cut churches of Tigray and Lasta. Other tombs consisted of carefully cut shafts leading beneath the stelae into vast roughly cut chambers (Shaft Tombs A, B, and C), or into long winding corridors (the Tunnel Complex), which may have belonged to tombs, or perhaps more likely were robber tunnels. Though pottery, cut stone, skulls and so forth could be seen lying in the rooms and corridors, little clearing could be done in the time available. Much more work is necessary in the tombs found by the British Institute expedition, but political events have precluded a return as yet.

Nothing significant was found in the tombs or buildings at Aksum which can be certainly attributed to a later date than the sixth or early seventh century AD. The archaeological record shows that the large residences were occupied or built around by squatters, even, apparently, in the time of the last coin-issuing kings, then gradually covered by material brought down by run-off from the deforested hills. The excavations thus confirm the theory suggested above that by about 630AD the town had been abandoned as a capital, although it continued on a much reduced scale as a religious centre and occasional coronation place until the present.

Bibliography

Further extensive bibliographies on all aspects of Aksumite studies are available in Kobishchanov 1979, and Sergew Hable Sellassie 1972 (see below).

Almagro, M., et al 1975 *Qusayr 'Amra*, Madrid.

Almeida, E. d', 1954 C.F.Beckingham and G.W.B.Huntingford, eds., *Some Records of Ethiopia, 1593–1646*, Being Extracts from *The History of High Ethiopia or Abassia* by Manoel de Almeida, London, Hakluyt Society, pp. 3–107, 163–202.

Almeida, E. d' *Historia da Ethiopia*; *Historia Aethiopiae*, in Beccari,*Rerum aethiopicarum scriptores occidentales inediti*, 15 vols., Rome 1905–1917, vols. V–VII;

Altheim, F., and Stiehl, R., 1971 'Äussere Geschichte bis zur Regierung Ezana's', *Christentum am Roten Meer*, II, Berlin – NY.

Alvarez, F., 1961 C.F.Beckingham and G.W.B.Huntingford, eds., *The Prester John of the Indies* 2 vols, Hakluyt Society, Cambridge.

Alvarez, F., *Ho Preste João das Indias. Verdadera Informaçao das Terras do Preste João das Indias*. Lisboa 1540. Trans. from a different ms. into Italian by Ramusio, G. B., *Delle navigationi et viaggi,* Venezia, 1550 and subsequent editions; French, Antwerp 1558; Spanish, Antwerp 1557 and Toledo 1588; also in Monneret de Villard, U., *Aksum*, pp.56–59.*Narrative of the Portuguese Embassy to Abyssinia during the years 1529–1527*, trans. and ed. by Lord Stanley of Alderley, Hakluyt, London 1881.*Wahrhaftigen Bericht von den Landen des Königs von Ethiopien*, Eisleben 1566 and 1567. Also translated into French in Temporal, G., *De l'Afrique, contenant la description de ce pays et la navigation des anciens capitaines portugais*, Paris 1830, t. III.

Anfray, F., 1963 'La première campagne de fouilles à Matara (Nov 1959 – Janv. 1960)', *AE* V, pp. 87–166.

Anfray, F. 1964 'Notre connaissance du passé Ethiopien d'après les travaux archéologiques recents', *JSS* 9, pp. 247–249.

Anfray, F., 1965i 'Chronique archéologique, (1960–1964)'. *AE* VI, pp. 3–26.

Anfray, F., 1965ii 'Notes sur quelques poteries axoumites', *AE* VI, pp. 217–20.

Anfray, F., 1966 'La poterie de Matara', *RSE* Vol XXII, pp. 5–74.

Anfray, F., 1967 'Matara', *AE* VII, pp. 33–88.

Anfray, F., 1968 'Aspects de l'archéologie éthiopienne', *JAH* IX, pp. 345–366.

Anfray, F., 1970 'Notes archéologiques', *AE* VIII, pp. 31–42.
Anfray, F., 1972i 'L'archéologie d'Axoum en 1972', *Paideuma* 18, pp. 60–78.
Anfray, A., 1972ii 'Les fouilles de Yeha, Mai–Juin 1972', *DSHCE* 3, pp. 57–63.
Anfray, F., 1973i 'Nouveaux sites antiques', *JES* XI no. 2 , pp. 13–20.
Anfray, F., 1973ii 'Les fouilles de Yeha, Mai–Juin 1973', *DSHCE* 4, pp. 35–38.
Anfray, F., 1974 'Deux villes Axoumites; Adoulis et Matara'. *VI Cong. Int. di Studi Etiopici, (Rome, 1972)* Rome, pp. 745–765.
Anfray, F., and Annequin, G. 1965 'Matara, deuxième, troisième et quatrième campagnes de fouilles', *AE* VI, pp. 49–92.
Anfray, F., Caquot A., and Nautin, 1970. 'Une nouvelle inscription grècque d'Ezana, Roi d'Axoum', *Journal des Savants* pp. 260–273.
Anzani, A., 1926, 1928 and 1941. Articles on Aksumite coinage in *Rivista Italiana di Numismatica*, serie III vols III, V, VI, serie IV vol I.
Atiya A. S., et al., 1943, 1948, 1950 *'History of the Patriarchs of the Coptic Church of Alexandria' by Sawirus ibn al-Mukaffa* Vols I–III, Cairo.
Avanzini, A., 1987 *Les inscriptions sud-arabes d'Ethiopie* paper read at the colloquium *L'Arabie Préislamique et son environnment historique et culturel, 24–27 juin 1987.*
Ayele Teklahaymanot, 1984 'The Egyptian Metropolitans of the Ethiopian Church', paper presented to the Eighth International, Conference of Ethiopian Studies, Addis Ababa, Nov. 1984, pp. 1–62; subsequently published as Ayele' Taklahaymanot, 'The Egyptian Metropolitan of the Ethiopian Church', *Orientalia Cristiana Periodica*, 54, 1988, pp. 175–222.
Bafaqih, M. A., 1983 *Le Yemen*, unpubl. doctoral thesis, Sorbonne, Paris.
Bafaqih, M. A., and Robin, C., 1980 'The Importance of the Inscriptions of Jabal al-Mis'al' (in Arabic), *Raydan* 3, pp. 9–29.
al-Battani, see Nallino, C. A.
Barkay, R., 1981 'An Axumite Coin from Jerusalem', *Israel Numismatic Journal*, 5, pp. 57–59.
Beckingham, C. F., 1980 'The Quest for Prester John', *Bulletin of the John Rylands University Library of Manchester*, Vol. 62, 2, pp. 290–310.
Beckingham, C. F., and Huntingford, G. W. B., 1954 eds., *Some Records of Ethiopia, 1593–1646*, Being Extracts from (*The History of High Ethiopia or Abassia* by Manoel de Almeida, London, Hakluyt Society.
Beckingham, C. F., and Huntingford, G. W. B., 1961 *The Prester John of the Indies; A True Relation of the Lands of the Prester John being the narrative of the Portuguese Embassy to Ethiopia in 1520 written by Father Francisco Alvares* 2 vols, Hakluyt Society, Cambridge.
Beek, G. W. van 1967 'Monuments of Axum in the light of South Arabian Archaeology', *Journal of American Oriental Soc.*, 87, no 2. pp. 113–122
Beeston, A. F. L., 1937 *Sabaean Inscriptions*, Oxford .
Beeston, A. F. L., 1980i 'The authorship of the Adulis throne text', *BSOAS* XLIII, part 3, pp. 453–458.
Beeston, A. F. L., 1980ii 'The South Arabian Collection of the Wellcome Museum in London', *Raydan*, 3, pp. 1–4.

Beeston, A. F. L., 1987 'Habashat and Ahabish', *Proceedings of the Seminar for Arabian Studies*, 17, pp. 5–12.

Bent, T., 1893 *The Sacred City of the Ethiopians* London.

Bent, Mrs. Theodore, 1898 'The Island of Sokotra', *The Scottish Geographical Magazine*', XIV, pp. 629–36.

Bermudes, J., 1565 *Breve relaçam de embaixada que ho Patriarcha D. João Bermudez trouxe do imperador da Ethiopia*, Lisboa (reprinted 1875); also Whiteway, R. S., *The Portuguese Expedition to Abyssinia 1541–3*, Hakluyt Society, 1902 (translation of the narratives of Castanhoso and Bermudes).

Bernand, E., 1982 'Nouvelles versions de la campagne du roi Ezana contre les Bedja', *Zeitschrift für Papyrologie und Epigraphik'*, Band 45, pp. 105–114.

Bersina, S.Y., 1984 'An Inscription of a King of Axumites and Himyarites from Meroe', *Meroitic Newsletter* 23, pp. 1–9.

Blake, R. P., and de Vis, H., 1934 eds. Epiphanius *De Gemmis*, The Old Georgian version and the Fragments of the Armenian Version (ed. Blake R. P.) *and the Coptic-Sahidic Fragments* (ed. de Vis, H.), London.

Blois, F. de, 1984 'Clan-names in ancient Ethiopia', *Die Welt des Orients*, XV, pp. 123–5.

Blois, F. de, 1988 'Problems in Axumite Chronology', paper presented to the 10th International Conference of Ethiopian Studies, Paris.

Boissonade, J. F., 1833 *Anecdota Graeca*, V, Paris.

Bowersock, G. W., 1983 *Roman Arabia*, Harvard.

Brandt, S. A., 1984 'New Perspectives on the Origins of Food Production in Ethiopia', *From Hunters to Farmers*, J. D. Clark and S. A. Brandt eds., Los Angeles and London, pp. 173–189.

Breton, J-F., et al., 1980 *Wadi Hadramawt, Prospections 1978–79*, Aden.

Breton, J-F., 1987 'Shabwa, Capitale antique du Hadramawt', *Journal Asiatique* 275, 1987, pp. 13–34.

Brooks, E. W., ed. 1923 *John of Ephesus. Lives of the Eastern Saints, X, The history of Mar Simeon the bishop, the Persian debater*, PO XVII, fasc. 1, pp. 137–58.

Brooks, E. W., ed., 1952, *Ioannis Ephesini Historiae Ecclesiasticae,* III, CSCO 106, Script. Syri. 55, Louvain.

Brooks, E. W., ed., 1953 *Historia Ecclesiastica Zachariae Rhetori Vulgo Adscripto*, CSCO 88, Script. Syri 41.

Browning, R., 1971 *Justinian and Theodora*, London.

Bruce, J., 1790 *Travels to Discover the Source of the Nile in the Years 1768, 1769, 1770, 1771, 1772, and 1773,* Edinburgh, another edition Dublin 1790.

Budge, E. A. W., 1922 *The Queen of Sheba and her only Son Menyelek* London.

Budge, E. A. W., 1928i *A History of Ethiopia, Nubia and Abyssinia,* 2 Vols, London

Budge, E. A. W., 1928ii *The Book of the Saints of the Ethiopian Church,* Vol I, London.

Burstein, S. M., 1980 'The Axumite Inscription from Meroe and late Meroitic Chronology',*Meroitica* 7, pp. 220–221.

Butzer, K. W., 1981 'Rise and Fall of Axum, Ethiopia: A Geo-Archaeological Interpretation', *American Antiquity* 40, pp. 471–95.

Buxton, D., and Matthews, D., 1974 'The Reconstruction of Vanished Aksumite Buildings', *RSE*, pp. 53–76.

Caquot, A., 1957 'La royauté sacrale en Ethiopie', *AE* II, pp. 205–9.

Caquot, A., 1965 'L'inscription éthiopienne de Marib', *AE* VI, pp. 223–6.

Caquot, A., and Drewes, A.J., 1955. 'Les monuments recueillis à Maqallé', *AE* I, pp. 17–41.

Caraman, P., 1985 *The Lost Empire*, London.

Carpentier, E., ed. 1861 *Acta Sanctorum*, T. X.

Casson, L., 1989 *The Periplus Maris Erythraei*, Princeton.

Cerulli, E., 1943 *Etiopi in Palestina*, Roma. 2 vols.

Cerulli, E., 1956 *Storia della letteratura etiopica*, Milano; 3rd ed., Milano 1968.

Cerulli, E., 1960 'Punti di vista sulla storia dell'Etiopia', *Atti del Convegno Internazionale di Studi Etiopici, Roma 2–4 aprile 1959*, Accad. Naz. dei Lincei, Quaderno 48, pp. 5–27.

Chaine, M., 1925 *La chronologie des temps chrétiens de l'Egypte et de l'Ethiopie*, Paris.

Chatterji, S. K., 1967 *India and Ethiopia from the Seventh Century*, Calcutta.

Chennafi, M. el- 1976 'Mention nouvelle d'une 'reine Ethiopienne' au IVe s. de Hégire/ Xe s. ap. J-C', *AE* X, pp. 119–121.

Chittick, H. N., 1973 'Archaeological Research by the BIEA; some conclusions with particular reference to Aksum'. Paper read to the International Congress of Africanists, Dec. 1973.

Chittick, H. N., 1974 'Excavations at Aksum, 1973–4; a Preliminary Report', *Azania* IX, pp. 159–205.

Chittick, H. N., 1975 'Excavations by the BIEA at Aksum 1973' *Etudes Sémitiques*, Paris, pp. 1–4.

Chittick, H. N., 1976i 'Radiocarbon Dates from Aksum', *Azania* XI, pp. 179–81.

Chittick, H. N., 1976ii 'Excavation by the BIEA', *AE* X, pp. 325–7.

Chittick, H. N., 1978 'Notes on the Archaeology of Northern Ethiopia', *Abbay* 9, pp. 15–19.

Chittick, H. N., 1981 'The *Periplus* and the Spice Trade', *Azania* XVI, pp. 185–190.

Clark, J. D., 1976 'The domestication process in sub-saharan Africa with special reference to Ethiopia', in *Origine de l'élévage et de la domestication*, ed. Higgs, E. S., Colloque XX, Union Internationale des Sciences Préhistoriques et Protohistoriques, Nice, pp. 56–115.

Clark, J. D., 1988 'A Review of the Archaeological Evidence for the Origins of Food Production in Ethiopia', *Proceedings of the Eighth International Conference of Ethiopian Studies, 1984*, Addis Ababa, vol. 1, pp. 55–69.

Connah, G., 1987 *African Civilisations*, CUP.

Contenson, H. de, 1959i 'Les fouilles à Axoum en 1957, Rapport préliminaire'. *AE* III, pp. 25–42.

Contenson, H. de, 1959ii 'Aperçus sur les fouilles à Axoum et dans la région d'Axoum en 1958 et 1959', *AE* III, pp. 101–106.

Contenson, H. de, 1961i 'Les fouilles à Ouchatei Golo près d'Axoum en 1958', *AE* IV, pp. 3–16.

Contenson, H. de, 1961ii 'Les fouilles à Haoulti-Melazo en 1958', *AE* IV, pp. 39–60.

Contenson, H. de, 1961iii 'Trouvailles fortuites aux environs d'Axoum (1957–9), *AE* IV, pp. 15–38.

Contenson, H. de, 1962 'Les monuments d'art Sud-Arabe découverts sur le site de Haoulti (Ethiopie) en 1959', *Syria*, XXXIX, pp. 64–87.

Contenson, H. de, 1963i 'Les fouilles à Axoum en 1958 -Rapport préliminaire', *AE* V, pp. 1–40.

Contenson, H. de, 1963ii 'Les fouilles à Haoulti en 1959. – Rapport préliminaire', *AE* V, pp. 41–86.

Conti Rossini, C., 1901 'L'evangelo d'oro de Dabra Libanos', *Rendiconti della R, Accad. dei Lincei*, ser. V. vol. 10.

Conti Rossini, C., ed., 1904 *Gadla Marqorewos seu Acta Sancti Mercurii*, CSCO, Script. Aeth., series altera, XXII, Paris.

Conti Rossini, C., ed., 1907 *Historia Regis Sarsa Dengel (Malak Sagad)*, CSCO, Script. Aeth., series altera, III, Paris.

Conti Rossini, C., 1909 'Les listes des rois d'Aksoum', *Journal Asiatique* pp. 263ff.

Conti Rossini, C., 1910 *Liber Axumae*, CSCO, Script. Aeth. series altera, VIII.

Conti Rossini, C., 1927 'Monete Aksumite', *Africa Italiana*, I, pp. 179–212.

Conti Rossini, C., 1928 *Storia d'Etiopia*, Milan.

Conti Rossini, C., 1931 'Antiche rovine sulle rore eritree', *Rassegna di Studi Etiopici*, ser. VI, vol. IV, fasc. II, 1931, pp. 241–78.

Conti Rossini, C., 1939 'L'iscrizione etiopica di Ham', *Atti della R. Accad. dei Lincei*, serie 7, Vol. l, pp. 1–4.

Corcoran, T. H., 1972 ed. Seneca, *Naturales Quaestiones*, Loeb, London.

Crawford, O. G. S., 1958 *Ethiopian Itineraries, circa 1400–1524*, Hakluyt Society, Cambridge.

Derrett, J. D. M., 1960 'The History of Palladius on the Races of India and the Brahmanes', *Classica et Mediaevalia* 21, pp. 64–135.

Desanges, J., 1969 'D'Axoum à l'Assam, aux portes de la Chine; le voyage du Scholasticus de Thèbes (entre 360 et 500 après J-C)', *Historia* XVIII, 5.

Dewing, H. B., 1914 ed. and trans. Procopios *History of the Wars*, Loeb, London.

Dictionary of Ethiopian Biography, 1975 (eds. Belaynesh Michael, Chojnacki, S., Pankhurst, R., Addis Ababa.

Dillmann, A., 1878 'Uber die Anfänge des Axumitischen Reiches', *Abh. der K. Preuss. Akad. der Wiss. zu Berlin, Phil-hist. Klasse*, Berlin, pp. 177–238.

Dillmann, A., 1880 'Zur Geschichte des Axumitischen Reiches im vierten bis sechsten Jahrhundert', *Abh. der K. Preuss. Akad. der Wiss. zu Berlin, Phil-hist. Klasse*, I, pp. 4–51.

Dombrowski, B. W. W., and Dombrowski, F. A., 1984 'Frumentius/ Abba Salama: Zu den Nachrichten über die Anfänge des Christentums in Äethiopien', *Oriens Christianus*, 68, pp. 114–69.

Donadoni, S., 1959 'Un'epigrafe greco-nubiana da Ikhmindi', *La Parola del passato* 14, p. 461.

Doresse, J., 1956 *Au Pays de la Reine de Saba*, Paris.

Doresse, J., 1957 *L'Empire du Prêtre Jean*, 2 Vols., Paris.

Doresse, J., 1960 'La découverte d'Asbi-Dera...' *Atti del Convegno Internazionale di Studi Etiopici, Roma 2–4 aprile 1959*, Accad. Naz. dei Lincei, Quaderno 48, pp. 411–34.

Doresse, J., 1971 *Histoire sommaire de la corne orientale de l'Afrique*, Paris.

Drewes, A. J., 1955 'Problèmes de paléographie éthiopienne', *AE* I, pp. 121–6.
Drewes, A. J., 1959 'Les inscriptions de Melazo', *AE* III, pp. 83–9.
Drewes, A. J., 1962 *Inscriptions de l'Ethiopie antique,* Leiden.
Drewes, A. J., 1978 'Kaleb and Himyar: another reference to HYWN'?', *Raydan,* 1, pp. 27–32.
Drewes, A. J., and Schneider, R., 1967 'Documents épigraphiques de l'Ethiopie', *AE* VII, pp. 89–106.
Drewes, A. J., and Schneider, R., 1976 'Origins et développements de l'écriture éthiopienne jusqu'à l'époque des inscriptions royales d'Axoum' *AE* X, pp. 95–108.
Dunlop, D. M., 1940 'Another 'Prophetic' Letter', *Journal of the Royal Asiatic Society*, pp. 54–60.
Epiphanius, see Blake R. P., and de Vis, H.
Evetts, B., ed. 1904 *History of the Patriarchs of the Coptic Church of Alexandria*, by Sawirus ibn al-Mukaffa', bishop of al-Ashmunein, Vol. I, IV, Menas I to Joseph, PO X, fasc. 5. pp. 357–551, Paris.
Fattovich, R., 1975 'The Contribution of the Nile Valley's Cultures to the Rising of Ethiopian Civilisation', *Meroitic Newsletter* 16, pp. 2–8.
Fattovich, R., 1977, 'Some data for the Study of Cultural History in Ancient Northern Ethiopia,' *Nyame Akuma* , 10, pp. 6–18.
Fattovich, R., 1978 'Traces of a Possible African Component in the Pre-Aksumite Culture of Northern Ethiopia', *Abbay* 9, pp. 25–30.
Fattovich, R., 1987 'Some Remarks on the Origins of the Aksumite Stelae', *AE* XIV, pp. 43–69.
Fattovich, R., 1988 'The Contribution of Recent Field Work at Kassala (Eastern Sudan) to Ethiopian Archaeology', paper read at the Tenth International Conference of Ethiopian Studies, Paris.
Fattovich, R., 1989i 'Remarks on the Pre-Aksumite Period in Northern Ethiopia', paper read at the Seminar on Aksum, Addis Ababa University, Oct. 4th–5th, 1989.
Fattovich, R., 1989ii 'Remarks on the Late Prehistory and Early History of Northern Ethiopia', *Proceedings of the Eighth International Conference on Ethiopian Studies*, Addis Ababa 1984, Institute of Ethiopian Studies, Addis Ababa 1989, I, pp. 85–104.
Fiaccadori, G., 1981 'Per una nuova iscrizione Etiopica da Aksum', *Egitto e Vicino Oriente,* IV, pp. 357–367.
Fiaccadori, G., 1984 'Teofilo Indiano', part II, *Studi Classici e Orientali*, 34, pp. 271–308.
Freese, J. H., 1920 trans. Photius, *The Library of Photius*, London.
Gallagher, J. P., 1974 'The Preparation of Hides with Stone Tools in South Central Ethiopia', *JES* XII, pp. 177–82.
Gatier, P.-L., and Salles, J.-F., 1988 'L'emplacement de Leuké Komé', *L'Arabie et ses mers bordières*, 1, GS – Maison de l'Orient, pp. 186–7.
Gebremedhin, N., 1976, 'Some Traditional Types of Housing in Ethiopia', in Oliver P., ed., *Shelter in Africa*, London.
Geddes, M., 1696 *The Church-History of Ethiopia*, London.
Gerster, G., et al 1970 *Churches in Rock*, New York.
Gezaou Haile Maryam, 1955 'Objects Found in the Neighbourhood of Axum', *AE* I, pp. 50–51.
Godet, E., 1977 'Repertoire des sites Pre-Axoumites et Axoumites du Tigré (Ethiopie)', *Abbay,* 8, pp. 19–58.

Grabar, A., 1967 *Byzantium*, Thames and Hudson, trans. from Paris edition, 1966.
Grohmann, A., 1911 'Eine Alabasterlampe mit einer Ge'ezinschrift', *Weiner Zeitschrift für Kunde des Morgenlandes*, 25, pp. 410–422.
Guidi, I., 1871, *Catalogue of the Ethiopian Manuscripts in the British Museum*, London.
Guillaume, A., 1955 *The Life of Muhammad; A Translation of Ibn Ishaq's 'Sirat rasul Allah'*, Oxford.
Hägg, T., 1984 'A New Axumite Inscription in Greek from Meroe; a Preliminary Report'. Meroitistiche Forschungen 1980, *Meroitica* 7, pp 436–41.
Hägg, T., forthcoming 'Sayce's Axumite Inscription from Meroe – Again', *Meroitic Newsletter*.
Hahn, W. R. O., 1983 'Die Münzprägung des Aksumitisches Reiches', *Litterae Numismaticae Vindobonenses*, 2, pp. 113–180.
Hahn, W. R. O., 1987 'Die Vokalisierung Axumitischer Münzaufschriften als Datierungselement', *Litterae Numismaticae Vindobonenses*, 3, pp. 217–25.
Hansen, O., 1986 'The king-title Βασιλισκοσ in Nubia in the fourth to sixth century AD', *Journal of Egyptian Archaeology* 72, p. 205.
Hartmann, M., 1895 'Der Nagasi Aṣḥama und sein Sohn Arma', *Zeitschrift der Deutschen Morgenländischen Gesellschaft*, 49, pp. 299–300.
Hasan, Y. F., 1967 *The Arabs and the Sudan*, Edinburgh; reprint, Khartoum 1973.
Henry, R., 1959 ed. and trans., Photius *Bibliothèque*, Vol. I, Paris.
Huntingford, G. W. B., 1965 *The Land Charters of Northern Ethiopia* Addis Ababa.
Huntingford, G. W. B., 1980 *The Periplus of the Erythraean Sea*, London.
Huntingford, G. W. B., 1989 *The Historical Geography of Ethiopia*, ed. R. Pankhurst, OUP.
Igonetti, G., 1973 'Un frammento di inscrizione etiopica da Zafar (Yemen)', *Annali dell'Istituto Orientale di Napoli*, 33, pp. 77–80.
Irvine, A., 1965 'On the identity of Habashat in the South Arabian inscriptions', *Journal of Semitic Studies*, 10, pp. 178–96.
Irvine, A., 1978 'Linguistic Evidence on Ancient Ethiopia...', (paper read at the Conference on Ethiopian Origins, SOAS, London, 1977), *Abbay*, 9, pp. 43–8.
Isaac, E., and Felder, C., 1988 'Reflections on the Origins of the Ethiopian Civilization', *Proceedings of the Eighth International Conference of Ethiopian Studies, 1984*, Addis Ababa, vol. 1, pp. 71–83.
Jamme, A., 1957 'Annales d'Ethiopie', Boekbesprekingen, *Bibliotheca Orientalis* 14, pp. 79–80.
Jamme, A. 1962 *Sabaean Inscriptions from Mahram Bilqîs (Mârib)*, Baltimore.
Jones, A., and Munroe, E., 1955 *A History of Ethiopia*, Oxford.
Judge, E. A., 1976 'The Date of Ezana, 'Constantine' of Ethiopia', *New Documents Illustrating Early Christianity*, Macquarie University, pp. 143–4.
Juel-Jensen, B., 1986 'Ousanas I-Ezanas-Ousanas II...', *Spink Numismatic Circular* Oct. 1986, pp. 255–8.
Juel-Jensen, B., 1989 'An Aksumite Survival in Late Mediaeval Ethio-

pian Miniatures', *Proceedings of the First International Conference on the History of Ethiopian Art*, London, pp. 41–3.
Kamil, M., 1964 'An Ethiopic Inscription Found at Mareb', *Journal of Semitic Studies*, 9, pp. 56–7.
Kammerer, A., 1929 *Le Mer Rouge*, Cairo.
Kebbédé Mikaël et Leclant, J., 1955 'La section d'archéologie (1952–1955),' *AE* I, pp. 1–6.
Kirwan, L. P., 1963 'A Little-known People of the Nubian Nile', *Vanished Civilisations*, London.
Kirwan, L. P., 1966 'Prelude to Nubian Christianity', *Mélanges offerts à K. Michalowski*, Warsaw, pp. 121–8.
Kirwan, L. P., 1972 '*The Christian Topography* and the Kingdom of Axum', *Geographical Journal* 138, pp. 166–77.
Kitchen, K., 1971 'Punt and How to Get There', *Orientalia*, 40, fasc. 2, pp. 184–207.
Kobishchanov, Y. M., 1979 *Axum*, Philadelphia.
Kramers, J. H., and Weit, G., 1964 *Ibn Haukal; Configuration de la terre*, 2 vols, Paris.
Kur, S., 1965 *Actes de Iyasus Mo'a*.. CSCO, Script. Aeth. 49, Louvain.
Leroy, J., 1963 'Les 'Ethiopiens' de Persépolis', *AE* V, pp. 293–5.
Lewcock. R. B., 1973–4 'Axum; Tentative conclusions and hypotheses', Architectural report to the BIEA.
Leclant, J., 1959i 'Les fouilles à Axoum en 1955–1956. Rapport préliminaire'. *AE* III, pp. 3–24.
Leclant, J., 1959ii 'Haoulti-Melazo (1955–1956)', *AE* III, pp. 43–82.
Leclant, J., 1965 'Note sur l'amulette en cornaline *J. E.* 2832', *AE* VI, 86–7.
Leclant, J., and Miquel, A., 1959 'Reconnaisances dans l'Agamé; Goulo-Makeda et Sabéa', *AE* III, pp. 107–130.
Lepage, C., 1989 'Bilan des Recherches sur l'Art Médiéval d'Ethiopie; Quelques Résultats Historiques', *Proceedings of the Eighth International Conference of Ethiopian Studies, 1984*, Addis Ababa, vol. 2, pp. 47–56.
Leslie, D., 1989 'The Sahaba Sa'd Ibn Abi Waqqas in China', paper presented to the Harvard Symposium *The Legacy of Islam in China*, 14–16 April.
Levine, D., 1974 *Greater Ethiopia: the Evolution of a Multi-Ethnic Society*, Chicago and London.
Littmann, E., et al. 1913 *Deutsche Aksum-Expedition*, Berlin, Band I–IV.
Littmann, E., 1947 'La leggenda del dragone del Aksum in lingua Tigrai', *RSE*, 6.
Littmann, E., 1950 'Aethiopische Inschriften', *Miscellanea Academica Berolinensis*, pp. 97–117.
Littmann, E., 1954 'An Old Ethiopic Inscription from the Berenice Road', *Journal of the Royal Asiatic Society*, pp. 119–123.
Littmann, E., and Krencker, D., 1906 'Vorbericht der deutschen Aksumexpedition', *Abh. der K. Akad. der Wissenschaften zu Berlin*, II, pp. 1–37.
Lobo. J., 1728 trans. by le Grand, J., *Voyage historique d'Abyssinia, du R.P. Jerome Lobo, de la Compagnie de Jesus, continuée et augmentée de plusiers Disserations, Lettres et Mémoires*, Paris (and The Hague); (including quotes from Mendes, Ludolph etc.). Translated into English as *A Voyage to Abyssinia, by Father Jerome Lobo, a Portuguese Jesuit*,

trans. by Dr. Samuel Johnson, London 1735. Portuguese original lost, but another version published as *Itinerário e outras escritos ineditos*, ed. da Costa, M. G., Barcelos, 1971.

Ludolf, J., (Ludolphus, I.,) 1681 *Historia Aethiopica* Francofurti ad Moenum.

Ludolf, J., 1691 *Commentarius ad historiam aethiopicam* Francofurti ad Moenum.

Ludolf, J., 1684 *A New History of Ethiopia*, made English by J(ohn) P(hillips), London.

Magie, D., trans., 1932 *The Scriptores Historiae Augustae*, Vol. III, London and New York.

Malalas, Ioannes., see Migne, J-P.

Marrassini, P., 1985 *'Ancora sulle 'origine' etiopiche'*, Studi in onore di Edda Bresciani, Pisa, pp. 303–15.

Mason, I., 1921 *The Arabian Prophet; a Life of Mohammed from Chinese Sources*, Shanghai.

al-Mas'udi, see Meynard, C. Barbier de, and Courteille, P. de.

Mathew, G., 1975 'The Dating and the Significance of the *Periplus of the Erythrean Sea*', in Chittick, H. N., and Rotberg, R. I., *East Africa and the Orient*, New York and London, pp. 147–63.

Meinardus, O., 1965 'The Ethiopians in Jerusalem', *Zeitschrift für Kirchengeschichte*, Vierte Folge, 14, pp. 113–232.

Mendes, A., 1908 *Expeditio Aethiopica*, in Beccari, op. cit., vol. VIII, and in U. M. de Villard, op. cit., pp. 63, 75–76.

Mendes, A., 1628 *Lettera dell'anno 1626*, in *Lettere annue di Ethiopia del 1624, 1625, e 1626*, Roma, in U. M. de Villard, op.cit., p 74.

Meshorer, Y., 1965–6 'An Axumite Coin from Caesarea', *Israel Numismatic Journal*, 3, p. 76 and pl. XV, 2.

Meynard, C. Barbier de, and Courteille, P. de, 1864 eds. al-Mas'udi, *Les prairies d'or*, Paris.

Michels, J., 1986 'The Axumite Kingdom; A Settlement Archaeology Perspective', paper presented to the Ninth International Conference on Ethiopian Studies, Moscow 1986, and published in the *Proceedings of the Ninth International Congress of Ethiopian Studies, Moscow, 26–29 August 1986*, Moscow 1988, pp. 173–83.

Michels, J., 1988 'Regional political organisation in the Axum-Yeha area during the pre-Axumite and Axumite era', paper presented to the 10th International Conference of Ethiopian Studies, Paris, 1988.

Migne, J-P., ed. 1849 Rufinus *Historia Ecclesiastica*, PL 21, 478–9.

Migne, J-P., ed. 1860 Ioannes Malalas *Chronographia*, PG 97, Paris.

Migne, J-P., ed. 1864 Philostorgios, *Historia Ecclesiastica*, PG. 65, pp. 482ff.

Miller, K., 1927 *Mappae Arabicae*, II, Stuttgart.

Minorsky, V., 1937 *Hudud al-'Alam*, Oxford.

Moberg, A., 1928 *The Book of the Himyarites*, Lund.

Mommsen, T., 1886 *The Provinces of the Roman Empire*, London.

Mordini, A., 1960 'Gli aurei kushana del convento di Dabra Dammo'. *ACISE* Rome, pp. 249–54.

Mordini, A., 1967 'Gold Kushana Coins in the Convent of Dabra Dammo'. *Journal of the Numismatic Society of India*, XXIX, pp. 19–25.

Muir, T. H., 1923 *The Life of Mohammad*, Edinburgh.

Müller, W. W., 1972 'Zwei weitere Bruchstücke der äthiopischen Inschrift aus Mareb', *Neue Ephemeris für semitische Epigrafik*, I, Weisbaden, pp. 59–74.

Munro-Hay, S. C. H., 1978 *The Chronology of Aksum: A Reappraisal of the History and Development of the Aksumite State from Numismatic and Archaeological Evidence*. Ph.D. thesis, S.O.A.S., London.

Munro-Hay, S. C. H., 1979i 'MHDYS and Ebana, Kings of Aksum. Some problems of Dating and Identity', *Azania,* XIV, pp. 21–30.

Munro-Hay, S. C. H., 1979ii 'Ezana and Ezanas: Inscriptions and Coins', *Abbay,* Cahier No. 10, pp. 87ff.

Munro-Hay, S. C. H., 1980i 'Ezana (Ezana and Ezanas): Some Numismatic Comments', *Azania,* XV, pp. 109–119.

Munro-Hay, S. C. H., 1980ii 'Axum, by Y. Kobishchanov', review article, *Azania*,XV, pp. 148–155.

Munro-Hay, S. C. H., 1980–81 'Aksumite Addenda: The Existence of 'Bisi Anioskal'', *Rassegna di Studi Etiopici,* XXVIII, pp. 57–60.

Munro-Hay, S. C. H., 1981–82 'A Tyranny of Sources: The History of Aksum from its Coinage', *Northeast African Studies,* 3,3, pp. 1–16.

Munro-Hay, S. C. H., 1982i 'The Foreign Trade of the Aksumite Port of Adulis', *Azania,* XVII, pp. 107–125.

Munro-Hay, S. C. H., 1982ii 'A New Issue of King Nezool of Aksum in the Collection of the American Numismatic Society', *ANS Museum Notes,* 27, pp. 181–184.

Munro-Hay, S. C. H., 1982–3 'Kings and Kingdoms of Ancient Nubia' *Rassegna di Studi Etiopici* XXIX, pp. 87–137.

Munro-Hay, S. C. H., 1984i *The Coinage of Aksum*, New Delhi.

Munro-Hay, S. C. H., 1984ii 'Aksumite Chronology; some Reconsiderations', *Jahrbuch für Numismatik und Geldgeschichte*,Band XXXIV, pp. 107–126; also published in *Proceedings of the Eighth International Conference of Ethiopian Studies, 1984*, vol. 2, Addis Ababa 1989, pp. 27–40.

Munro-Hay, S. C. H., 1984iii 'The Ge'ez and Greek Palaeography of the Coinage of Aksum', *Azania*, XIX, pp. 134–144.

Munro-Hay, S. C. H., 1984iv 'An African Monetarised Economy in Ancient Times', *Proceedings of the Second International Conference on Indian Ocean Studies, Perth*, Section E.

Munro-Hay, S. C. H., 1986 *The Munro-Hay Collection of Aksumite Coins,* Supplemento 48, Annali, (Naples) vol. 46 fasc 3.

Munro-Hay, S. C. H., 1987 'Aksumite Silver Coinage: Some Variant Types in the Brereton Collection', *Numismatic Chronicle* 147, pp. 174–5.

Munro-Hay, S. C. H., 1989, *Excavations at Aksum*, Memoir no. 10, British Institute in Eastern Africa.

Munro-Hay, S. C. H., 1989i, 'The British Museum Excavations at Adulis, 1868', *Antiquaries Journal*, vol. 69i, pp 43–52.

Munro-Hay, S. C. H., 1989ii, 'The al-Madhariba Hoard of Gold Aksumite and Late Roman Coins', *Numismatic Chronicle*, pp 83–100.

Munro-Hay, S. C. H., 1990. 'The dating of Ezana and Frumentius', *Rassegna di Studi Etiopici*, XXXII, 1988, pp 111–127.

Munro-Hay, S. C. H., forthcoming, 'Brick Architecture at Aksum', *Rassegna di Studi Etiopia.*

Munro-Hay, S. C. H., forthcoming, 'The Coinage of Shabwa', *Syria.*

Munro-Hay, S. C. H., forthcoming, 'Forgeries of the Aksumite Series',

ANS Museum Notes.
Munro-Hay, S. C. H., forthcoming, *The Metropolitan Episcopate of Ethiopia and the Patriarchate of Alexandria, 4th to 14th Century.*
Munro-Hay, S. C. H., Oddy, W. A., and Cowell, M. 1988 'The Gold Coinage of Aksum; New Specific Gravity and XRF Measurements and their Chronological Significance', *Metallurgy and Numismatics*, II.
Nallino, C. A., 1907 ed. al-Battani, *Opus Astronomicum*, Milan.
Oddy, W. A. and Munro-Hay, S. C. H., 1980 'The Specific Gravity Analysis of the Gold Coins of Aksum', *Metallurgy and Numismatics* I, OUP, pp. 73–82, pls.2–4.
Olderogge, D. A., 1974 'L'Armenie et l'Ethiopie au IV sicle...' *IV Congresso Internazionale di Studi Etiopici*, I, pp. 195–204.
Paez, P., (see also Pais), *Historia Aethiopiae*, in Beccari, vols II–III and U.M. de Villard, op. cit., pp. 67–8
Page, T. E., 1930 ed. Strabo, *Geography*, Loeb, London, vol. VII.
Pais, P., 1945–6 *Historia da Ethiopia*, 3 vols., Porto.
Pankhurst, R., 1961 *An Introduction to the Economic History of Ethiopia from early times to 1800*, London.
Pankhurst, R., 1974 'The History of Ethiopia's Relations with India prior to the Nineteenth Century', *IV Congresso Internazionale di Studi Etiopici*, I, pp. 205–311.
Paribeni, R., 1907 'Richerche nel luogo dell'antica Adulis', *Monumenti Antichi, Reale Accademia dei Lincei*, Vol XVIII, Rome, pp. 438–572,
Paul, A., 1954 *A History of the Beja Tribes of the Sudan*, CUP.
Pearce, N., 1831, new reprint London 1980. *The Life and Adventures... during a residence in Abyssinia from the years 1810 to 1819*, London .
Perruchon, J., 1893 *Les Chroniques de Za'ra Ya'eqob et de Ba'eda Maryam*, Paris.
Perruchon, J., 1894 'Note pour l'histoire d'Ethiopie, vie de Cosmas, patriarche d'Alexandrie de 923 à 934', *Revue Sémitique*, p. 84.
Pétrids, S. P., 1972 'Essai sur l'évangelisation de l'Ethiopie, sa date et sa protagoniste', *Abba Salama* III, pp. 208–232.
Petrie, W. M. F., 1888 *Tanis II*, London.
Pharr, C., 1952 *The Theodosian Code...*, Princeton.
Philby, H. St J. B., 1950 'Note on the Last Kings of Saba',*Museón* 63, pp. 269–275.
Philby, H. St J. B., 1960 'Note on Ryckmans 535', *Museón*, pp. 396–417.
Phillipson, D. W., 1977 'The Excavation of Gobedra Rock-shelter, Axum.' *Azania,* XII, pp. 53–82.
Phillipson, D. W., 1989 'Axum in Africa', paper read at the Seminar on Aksum, Addis Ababa University, Oct. 1989.
Philostorgius, see Migne J-P, and Walford, E.
Photius, see Freese, J. H., and Henry, R.
Pirenne, J., 1956 *Paléographie des inscriptions sud-arabes* I, Bruxelles.
Pirenne, J., 1961 'La date du Périple de la Mer Erythrée', *Journal Asiatique* 249, pp. 441–459.
Pirenne, J., 1967 'Haoulti et ses monuments, nouvelle interpretation', *AE*, VII, pp. 125–140.
Pirenne, J., 1970 'Haoulti, Gobochéla (Mélazo) et le site antique', *AE* VIII, pp. 117–127.
Pirenne, J., 1975 'Le cadre chronologique de l'histoire ethiopienne du IVe au VIe siècle', *Actes du XXIXe Congrès Internationale des Orientalistes*, Section; *Etudes Semitiques*, Paris, pp. 48–54.

Pirenne, J., 1975 'L'imbroglio de trois siècles de chronologie aksumite, IVe à VIe s.' *Documents pour servir a l'histoire des civilisations éthiopiennes*, fasc. 6, pp. 49–58.

Pirenne, J., 1977 *Corpus des Inscriptions et Antiquités Sud-Arabes*, Louvain.

Pirenne, J., 1987 'La Grece et Saba après 32 ans de nouvelles recherches', paper read to the colloquium L'Arabie Préislamique et son environnement historique et culturel 24–27 juin, Univ. of Strasbourg 1987.

Pirenne, J., and Tesfaye, G., 1982 'Les deux inscriptions du negus Kaleb en Arabie du Sud', *JES* XV, pp. 105ff.

Piva, A., 1907 'Una Civiltà scomparsa dell'Eritrea e gli scavi archeologici nella regione di Cheren', *Nuova Antologia*, pp. 323–335.

Plant, R., 1973, 'Notes on the Architecture of Aksum, Tigré, Ethiopia', Jan–April 1973, unpublished note.

Plant, R., 1978 'A Hypothesis on Origins of Ethiopian Architecture', *Abbay*, 9, pp. 21–24.

Plant, R., 1983 'Architecture of Aksum', report to the BIEA Nov. 1983.

Plant, R., 1985, *The Architecture of the Tigré, Ethiopia,* Worcester.

Playne, B., 1965 'Suggestions on the Origin of the False Doors of Aksumite Stelae', *AE* VI, pp. 279–80.

Pliny, (Plinius Secundus), see Rackham.

Plowden, W. C., 1868 *Travels in Abyssinia*, London.

Polotsky, I., 1940 *Kephalaia*, Stuttgart.

Poncet, C. J., *Relation abrégée du voyage que M. Charles Jacques Poncet, médecin français, fit en Ethiopie en 1698, 1699, et 1700*, in *Lettres édifiants et curieuses écrites des missions étrangres*...Recueil, Paris 1704. Trans. into English as *A Voyage to Ethiopia made in the years 1698, 1699, and 1700*, London 1709, and *A Voyage to Ethiopia, 1698–1701*, Hakluyt Society 1949.

Procopius, see Dewing, H. B.

Ptolemy (Claudius Ptolomaeus), see Stevenson, E. L.

Puglisi, G., 1969 'Alcuni vestigi dell'isola di Dahlac Chebir e la leggenda dei Furs', *Proceedings of the Third International Conference of Ethiopian Studies*, I, Addis Abeba, 1969, pp. 35–48.

Puglisi, S., 1941 'Primi risultati delle indagini compiute dalla Missione archeologica di Aksum', *Africa Italiana* VIII, pp. 95–153.

Rackham, B. H., 1947–56 ed. and trans. Pliny, (Plinius Secundus), *Naturalis Historia,* , 4 vols, London.

Rey, C. F., 1929 *The Romance of the Portuguese in Abyssinia*, London.

Ricci, L., 1974 'Scavi archeologici in Etiopia', *Africa,* XXIX, pp. 435–41.

Ricci, L., 1976 'Communication', *AE* X, pp. 327–8.

Ricci, L., and Fattovich, R., 1984–6 'Scavi archeologici nella zona di Aksum. A. Seglamien', *Rassegna di Studi Etiopici*, XXX, 1984–6, pp. 117–69.

Ricci, L., and Fattovich, R., 1987 'Scavi archeologici nella zona di Aksum. B. Bieta Giyorgis *Rassegna di Studi Etiopici*, XXXI, 1987, pp. 123–97.

Robin, C., 1981 'Les inscriptions d'al-Mis'al et la chronologie de l'Arabie méridionale au IIIe siècle de l'ère chrétienne' *Comptes rendus; Académie des Inscriptions et Belles-Lettres*, (Avril–Juin), pp. 315–339.

Robin, C., 1984, 'Les Abyssins en Arabie meridionale (IIe–IVe s)', paper read to the Eighth International Conference of Ethiopian Studies, Addis Ababa.

Rodinson, M., 1969 'Sur une nouvelle inscription du règne de Dhoû Nowâs', *Bibliotheca Orientalis* XXVI, 1/2, pp. 26–33.

Rufinus, see Migne J-P.

Ryckmans, G., 1946 'Une inscription chrétienne sabéenne aux musées d'Antiquités d'Istanbul', *Muséon*, 59, pp. 171–2.

Ryckmans, G., 1951 *Les Religions Arabes Préislamiques*, Louvain.

Ryckmans, G., 1953 'Inscriptions sud-arabes', *Muséon*, 66, pp. 267–317.

Ryckmans, G., 1958 'Découvertes épigraphiques en Ethiopie', *Muséon* 71, pp. 142–4.

Ryckmans, J., 1951 *L'institution monarchique en Arabie Méridionale avant l'Islam*, Louvain.

Ryckmans, J., 1976 'L'inscription Sabéene chrétienne Istanbul 7608 *bis*', *Journal of the Royal Asiatic Society*, pp. 96–99.

Salt, H., 1812 *Voyage en Abyssinie...Traduit de l'anglois et extrait des voyages de lord Valentia*, Paris; and in de Villard, U. M., op. cit., pp. 82–87.

Salt, H., 1814 *A Voyage to Abyssinia*, London; and in de Villard, U. M., op. cit., pp.88–89.

Säve-Söderbergh, T., 1946 *The Navy of the Eighteenth Egyptian Dynasty*, Uppsala and Leipzig.

Sayce, A. H., 1909 'A Greek Inscription of a King(?) of Axum Found at Meroë', *Proc. Soc. Bibl. Arch.*31, pp. 189–90.

Sayce, A. H., 1912 'Second Interim Report on the Excavations at Meroë in Ethiopia; II. The Historical Results', *Liverpool Annals of Archaeology and Anthropology*, 4, pp. 53–65.

Schneider, M., 1967 'Stèles funéraires arabes de Quiha', *AE* VII, pp. 107–118.

Schneider, R., 1961 'Inscriptions d'Enda Čerqos', *AE* IV, pp. 61–5.

Schneider, R., 1963 'Une page du Gadla Sadqan', *AE* V, pp. 167–9.

Schneider, R., 1965 'Notes épigraphiques sur les découvertes de Matara', *AE* VI, pp. 88–92.

Schneider, R., 1973 'Deux inscriptions Sudarabiques du Tigré', *Bibliotheca Orientalis*, XXX, 5/6, pp. 385–9.

Schneider, R., 1974 'Trois nouvelles inscriptions royales d'Axoum', *IV Congresso Internazionale di Studi Etiopici*, Accad. dei Lincei, Rome, pp. 767–86.

Schneider, R., 1976i 'Les débuts de l'histoire Ethiopienne', *DSHCE* 7, pp. 47–54.

Schneider, R., 1976ii 'L'inscription chrétienne d'Ezana en écriture sud-arabe', *AE* X, pp. 109–117.

Schneider, R., 1976iii 'Documents épigraphiques de l'Ethiopie- V', *AE* X, pp. 81–93.

Schneider, R., 1978 'Documents épigraphiques de l'Ethiopie- VI', *AE* XI, pp. 129–32.

Schneider, R., 1982 'Deux inscriptions éthiopiennes. I. 'WM, AVA, YEHA et ADUA', *JES* XV, pp. 125–8.

Schneider, R., 1984 'Yuri M. Kobischanov. Axum', review article, *JES* XVII, pp. 148–74.

Schneider, R., 1987 'Notes sur les inscriptions royales aksumites', *Bibliotheca Orientalis*, XLIV no. 5/6, pp. 599–616.

Schneider, R., 1988 'A New Axumite Chronology', *Journal of Ethiopian Studies*, XXI, pp. 111–20.

Schoff, W. H., 1912 *The Periplus of the Erythraean Sea*, New York etc.

Schur, W., 1923 'Die Orientpolitik des Kaisers Nero', *Klio* 25, pp. 40–45.
Sergew Hable Sellassie, 1972 *Ancient and Medieval Ethiopian History to l270,* Addis Ababa.
Sergew Hable Sellassie, 1989 'A New Literary Source for Aksumite History; the Case of EMML 8509', paper read at the Seminar on Aksum, Addis Ababa University, Oct. 4th–5th, 1989.
Seneca, see Corcoran, T. H.
Shahid, I., 1971 *The Martyrs of Najran*, Subsidia Hagiographica 49, Bruxelles.
Shahid. I., 1979 'Byzantium in South Arabia', *Dumbarton Oaks Papers* 33, pp. 27–94.
Shinnie, P. L., 1967 *Meroe*, London.
Sleeswyk, A. W., 1983 'On the location of the land of PWNT on two Renaissance maps', *The International Journal of Nautical Archaeology and Underwater Exploration*, 12.4 pp. 279–91.
Smith, S., 1954 'Events in Arabia in the Sixth Century AD', *BSOAS* 16, pp. 425–68.
Snowden, F. M., 1970 *Blacks in Antiquity,* Harvard.
Stevenson, E. L., 1932 ed. and trans. Ptolemy (Claudius Ptolomaeus), *The Geography of Claudius Ptolemy,* New York.
Strabo, see Page, T. E.
Sundström, R., 1907 'Letter to Dr. Enno Littmann', in Littmann, E., 'Preliminary Report of the Princeton University Expedition to Abyssinia', *Zeitschrift für Assyriologie*, XX, pp. 170–82.
Szymusiak, J. M., 1958 *Athanasius, Apologia ad Constantium Imperatorem,* Paris.
Taddesse Tamrat, 1970 'The Abbots of Däbrä Hayq 1248–1535', *Journal of Ethiopian Studies*,VIII, I, pp. 87–117.
Taddesse Tamrat, 1972 *Church and State in Ethiopia 1270–1527*, Oxford.
Tedeschi, S., 1971 'Venise et l'Ethiopie à travers les siècles' paper presented to the conference *Sauvegarde de Venise*, Addis Abeba, Feb. 16th, and published as a pamphlet (no. 6) by the Istituto Italiano di Cultura, Addis Abeba.
Tedeschi, S., 1988 'La première description de l'Ethiopie imprimeé en Occident', paper presented to the Tenth International Conference of Ethiopian Studies, Paris.
Taddesse Tamrat, 1972 *Church and State in Ethiopia l270–l527,* Oxford.
Tellez (Teles), B., 1660 *Historia geral de Ethiopia a alta...pelo Padre Manoel d'Almeyda*, Coimbra , (partly abridged and revised from de Almeida (unpublished) itself revised from Paez' unpublished work). English version *The Travels of the Jesuits in Ethiopia... by F.Balthazar Tellez*, 1710 London,.
Thomas, H. and Cortesão, A., trans. 1938 *The Discovery of Abyssinia by the Portuguese in 1520*, a Facsimile of the Relation entitled *Carta das novas que vieram a el rey nosso senhor do descobrimento do Preste Joham*, Lisbon 1521, British Museum, London.
Tolmacheva, M., 1986 'Toward a Definition of the Term *Zanj*', *Azania,* XXI, pp. 105–114.
Török, L., 1988 *Late Antique Nubia*, Antaeus, Communicationes ex Instituto Archaeologico Academiae Scientiarum Hungaricae, no. 16, Budapest.
Trimingham, J. S., 1954 *Islam in Ethiopia,* London.

Tringali, G., 1965 'Cenni sulle "Ona" di Asmara e dintorni', *AE* VI, pp. 143–152.

Tringali, G., 1987 'Reperti antichi di scultura minore e di ornamenti dall'Eritrea e da Aksum', *Rassegna di Studi Etiopici*, XXXI, 1987, pp. 213–8.

Tubiana, J., 1958 'Les noms de Gondar et d'Aksum', *Comptes rendus du Groupe Linguistique d'Etudes Chamito-Sémitiques* VIII, pp. 25–6.

Tzadua, P., 1968 *The Fetha Nagast*, Addis Ababa.

Ullendorff, E., 1949 'Note on the Introduction of Christianity into Ethiopia',*Africa* 19, pp. 61–2.

Ullendorff, E., 1951 'The Obelisk of Matara',*JRAS*, pp. 26–32.

Ullendorff, E., 1955 *The Semitic Languages of Ethiopia*, London.

Ullendorff, E., 1955 'The Ethiopian Inscription from Egypt', *Journal of the Royal Asiatic Society*, pp. 159–161.

Ullendorff, E., 1968 *Ethiopia and the Bible*; the Schweich Lectures of the British Academy 1967, London.

Ullendorff, E., 1973 (1st ed. 1960) *The Ethiopians*, OUP, London, Oxford, New York.

Urreta, L. de *Historia Ecclesiastica, politica, natural y moral de los grandes y remotos Reynos de la Etiopia, Monarchia del Emperador llamado Preste Iuan de las Indias*, Valencia 1610.

Vaccaro, F., 1967 *Le Monete di Aksum,* Mantua .

Valentia, viscount (G. Annesley) 1809, *Voyages and Travels to India, Ceylon, the Red Sea, Abyssinia and Egypt*, 3 vols., London, reprinted 1811 (containing Salt's original account).

Vantini, G., 1975 *Oriental Sources Concerning Nubia*, Heidelberg and Warsaw.

Vavilov, N. I., 1931. *The Wheats of Abyssinia and their place in the General System of Wheats*, Supplement 51, *Bulletin of Applied Botany, Genetics and Plant Breeding*, Leningrad.

Villard, U. Monneret de 1938 *Aksum; richerche di topografia generale,* Rome.

Villard, U. Monneret de 1940 'L'inscrizione etiopica di Ham', *Aegyptus* 20, pp. 61–8.

Villard, U. Monneret de 1948 'Aksum e i quattro re del mondo' *Annali Lateranesi* 12, pp. 125–80.

Walford, E., 1875 trans. Philostorgios, *The Ecclesiastical History*, London.

Williams, S., 1985 *Diocletian and the Roman Recovery*, London.

Wolska-Conus, W., 1968, 1973 *La Topographie chrétienne,* Sources chrétiénnes, Paris.

Yusuf Kamal, 1930–35 *Monumenta Cartographica Africae et Aegypti*, Cairo.

Zarins, J., 'Prehistoric Trade in the Southern Red Sea – The Obsidian Evidence', paper read at the British Museum Conference *The Indian Ocean in Antiquity*, July 1988.

Zotenberg, H., 1877 *Catalogue des manuscrits ethiopiens de la Bibliothéque Nationale,* Paris.

Zotenberg, H., 1919 *Tabari; Chronique,* Paris.

Index